THE
HISTORICAL ATLAS
OF THE
CELTIC WORLD

A CARTOGRAPHICA BOOK

This updated edition published in 2010 by
CHARTWELL BOOKS, INC.
A division of BOOK SALES, INC.
276 Fifth Avenue Suite 206
New York, New York 10001
USA

Copyright © 2009 Cartographica Ltd

Reprinted in 2011

ISBN 13: 978-0-7858-2749-8
ISBN 10: 0-7858-2749-8

QUMHA12

This book is produced by
Cartographica Ltd
6 Blundell Street
London N7 9BH

Project Editor: Samantha Warrington
Production Manager: Rohana Yusof
Publisher: Sarah Bloxham

Cartography:
Red Lion Mapping

Printed in Singapore by
Star Standard Industries Pte Ltd.

THE HISTORICAL ATLAS OF THE CELTIC WORLD

DR. IAN BARNES

CHARTWELL
BOOKS, INC.

CONTENTS

Map List

INTRODUCTION

"THE RIVER ISTER RISES AMONG THE CELTS AND THE TOWN OF
PYRENE AND CROSSES THE WHOLE OF EUROPE. THE CELTS ARE
BEYOND THE PILLARS OF HERCULES, NEXT TO THE CYNETES, WHO
LIVE FURTHEST WEST OF ALL THE PEOPLE OF EUROPE."

HERODOTUS, *HISTORY*, II.33

The Celts dominated large areas of Europe for many centuries. Several European countries
are influenced by Celtic origins while Celtic languages are still used in Brittany, Ireland,
Scotland, and Wales. The Isle of Man states its new laws annually in Manx. Thriving
communities of expatriate people of Celtic origin exist around the world in such places as the United
States, Canada, South Africa, New Zealand, and Australia. There is even a Welsh community in
Argentine Patagonia, and Bretons have helped discover the Americas and build the cities of Québec
and Montréal in Canada.

From the emergence of the historical Celts with their Hallstatt and La Tène civilizations, their
fate as warriors and mercenaries was iconized by resistance to Rome in the hands of Caratacus,
Vercingetorix and Boudicca while being eulogized in the cartoon Asterix the Gaul. Rome and the
Germanic tribes jointly squeezed Celtic territories until Roman power subjugated the Celts of
northern Italy, France and the Iberian Peninsula. The population of France was Romanized but
retained a Celtic peninsula in Brittany. In the British Isles, invading Angles, Saxons, and Jutes pushed
the Romano-Britons into Cornwall, Wales, and Scotland. Ireland and the Isle of Man developed a
Hiberno-Norse, while Norse-controlled Mann developed differently.

The Middle Ages saw the British islands invaded by William the Conqueror and Norman authority
was established over England and then projected into Wales, Scotland, and Ireland. Eventually, the
first two were united with England by force, with the Scottish king inheriting England from Elizabeth
I. The stories of Scots rebellion under the Old and Young Pretender in 1715 and 1745 are well known,
with legends of Highland clansmen charging Hanoverian troops from England with the verve and

vigor seen as far back as the Battle of Telamon (225 BC) when charging Celtic swordsmen were hacked down by Roman military discipline.

Celtic artistry is demonstrated in metal work, enamels, jewellery, and coins using a variety of images. Hill-forts and city states were built at the junction of trade routes, their fortified sites becoming modern Milan, Turin, Amiens, Paris, Geneva, Bratislava, Budapest, and Salamanca. The role of regiments raised from Celtic environments with their incredible fighting spirit is displayed in the context of a series of wars, especially the two world wars. Simultaneously, the story of how Scots, Welsh, and Irish helped in the creation of the British Empire receives treatment, as do the widespread Celtic diasporas all over the world.

The modern world depicts the history of a Celtic revival not just through the antics of would-be druids but by contemplating new Celtic nationalism, the growth of the state of Eire, and the recent devolution processes allowing Wales and Scotland to have their own assemblies with degrees of sovereignty. The long-lived Manx Tynwald is placed in context here, with the Isle of Man's unusual history surrounded in legend by mists generated by the god Manannan keeping the island unseen and unharmed. This island sports the oldest working democracy in the world and is an example of how a small nation can keep its independence despite various would-be arbitrary rulers. On the other hand, the case of Brittany is less pleasant, with part of the traditional Breton territory around Nantes being removed from the Breton regional council. The Breton council has very limited authority, being treated just like any other region in France. The other Celtic people confronting the British state are the Cornish, whose Duchy has an unusual constitutional status, as do the old Stannery democratic institutions. The tale of the Celtic peoples is augmented by discussing religion and folklore, with examples of teaching stories and fables and descriptions of various legends, such as fairies, monsters, and mermaids.

The ruins of a 12th-century Norse-Celtic Christian chapel on St Michael's Isle, on the Isle of Man.

OUT OF THE MISTS OF TIME

"AFTER IBERIA, WE COME TO CELTIC TERRITORY, WHICH REACHES EASTWARDS AS FAR AS THE RHINE. ITS ENTIRE NORTHERN EDGE IS BATHED BY THE BRITISH CHANNEL ... THE EASTERN BOUNDARY OF CELTICA IS DEFINED BY THE RIVER RHINE WHICH RUNS PARALLEL TO THE PYRENEES." STRABO, *GEOGRAPHY*, II.5.28

The Celtic Iron Age world emerged somewhere out of the cultures of the Bronze Age, some of which must have been Celtic-speaking. The European Bronze Age lasted from about 2,500 to 800 BC. The first civilizations enjoyed revolutions in metal technology, moving from gold to copper to bronze and then iron. Copper was used as a material for weapons and tools. Neolithic communities commenced making simple knives and sickles from copper from approximately 7,000 BC. Copper and flint technologies co-existed for ages, generating a name for this particular period. This Chalcolithic era is named after the Greek *chalcos*, copper, and *lithos*, stone.

Metal working probably began around 4000 BC with gold worked cold or smelted. Copper can be produced from various ores including azurite and malachite. The processing of copper ore begins with small pieces of ore being placed in a furnace on a bed of charcoal. These furnaces were generally basin-shaped to capture the liquid metal flowing from the melted stone, resulting in pudding-shaped ingots. Bellows were used to provide a draft strong enough to achieve the smelting temperature. The ingot needed much hammering and re-smelting to beat out all the impurities. Eventually, smiths prepared clay molds into which metal could be poured. Many mineral ores are found on the earth's surface in rock outcrops but eventually communities learned to pursue metal-bearing lodes underground thereby creating the first mines. Copper was superseded by bronze, an alloy of copper and tin. The new metal provided blades which could take sharper edges than copper and could be cast more delicately. Iron might have been first discovered in the impurities left after smelting copper ores. These bits of detritus could be reheated and hammered to produce a soft metal. Some historians suggest that tin was so scarce that the more abundant iron-bearing ores were used in preference and out of necessity.

The gradual use of a bronze technology generated an increase in long-distance trade as settlements and larger communities that had become self-sufficient now needed to travel widely to access copper and tin deposits. Trade routes carried more than goods. Ideas, art techniques, and design fostered development and as these attributes were exchanged, a greater level of cultural uniformity occurred. Early European metallurgy started in the Balkan mountain region when copper smelting began around 4500 BC. Bronze Age cultures include diverse groups such as the Bell Beaker people, who placed a specifically designed pottery drinking vessel in their burials, the Unetice, and the widespread Urnfield culture, which became important from 1300 to 800 BC.

The Urnfield culture is so named because its burial practice required that the deceased be cremated and their ashes placed inside funerary urns for burying. Spreading from the Hungarian steppe to eastern France and from Poland to northern Italy, the culture was connected by extensive trade routes, which linked the region together while having direct contact with the amber bearing Baltic and the civilizations of the Mediterranean. Control of raw materials and patronage of craftsmen to produce metal artifacts created a socio-economic political elite which became the origins of a hierarchical order, a proto-aristocratic society developed fully by the Hallstatt Celts when their culture spread over Europe

The first millennium BC witnessed iron replacing bronze as a preferred weapon and tool material which can take a harder cutting edge than bronze. Crossing the Dardanelles to the Greek world from Asia Minor in about 1200 BC, iron works spread across the Mediterranean and into the Danube Valley. The technological switch was complete by 800 BC in central and southern Europe but would take longer to reach the peripheries of Scandinavia, the Iberian Peninsula, and Britain. The Hallstatt Iron Age culture emerged among the Urnfield culture in southern Germany, Austria, and Bohemia and then spread outward but never reached Ireland.

A Celtic menhir, or standing stone, at St. Guenole in the Cornouaille area of Brittany, France. Menhirs are located across the world but are most numerous and most varied in style in Britain and Brittany. No one is really sure of the exact purpose of menhirs. Some experts believe that they were used for human sacrifice, others claim that they are territorial markers or early calendars.

Hallstatt Culture, 750–450 BC

THE HALLSTATT PERIOD IS THE EARLIEST CULTURE OF THE CELTS, EMERGING WITHIN THE URNFIELD REGION OF SOUTHERN GERMANY, AUSTRIA, AND BOHEMIA BUT SPREADING TO WESTERN EUROPE, IBERIA, AND SOUTHERN BRITAIN.

The Hallstatt culture (750–450 BC, named after a burial ground in the Salzkammergut in Austria) spread its Iron Age technology and civilization throughout the Balkans, central Europe, France, Spain, and into south-east England. Artifacts recovered at the Hallstatt necropolis, containing some 2,000 graves, demonstrate elaborate funeral rites, whether by cremation or interment. Some graves contain four-wheeled carts and bronze harness mounts and bits, suggesting economic and cultural links with the Russian steppes, whether by origin or by the absorption of peoples moving westward from a steppe homeland. Finely decorated burial sites in Bohemia, complete with a Greek wine amphora and pottery, in southern Germany, and in north-eastern France would appear to be those of chieftains.

The increasing use of iron and technological skills in its work and smithing characterize the Hallstatt Age. However, this culture continued to use Bronze Age materials and the techniques of the earlier Urnfield culture. The widespread use of iron allowed the Celts to fell forests and clear land for agriculture as well as engaging in raids and warfare among themselves or with other peoples such as the Iberians, who settled in the Iberian Peninsula. An indication of increasing warfare can be seen in the construction of strongly fortified settlements and the later hill forts. The first fortified "castle" of the late Hallstatt period was found at Heuneburg on the Danube, where rich grave finds were uncovered by archeologists. The late Hallstatt period saw many small hill forts being abandoned with a drift of population westward to the upper Danube, the upper Rhine, and eastern France. A reduced number of very large hill forts were created where very prestigious and powerful high chiefs resided. This move westward might be attributed to the Greek trade goods

Opposite: Celtic peoples were well established during the European and Bronze Age. However, it was not until the emergence of the Hallstat culture that the period could be linked directly to the Celts.

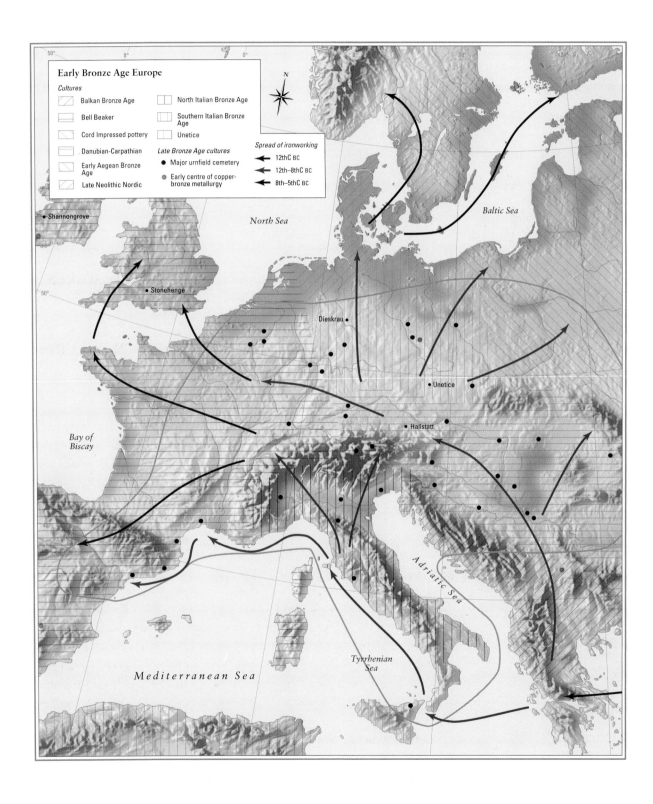

Early Bronze Age Europe

Cultures

Balkan Bronze Age

Bell Beaker

Cord Impressed pottery

Danubian-Carpathian

Early Aegean Bronze Age

Late Neolithic Nordic

North Italian Bronze Age

Southern Italian Bronze Age

Unetice

Late Bronze Age cultures

● Major urnfield cemetery

● Early centre of copper-bronze metallurgy

Spread of ironworking

◀ 12thC BC

◀ 12th–8thC BC

◀ 8th–5thC BC

N

North Sea

Baltic Sea

Shannongrove

Stonehenge

Dieskrau

Unetice

Hallstatt

Bay of Biscay

Adriatic Sea

Tyrrhenian Sea

Mediterranean Sea

emanating from Massilia forming a major attraction. The routes along the river valleys of the Seine, Rhine, Danube, and Rhône link together major centers.

The wealth of Celtic chieftains is demonstrated by the interred works of art. Greek bronze, northern amber, gold, and wine vessels point to a significant increase in trade. Indeed, Greeks certainly acted as merchants at Massilia (Marseille). The grave furniture of an aristocratic young woman at Vix, near Châtillon-sur-Seine in the Côte d'Or, contained a five-foot high bronze wine container (krater), emphasizing the huge importance of trade between the Hallstatt Celts and Greece. Other sites provide evidence of links with the Etruscan civilization in Italy. During and after the heyday of Hallstatt culture, there is evidence for an increase in salt extraction, both for domestic use and as a trade product, as is demonstrated by the Hallstatt mines with long shafts boring down to a depth of 1,300 feet.

Although inter-tribal rivalry was prevalent, the Hallstatt Celts made a great contribution to European art, inheriting their techniques from the Urnfield culture and thus laying the foundations for the blossoming of art during the La Tène Celtic period. Hallstatt artifacts were normally adorned with repeated, rigidly designed, symmetrical patterns, as can be seen on the pottery vessel in the Württembergisches Landesmuseum in Stuttgart. Their stylization of chevrons and curves derives from the Scythians and other steppe peoples but this did not preclude the Hallstatt Celts from occasionally creating artwork with images of animals and people. A 35-centimeter-long vehicle was found at Strettweg in Austria, this comprising a group of bronze figures on a wheeled platform. In the center stands a goddess surrounded by mounted warriors and sacred animals, including a horned god. The culture is also represented in grave finds of long, weighty swords of bronze and iron, the winged Hallstatt axe, and dagger swords with horseshoe hilts.

As far as Hallstatt Celtic society is concerned, it appears that it comprised tribes which subdivided into families, with loyalty being given to a chieftain. Society was made up of chiefs, warriors, druids, craftsmen, farmers, servants, and slaves. The burial at Vix seems to demonstrate that aristocratic women were given parity with men, this theory being confirmed by the existence of Cartimandua, queen of the Brigantes, and Boudicca, Queen of the Iceni in a later period in Britain.

The late Hallstatt period witnessed the growth of princely residences, those built with the proceeds of trade following that already mentioned westward population drift. One residence ,discovered in 1973, was revealed when an amateur archeologist found some fragments of Attic pottery at Châtillon-sur-Glâne in Switzerland. Pottery shards show Greek kraters, amphorae from southern France, and Phocaean ware. The settlement has been dated to a period between 550 and 480 BC and was founded on a trade route that linked Greece to Brittany and Cornwall, which produced tin, so important for making Greek bronze. This route from Greece to Italy, over the St. Bernard Pass, the Saane River, the Swiss plateau, the rivers Saône and Seine, to Brittany and Britain. Châtillon was a probable way-station between the Rhine and the Saane and Aare valleys. The area contains burial barrows which are still to be excavated, themselves being evidence of a high status site. The site is thought to be one of a series of entrepôts, with others being Le Camp-du-Château de Sallin with its port at Lesny on the Loue, Bragby where the Doubs and Sâone join, and Mont Lassois with a port at Vix on the upper Seine.

Opposite: The Hallstatt culture of central Europe produced superb craftmanship, gloriously furnished burials, and dominating hill forts. This is the earliest culture which can be specifically recognized as being Celtic.

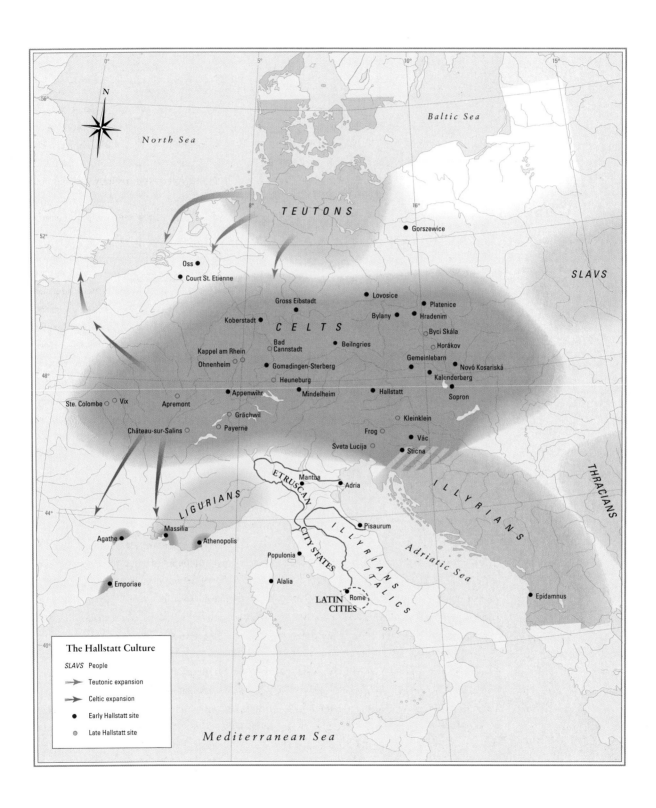

The following labels appear on the map:

North Sea

Baltic Sea

TEUTONS

● Gorszewice

SLAVS

Oss ●
● Court St. Etienne

● Lovosice
Gross Eibstadt ●
● Platenice
Bylany ○ Hradenim
Koberstadt ● *C E L T S*
○ Byci Skála
Kappel am Rhein Bad ○ ● Beilngries ○ Horákov
Cannstadt Gemeinlebarn ●
Ohnenheim ○ ○ ● Gomadingen-Sterberg ● Novó Kosariská
○ Heuneburg ● Kalenderberg
Ste. Colombe ○ ○ Vix ● Appenwihr ● Mindelheim ● Hallstatt
Apremont ○ ○ Sopron
○ Grächwil ○ Kleinklein
Château-sur-Salins ○ ○ Payerne Frog ○
Sveta Lucija ○ ● Vác
Sticna ●

LIGURIANS

ETRUSCAN Mantua ○
● Adria *I L L Y R I A N S*

CITY STATES
● Pisaurum
Massilia ● *I L L Y R I A N S*
Agathe ○ *I T A L I C S*
● Athenopolis Adriatic Sea
Populonia ●
● Alalia
● Emporiae *LATIN CITIES* Rome ○
● Epidamnus

THRACIANS

Mediterranean Sea

The Hallstatt Culture

SLAVS People
Teutonic expansion
Celtic expansion
● Early Hallstatt site
○ Late Hallstatt site

HILL FORTS

HILL FORTS WERE IMPRESSIVE STRUCTURES OFTEN INCORPORATING SEVERAL RAMPARTS, BRIDGES, AND BASTIONS AND REINFORCED WITH LARGE QUANTITIES OF TIMBER. SEVERAL SITES SHOW AN ORDERLY ARRANGEMENT OF BUILDINGS, SUGGESTING AN ELEMENT OF SETTLEMENT PLANNING.

Celtic hill forts are extremely commonplace as one drives around Europe. A journey through the Downs in England on the way to the coast will see several of these constructions on the tops of hills with their distinctive outlines. Hill forts were used either as a sanctuary during a time of war or raiding or became the residences of chiefs and acted as administrative centers or distribution points for trade goods with fairs and even religious festivals. However, the latter task could also be fulfilled by a promontory fort such as Hengistbury Head in Dorset, England.

Some hill forts were built during the Bronze Age but the period of the Iron Age from the seventh to the first century BC saw heavy use of such constructions whether covering a large or very small area. Eventually, the Celts also used *oppida* as a semi-urban lifestyle developed in some parts of Europe. Hill forts did not always occupy a hill, especially in non-hilly regions such as eastern lowland Britain where an extremely low lying hill-fort can be found at Stonea in Cambridgeshire.

The main examples of hill forts are located on the summits of hills with enclosure ramparts adapted to the contours of the upper hill slopes, thus being called contour forts. The major characteristic of such a fort is a whole or partial circuit of man-made enclosing defense works. Some forts possess several ramparts and these multi-vallate forts often have very cleverly constructed gateways designed to deter attacks by building killing grounds. Such a fort is Maiden Castle in England. Hill forts can also be found with a series of ditches with ramparts surmounted with palisades.

Very few hill forts have been excavated archeologically but various buildings and post-holes have been found suggesting inhabitation, large storage pits, or four-post edifices acting as granaries. Hill forts close to the Mediterranean sometimes possess large storage jars, called pithoi. Some mainland

Opposite: In southern Britain many hill forts were constructed along the South Downs in the 6th century BC. As power became more centralized there were fewer hill forts in occupation. These were generally more heavily fortified. One of these, Danebury, came to an abrupt end, probably caused by war around 100 BC.

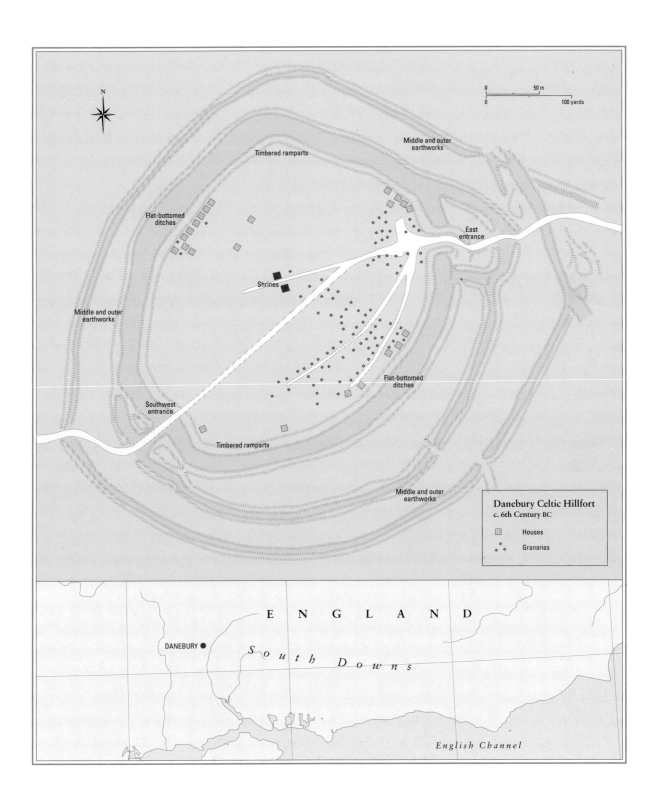

Timbered ramparts

Middle and outer
earthworks

Flat-bottomed
ditches

East
entrance

Shrines

Middle and outer
earthworks

Southwest
entrance

Flat-bottomed
ditches

Timbered ramparts

Middle and outer
earthworks

0   50 m
0   100 yards

N

Danebury Celtic Hillfort
c. 6th Century BC

Houses

Granaries

E N G L A N D

DANEBURY ●

South Downs

English Channel

European forts also have dry-stone or timber-built cellars which can only be accessed via staircases like that at Mont Beuvray in French Burgundy. The fort at Châteaumeillant in Berry in central France was found with its cellars full of wine amphorae.

Many hill forts provide animal bones demonstrating the likelihood of animals being butchered and probably sheltered within the enclosure. Some forts are so huge that animals could graze within them. The issue of how livestock or people were watered is still open for discovery although some forts have dew ponds. Hill forts can be industrial centers because some in north-west Wales provide evidence of smelting and smithing iron. The mining and refining of ore were also carried out at the forts at Sticna in Slovenia and Kelhelm in Bavaria, Germany. So fort inhabitants could be processing raw materials and manufacturing items, but this was certainly not always the case.

Trade was another important factor in the life of forts that were located adjacent to trade routes by land or by river. Southern Britain and European sites have found coins, often cast copper, which show a market-oriented economy. Economic transactions took place within forts, and the temperate areas of Europe were interested in acquiring Mediterranean products of high quality. Evidence of long-distance trade and relay-marketing are pottery fragments from Italian wine amphorae discovered on sites from Bavaria to the Atlantic coasts of Europe and southern Britain. The presence of amber demonstrates the movement of goods southward from the Baltic.

However, perishable products are impossible to provide archeological evidence such as slaves and livestock. It is impossible to estimate the populations of hill forts in times of peace. The exemplary hill-fort at Danebury in England is considered as a sanctuary and storage center which might have housed 200 to 350 people.

In England, as in most of Europe, hill forts were mainly constructed during the fifth and sixth centuries BC and abandoned after about 400–350 BC. Some 2,000 have been identified in England and over 20,000 across Europe. Most historians believe that British hill forts were expressions of status and prestige or delineated territory or spheres of influence rather than being concerned with actual conflict. Nevertheless, Danebury provides evidence of two fires suggesting warfare.

Maiden Castle, near Dorchester, England, has been excavated in 1934 and 1937, with more digs carried out in 1985–86. Developed at different times, the fort eventually encompassed 46 acres (18.5 hectares) with various types of Celts adding to the fortifications. The earlier Celts built ramparts to defend against javelin attack but later newcomers, arriving about 250 BC, used the sling as an offensive weapon and therefore improved the ramparts extensively, adding secondary banks and ditches to counter the power of sling-shot. The twin gateways were strengthened, being given stone revetments, as was the north-western entrance to the gateway where it passed the first line of outer defenses. However, Maiden Castle proved incapable of repelling the Roman army, which made short work of the fort and destroyed the gateways.

The Durotrigii, the local Celtic tribe, probably used Maiden Castle as a center for farming rather than trade or manufacture. Livestock was raised within the ramparts: the remains of a variety of animals including cattle, sheep, pigs, and chickens have been found there. Historians have suggested that Iron Age Celts would drive their animals or carry their grain to the fort where it could be exchanged, sold, or even handed to a local chieftain as a type of taxation.

Opposite: Photograph of the southern ramparts of Maiden Castle, England. The castle was first built in 600 BC, above the remains of a Neolithic settement. This multi-vallate fort was, at one point, home to several hundred people.

ZÁVIST, BOHEMIAN FORTRESS

THE FORTIFIED SETTLEMENT OF ZÁVIST WAS SURROUNDED BY
COMPLICATED DEFENSE SYSTEMS AND CONTAINED AN ACROPOLIS
WITH A CULT SANCTUARY. UNCOVERED ARTIFACTS SHOW THE
HILL-FORT AS A FOCAL POINT FOR INTERNATIONAL TRADE IN ITS
DAY. IT IS LOCATED NEAR PRAGUE, CZECH REPUBLIC.

The Celtic fortress at Závist overlooks a bank of the River Vitava some seven miles from Prague while facing the juncture with the River Berounka. The site has been occupied from Neolithic times and witnessed several periods of occupation with some interruptions. Filling 125 acres (50 hectares) in the Bronze Age, the fortress grew to 250 acres (100 hectares) toward the end of the sixth century BC. The site, 200 meters above the river, has been carefully excavated and ramparts constructed from wood, earth and dry-stone have been revealed. Archeologists spent some 20 years uncovering the defenses and various buildings, including an 'acropolis' showing Závist was a religious sanctuary as well as a distribution point for goods and a market. Eventually reaching 370 acres (150 hecatres), the *oppidum* possessed defense lines extending 6.2 miles (10 kilometers). The fortress belonged to the Celtic Boii and dominated and served a large territory, and by the fifth century BC the center was enclosed by a large trench dug out of the living rock. Inside were high dry-stone platforms some 16 feet high; five were rectangular and one triangular serving as probable observation points. The 'acropolis' or sanctuary evolved over time. Between the sixth and fifth centuries BC, the original palisaded sanctuary was enhanced by several large timber-constructed buildings. These were placed symmetrically along a central street leading to the entrance of the cult/sanctuary centre. The whole religious complex was incinerated during the first half of the fifth century and was rebuilt soon after. A new central building was created with twin naves with wooden pillars supporting a pitched roof. Beautiful artifacts have been found from the early La Tène period.

Behind the line of defenses were buildings and shops planned around a grid street system. Excavations show that the population engaged in metal-working, iron-smithing and produced silver and gold coins,

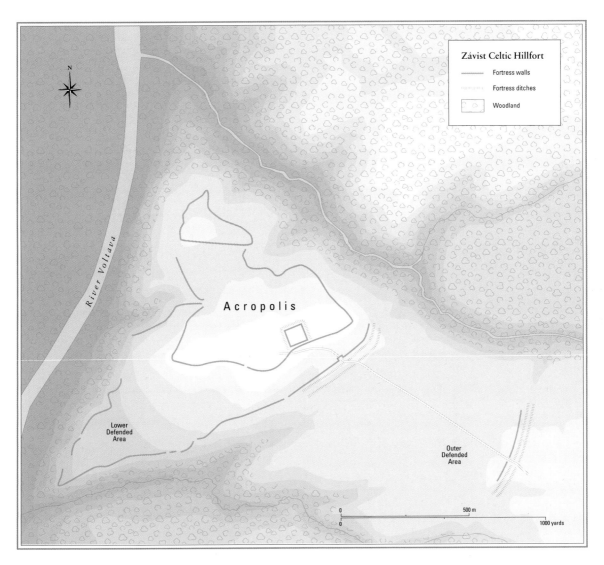

The fortress at Závist covered some 370 acres (150 hectares). This fine *oppidum* offered a meeting place for religious, social and trade purposes, securely protected by its defensive walls.

demonstrating the political and administrative importance of the fortress. The fortress vanished between 25 and 20 BC, resulting from a fire which could be attributed to a decline in Celtic power and fortunes as Germanic peoples encroached upon and squeezed Celtic lands.

When Závist led the network of *oppida*, Bohemian trade and trade routes were therefore controlled. This trade policy was apparently a carefully devised plan in an imperial sense with the *oppida* built on new sites, only Závist being on an old site. The first colony was planted at Hrazany, the next being at Nevezice, upstream on the River Vitava, followed by an *oppidum* at Stradonice on the River Berounka. Eastern Bohemia was home to Ceské Lhotice, which was halfway between Závist and Staré Hradisko, a fortification on the Amber Route. The Celts wanted to link the Boii network with a similar system in the Danube Valley but this scheme failed except for an *oppidum* at Trísov further along the Vitava.

CELTS OF CHAMPAGNE

THE CHAMPAGNE REGION OF THE RIVER MARNE SUFFERED DEPOPULATION DURING MIGRATION MOVEMENTS AND DEVELOPED A MIXED CULTURE AS DANUBIAN CELTS MOVED INTO EMPTY LANDS. THE REGION IS NOTED FOR THE RICHNESS OF ITS CHARIOT BURIALS.

The Champagne region of Gaul was inhabited by the Lingones, who left many cemeteries, some 140 cart burials, and some chariot burials. Unfortunately, many sites were prospected and raided during the nineteenth century and the woodwork in grave finds has rotted. The Lingones are particularly well known for sending some of their people, maybe surplus population, in the Celtic invasion of Italy when they joined the Senones and Boii in this migration. They settled in the Po Valley near Spina. In Champagne, the decrease in population meant that the inhabitants were reduced to living in two areas: Beine-Suippes, east of Rheims, and Senna-Yonne, north-east of Sens. The region has offered up some women's tombs containing chariots but more importantly two types of female funerary costumes in styles of torques, bracelets, and fibulae, the brooches used to hold textiles together. These differences are probably a reflection of a population increase after 350 BC when lands abandoned in the Italian migration were acquired by a different population moving in from the Danube region. The incoming groups were aggressive and re-conquered agricultural lands, probably being Belgae who conflicted with the Celts of the Seine and Marne. The violence in the region is attested by the hordes of weapons and the monuments and sanctuaries at Gournay-sur-Aronde and Ribemont-sur-Ancre.

The burial sites in the Champagne show that elite tombs often contained the aforementioned wagons and chariots. The Somme-Bionne grave contained a deceased warrior wearing a gold ring on his right hand who lay on his back under the chariot's carriage which had been dismantled and overturned. The two wheels were held upright by grooves cut in the ground to take them. The iron rims of the wheels and the metal parts of the yoke remained in place. The harness was well decorated and perforated bronze discs, which had been attached to the leather, were superb pieces of art work. The warrior's belt had a

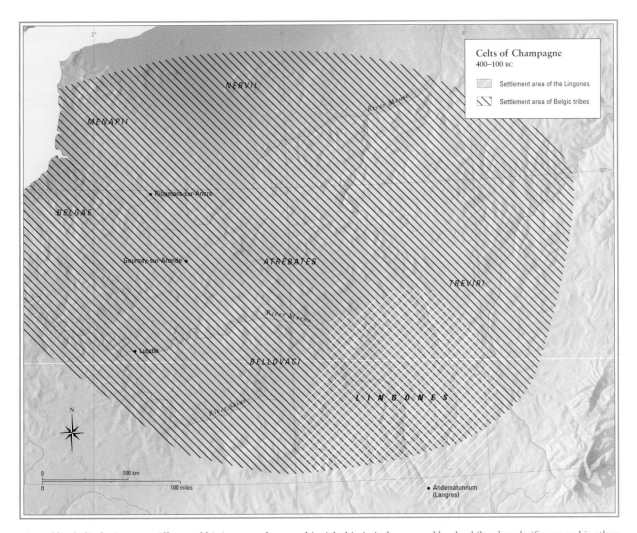

pierced hook displaying two griffons and his iron sword was on his right hip in its bronze scabbard, while a long knife was on his other hip. Metal bars were on his left and they may have been roasting spits. There was an Etruscan jug, a vase made from local pottery, and an Attic cup, which shows the sources of trade goods. A drinking horn was adorned with a band of embossed gold leaf. Another important find was excavated in 1876 at Le Gorge Meillet. A large trapezoid pit was hollowed out of the chalk soil, and the deceased warrior was accompanied by his two-wheeled chariot. He was surrounded by La Tène-style burial goods.

The Lingones capital was at Andematunnum, now Langres, situated on a rocky promontory above the River Marne. They succumbed to Roman rule and were grateful for Caesar's treatment of the Belgae because it increased their security with their enemy defeated. They became Romanised and managed to survive, entering the Batavian revolt in AD 69. Two cohorts of Lingones were stationed in Roman Britain and inscriptions at High Rochester, Northumberland and Lanchester, Durham attest to this. One inscription reads: "For the emperor Caesar Marcus Antoninus Gordianus Pius Felix Augustus, the bath house and the basilica were built from the ground up during the governorship of Egnatius Lucilianus, pro-praetorian legate of the emperor, under the direction of Marcus Aurelius Quirinus, prefect of Gordian's First Cohort of Lingones."

La Tène Culture

THE SITE AT LA TÈNE ON LAKE NEUCHÂTEL APPEARS TO BE AN
OPEN-AIR SANCTUARY WHERE THE CELTS MADE OFFERINGS
OF WEAPONS INTO THE WATER, PARALLELING THE TRADITION
FOUND AT THE SPRINGS AT CHAMALIÈRES, PUY-DE-DÔME, AND
THE HEADWATERS OF THE SEINE.

The La Tène culture, named after a Celtic archeological site on Lake Neuchâtel in Switzerland, existed in mainland Europe from about 450 BC to the conquest of Gaul by Julius Caesar in 58 BC. The homeland of this Celtic development lay between the valleys of the Marne and Moselle in the west and Bavaria and Austria in the east.

During this period many Celts left their homeland in central Europe to cross the Alps and settle in the fertile river valleys of northern Italy, fighting and destroying many Etruscan cities on their way. In 38 BC, the Celts sacked Rome and raided down to Sicily; the Romans eventually recovered under Marcus Furius Camillus and drove the invaders back to the Alpine foothills. The Celts next enlarged their control in Europe, overtaking the Hallstatt culture while spreading into Gaul, Spain, the Carpathians, and the Balkans. The Roman historian Livy, as well as recounting the sack of Rome, describes how branches of the Celts settled in southern and central Germany. Under their leader, Brennus, some tribes stormed into Bulgaria, Thrace, and Macedonia. In 279 BC, Brennus fought the Greeks while attempting to raid the temple of the god Apollo at Delphi. Eventually, the Celts were driven out. After this defeat, surviving Celts built a fortress on the eventual site of Belgrade, and one band crossed the Dardanelles into Anatolia, where they established themselves, giving their name to Galatia. Some even reached the Sea of Azov in Russia. Eventually, the Celts were squeezed between the military might of Rome and the pressure of expanding Germanic tribes, which forced many Celts to the south and west, where they would later be conquered by the Romans; the absence of political unity contributed to the Celts' ultimate downfall. The La Tène culture in Britain was brought under Roman control in the first century AD.

The La Tène culture developed the Hallstatt art forms and incorporated Greek and Etruscan styles but eventually Celticized these onto its own legendary animals, plant motifs, and human masks. The designs appeared on military accoutrements, bowls and vessels, and mirrors. Examples of Celtic arts are neck rings or torques, brooches, and particularly the silver Gundestrup cauldron (in the Danish National Museum in Copenhagen), on which the figures were hammered out from behind using the repoussé method. The images on the cauldron are thought to be partially oriental, maybe of Scythian origin. An inside plaque depicts the bust of a woman flanked by wheels and fantasy animals. Other plaques show: three bulls with figures pointing swords at their throats; a line of horsemen with decorated helmets; the bust of a young goddess with two male figures behind her while she wears a buffered torque around her neck; a small figure riding a large fish; and a god with the horns of a stag, holding a torque and a serpent with ram's horns. Other well-known finds are in the British Museum, including a bronze lozenge-shaped shield with medallions and enamel work and a bronze mirror with enamel decorations. This first-century BC Battersea shield was recovered from the Thames. More shields have been found: two third-century BC examples, one from the River Witham near Washingborough, England, and an oval bronze shield from Chertsey, London. The Desborough Mirror in the British Museum in London has lace-style patterning with lyre-palmette formations and triskellis. In Ireland, La Tène arts acquired a different style, especially in metalwork such as the Tara brooch and Ardagh chalice. The art was mainly for the tribal elites for conspicuous display and for grave goods. La Tène art is a wonderful amalgam embodying the geometric pattern of the Hallstatt culture which is allied to stylized curved lines and animal and vegetal designs embellished with Scythian animal designs from the steppe lands of the Ukraine.

When the La Tène village was revealed on the lakeshore of Neuchâtel, various excavations uncovered houses and bridges and uncovered some 2,500 artifacts including unused swords, spearheads, shield bosses, hundreds of brooches, tools, and bits of chariots. Historians have suggested that the site was a place of sacrifice where metalware was offered to water gods as thanks for a victory in battle. The complete civilization developing has been understood through extensive archeological evidence and the writings of Greek and Roman commentators and historians. Ethnological evidence has also been useful when analyzing evidence in surviving Celtic regions on the periphery of western Europe.

The Celts have left a substantial legacy in Wales, Scotland, Ireland, Isle of Man, Brittany, and Cornwall. Irish monks preserved knowledge by keeping learning and the Christian religion alive. Eventually, Irish monks, later to be saints, were important in returning Christianity to mainland Britain and also establishing missions in mainland Europe. The manuscripts they created are beautifully illuminated, such as the *Book of Kells*, while the Celtic crosses surviving in Ireland and the Isle of Man have a beauty of their own. Among the best examples are the Manx crosses at Maughold, the Isle of Man, on an ancient monastic site. A second inheritance is the survival of Celtic literature and stories. Although the Celts did not write, they passed on law, history, and stories through a rich oral tradition, and parts of these are preserved in the Welsh *Mabinogion*, the Irish legends of Cuchulainn, and the story of Bricriu's feast.

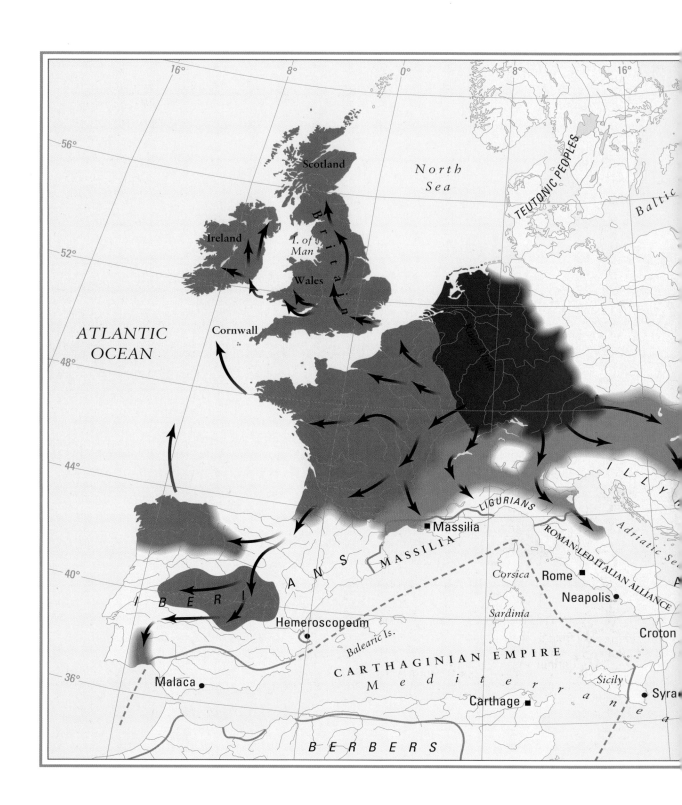

16° 8° 0° 8° 16°

56°

*North
Sea*

Scotland

52°

Ireland   I. of
Man

ATLANTIC
OCEAN   Wales

Cornwall

TEUTONIC PEOPLES

Baltic

48°

44°

ILLY

Adriatic Sea

LIGURIANS

Massilia

MASSILIA

ROMAN-LED ITALIAN ALLIANCE

Corsica   Rome
Neapolis

IBERI

ANS

40°   Hemeroscopeum   *Sardinia*   Croton

Balearic Is.

CARTHAGINIAN EMPIRE

36°   Malaca   *Sicily*   Syra
Mediterra

Carthage   *ne*
a

BERBERS

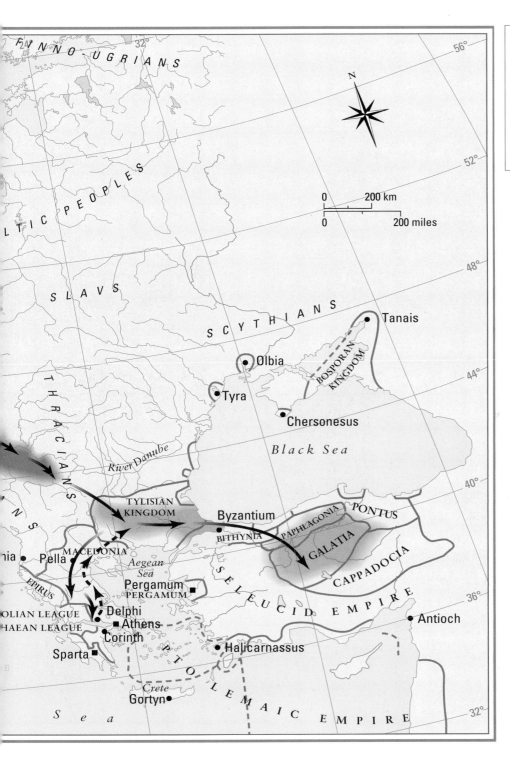
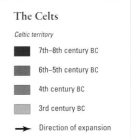

The Celts

Celtic territory

■ 7th–8th century BC

■ 6th–5th century BC

■ 4th century BC

■ 3rd century BC

→ Direction of expansion

FINNO-UGRIANS

BALTIC PEOPLES

SLAVS

SCYTHIANS

THRACIANS

TYLISIAN KINGDOM

River Danube

Black Sea

Tanais

BOSPORAN KINGDOM

Olbia

Tyra

Chersonesus

Byzantium

BITHYNIA

PAPHLAGONIA

PONTUS

GALATIA

CAPPADOCIA

SELEUCID EMPIRE

Antioch

MACEDONIA

Pella

Aegean Sea

Pergamum

PERGAMUM

EPIRUS

ia

Delphi

Athens

Corinth

Sparta

OLIAN LEAGUE

HAEAN LEAGUE

Halicarnassus

PTOLEMAIC EMPIRE

Crete

Gortyn

Sea

0   200 km

0   200 miles

N

The La Tène culture developed
in west-central Europe in the
middle of the fifth century BC.
The culture takes its name
from a ritual site and settlement
on the shores of lake
Neuchatelle, Switzerland, first
excavated in 1857.

CELTIC TRADE

CELTIC TRADE WAS INTERNATIONAL, USING SOPHISTICATED SHIPPING ON THE ATLANTIC COAST AND THE BRITISH CHANNEL TO BRING TIN TO THE MEDITERRANEAN WHILE THE DANUBE SETTLEMENTS CONTROLLED THE AMBER ROUTE FROM THE BALTIC SOUTHWARD TO THE ADRIATIC.

Trade in the Celtic world was widespread and commercial networks linked into international trade routes in the Mediterranean and the Silk Route to China as attested by silk threads being a Celtic grave find. Commerce was important because the raw materials controlled by the Celts could be exchanged for luxury goods which could be conspicuously displayed to raise the status of elite groups such as chieftains and priests even higher.

Celtic technology was extensive, being capable of making charcoal and smelting iron, and with ingots and bars of iron being used as an early medium of exchange before Celtic kings commenced minting their own coinage. Wheeled vehicles of various designs were made with iron tires which made Celtic society extremely mobile in times of migration or could be used to move goods as well as being used in burials as with chariots. Ship building was extensive with the Celts capable of crossing the English Channel and Irish Sea in order to populate the British Isles. Indeed, a complete communication system allowed the Atlantic Celts to sail the seas and construct very stout ships like those which Julius Caesar fought in the Battle of the Loire during his Gallic wars.

The Celtic tribes were self-sufficient in food and produced nearly all they needed. Agricultural production in terms of grain and cattle developed a surplus which could be exchanged or sold. Initially, trade was simple with certain basic necessities being bought and sold, such as tin, salt, iron, flint, and copper, these not always being found in a tribal locale. Brittany was known for its salt pans and the axe heads its inhabitants made. Tin was mined in Cornwall and merchants sailed from the Mediterranean to get it. In return for these basics, trade in cattle, hides, and slaves developed. Eventually, the wealth produced could buy products from Greece, Cartage, Etruria, and Rome.

Opposite: Celtic trade linked most of north-western Europe, exchanging materials like amber and tin for luxury goods.

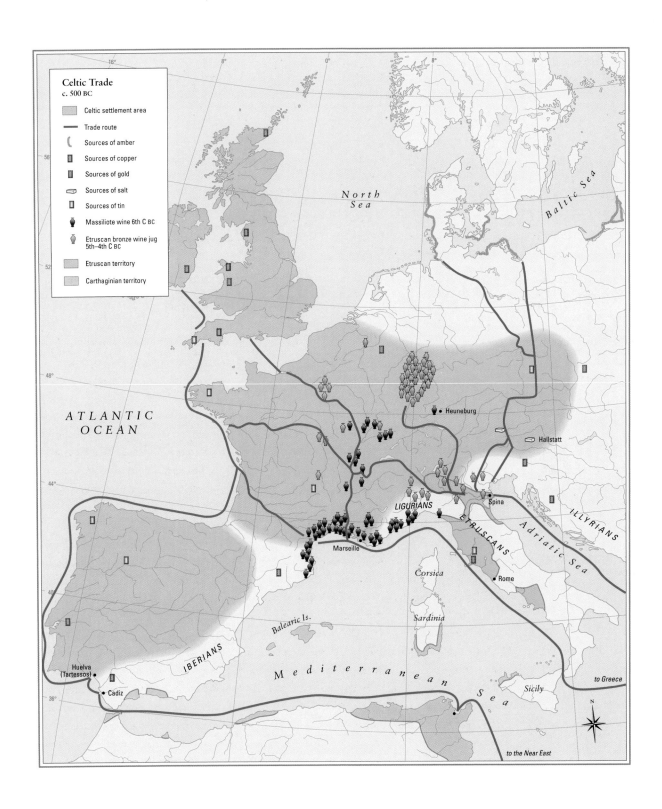

Celtic Trade
c. 500 BC

Celtic settlement area

Trade route

Sources of amber

Sources of copper

Sources of gold

Sources of salt

Sources of tin

Massiliote wine 6th C BC

Etruscan bronze wine jug
5th–4th C BC

Etruscan territory

Carthaginian territory

North Sea

Baltic Sea

ATLANTIC OCEAN

• Heuneburg

Hallstatt

LIGURIANS

Spina •

ETRUSCANS

ILLYRIANS

Adriatic Sea

Marseille

Corsica

• Rome

Sardinia

Balearic Is.

IBERIANS

Mediterranean Sea

Sicily

to Greece

Huelva
(Tartessos) •

• Cadiz

to the Near East

Much evidence exists of commercial traffic between European ports and Britain as early as 800 BC. By Roman times and before the Roman conquest, British kings were minting their own coinage and were importing wine, Roman silver and glass ware, Arretine pottery, and fish sauce from either southern Iberia or Brittany. Strabo, the Greek historian and geographer, stated that Roman trade with Britain produced more revenue than if it had been a Roman province, a better option than the cost of conquering, occupying, and administering the islands. The flow of goods saw artwork, wine, and drinking goods emanating from the Mediterranean, amber from the Baltic, gold and copper from Wales, iron from the Severn Valley, hunting dogs, pearls, wheat, timber, gold from Ireland and slaves. Many of the goods exported from Britain were bought for use by the Roman army. The exchanges and the growth of settlements around trading centers allowed for the development of craftsmen, leading to improved pottery, stylish jewellery, and enamel work.

Archeology provides evidence of Celtic–Mediterranean interactions through excavated finds. The Hallstatt Celtic culture saw a move from bronze to iron which was helped by the development of an iron industry in Etruria which was adjacent to the Golasecca Celts of the Ticino. Goods moved around Europe with three major trade routes developing.

The Tin Road started in Massilia and either went up the Rhône Valley and the Loire to the Breton sailors who linked the road to Cornwall. Or the road traveled along the Garonne before it reached the sea and its mariners.

An alternative road left the Near East and Phoenicia, sailing to Carthage, Cadiz, Tartessos and through the Bay of Biscay to south-west England. Another road saw an Amber Road tying Italy to Denmark and the Baltic coast. The road moved down the rivers Oder and Elbe through the Weichsel Valley and Moravian Gate. The Celts in southern Germany drew these two routes together with the Danube route. A testament to this period is the Celtic castle of Heuneburg, near the source of the Danube, being probably the most important Celtic trade center through which poured Etruscan wine and pottery.

When the La Tène culture developed, the region around Hunsrück-Eifel became very important. The area was prosperous as reflected in the art and gold work found by archeologists in the graves of the social elites of the period. The prince's grave at Schwarzenbach-Hunsrück produced a gold drinking cup while the princess of Waldalgesheim/Nahe had a grave containing gold rings of a tendril style. Raw iron was traded in bars about 50 centimeters in length, while iron ore could be surface mined in Schwarzenbach. A well-traveled trade route crossed the Hunsrück hills and led to the Rhine; today this is known as the Via Ausonia. A north-south alignment was formed over the San Bernadino Pass, allowing the Hunsrück area to be directly accessed by water —the Walensee, Lake Zurich and the Limmat, the Aare, and the Rhine through to the mouths of the Nahe and Mosel rivers. The trans-alpine trade routes and trade centers led to the economic and social system of the urban *oppida*. These settlements specialized in craftsmanship, and the town planning and architecture was sophisticated as these towns became centers of political and religious activities in the Celtic world or Celtic cultural federation, which never united to form a state, even though Caesar regarded these political units or *oppida* as a state, a *civitas*.

Opposite: The Celts of southern Britain exported tin, copper, and silver to eager customers within the Roman Empire in exchange for highly valued Mediterranean wine.

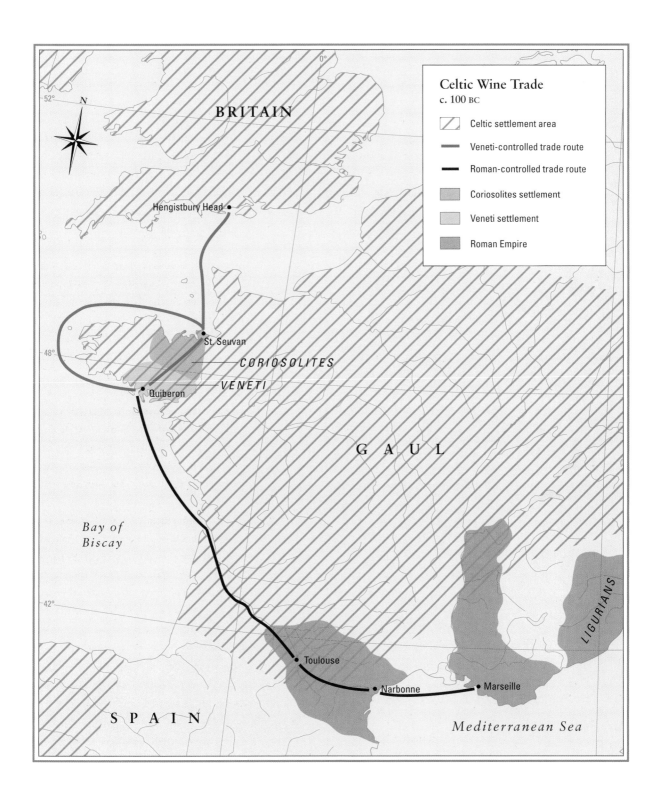

Celtic Wine Trade
c. 100 BC

Celtic settlement area
Veneti-controlled trade route
Roman-controlled trade route
Coriosolites settlement
Veneti settlement
Roman Empire

BRITAIN

Hengistbury Head

St. Seuvan

CORIOSOLITES

VENETI

Quiberon

GAUL

Bay of
Biscay

LIGURIANS

Toulouse

Narbonne

Marseille

SPAIN

Mediterranean Sea

N

GRAVE FINDS

THE GRAVES OF ELITE CELTS, BOTH MEN AND WOMEN, PROVIDE
RICH EVIDENCE OF A MAGNIFICENT MATERIAL CULTURE IN
THE DESIGNS INCORPORATED INTO IRON-WORK AND THE ART
OF SILVER AND GOLDSMITHS, SHOWING THE INFLUENCE OF
ETRUSCAN, GREEK, AND SCYTHIAN DESIGN.

Burial practices in the Hallstatt Culture see bodies being placed in graves with possessions and four-wheeled wagons, which suggests an earlier steppe culture. Such finds have been evident in Bavaria and northern Austria and are extremely useful because material culture can be assessed via the personal effects placed near the deceased's body. The La Tène Culture switched from wagons to chariot burials, and the rich character of elite figures can be seen in the rich design of jewellery. Warrior graves see weapons being placed next to bodies but graves also contain cauldrons, drinking horns, and cups and eating utensils, attesting to the Celtic love of feasting. Bronze drinking vessels would be used to quaff beer and mead in the afterlife or even wine.

Sieves to filter wine have been found, as have pieces of silk-embroidered cloth that must have traveled the Silk Road or entered the Mediterranean after traveling the Indian Ocean and the Arabian desert. Ivory appliqués were once attached to wooden furniture imported from northern Italy and Greece. A bronze couch with little figurines mounted on wheels that support the bed was found in the princely burial chamber at Hochdorf near Stuttgart, Germany. The bed was also inlaid with coral, another product traveling from afar. Even more interesting are the medical instruments associated with trepanning. In fact, sites with medical artifacts are not unusual and point to a sophisticated understanding of physiology.

Grave finds attest to the quality of material wealth enjoyed by elite members of society and demonstrate the extent of a trading network linked to China, the Baltic, and the Mediterranean world. Finds include bracelets and diadems of bronze and gold, as well as fish hooks, arrowheads, horse harnesses, and iron axe spears. The sophistication in taste shows that early Celtic culture was as vibrant as the later La Tène and Etruscan style, and furniture was imported as object of status.

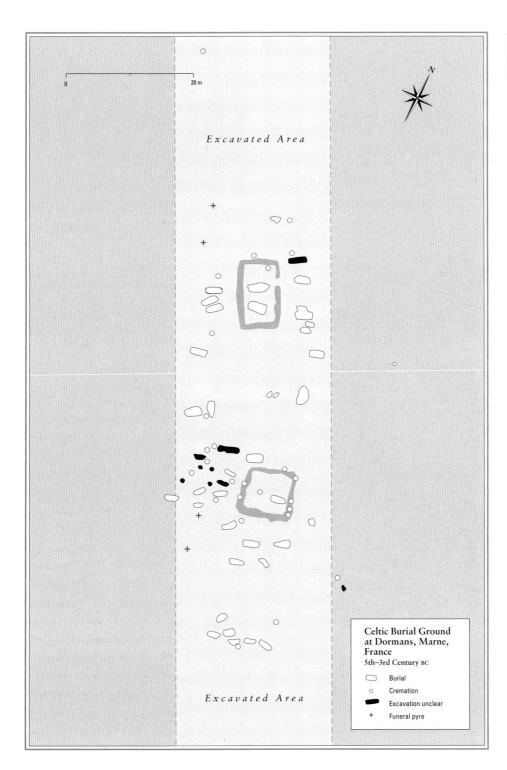

The grave excavation at Dormans has revealed both inhumation and cremation burials.

Excavated Area

N

0   20 m

Excavated Area

Celtic Burial Ground at Dormans, Marne, France
5th–3rd Century BC

▭ Burial
○ Cremation
▬ Excavation unclear
+ Funeral pyre

CELTIC LANGUAGES

THE CELTIC WORLD SPOKE CELTIC TONGUES WHICH DEVELOPED
REGIONAL VARIATIONS, AND CULTURES FORMED SUCH AS
THE CELTIBERIAN IN SPAIN AND THE GOLASCCAN IN ITALY.
ROMANIZATION KILLED OFF MOST GAULISH LANGUAGES, LEAVING
THE FRINGE OF CELTICA TO KEEP THE LANGUAGE ALIVE.

I n the mists of time, a Proto-Indo-European root language developed which parented a whole series of other languages. The existence of an extensive Sanskrit and ancient Greek literature, in addition to the more recently deciphered Hittite, shows common characteristics. By 2000 BC, ancient literatures were the product of distinct languages, suggesting that the original language was fairly unified some thousand years earlier. The Indo-European language evolved into a variety of sub-families as people migrated across the face of Eurasia. Albanian, Armenian, Baltic, Celtic, Italic (Romance languages), Slavic, and Tocharian developed a life of their own.

The Celtic tongue was first identified in south-central Europe, from where it spread over much of Europe. Settlement names and personal names provide linguists with the evidence to identify a variety of Celtic dialects. The Iberian Peninsula witnessed the spread of Celtiberian being spoken over large parts of central, northern, and western Iberia. On the western littoral and in the south-west, Lusitanian was the tongue while Gaulish was the language used in France, Belgium, and the Rhine Valley. Julius Caesar remarked that there were three Gaulish sub-dialects because he divided the inhabitants of Gaul into the Belgae, Celtae, and Aquitani. Italy north-west of the Po Valley was home to an early form of Celtic known as Lepontic, a form of Cisalpine Gaulish. The dialect has spawned some inscriptions which were written in an alphabet based on the Etruscan one. The migration into Asia Minor allows another Celtic dialect to be identified in Galatian. However, Celtic in mainland Europe disappeared under the impact of the Roman Empire, leaving the British Isles and Brittany. However, some Celtic dialects left elements behind that affected French and Spanish and Gallo in Brittany.

The Insular Celtic languages can be split into two types: Brythonic, which used to be spoken in England

Opposite: Celtic languages entered Europe as part of the indo-european migration. Celtic itself is part of the family tree of European languages descending from an archaic proto-indo European.

Development of Indo-European Languages

(After Tomas Gamkrelidze and Vyacheslav Ivanov, 1985)

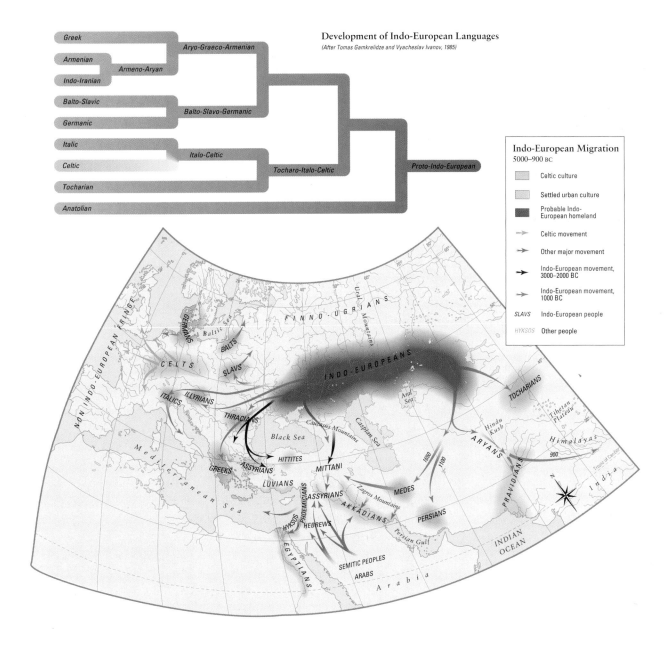

Greek
Armenian
Indo-Iranian
Aryo-Graeco-Armenian
Armeno-Aryan
Balto-Slavic
Germanic
Balto-Slavo-Germanic
Italic
Celtic
Tocharian
Italo-Celtic
Tocharo-Italo-Celtic
Anatolian
Proto-Indo-European

Indo-European Migration
5000–900 BC

- Celtic culture
- Settled urban culture
- Probable Indo-European homeland
- Celtic movement
- Other major movement
- Indo-European movement, 3000–2000 BC
- Indo-European movement, 1000 BC
- *SLAVS* Indo-European people
- *HYKSOS* Other people

and Wales but now only in parts of the latter and was exported to Brittany by British migrants where it superseded Gaulish; and Goidelic, which is still spoken in Ireland and which migrated to Scotland and the Isle of Man. The other ancient language spoken in Scotland was Pictish, which is thought to have been a non-Indo-European language. Another way of dividing the Insular Celts is by the nomenclature: P-Celtic and Q-Celtic. Here, an early 'q' sound was replaced by a 'p' sound. Hence the word for son in Brythonic Welsh is 'map' whereas in Goidelic Irish or Scots it is 'mac'. Brythonic, Gaulish and Lepontic belong to the P-Celtic group, likewise Galatian. The Q-Celtic group includes, among others, Goidelic, Celtiberian, and Lusitanian.

Modern Breton (*Brezhoneg*) was fathered by British immigrants who crossed the Channel to Armorica in the fifth and sixth centuries after the fall of Rome when the Celtic population of England was being pressured by alien raids. Despite the Bretons having their own old literature, generally medieval poetry, it is the only Celtic language which is not recognized as an official language because the French state has French enshrined in the constitution as the language of the Republic.

Cornish (*Kernewek*) in south-west England has literature in the form of passion plays and medieval texts. The language died out in the eighteenth century but modern enthusiasts are rebuilding the language using medieval Cornish texts and vocabulary comparisons with Welsh and Breton. The United Kingdom government recognized Cornish as a language according to the European Charter for Regional or Minority Languages in November 2002.

Welsh (*Cymraeg*) is still spoken, especially in north-eastern and south-eastern, Wales with some half a million speakers, but few Welsh do not speak English. A Welsh literature developed in the early Middle Ages with much medieval poetry and prose. From the time of the Reformation the Church became a bastion of the language and 1588 saw the production of a Welsh Bible. Welsh has many supporters and Welsh-speaking migrant communities around the world, especially in Argentina. British law states that all public bodies must develop policies to help the language. The Welsh TV channel, *Sianel Pedwar Cymru* (S4C) helps here.

Irish (*Gaeilge*) was the one Celtic tongue not under the boot of Rome and developed its own writing system in Ogham. Irish literature is available in large quantities and the Irish experience allowed Gaelic to absorb Norse influences during Viking times. The years spent under British rule meant that Irish remained the language of the poor Catholics whereas English was the language of politics, whether spoken by English or Irish fellow-travelers. Irish nationalism, however, after statehood was achieved, made Irish the first national language. Irish studies keep the language alive and flourishing although the numbers of Irish speakers in the Gaelic-speaking areas of Munster, Connemara, and Donegal are declining. Scottish Gaelic (*Gàidhlig*) was exported to Scotland from Ireland during the fourth to sixth centuries and became the dominant language as Pictish died out. As Norman forms of feudalism were introduced into Scotland, Gaelic receded into the Highlands and Western Islands, where its home is today. Fewer than 60,000 Gaelic speakers remain but the educational system is seeking to secure the language's future. Manx (*Gailck*) was the language of the crofts and fishing villages and remains alive among a few people, and all new laws must be read out in Manx on Tynwald Hill every year. Some Manx-born people still use the occasional Manx word in everyday parlance and place names and streets remain in Gaelic.

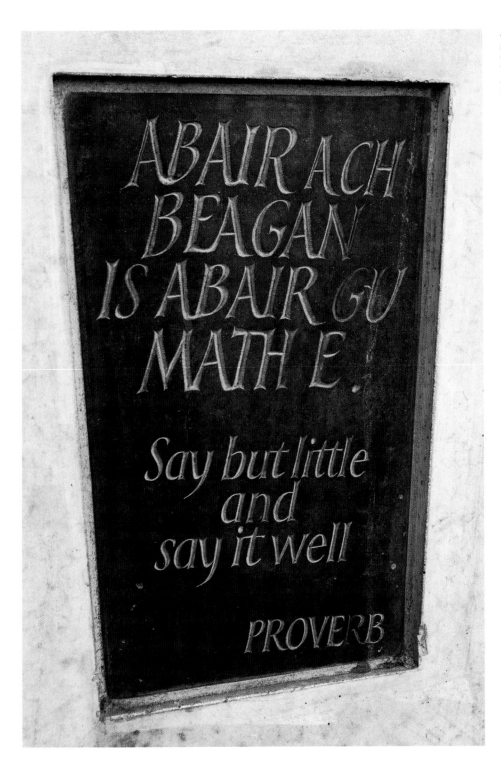

A stone plaque with a Scottish proverb written primarily in Gaelic and translated into English. This photograph was taken outside the Scottish Parliament at Holyrood, Edinburgh

CHARIOT BURIALS

"IN CHARIOT FIGHTING THE BRITONS (OF BRITAIN) BEGIN BY DRIVING ALL OVER THE FIELD HURLING JAVELINS. GENERALLY, THE TERROR INSPIRED BY THE HORSES AND THE NOISE OF THE WHEELS IS SUFFICIENT TO THROW THEIR OPPONENTS' RANKS INTO DISORDER." JULIUS CAESAR, *THE CONQUEST OF GAUL*, IV.33

The Celtic chariot was a weapon of great mobility which could be used as a mobile missile launching vehicle or a delivery system getting a warrior in and out of battle. Useful for skirmishing, a chariot charge could be frightening, and Julius Caesar commented how useful the vehicle was against foraging parties and small patrols. A grave stele at Padua and coins show chariots being the same general shape while a Galatian chariot yoke is depicted on Pergamese reliefs.

The chariot was a light two-horsed vehicle with a crew of a driver and one warrior noble carrying javelins. The chariot wheels were three feet (90 centimeters) in diameter, with iron tires shrunk on. The body was approximately three feet across and the Padua stele suggests it was the same length. The driver sat or squatted at the front of the chariot and carried a whip with the warrior standing behind him. The chariot sides were double wooden arches, partially covered in leather and might be decorated with circular discs (phalerae) of great artistic merit. The horses were harnessed with a wooden yoke, with the pole reinforced with iron where the yoke was attached, a girth, and breast straps and with side traces probably attached via long rods to the axle. The leather work was often highly decorated. The chariot was an elite status symbol and was therefore highly suitable as a burial item.

In Britain, the earliest sites date to around 500 BC, probably coinciding with the Celtic immigration to the British Isles. Burial finds are quite rare, and the persons interred were presumably chieftains, wealthy nobles, or other figures of social standing.

Two chariot burials have been found in Yorkshire, England, at Garton Slack and Ferry Fryston. The second chariot was found with its wheels upright in the ground. The leather and wood had rotted away but the archaeologists were able to identify the position, size, and location of wooden components, such as the

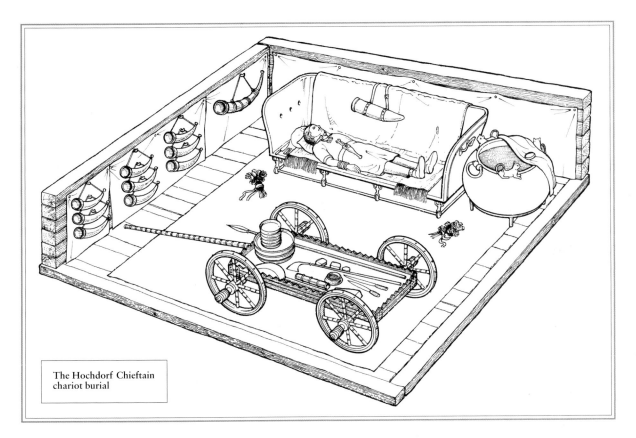

The Hochdorf Chieftain chariot burial

chariot pole, by filling voids with plaster or by recording darker stains on the soil left from wood tannins. This chariot is the westernmost example of a type known as the Arras Culture of the Yorkshire Wolds, which was much further east. Forensic analysis proves that the deceased was a man aged around 40 years and the bones suggest he was in good health and had a fine set of teeth. Analysis of the radio-strontium from his tooth enamel suggested that his origins were in Scotland. The remnants of a brooch appear to be there and radio-carbon dating states that the body and chariot come from the fourth century BC. Burial pits around the grave contain over 12,000 bone fragments from over 180 cattle. One interpretation argued that these were the remains of a large sacrificial feast for a high-status male. However, further testing revealed that bones were added until the second century AD, showing repeated visits to the site for some five hundred years. Another burial is the Wetang of c. 300 BC, exceptional in that a woman was interred with the chariot. The Ferrybridge and Newbridge chariots are unusual in Britain, as they are the only ones to be buried intact. The burial custom seems to have disappeared with the Roman occupation of Britain.

Another grave at Fas in Thrace provided parts of the fittings of a chariot, including five bridle rings, the lower part being bronze and depicting a stylized human head, two flower ornaments with anthropomorphic patterns and a flat back, a rosette with the stalk ending in a stylized head, and an ornament forked at one end decorated with an animal head. These Celtic objects suggest the burial of a nobleman who came from a Celtic state with its capital at Tule.

The Hochdorf chieftain was buried with lavish funeral rites and offerings, perhaps to be enjoyed in the after-life.

THE GREAT EASTWARD ADVENTURE

"BRENNUS AND HIS ARMY WERE NOW FACED BY THE GREEKS WHO HAD MUSTERED AT DELPHI ... NO GOODS WERE SENT BY THE GOD ... FOR THE GROUND OCCUPIED BY THE GALLIC ARMY WAS SHAKEN VIOLENTLY ..." PAUSANIAS, *DESCRIPTION OF GREECE*, XIII.I

Celtic migrations into the Danube River valley and the Balkans commenced in the late fifth century. Some historians have suggested that the Celts wished to control north–south trade along the Amber Road. Central Europe provides evidence of Celts moving into modern Slovakia, Hungary, Serbia, and southern Poland, while archeology has uncovered La Tène products in Scythian graves in Moldova and Ukraine. Trade or the movement of warrior bands on raids could equally explain their presence so far east. Certainly, the Greek colonies and lands record the fear concerning possible attacks by Celt fighters.

The Celts had settled successfully in Italy and were fully capable of planning large-scale military operations, especially when the Mediterranean world was in a state of flux after Alexander the Great's conquests followed by the political chaos after his death. Whether the tribes wanted to settle in Greece and the Balkans or just engage in battle, the later stages of the fourth century saw a Celtic invasion of the Balkans from the middle Danube region, where the Celts were the dominant people in an ethnically mixed region.

An incursion into Macedonia in 298 BC was turned back and another invasion occurred in 281 BC. The Macedonian army was severely defeated and the Macedonian King, Ptolemy Ceraunos was killed and beheaded. Meanwhile, another Celtic army had invaded Thrace and destroyed and plundered Seuthopolis, a seat of Thracian tribal power. Celtic tribes moved into Macedonia, a collection of many peoples, possibly including many who had left Italy after being defeated by the Romans. In 279 BC, some Celts split off from the main body under their leaders, Leonorius and Lutorios. They moved into Thrace and were then invited into Asia Minor, eventually becoming known as the Galatians.

Opposite: The great eastward migrations brought the Celts into contact with Greek civilization.

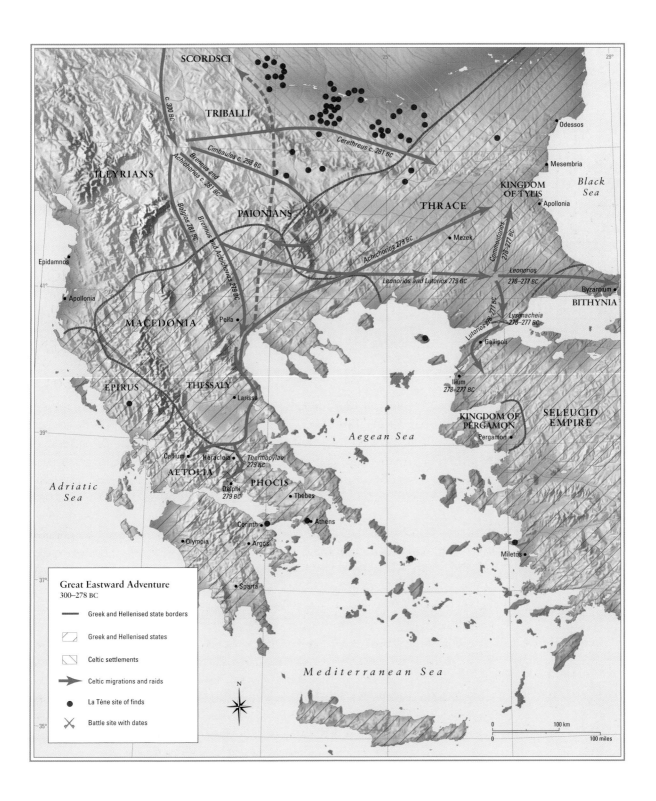

SCORDSCI

TRIBALLI

ILLYRIANS

c. 300 BC

Cimbaules c. 298 BC

Brennus and Achichorios c. 281 BC

Cerethreus c. 281 BC

Odessos

Mesembria

Bolgios 281 BC

Brennus and Achichorios 279 BC

PAIONIANS

THRACE

KINGDOM OF TYLIS

Black Sea

Apollonia

Epidamnos

Achichorios 279 BC

Mezek

Apollonia

Leonorios and Lutorios 279 BC

Commontorios 278–277 BC

Leonorios 278–277 BC

Byzantium

BITHYNIA

MACEDONIA

Pella

Lutorios 278–277 BC

Lysimacheia 278–277 BC

Gallipoli

EPIRUS

THESSALY

Larissa

Ilium 278–277 BC

KINGDOM OF PERGAMON

Pergamon

SELEUCID EMPIRE

Aegean Sea

Callium

Heracleia

Thermopylae 279 BC

AETOLIA

PHOCIS

Delphi 279 BC

Thebes

Adriatic Sea

Corinth

Athens

Olympia

Argos

Miletos

Sparta

Mediterranean Sea

N

Great Eastward Adventure
300–278 BC

— Greek and Hellenised state borders

▱ Greek and Hellenised states

◩ Celtic settlements

➤ Celtic migrations and raids

● La Tène site of finds

✕ Battle site with dates

0   100 km
0   100 miles

GALATIA

THE GALATIAN CELTS IN ANATOLIA BECAME STRONGLY
HELLENIZED, BUT FORMED AN ENCLAVE IN THE POOREST AREA
OF ASIA MINOR FROM WHERE THEY CONDUCTED RAIDS ON
PERGAMUM. ANCIENT WRITERS SAY THEY PRESERVED THEIR
LANGUAGE DEEP INTO THE CHRISTIAN ERA.

Those Celts who did not join Brennus and Acichorios in their hapless great expedition in Greece crossed the Hellespont into Anatolia under the leadership of Lutorios and Leonorios. Invited by Nicomedes, King of Bithynia in 278 BC, the Celts were desirous of settling new lands rather than merely engaging in a vast looting campaign like Brennus. This group was small, comprising some ten thousand warriors with as many women and children. The three tribes of Tectosages, Trocmii, and Tolistobogii were to be used by Nicomedes as mercenaries against the Seleucid King of Syria, Antiochus I, whose domain included most of Asia Minor. Known in Greek as the Galatoi, the Celtic Galatians suffered a defeat at the hands of Antiochus in 275 BC, being terrified and shocked at the use of war elephants. Then, allied with Mithridates, King of Pontus, they made their new home on the plateau area along the River Halys, where they fought off all Seleucid attempts to oust them.

The Galatians rapidly became Hellenized but retained their language, as evidenced by St. Jerome (347–419). who stated that they spoke the same tongue as the Gauls. This Celtic elite, reinforced by other Celtic clans from Thrace, enforced its rule over Galatia, eventually invading and conquering Bithynia. They raided surrounding regions, dividing their neighbors between their tribes as targets. The Trocmii raided the Dardanelles area, the Tolistobogii the Ionian coastal Greek cities, and the Tectosages attacked inland. That they sacrificed captives, fought with the utmost savagery, and were great slave traders reinforced their reputation as a determined people to be respected. Many Galatians also became mercenaries. The Galatians were clearly described by Greek observers, such as Strabo (63 BC–AD 24). The Tectosages dwelt around their capital at Ancyra, modern Ankara, the Tolistobogii near Pessinmus, and the Trocmii in the east by Tavium. Each tribe was divided into four clans or cantons, led by a tetrarch. The

Opposite: As the Celts settled in Anatolia they had absorbed Hellenistic culture but retained enough of their Celtic identity to be recognised as a distinct people for hundreds of years.

twelve tetrarchs each had a judge and a general, with the whole federation owning a council comprising the tetrarchs and 300 senators who met at Drynemeton (a sacred place, the oak sanctuary), a short distance from Ancyra. The tribes were jealous of their independence, failing to unite, with each tetrarch regarding himself, ultimately, as a king.

The Romans first met the Galatians at the Battle of Magnesia in 190 BC when they comprised units of infantry and light cavalry in the army of the Seleucid King, Antiochus III. The Romans were allied with Eumenes II of Pergamum, a frequent target of raiding Galatians. As punishment, the Romans mounted an expedition against Ancyra and severely damaged the Galatians militarily. Rome kept Galatia as a virtual client under its hegemony. These Celts then directed their raiding against Pontus and Cappadocia. A new challenge to Roman power developing in Asia Minor saw Mithridates of Pontus attacking Roman allies. He lured the leadership of the Galatians with their families to Pergamon where he had them all murdered. The Galatians responded by joining the Roman General, Pompey, in his campaigns against Mithridates, and the latter was defeated in 66 BC.

Galatia became a client state, with Deiotarus of the Tolistobogii being regarded as the pre-eminent king. His grandson, Amyntas, died in 25 BC and Caesar Octavian Augustus incorporated Galatia into the Roman Empire as a province. The Galatians appear to have adopted the material culture of the Greeks and then became Romanized, leaving no real Celtic artifacts for the archaeologist.

Celtic Anatolia
c. 270 BC

➜ Celtic migrations and raids

— State borders c. 270 BC

⛆ City attacked by Galatians

✕ Battle site with dates

▨ Trocmi area

▨ Tectosages area

▨ Tolistobogii area

▥ Celtic hillforts

● Celtic sites of interest

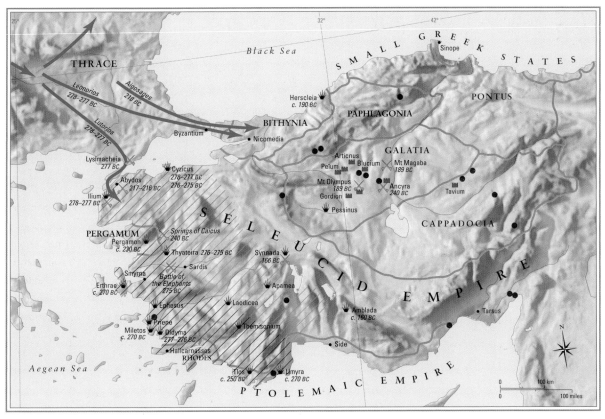

CELTIC WARFARE

"WHEN [THE CELTS] KILL ENEMIES IN BATTLE, THEY CUT OFF THEIR HEADS AND ATTACH THEM TO THE NECKS OF THEIR HORSES. THEY LEAVE THE OTHER BLOODY REMAINS TO THEIR SERVANTS TO CARRY OFF AS PLUNDER, AND SING HYMNS OF PRAISE AND VICTORY SONGS ..." DIODORUS SICULUS, *WORLD HISTORY*, V. 29

The Celts were a warlike group of tribes, as evidenced by the number of weapons found in graves. The warrior sought to emulate the heroes of myth and legend on the battlefield and in inter-tribal raids and conflicts. Personal weapons were so important that a Celt would often prefer to commit suicide than surrender his weapons to someone. The feats of Cuchulainn in Irish legend are redolent of the role models followed by young fighters, as were the actions of the naked Gaesatae at Telemon as they charged to their death in a hail of Roman javelins.

The warriors enhanced their appearance by wearing bright clothes, often with a checked pattern, tattoos, and gold jewellery in the form of arm bands and torques. The main battle equipment of the warrior was the spear and sword together with a shield and helmet. The swords were used for slashing while different types of spear could be used for casting or hand to hand combat. Some spears were as long as 2.5 meters (8 feet 2 inches). Blades and spearheads were sometimes etched or decorated with bronze appliqué. The quality of the weapons was so fine that the Roman army adopted the straight sword used by Spanish soldiers in the Punic Wars. Of particular interest was the short slashing Iberian *falcate,* similar to the curved Greek *machaira* and as devastating as the Catalan *colltell*. The figure of the fierce Celtic warrior has become legendary. A Roman statue 'The Dying Gaul' typifies the popular image of the Celtic warrior: fighting to his death, refusing to accept his fate.

To protect himself, the warrior carried a shield and ring mail, which could sometimes deflect blows but could be punctured. Different helmet types have been revealed by grave finds or finds in rivers, such as the pot helmet with a neck guard dredged from the Thames and the very ornate Amfreville helmet found in northern France. Large shields were used but the most spectacular shield was the

Battersea Shield, on display in the British Museum.

This disorganized, undisciplined form of fighting was of little use against the Romans, who could fight better as a team with their standardized weaponry and battle tactics. They learned to break a mass charge with javelin volleys and then fought in relays with orders dictated by trumpet. The Celts preferred to fight in open terrain where their massed forces would give weight to a charge. Mountain country or forests did not suit them, although a Celtic ambush in the Litana forest in 216 saw a Roman defeat and their leader, Lucius Postumius, was killed. "The Boii stripped off the body, cut off the head, and carried their spoils in triumph to the most hallowed of their temples. There they cleaned out the

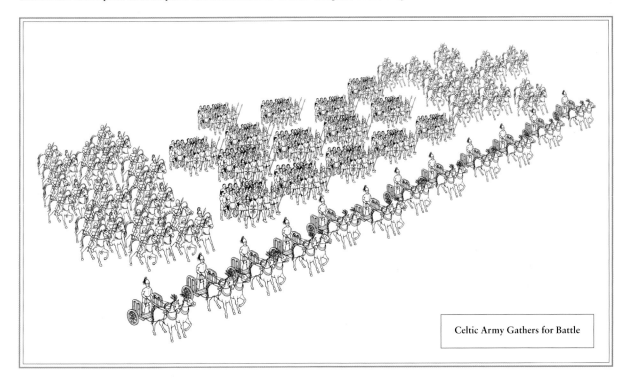

Celtic Army Gathers for Battle

head, as their custom is, gilded the skull, which thereafter served as a holy vessel to pour libations from and as a drinking cup..." (Livy).

Celtic warriors sometimes gave up if a charge did not break the enemy line, and they could easily be outflanked and did not have light infantry to fight off skirmishers. On occasions, the Celts could observe steady discipline, as at the Battle of Telemon when they were caught between two forces and turned to face both fronts simultaneously and died where they stood. The Celts eventually created large cavalry formations which would be mustered on the flanks and would often open a battle by charging the enemy cavalry or seizing key high ground to prevent the enemy deploying there. The Galatians even dismounted on the rough ground of Mount Magaba. The aristocracy tended to form the cavalry force and some units were so professional that they became *oppida* troops.

Chariots generally supported the cavalry, but at the battle of Sentinum (295 BC) in the Third

Celtic warfare is a mirror of Celtic society, family and clan chiefs lead their men into battle, they in turn hold allegiance to higher nobles. The warrior elite may chose to fight on foot or horseback and a few fought with chariots.

Samnite War when the Gauls and Samnites allied, a chariot charge broke the Roman line. The Romans only survived when their leader, Decius, charged his cavalry into the Celts, dying in the process but saving the day. A peculiar Celtic trait was that poorer warriors sought a patron. and these men became a retinue of a chief. Sometimes their loyalty was so great that they would die with their chief in an act of pure devotion. This activity was especially noticeable in Iberia. It compares favorably with Japanese samurai dying for their lords or the Saxon hearth-troop dying with their Ealdorman Brihtnoth at the Battle of Maldon against the Vikings. The Gauls learned new methods of warfare from the Romans. During Caesar's Gallic wars, the Nervii attacked Cicero's winter camp, surrounding it with a rampart ten feet high and a trench 15 feet wide and using red-hot clay sling-shots to torch the camp's huts.

The heroic cycles of Ireland were written down in the medieval period, some time after the pre-Christian era they were supposed to depict. Ireland was the last region to adopt the La Tene version

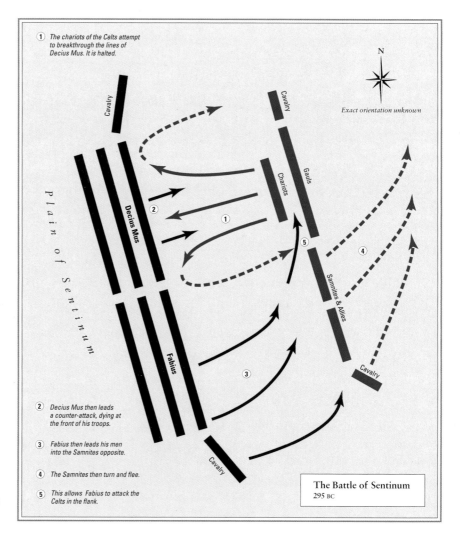

The battle of Sentinum, Italy, 295 BC. A critical battle in the rise of Rome, the Celts in this battle were part of an anti-Roman alliance and surged into battle led by a chariot charge.

A gold torque, similar to those worn by the celtic warriors fighting off the invading Romans. Depending on their size, torques could be worn as an arm ring, a necklace or a bracelet. The torque was a symbol of high social status and nobilty; warriors were awarded with a decoration for courageous acts on the battlefields.

of Celtic technology, and because its population was smaller than the regions of the British or Continental Celts, Ireland probably kept to small-scale elite combat for longer. The tales of the Ulster hero Cuchulain portray individual combats centered on the use of the spear (gae) and javelin (ga-in), with no mention at all of metal armor or helmets. This matches the archeological evidence available. A large role is played by chariots in the stories, although this may have been a later invention of Homeric literature. No remains of chariots from this period have yet been discovered. Viking invasions also had their influence on warfare in Ireland, but the Norman invasion caused the Irish to move toward more medieval methods of warfare.

CITY STATES: THE *OPPIDUM*

THE *OPPIDUM* DESCRIBED THE CITY STATES CREATED BY THE CELTS, TAKING OVER THE ORIGINAL HILL FORTS AS THEY AQUIRED MORE URBAN TASTES. "*OPPIDUM*" IS A ROMAN WORD USED BY JULIUS CAESAR TO DESCRIBE THESE CITIES. *OPPIDA* WERE USUALLY LOCATED ON MAJOR TRADE ROUTES OR NEAR RIVERS. THE OPPIDA WERE THRIVING CULTURAL AND COMMERCIAL CENTERS.

The La Tène Celts developed an urban lifestyle which demonstrates the economic growth, trade, and wealth of Europe. The settlements they now created were recognized by both Greek and Roman as towns, and Julius Caesar used the term *oppidum* to describe them. Their origins can be seen in the hill-forts of the Bronze Age and the Hallstatt Celt princedoms. Many of these *oppida* were located by major trade routes, by river crossings, or at river ports. They were large fortified urban centers thought to be tribal centers where commerce, manufacturing, religious observances, and administration could take place. Over 200 *oppida* have been located in Europe, in Britain, Spain, France, Italy, and the Danube region. Many of them were so carefully situated that they constitute the locations for contemporary important European cities, such as Salamanca, Budapest, Belgrade, Geneva, Basel, Berne, Bratislava, Milan, Bergamo, Brescia, Como, Turin, Paris, Amiens, Besançon, Bourges, Poitiers, Rheims, and Colchester.

A photograph of a Celtic Coin (far right) of Apollo from the Celtic Ambiani tribe of northern Gaul (France). It shows Apollo with laureled hair, and dates from the 2nd century B.C. Coinage signified the development of urban life, and coins like this one were considered to be a symbol of power and wealth.

One important *oppidum* is Bibracte, which is located on an outcrop known as Mount Beuvray and was the capital of the Aedui. This tribe remained loyal to Julius Caesar in his wars against Vercingetorix. He used Bibracte as a base for his winter quarters, knowing its importance for controlling goods through the Loire and Sâone river valleys. The tribe was rewarded with a new capital at Augustudunum, modern Autun. Bibracte possessed a 5.25-kilometer boundary (just over 3 miles) with an area of 135 hectares (334 acres) and a rampart running for 5 kilometers (3 miles). The town was divided into quarters, one housing craftsmen who achieved high levels of technical

skill when working in iron, bronze, and enamel. The center of the town was a large oval market place with an area for sacred ceremonies. Streets and houses with paved roadways over eight meters wide linked residencies, with the roads bordered by colonnades and arcades. The town was adorned with a central pond and some houses were built in the Roman manner with atrium, peristyle, garden, and bathroom. Populated by several thousand people, the *oppida* still shows its *murus gallicus* fortifications.

A significant feature of the urban life was the appearance and use of coinage with precious metals being used as a medium of exchange. Coins were firstly used to pay mercenaries. Chieftains were contracted to provide a given number of warriors and were paid in gold staters or silver drachmas. This money appeared in the third century BC in the Rhône Valley simultaneously with Gaesatae mercenaries. From the second century coins became identified with regional communities as chieftains minted money, a sign of political power and assertiveness. The creation of these city states was the last fling of tribal confederations as they faced the might of Rome. That they existed prior to submitting to the Roman Empire shows that Roman conquest was not the cause of urbanization.

Another aspect of the city-states was the formation of bands of elite warriors as a response to mercenary bands and raids. The towns were noted for the foundation of cavalry regiments whose soldiers were recruited from the nobility. These troops were armed with a long sword, spear, helmet, and shield and wore a light breastplate or mail coat. They were trained to ride in formation and maneuver together and relied on the charge to break the enemy. Warriors such as these were represented on tribal coins, thereby carrying the prestige of the city into battle. The problem with *oppida* was that their capture would bring down the focal point of a tribe, leaving it powerless to prevent the capture of its territory.

The Celtic power structure changed: authority passed from the Hallstatt kings and princes into a more egalitarian diffusion of sovereignty. A tribal oligarchy developed as an aristocratic oligarchy, known as the tribal senate, ruled the tribe through an assembly of free men. Instead of electing a king annually, they selected a magistrate, named a vergobretos in Gaul, who directed

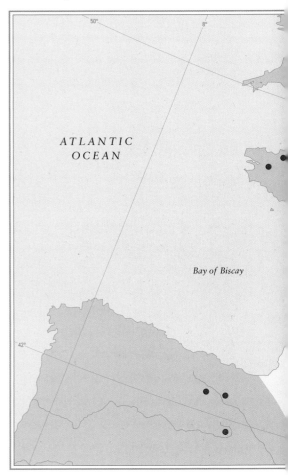

daily affairs. Anything of signal importance would be debated by the senate while the assembly of all freemen together would rarely be called to take a decision. The magistrate's term of office and any specific responsibility of a nobleman would last a year and the former could not stand for another term, nor could he vacate tribal territory during his term of office. No man was allowed to concentrate too much power and authority in his hands and severe penalties could be incurred for the overly ambitious, even death. The *oppida* differed from region to region. Those near the Mediterranean were more likely to take on foreign influences such as Entremont near Masilia, which became a Greek-style town. The towns of southern Germany and Bohemia showed a much less Mediterranean influence while the Galatians of Anatolia became rapidly Hellenized. Less well known are the *oppida* of the Iberian Peninsula. That at Ulaca of the Vettones occupied 70 hectares and is famous for the monumental nature of some of its architecture. The central-western sector of the town possesses two large constructions. One is a large rectangular space with a double staircase leading to a platform with two connected hollows. This is thought to be a sacred space, an altar. Other settlements are much smaller but are noted for defences of towers and *chevaux-de-frise*.

Though the Celts remained a largely rural people, some discovered a taste for a more urban lifestyle as their hill forts developed as places of commerce and culture, the *oppidum*.

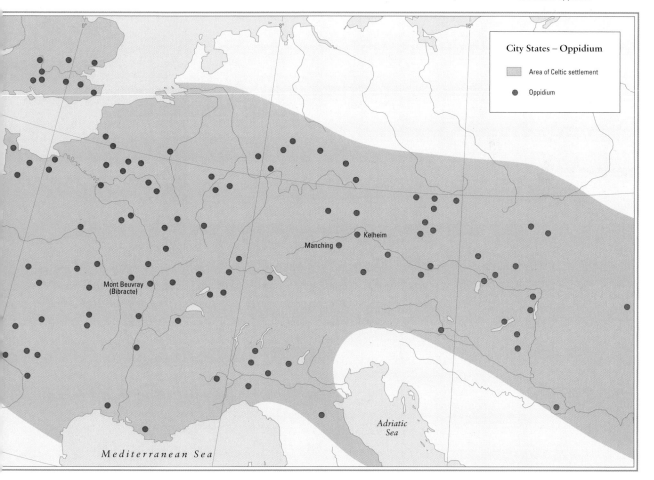

City States – Oppidium

Area of Celtic settlement

Oppidium

Kelheim

Manching

Mont Beuvray
(Bibracte)

Adriatic
Sea

Mediterranean Sea

Manching Oppidum, Bavaria

MANCHING DEVELOPED INTO AN IMPORTANT *OPPIDUM* IN GERMANY. IT HAS A GRID-PATTERN STREET PLAN, A RELIGIOUS SANCTUARY, AND BUILDINGS FOR CRAFTSMEN. THE CITY WAS RENOWNED FOR ITS MAJOR GATE, ITS MINT, AND ITS TRADE.

Manching *oppidum* is unusual in not occupying high ground. Instead, the settlement was located on a riverine plain near Ingoldstadt in Bavaria. The *oppidum* was strategically important, being the main center of the Vindelici tribe. In addition to this it was a place where two trade routes crossed, one with a north-south axis, the other being east-west. Manching is placed at the confluence of the rivers Danube and Paar, also being close to a tributary of the Danube where a port was constructed.

The Manching site shows several periods of development, finally reaching a size of 939 acres (380 hectares). The settlement was originally not fortified, and functioned as an agricultural and craft center with two necropolises. Eventually, the place was fortified, being partially defended anyway by a swamp on the northeast side. The first ramparts were the murus gallicus type, with timber-laced ramparts with a ditch outside. Later, the walls were rebuilt using the Pfostenschlitzmauer method. This building system sees vertical earth-fast posts interspersed with dry-stone walls. The main gate of the circular ramparts was placed within receding walls, making it more defensible, and the totality was surmounted by a large gatehouse which was capable of taking two wagons going through it simultaneously. The walls extended for 4.3 miles (7 kilometers), were 13 feet (4 meters) high and 82-98 feet (25-30 metees) wide at the base. The new wall incorporated the old within its body. The Igelsbach stream on the southwest approaches was channeled to flow into the River Paar while running along the wall. The southwest portion of the wall had an external moat for extra defense.

The town plan involved dividing the land into individual plots, each with a fence, which were probably designed for carrying out specialized functions. Iron weapons, the head of an iron equestrian statue, and

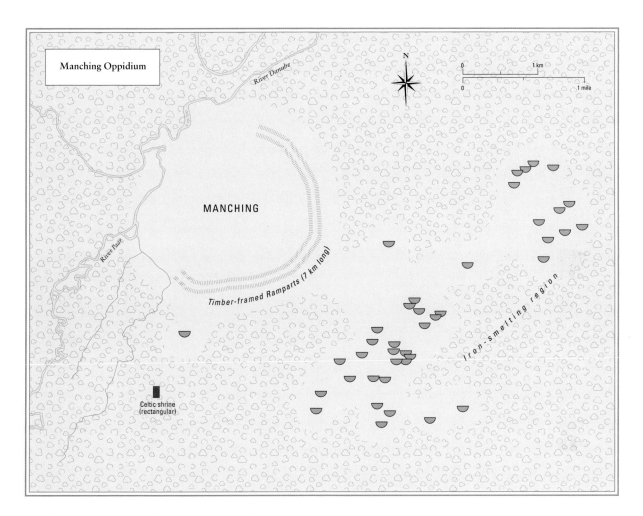

Manching Oppidium

MANCHING

River Danube

River Paar

Timber-framed Ramparts (7 km long)

Iron-smelting region

Celtic shrine
(rectangular)

N

0   1 km

0   1 mile

a small tree sculpture with gold leaves have been found.

The crafts carried out at Manching are evidenced by archeological finds. Tools were made from iron, glass was made, especially blue glass beads, and workshops existed for making textiles, leather goods, and ceramics, whether of coarse construction or wheel thrown. Products were imported from the Mediterranean, including Roman wine amphorae. Coins have been found, as have been tools for minting coinage. The Celts at Manching probably cultivated land inside the *oppidum* and certainly outside. Plants included barley and spelt, with millet, eihkorn, emma, avena, wheat, and rye also grown. Lentils, vicia faba, poppies, hazelnuts, and fruits were eaten. Evidence of eating fish has been found as well as the fish sauce called garum which was produced and exported by Celts in Brittany. Livestock was raised, including pigs, cattle, sheep, and goats. Horses and dogs were also eaten. Important finds include amber, a collection of concave gold Manching-minted coins, weighing scales for coins, and a large number of different types of locks and keys. The harbor has offered up a hoard of 483 Boian *staters* and a 217-gram lump of gold.

The *oppidum* of Manching in Bavaria began as a small settlement during the second century BC and became the largest center in the region, covering almost 200 acres.

IBERIAN CELTS

THE PRESENCE OF CELTS IN IBERIA IS ATTESTED BY A COMBINATION OF ANCIENT TEXTS, LINGUISTICS, AND PLACE NAMES. CELTIBERIANS OCCUPIED THE CENTRAL AREAS OF THE PENINSULA BUT TRACES OF AN ARCHAIC CELTIC DIALECT HAVE BEEN FOUND IN LUSITANIA, AS HAS EVIDENCE OF A LATER WAVE OF CELTS IN GALICIA.

The Greek Historian Herodotus mentions that Celts lived beyond the Pillars of Hercules, that is, beyond Gibraltar in the Iberian Peninsula. Normally, the presence of Celts in Iberia has received little academic discussion because their history is different from the rest of Europe. However, Spanish academics have more recently engaged in intense research, concentrating their energies upon archeological, cultural, and linguistic research in an analysis of Celts in Spain. These Celts were based around a central area with population outflows into adjacent areas. Iberian Celts developed independently of the Hallstatt and La Tène cultures in a very similar way to the Golasecca Celt culture in northern Italy.

The Iberian Celts or Celtiberians inhabited areas in the south-west, north-west and the eastern Meseta whereas the remainder of Iberia facing the Mediterranean was non-Celtic-speaking, non-Indo-Europeans. The two communities borrowed cultural aspects from each other to create the Celtiberians generating a Celtic-speaking blend which developed that non-Hallstatt and non-Latenian culture drawn from the original Iberians. Nevertheless, the religious and artistic tendencies were similar and the social structures which developed were of a piece. Julius Caesar mentions that his conquest of Gaul caused several thousand Gauls to migrate to the Ebro valley but their impact on the region appears very limited. The Celtiberians inhabited hill-top villages which were heavily fortified with walls and stones sunk into the ground. These *castors* were prevalent in the Douro valley, with some developing into large urban communities like Numantia, which had symmetrical street plan like *oppida* in other parts of Celtic Europe. The Celtiberians were isolated from the Mediterraean until Carthage began to develop an empire and control much of Spain. Many Celtiberians fought as mercenaries in the Punic Wars and thousands

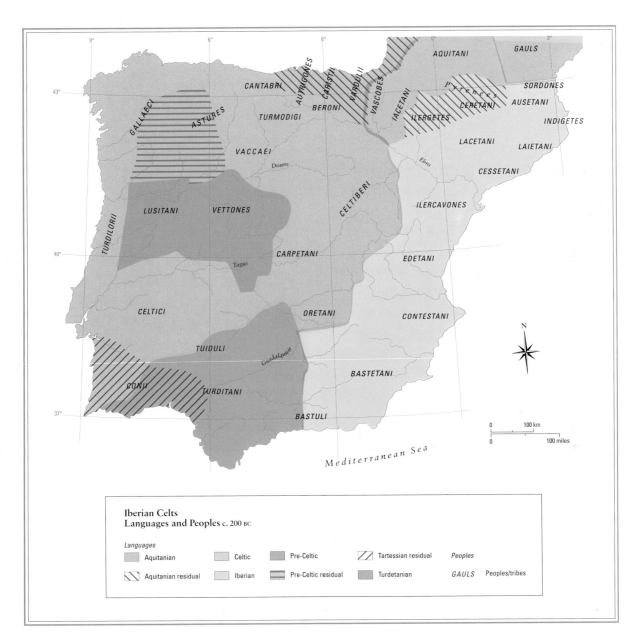

Iberian Celts
Languages and Peoples c. 200 BC

Languages

- Aquitanian
- Aquitanian residual
- Celtic
- Iberian
- Pre-Celtic
- Pre-Celtic residual
- Tartessian residual
- Turdetanian

Peoples

GAULS Peoples/tribes

served Hannibal and other Carthaginian generals in the conflict with Rome. Their ferocity was legendary and their skill in guerrilla warfare was well known.

The Celtiberians' metalwork utilized bronze, silver, and gold and developed some unique features. Some graves contain spears, shields with protective discs, helmets, and swords with antenna-shaped hilts. Like other Celtic domains, the Celtiberians possessed an elite warrior aristocracy which became an hereditary class. Evidence suggests a pyramid-style social organization under the warrior elite.

The exact arrival of Celtic peoples in Iberia is unknown, but they are mentioned in many ancient histories as attested by Strabo.

HIBERNIA

"I HAVE OFTEN HEARD HIM [AGRICOLA] SAY THAT A SINGLE LEGION AND A FEW AUXILIARIES COULD CONQUER AND OCCUPY IRELAND, AND IT WOULD HAVE A SALUTARY AFFECT UPON BRITAIN FOR THE ROMAN ARMS TO BE SEEN EVERYWHERE AND FOR FREEDOM ... TO BE BANISHED FROM SIGHT." TACITUS, *AGRICOLA*, 24

No record exists to suggest when the Celts entered Ireland and no theory adequately explains why Irish Gaelic came to be spoken by its entire population, including the pre-Celtic peoples. The outside world knew little about the Celts, and Pytheas of Massilia (fl. 300 BC), a navigator and geographer who is thought to have circumnavigated the British Isles, called the island Ierne. A later account by the Greek Ptolemy of Alexandria (C. AD 100–170), the astronomer and mathematician, most likely assembled information from Roman or British sailors who traded in Ireland. His map bears a passing resemblance to the island to which he appended a variety of place names and tribal areas. Some of these names can be matched with dynasties. He places the Brigantes in the south-east where they might have escaped from Rome from northern England. Also, Emain Macha, the northern cult site, is called Isamnion. He shows the Manapii, who were also resident in France. He fails to mention the Dumnonii, who also dwelt in Devon and Cornwall, and his Gangani inhabited part of north Wales. Hence, his geography has some relevance but it also suggests that Celtic peoples were moving around across the Irish Sea just as the Irish colonized parts of England, Wales, and Scotland as the Roman Empire collapsed in the British Isles.

The Irish Sea comprised part of a communication network linking the Celts of Britain, Wales, Ireland, and Scotland. Anglesey, Celtic *Ynys Môn*, was the focal point of Druid religious culture. The destruction of the cult site by the Romans under Suetonius Paulinus (AD 60) would have reverberated through the seaways, bringing knowledge of the Romans to Ireland. So although the Roman Empire marched across the mainland British Isles, it failed to cross the Irish Sea. However, Ptolemy suggests that an Irish-Roman relationship may have existed through trade, through a Romano-British link.

Opposite: Celtic language and culture came to dominate the island of Ireland. The exact process is unclear but it now gives most of Ireland's population its sense of identity.

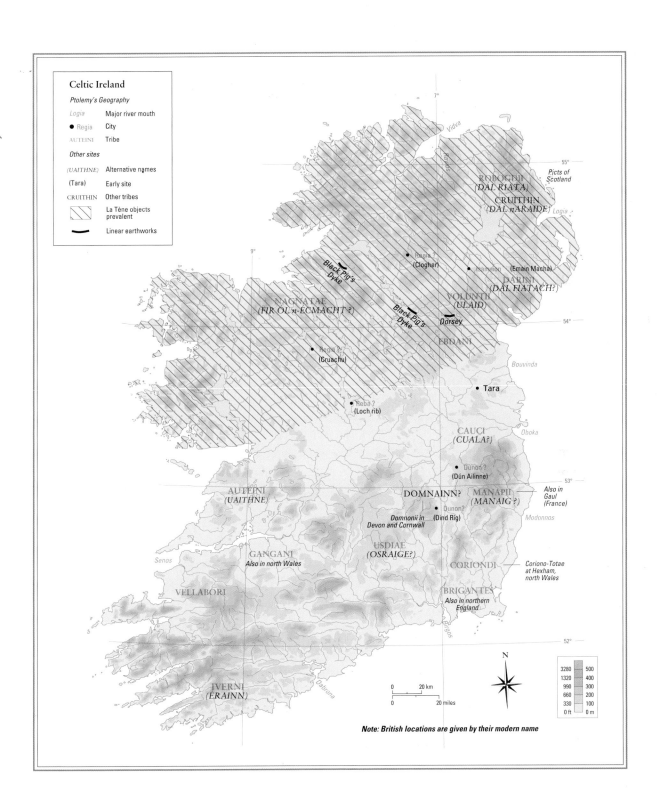

Celtic Ireland

Ptolemy's Geography

Logia	Major river mouth
● Regia	City
AUTEINI	Tribe

Other sites

(UAITHNE)	Alternative names
(Tara)	Early site
CRUITHIN	Other tribes
▨	La Tène objects prevalent
━	Linear earthworks

Vidva

Picts of Scotland

55°

RODOGDII
(*DAL RIATA*)

CRUITHIN
(*DAL nARAIDE*)

Logia

7°

9°

● Regia ?
(Clogher)

● Isamnion   (Emain Macha)

DARINI
(*DAL FIATACH?*)

Black Pig's Dyke

NAGNATAE
(*FIR OL n-ECMACHT ?*)

Black Pig's Dyke

VOLUNTII
(*ULAID*)

● Dorsey

54°

EBDANI

● Regia ?
(Cruachu)

Bouvinda

● Tara

● Reba ?
(Loch rib)

CAUCI
(*CUALA?*)

Oboka

● Dúnon ?
(Dún Ailinne)

53°

AUTEINI
(*UAITHNE*)

DOMNAINN?

MANAPII
(*MANAIG ?*)

Also in Gaul (France)

● Dunon?
(Dind Ríg)

Modonnos

Domnonii in Devon and Cornwall

USDIAE
(*OSRAIGE?*)

GANGANI
Also in north Wales

CORIONDI

Coriono-Totae at Hexham, north Wales

Senos

VELLABORI

BRIGANTES
Also in northern England

Birgos

52°

N

3280	500
1320	400
990	300
660	200
330	100
0 ft	0 m

IVERNI
(*ERAINN*)

Dabrona

0   20 km

0   20 miles

Note: British locations are given by their modern name

Eilan Vannin (Isle of Man)

BY THE FIRST CENTURY BC, IRON-WORKING CELTS WERE SPREADING TO THE ISLE OF MAN. THE ISLAND HAD ENTERED A PERIOD OF CULTURAL DEVELOPMENT WHICH SAW THE POVERTY OF THE EARLY IRON AGE END AND THE GROWTH OF AN ECONOMY, WITH MANY SETTLEMENTS RUN BY LOCAL CHIEFTAINS.

The Isle of Man was inhabited during the Bronze Age by a non-Celtic population, which was killed off — or more likely absorbed — by Celtic invaders who introduced the Iron Age. Celtic finds can be found on the island, especially the Ballcagan roundhouse. The Celtic period witnessed many exchanges around the Celtic world, especially the influence of Ireland through its ogham script and export of Christianity. The characters have been incised in stone, with each letter made by a given number of strokes cut on the stone around a stem-line. The stones are generally found in burial sites and sometimes in churchyards with the addition of a cross. Normally the inscriptions state the name of the person buried and that of his father. Script has been found at Rushen, Arbory, and very recently at the Speke Farm keill. The last message was an eleventh-century ogham and is thought to have been a record of a warrior band but this is pure conjecture from minimal evidence. Celtic Christianity spread from Ireland as missionaries sent monks, later known as saints, to other parts of the British Isles. St. Patrick's name is found in the two different churches of Kirk Patrick, and there are other churches named after saints. Although the Isle of Man owed its church to the Celts, the current political system dates from the Viking period. Celtic politics was probably centered around chiefdoms of a traditional nature. However, Celtic tradition had lasted in the land tenure system. Land was owned in small quantities by families, as is reflected in places names with the prefix *balla*, a homestead. Thus, you can still find farms called Ballakelley, Ballaterson, Ballakillingan, Ballacooley, or Ballachrink; there are dozens of these names. The land system was never feudalized. The small land parcels or *udal* were amalgamated into one *treen*, four 'quarterlands', or *kerroos*. Each *treen* was responsible for the upkeep of a *keill* or small chapel of which at least 200 sites are known. The *treen* names remain to this day.

Opposite: The Bronze age in the Isle of Man was a time of change with the new Celtic population culturally submerging the previous inhabitants.

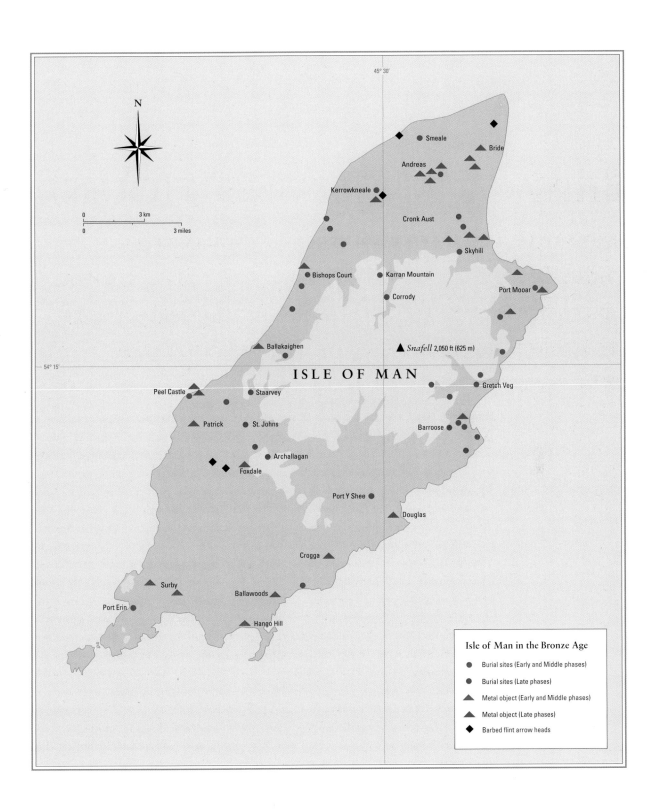

N

0   3 km
0   3 miles

45° 30'

Smeale
Bride
Andreas
Kerrowkneale
Cronk Aust
Skyhill
Bishops Court
Port Mooar
Karran Mountain
Corrody
Ballakaighen
▲ *Snafell* 2,050 ft (625 m)
54° 15'

ISLE OF MAN

Peel Castle
Staarvey
Gretch Veg
Patrick
St. Johns
Barroose
Archallagan
Foxdale
Port Y Shee
Douglas
Crogga
Surby
Ballawoods
Port Erin
Hango Hill

Isle of Man in the Bronze Age

● Burial sites (Early and Middle phases)
● Burial sites (Late phases)
▲ Metal object (Early and Middle phases)
▲ Metal object (Late phases)
◆ Barbed flint arrow heads

BALLACAGAN ROUND HOUSE

BALLACAGAN AND ITS NEIGHBORING HOUSE CAN BE REGARDED
AS A SPECIALIZED DEVELOPMENT OF AN IRON AGE FARM WHERE
CATTLE RAISING WAS THE MAIN ACTIVITY. THIS DEVELOPMENT
AROSE WHEN BUILDING BY SWAMP LAND MEANT IT WAS
UNNECESSARY TO HAVE AN ENCLOSED YARD.

The Celts of the Isle of Man dwelt in enormous round houses. In 1942, a series of excavations was carried out. Earthworks once thought to be a fort were seen to be the mounds over two round houses in the meadows by the River Dumb at Ballakaighen near Castletown. Two large circular houses were found, so large that they probably belonged to high-status chiefs of the Celtic Iron Age some 1,800 years ago. The larger of the two houses had a diameter of almost 90 feet and the whole building was covered by a slightly domed turf roof approximately ten feet high at the center. The whole structure was supported by five concentric rings of huge oak posts. These pillars were eight inches thick and the parent trees were between one and two hundred years old.

The main living area was located around a central hearth constructed from Poyllvaish limestone and separated from the rest of the building by a circular wattle screen braced by slender posts of elm or pine, while the remaining parts of the structure held stabling for animals and storage rooms. The outer wall of the round house comprised a single wall of continuous posts concealed by a bank of earth mounded against it. Away from the walls by some ten feet was a fence which would prevent animals climbing or eating the roof. The north-east part had a gap which led to a paved entrance hall and there was another smaller entrance to the south.

The Dumb River would be the water supply and the marshy environment would offer a degree of security. Discovered on the site were granite rotary querns for grinding grain, but the large quantity of animal bones demonstrated that the Celts farmed horses, cattle, pigs, sheep, and goats. Glass beads, colored blue, yellow, and white were worn as bracelets. Iron artifacts have not survived rust but some bronze articles were found.

The Ballacagen house was in continuous occupation for several generations during the first to third centuries AD. The sheer dimensions of the structure suggest an elite family, and the building was altered over time. That other such sites exist suggests that rule by local chieftains was normal. The sites are undefended and occupied for long periods; the times were probably peaceful. Manx Celtic houses are similar to others found in Britain. Those in North Wales are called concentric circles, those in Ireland are referred to as *raths*, and those in Scotland and the Hebrides are referred to as wheel houses.

The Ballacagen round house is a truly enormous structure. The earth works were so large that they were once thought to have been a fort.

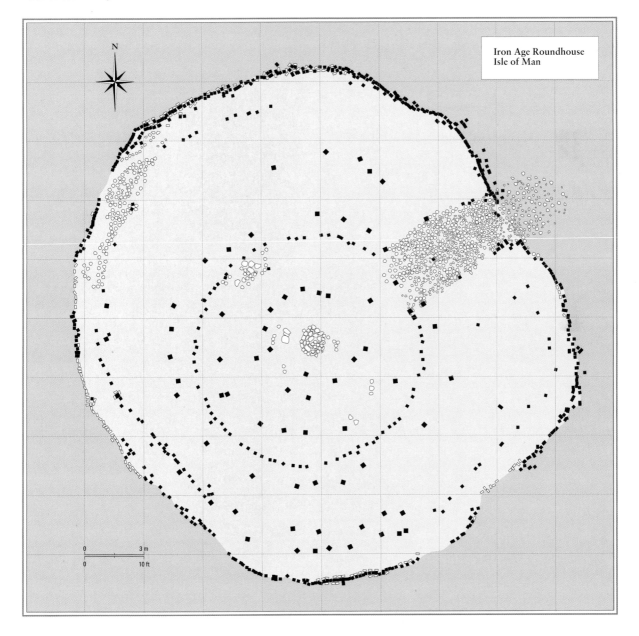

Iron Age Roundhouse
Isle of Man

N

0   3 m
0   10 ft

CELTIC TWILIGHT

"THEIR VANITY THEREFORE MAKES THEM UNBEARABLE IN VICTORY, WHILE DEFEAT PLUNGES THEM INTO DEEPEST DESPAIR. THEIR THOUGHTLESSNESS IS ALSO ACCOMPANIED BY TRAITS OF BARBARITY AND SAVAGERY, AS IS SO OFTEN THE CASE WITH THE POPULATIONS OF THE NORTH." STRABO, *GEOGRAPHY*, IV. 4.5

The end of the first century witnessed the ending of the Celtic world, which had existed for some five hundred years. The domination of Rome had swept across Europe from the Balkans to the Atlantic and only Celts in parts of Scotland and Ireland were free of the Roman boot. Across the Rhine and the Danube lurked Germanic and Dacian tribes, and the former would one day surge across Roman borders, causing the destruction of the western half of the Roman Empire. In combination, these two forces pushed the remnants of the Celts into the peripheral areas of the British Isles and into Brittany.

The Roman acculturation process ensured that Latin was learned by Celtic elites while Celtic languages petered out. Status could no longer be achieved by military worth but by education, service to Rome, and conspicuous consumption of Roman-valued goods and homes. The Celtic warrior had been at the apex of society, and those who resented being conquered could leave their homelands and become mercenaries in non-Roman lands. This had been a traditional occupation of many Celts, as evidenced by the numbers serving Hannibal in the past. Service with an enemy of the conqueror was no different from the later Wild Geese leaving Ireland for service in Spain and France, as did many Scots fighting for Roman Catholic or Protestant countries after the Reformation, split the country into two faith communities. Traditionally, the Celts had enjoyed being cavalry and had run Julius Caesar ragged in his conquest of Gaul. Many young Celtic aristocrats joined auxiliary cavalry formations and became Romanized by the military, and could achieve citizenship upon discharge after a given number of years' service. Gaul's experience before being overrun by Germanic tribes was curious when the Gauls established their own Gallic empire because they feared that Rome was ignoring their security needs (260). Their leader, Postumus, governor of Lower Germany, ruled Gaul, Spain, and Britain until he was assassinated. Spain acknowledged its allegiance to Rome, and his successor, Victorinus, lost lands east of the Rhône to Emperor Claudius II while the last Gallic Emperor, Tetricus, was defeated in 274 at the Battle of Châlons-sur-Marne, leaving his empire to be reintegrated into the Empire proper by Emperor Aurelian.

Later, a Gallo-Roman, Avitus, became emperor. Generally, Gallo-Romans were proud of their heritage but saw their future with Rome. However, the increasingly enserfed peasantry were taxed, and defense fell upon their shoulders. Poverty was so dire that many engaged in brigandage, forming bands of *baugaudae*; this phenomenon was prevalent in Spain too during the third century. The peasant insurgents were crushed but a recurrence in the fifth century saw these rebel armies being defeated by Aëtius, the opponent of Attila the Hun. When the Germanic invaders arrived, the Celts were relieved to no longer pay imperial taxes. However, the Celtic identity vanished except in Brittany, and Gaul became Francia, a word of the invaders.

In Britain, the region north of a line from the Severn to the Wash was less Romanized than the south, which developed a villa-led economy. The Irish, of course, never experienced Roman conquest.

The power of Rome absorbed the Celtic world, drawing Celtic peoples into a new social order and eclipsing some but not all Celtic culture.

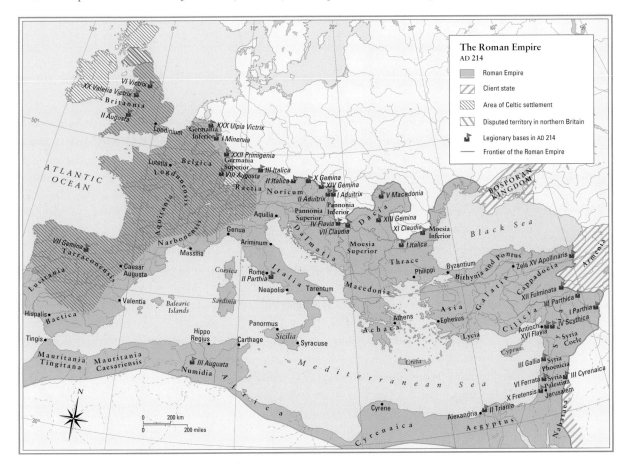

GALLIC INVASION OF ITALY, C. 400 BC

"THE CELTS, BEING CLOSE NEIGHBORS OF THE ETRUSCANS ... CAST COVETOUS EYES ON THEIR BEAUTIFUL COUNTRY ... AND SUDDENLY ATTACKED THEM WITH A LARGE ARMY AND, EXPELLING THEM... OCCUPIED IT THEMSELVES." POLYBIUS, *THE HISTORIES*

The year 400 BC witnessed Celts debouching into Italy in huge numbers, probably the result of over-population in their homelands or the disappearance of the Halstatt culture in the face of the new La Tène culture. No one knows where the migrating Celts originated but it seems likely that the Marne-Moselle area of northern France was their home. However, when Bellovesus of the Bituriges tribe led his people south, he collected other Celtic groups along the way: Arverni, Senones, Aedui, Ambarri, Carnutes and Aulerci, and other surplus populations. Some of these people originated from the Seine and Loire areas. Elsewhere, the Boii from Bohemia sifted into Italy via the Po Valley. Investigations of Celtic burial sites in the Marne area show their rapid abandonment, again suggesting a migrant point of origin.

Archeology has tracked the Celtic migration and settlement in Italy across the Po Valley from the Alps to the Apenines except for the already existing Golaseccan Celtic culture. Before entering Italy, the Celts had engaged in careful preparations, probably in collaboration with the Golaseccans and even the Greeks in Sicily, whose eventual ruler Dionysius recruited many Celtic mercenaries. The invasion route bypassed the Golaseccan/Insubres around Milan and journeyed south and southeast. The Cenomani made home around Brescia and Verona, hemmed in by the Insubres and the non-Celtic Veneti. The Boii crossed the Po and invaded Etruscan and Umbrian territory, engaging in warfare when necessary, such as the engagement near Felsina (Bologna). The Senones moved even further south along the Adriatic coast settling between Ariminium and the River Aso. The Romans soon named these Celtic dominated regions Gallia Cisalpina, "Gaul on this side of the Alps.""

Celt ambitions grew when Brennus led the Senones against Etruscan Clusium. The Romans moved

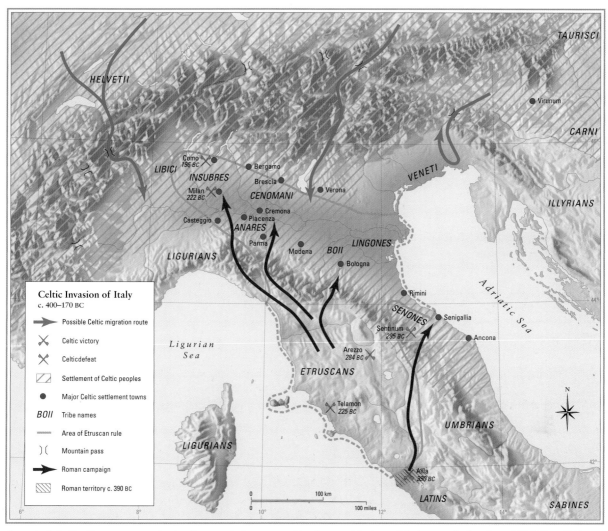

Celtic Invasion of Italy
c. 400–170 BC

➤ Possible Celtic migration route

✕ Celtic victory

✕ Celticdefeat

▨ Settlement of Celtic peoples

● Major Celtic settlement towns

BOII Tribe names

‒‒‒ Area of Etruscan rule

)(Mountain pass

➤ Roman campaign

▨ Roman territory c. 390 BC

forces to help the Etruscans, occasioning Brennus to leave a masking force at Clusium while he marched on Rome, punishing the Romans dearly at the Battle of Allia, nine miles from Rome. The Celts entered Rome and thoroughly sacked it, burning all the state records. They were finally bought off with a hundred pounds weight of gold. The Celtic invasion of Italy did not involve the expulsion of the native populations, which remained a majority. Instead assimilation and cultural exchanges took place. Celtic art absorbed Italic and Etruscan traits as well as styles adopted from the eastern Mediterranean.

The Celts still feuded with the Boii who were hostile to the Insubres and the Cenomani made friends with the Veneti. Celts traveled to be mercenaries in the Balkans, especially when the Alexandrine Empire fractured after Alexander's death in 323 BC. Conflict between the Senones and Romans continued, with the former gradually weakening until they were crushed in 283 BC. The Boii, who allied with their fellow Celts were also defeated. The Romans dictated harsh terms, which generated a long period of peace.

Around 400 BC large Celtic populations were on the move, heading south through the Alpine passes into northern Italy. This brought them into contact with the Etruscans and the growing power of Rome.

BATTLE OF TELAMON

"NO LESS TERRIFYING WERE THE APPEARANCE AND GESTURES OF
THE NAKED WARRIORS IN FRONT, ALL OF WHOM WERE FINELY
BUILT MEN IN THE PRIME OF LIFE, AND ALL IN THE LEADING
COMPANIES RICHLY ADORNED WITH GOLD TORQUES AND
ARMLETS."   POLYBIUS, *THE HISTORIES*, II. 28-30

After Rome defeated the Senones and Boii in northern Italy, the city increased in power after conquering all of central and southern Italy. Rome then became embroiled in Sicily after being invited in by the city of Messina, and it eventually clashed with Carthaginian interests. During the first Punic War (264–241 BC) that followed, Rome gained Sicily, Corsica, and Sardinia, effectively transforming the Roman republic from an Italian to a Mediterranean power.

Resenting their past defeat the Celts invaded Roman territory and marched on Rome. Gaesatae (spearmen) flooded into north Italy. Attempting to block the Celts' approach, the Romans occupied a position overlooking Telamon. Celtic cavalry and infantry were sent to push the Romans from the hill. The Roman commander, Atilius, was killed and his head taken to the Celtic leadership. The infantry battle commenced with the Gaesatae fighting naked and advancing into a hail of javelins as the legions retaliated. These warriors believed that they had divine protection and therefore did not require armor or clothing. The Gaesatae were slaughtered, having no protection apart from small shields. Some hurled themselves at the Roman lines and were cut down while others fled into the Insubres, badly disturbing their supporters' ranks. After the Romans secured the hill, their cavalry charged down into the Celts, who were slaughtered, including their Concolitanus.

The defeat of the Celts meant that they were seriously weakened and were pushed back into the Po valley. Roman policy became more expansionist and the republic decided that its borders should be pushed north and Cisalpine Gaul should be cleansed of all Celts. The battle also meant that elsewhere the Celts were less able to resist the pressure of encroaching Germanic tribes.

Opposite: Fresh from their victory at Faesulae, the Gauls pushed on, to be met at Telamon, near Rome, by a fresh Roman army commanded by Caius Atilius Regulus and Aemilius Papus. The Gauls were completely defeated, with 40,000 slain and 10,000 captured. Some 20,000 escaped northward to the Po Valley.

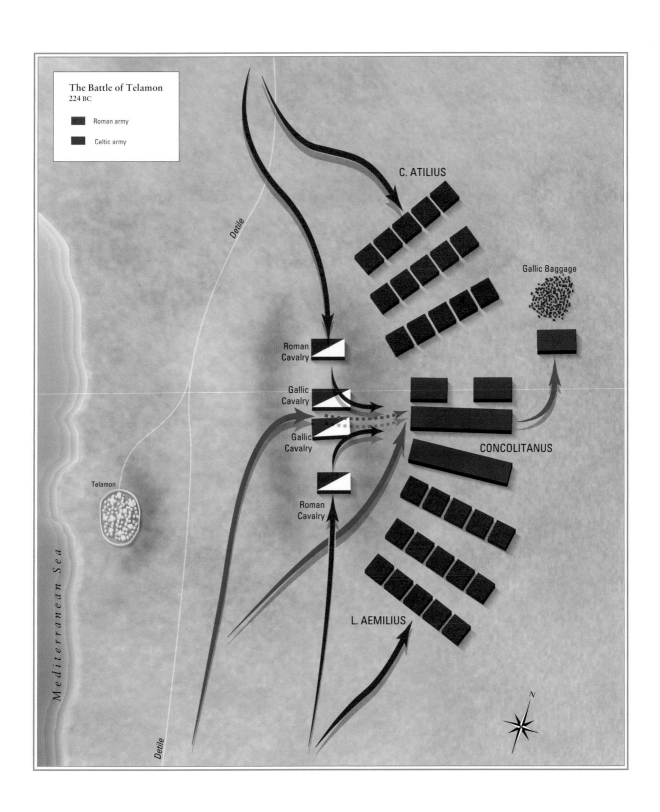

The Battle of Telamon
224 BC

Roman army

Celtic army

C. ATILIUS

Detile

Gallic Baggage

Roman
Cavalry

Gallic
Cavalry

Gallic
Cavalry

CONCOLITANUS

Roman
Cavalry

Telamon

L. AEMILIUS

Mediterranean Sea

Detile

N

HANNIBAL AND THE GAULS

"... THERE WAS NO LONGER ANY ROMAN CAMP, ANY GENERAL, ANY SINGLE SOLDIER IN EXISTENCE; APULIA, SAMNIUM, ALMOST THE WHOLE OF ITALY LAY AT HANNIBAL'S FEET. CERTAINLY, THERE IS NO OTHER NATION THAT WOULD NOT HAVE SUCCUMBED BENEATH SUCH A WEIGHT OF CALAMITY." LIVY, *HISTORY OF ROME*, 22

In 264 BC, Rome was invited to intervene in the politics of Messina in Sicily, which was in direct conflict with the policies of the North African empire of Carthage. Rome was happy to fish in troubled waters since it had gained control of all Italy south of the River Rubicon by 266 BC. This First Punic War (264-241 BC) against the Carthaginians (*Poeni* in Latin) was fought largely at sea and in Sicily. The Carthaginian fleet was annihilated at the battle of the Aegates Islands in 241 BC and the Romans acquired Sicily. By 238 BC, the Carthaginians were driven out of Sardinia and Corsica too.

The Second Punic War (218-201 BC) sprang from Rome's jealousy of Carthaginian expansion in Spain with its exploitation of the peninsula's copper, silver, and iron resources. A treaty with Rome gave Carthage a free hand south of the River Ebro, provided that the Greek city-colonies of Emporiae and Saguntum remained sovereign. However, the Romans so manipulated Saguntum's internal politics that an anti-Carthaginian coalition came to power. Hannibal Barca, the Carthaginian general in Spain, fearing that Saguntum would become another Messina, besieged and captured it and planned to advance to the Pyrénées. War inevitably followed.

Owing to Roman control of the sea routes, Hannibal decided to march overland from Spain and cross the Alps into Cisalpine Gaul en route to Rome. He mustered 20,000 infantry and 6,000 cavalry, backed up by 60 elephants and reinforced by Celtiberians and Gallic tribesmen, and invaded Italy generating sixteen years of intense combat.

Celts became involved in this conflict, fighting on both sides. Half his entire army comprised Celtiberians and Celts from southern Gaul. Hannibal was highly reliant upon the Celts as heavy infantry and cavalry, and many stayed loyal to him until his defeat at Zama (202 BC) in North Africa.

Opposite: Hannibal's army as it marched on Rome was a multi-ethnic organization and contained Celtiberians and Gallic tribesmen.

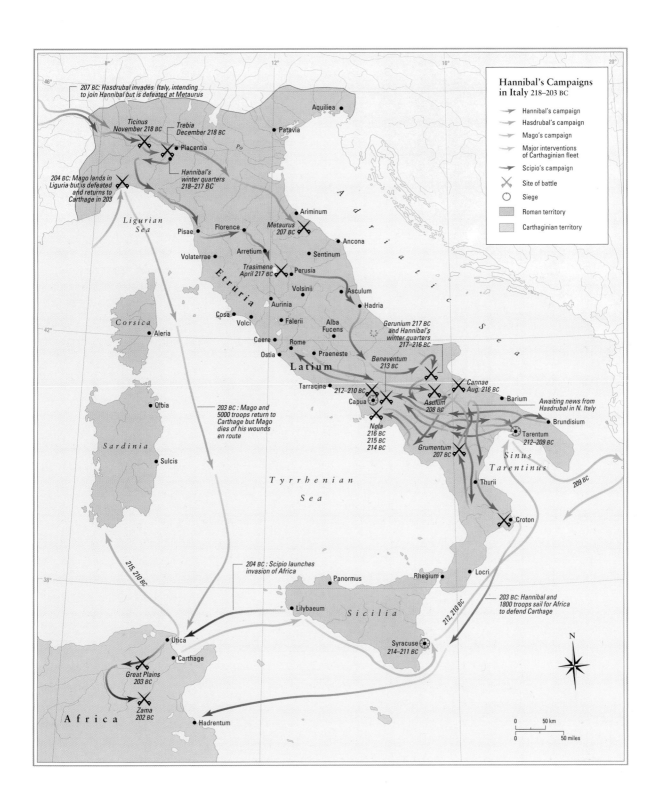

Hannibal's Campaigns in Italy 218–203 BC

Legend:
- → Hannibal's campaign
- → Hasdrubal's campaign
- → Mago's campaign
- → Major interventions of Carthaginian fleet
- → Scipio's campaign
- ✗ Site of battle
- ○ Siege
- Roman territory
- Carthaginian territory

207 BC: Hasdrubal invades Italy, intending to join Hannibal but is defeated at Metaurus

Ticinus November 218 BC

Trebia December 218 BC

Placentia

Hannibal's winter quarters 218–217 BC

204 BC: Mago lands in Liguria but is defeated and returns to Carthage in 203

Aquileia

Patavia

Po

Ligurian Sea

Pisae

Florence

Metaurus 207 BC

Ariminum

Ancona

Volaterrae

Arretium

Sentinum

Etruria

Trasimene April 217 BC

Perusia

Volsinii

Asculum

Aurinia

Hadria

Cosa

Volci

Falerii

Alba Fucens

Gerunium 217 BC and Hannibal's winter quarters 217–216 BC

Caere

Rome

Corsica

Aleria

Ostia

Praeneste

Latium

Beneventum 213 BC

Tarracina

212–210 BC

Capua

Cannae Aug. 216 BC

Asculum 208 BC

Barium

Awaiting news from Hasdrubal in N. Italy

Nola 216 BC 215 BC 214 BC

Grumentum 207 BC

Brundisium

Tarentum 212–209 BC

203 BC: Mago and 5000 troops return to Carthage but Mago dies of his wounds en route

Olbia

Sardinia

Sulcis

Thurii

Sinus Tarentinus

209 BC

Tyrrhenian Sea

Croton

Locri

215, 210 BC

204 BC: Scipio launches invasion of Africa

Panormus

Rhegium

Lilybaeum

Sicilia

203 BC: Hannibal and 1800 troops sail for Africa to defend Carthage

212, 210 BC

Utica

Syracuse 214–211 BC

Carthage

Great Plains 203 BC

Zama 202 BC

Africa

Hadrentum

N

0   50 km
0   50 miles

At the battle of Cannae Hannibal's skillfully handled multi-ethnic army, which included large numbers of Celtic Gauls, cavalry, and infantry, defeated the Roman army, which left 60,000 of its dead on the battlefield. It was the height of Hannibal's military achievements and still serves as an example of tactical perfection.

In November 218 BC, Hannibal confronted Roman forces under Publius Cornelius Scipio in Cisalpine Gaul, with both sides firstly making camp near the River Ticinus during the Carthaginians' advance toward the Po. A confused cavalry and skirmisher conflict emerged, with the Romans hastily retreating to their camp. This minor battle showed the Cisalpine Gauls that Rome could be beaten. These Celts were smarting from the defeat at Telamon, with the follow up of two Roman colonies being founded among them at Placentia (Piacenza) and Cremona, which were rightly seen as the initial stage of integrating Cisalpine Gaul into the Roman territories. The Gauls rebelled and northern Italy was now actively supportive of Hannibal or decidedly not pro-Roman. The acquisition of Gallic and Ligurian troops raised the Carthaginian forces to 40,000 men, more than making up for the losses marching through the Alps.

A wounded Scipio retreated across the Trebia River and concentrated his troops at Placentia while awaiting reinforcements. Another Roman army under the hotly impatient general, Publius Cornelius

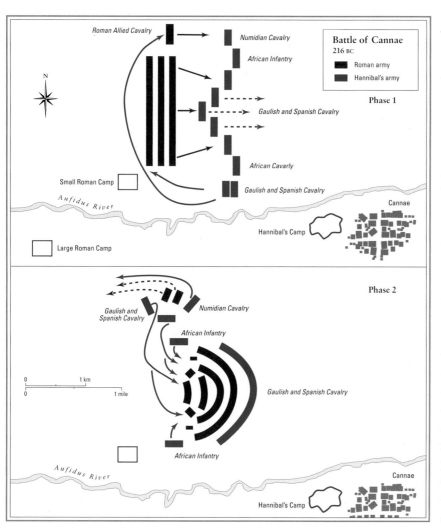

Battle of Cannae
216 BC
- ■ Roman army
- ■ Hannibal's army

Phase 1

Roman Allied Cavalry
Numidian Cavalry
African Infantry
Gaulish and Spanish Cavalry
African Cavalry
Gaulish and Spanish Cavalry
Small Roman Camp
Aufidus River
Cannae
Hannibal's Camp
Large Roman Camp

Phase 2

Gaulish and Spanish Cavalry
Numidian Cavalry
African Infantry
Gaulish and Spanish Cavalry
African Infantry
Aufidus River
Cannae
Hannibal's Camp

0   1 km
0   1 mile

Longus, outflanked Hannibal and joined forces with Scipio. Hannibal used Gallic spies to pinpoint the Roman position and prepared his battle ground by concealing some forces, commanded by his brother Mago, in a hidden defile. The rash Sempronius wished to engage before Scipio was well so he could win sole glory. His unfed troops crossed the Trebia, numbering 36,000 Roman infantry, 4,000 auxiliary cavalry, and 3,000 Gallic auxiliaries. Hannibal used 1,000 skirmishers in front of 20,000-heavy infantry comprising Libyan, Iberian, and Celtic mercenaries with 10,000 cavalry and 15 elephants on the flanks. The Romans adopted their standard three-line formation, with flanking cavalry and allied Gauls placed on their left flank. The advancing elephants broke the Roman Gallic allies, causing utmost panic and rout while the Punic mercenaries pinned the Roman center, allowing Carthaginian cavalry to flank attack the Romans. Mago's force emerged from hiding and attacked the Roman rear. Roman losses numbered some 20,000. The battles gave a lie to the notion of Celts being beaten by disciplined Romans as at Telamon. At Trebia, the Gauls helped hold the line in a totally disciplined fashion. However, Hannibal tended to intersperse his mercenaries so tjat one group might steady the other. The Celts were involved in two other major Punic victories: Lake Trasimene and Cannae. On 24 June 217 BC, Hannibal trapped a 40,000-man Roman force along a road traveling by Lake Trasimene. The Romans were strung out in marching order and attacked from a range of wooded hills along this Malpasso route. The Iberians, Celts, and Africans made a charge at the head of the Roman column while the tail was forced into the lake by cavalry. Elsewhere, the center was savaged by Hannibal's Gauls. Some 10,000 Romans reached Rome afterward, the rest being killed or captured.

The Romans faced a worse disaster at Cannae in August 216 BC. A new Roman army comprising some 86,000, half Roman, half allies, faced 54,000 Punic forces. Hannibal utilized a double envelopment

movement, which encircled and destroyed the Romans, who lost up to 75,000 men. Many Romans were brutally hamstrung and left for killing at leisure later. Hannibal used 16,000 Gallic infantry and 4,000 cavalry in this battle. Celts continued to be a component in Hannibal's forces even at the final battle of Zama in North Africa in October 202 BC. Here, Hannibal's defeat involved 47,000 killed, wounded, or captured out of approximately 54,000 troops at the battle's commencement. In 201 BC, the Romans resumed their campaign against Cisalpine Gaul, a campaign interrupted by the Second Punic War and fueled by a desire to punish the Celts for supporting Hannibal.

Storm clouds gather over Lake Trasimene, Italy, the site of a major Punic victory on 24 June 217 BC. 40,000 Roman troops suffered heavy losses as they were attacked and defeated by Hannibal and his army.

CISALPINE GAUL CAPTURED

CELT MERCENARY INVOLVEMENT IN HANNIBAL'S ARMIES DURING THE PUNIC WARS AND MEMORIES OF THE CELTIC SACK OF ROME ENSURED THAT ROME WOULD SEEK REVENGE AND PUNISH THE INHABITANTS OF CISALPINE GAUL IN ORDER TO IMPROVE ROMAN SECURITY AND ASSIMILATE THIS PAST ENEMY.

After Hannibal's defeat the Cisalpine Gauls realized that Roman retribution would follow since they had supported the Carthaginians. To forestall punishment, the Insubres, the Cenomani around Verona, and the Boii attacked the fortresses of Placentia and Cremona, successfully destroying the former. Here, their campaign stalled but they managed to prevent much damage from the rather low-grade Roman detachments sent against them. The Romans were still smarting from the cost in manpower incurred by the Punic War.

197 BC witnessed two consular armies mounting a converging attack upon the Celts. One army crossed the Apennines near Genua (Genova) and marched down the Po Valley while the other advanced beyond the Po and defeated the main force of Cenomani and Insubres on the banks of the River Mincio. Next year, Claudius Marcellus defeated another large Gallic army near Lake Como, which forced the Insubres and Cenomani to sue for peace. These tribes were allowed to hold their land with conditions attached; most likely, they were obliged to render military aid to Rome. Then, Valerius Flaccus is reported to have defeated another large Gallic army at Mediolanum (Milan) in 194 BC. The Boii were left alone for a while but they were eventually engaged by Cornelius Scipio Nasica at Mutina (Modena) in 194 BC; this Roman victory saw 14,000 Boii and 5,000 Romans killed. The peace treaty required the Boii to surrender half their territory. The dispossessed Boii flowed back to the Danube region, giving their name to Bohemia. Some of these moved west to land vacated by the Senones, evidenced by the finds of Danubian-style Celtic jewelry. The Romans had taken a long time to bring north Italy under control militarily because recuperation was necessary after the Second Punic War and there were new commitments in Spain and the East, with demands upon manpower resources.

Roman dominance in Cisalpine Gaul was now consolidated by colonization and road building. Boii territory was reserved for colonial settlement. Placentia and Cremona received increased drafts of settlers while three new colonies were founded at Bononia with Latin citizens (189 BC), and at Mutina and Parma (183 BC) with Roman citizens. The important military highway, the Via Flaminia, constructed from Rome to Ariminum (Rimini) in 220 BC, was extended under the name of Via Aemilia to Placentia via Bononia in 187 BC. In places, this road was built on a raised causeway because the adjacent land was subject to flooding. The Via Cassia linked the other colonies to one at Aquileia (181 BC) with Latin settlers after the Romans overran Istria. This latter border fortress was settled by soldiers and families from Samnium and by Veneti who had been loyal to Rome during the Punic War. The fortress also defended the southern outlet of the Amber Route. Bononia is interesting because Rome was now a successor of a town previously Villanovan, Etruscan, and Gallic. The colony was endowed with 600 square miles of estate.

Much of the sequestered land was given in viritane dispositions whereby poor Romans received ten acres of land. These individual allotments peppered the Po Valley and the new Roman roads and had very limited powers of self-government. This intensive resettlement of Northern Italy ensured the rapid assimilation of the remaining Celtic population. Fifty years later, the Greek historian Polybius traveled through the Po Valley and stated that the roadside districts were already Italianized and that the common term for Cisalpine Gaul was 'Italia.'

The destruction of Hannibal removed the greatest threat to Roman security. Their next move was to secure the Italian peninsula. The fate of Cisalpine Gaul and its Celtic population was to be part of the Roman state.

Cisalpine Gaul
c. 400 BC

▪ Find of Celtic material

BOII Celtic tribes

Laevi Non-Celtic tribes or origins unknown

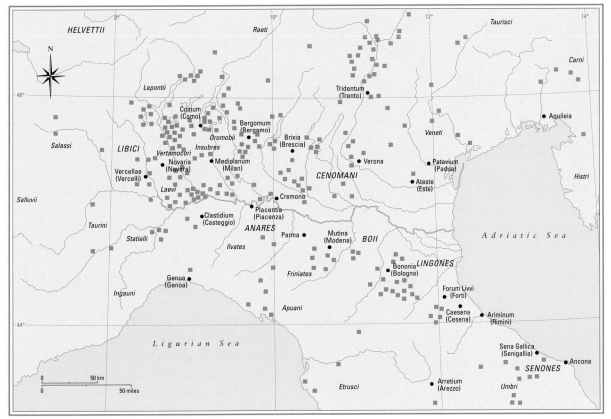

ROME AND THE CELTIBERIANS

"NOT MANY OF THE CANTABRI WERE TAKEN PRISONER, FOR WHEN THEY SAW THAT THEY HAD LOST ALL HOPE OF FREEDOM, THEY ALSO LOST ALL DESIRE TO PRESERVE THEIR LIVES. SOME SET FIRE TO THEIR FORTS AND CUT THEIR OWN THROATS; OTHERS WILLINGLY... DIED IN THE FLAMES OR TOOK POISON..." CASSIUS DIO, *HISTORY OF ROME*

During the Second Punic War, Roman armies fought Carthaginian forces in Spain, with Celtiberian mercenaries fighting on both sides. 206 BC witnessed Punic power in Spain being broken at the battle of Ilipa by the Roman general Scipio Africanus. In 197 BC, Roman-controlled Spain was divided into two different colonies: Hispania Citerior (Hither Spain) and Hispania Ulterior (Further Spain). The Roman Senate considered the colonies pacified and minimal Italian auxiliaries were left as garrisons.

Roman rule was oppressive and cruel ,with Roman governors extorting wealth out of the native peoples. In response, the Turdenati in southern Spain rebelled, routing the garrison and killing its commander. A general rising among the Celtiberian tribes saw a Roman army destroyed at Turda with the loss of 12,000 men (195 BC). However, that same year saw Marcus Helvius defeating Celtiberians near Iliturgi, concluding with the massacre of that town's entire population. This act introduced an intense bitterness into the conflict, with such slaughter occurring several times at Roman hands. However, a measure of control was reached after Cato the Elder landed his consular army at Ampurias, with a subsequent victory bringing Roman consolidation north of the River Ebro. Ultimately, the greed of governors in extracting mineral wealth for their own pockets fueled more warfare in the Iberian peninsula. In 154 BC, the Lusitanians invaded Roman territory followed by a Celtiberian uprising in 153 BC. The Romans were defeated at Numantia but Consul Claudius Marcellus made peace with the Celtiberians (151 BC). Under Licinius Lucullus, the Romans launched an unprovoked onslaught against the Celtiberian Vaccaei and killed all the men in the town of Cauca. He then joined Galba in the Lusitanian war, using fire and looting to coerce the Lusitanians into peace negotiations. They were promised peace and better farmland

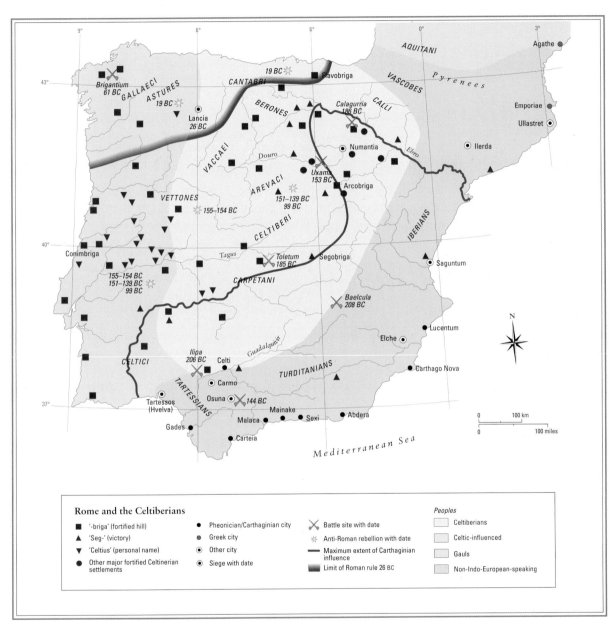

Rome and the Celtiberians

- ■ '-briga' (fortified hill)
- ▲ 'Seg-' (victory)
- ▼ 'Celtius' (personal name)
- ● Other major fortified Celtinerian settlements
- ● Pheonician/Carthaginian city
- ● Greek city
- ◉ Other city
- ◉ Siege with date
- ✕ Battle site with date
- ✳ Anti-Roman rebellion with date
- ▬ Maximum extent of Carthaginian influence
- ▬ Limit of Roman rule 26 BC

Peoples
- Celtiberians
- Celtic-influenced
- Gauls
- Non-Indo-European-speaking

in a re-settlement process but all men of fighting age were killed, some 9,000. One Lusitanian escaping the butchery was Viriathus, who became the Lusitanian leader in several victories against five different Roman leaders between 146 and 141 BC. This stimulated the Celtiberians to re-enter the fray. Viriathus dealt a crushing blow to Roman arms and prestige. A Roman murder plot saw Viriathus assassinated, leaving the Lusitanians so distraught that their resistance crumbled (139 BC). In 134 BC, Scipio Aemilianus Africanus was granted the consulship of Hispania Citerior. His task was to pacify the Celtiberians.

The fate of the Celtiberians would be as subjects of Rome. The process would take time and much savage fighting but in the end Roman discipline and resources would ensure victory.

CAESAR'S GALLIC WARS

"GAUL COMPRISES THREE AREAS, INHABITED RESPECTIVELY BY THE BELGAE, THE AQUITANI, AND A PEOPLE WHO CALL THEMSELVES CELTS, ALTHOUGH WE CALL THEM GAULS. ALL OF THESE HAVE DIFFERENT LANGUAGES, CUSTOMS, AND LAWS."

JULIUS CAESAR, *THE CONQUEST OF GAUL*, I.1.10

After Carthage was destroyed in the Third Punic War in 146 BC and Numantia was taken in Spain, Rome became the hegemonic power in the western Mediterranean. Its Spanish possessions could only be reached by sea, but this situation was soon changed when Rome's Greek ally, Massilia, requested aid to defend this colony against the Saluvii. Rome responded by conquering them and their allied Celts, the Allobroges, and attacked the Arverni. Within a few years Rome acquired a band of territory along the Mediterranean linking Italy with Spain with a strong presence in the Rhône Valley. These new gains became the province of Gallia Transalpina, which contained a Roman colony at Narbo.

Elsewhere, Germanic tribes were on the move, compressing the Celts into a more cramped geographical area. The Cimbri, Teutones, and the Suebi put pressure on the Rhineland area and one Celtic tribe, the Helvetii, planned a migration from Switzerland to the Gallic Atlantic coast. Gaul was unstable politically, and the situation was exacerbated when the Sequani used German mercenaries against the Aedui but were attacked in turn by the Suebi under Ariovistus.

In Rome, Julius Caesar (58 BC) had become one of the most powerful Romans and was awarded the governorship of Cisalpine Gaul, Illyricum, and Transalpine Gaul, with the use of four legions and the right to raise more. At this point, the Helvetii moved from their homeland, burning their towns and villages, and pushed into the lands of the Allobroges, who were themselves under the power of Rome. The Helvetii asked for safe passage through Gaul but Caesar refused. However, the Helvetii crossed Sequani lands and looted the Aedui, Ambarri, and Allobroges. These tribes subsequently requested Caesar's help. Caesar's legions destroyed a quarter of the Helvetii at the battle of the Arar. A subsequent

Detail from a sculpture depicting a Gallic warrior.

battle at Bibracte and its aftermath saw the defeat of the Helvetii. Only 110,000 out of an initial 368,000 returned to their homeland in Switzerland.

Caesar's plans demanded a war against the Suebi, who now occupied Sequani territory. Gallic leaders had congratulated Caesar for his victory against the Helvetii and pressured him to handle the Suebi. Caesar defeated the Suebi at the battle of Vosges, driving back Ariovistus and the remaining Germanic tribes across the Rhine. Caesar's ambition to seize all of Gaul and its wealth in order to clear his debts and boost his standing in Rome probably took hold then. Alliances were strengthened with the Aedui and the Remi, the latter being a major Belgic tribe of the Celts. Other Belgic tribes were restless and Caesar marched against them. Among these were the Nervii who, with the Atrebates and Viromandui, raised 60,000 warriors and surprised the Romans as they were making camp near the River Sambre. Caesar's personal intervention and Roman discipline won the day, with the Belgae receiving heavy losses. The threat of their towns being destroyed made them surrender. In 56 BC, Caesar marched against the Atlantic coastal tribes, especially the Veneti in Armorica (Brittany). The Romans built galleys on the River Loire to combat the Veneti fleet. Being sail-propelled, the Gallic fleet was caught becalmed by the Romans, whose oared galleys destroyed the Veneti ships. In 55 BC, Caesar raided across the Rhine but failed to engage the Suebi. The same year saw a reconnaissance in force to Britain to prevent the Britons continuing to give aid to their Celtic kin in Europe. Extreme weather destroyed much of the Roman fleet and the Romans withdrew to return in considerable force next year to defeat the powerful Catuvellauni.

Winter 54-53 BC saw an uprising when the Eburones of north-eastern Gaul rebelled commanded by Ambiorix, who was resentful at the Roman requisitioning stocks of grain. 15 cohorts, a cohort being approximately 480 men, were wiped out at Atuatuca Tungrorum in modern Belgium. Caesar managed to lift the siege of a Roman camp commanded by Quintus Tullius Cicero in Nervii territory. The Treveri were also rebelling, and requested aid from Germanic tribes and the Senones but the fourth legion survived a Treveri siege of their camp killing the Treveri leader. Caesar next led four legions against the Nervii, devastating the land and seizing cattle and prisoners. The Menapians then received the attention of five legions and were subjugated and placed under the authority of Commius of the Atrebates, an ally of Caesar. The Treveri's Germanic allies across the Rhine were punished and then Caesar led 50,000 soldiers against the Belgae until they capitulated five years later, with the Eburones ceasing to exist by the end.

Setting out once more to harass the Eburones, Caesar sent out in all directions a large force of cavalry that he had collected from the neighboring tribes. Every village and every building they saw was set on fire; all over the country the cattle were either slaughtered or driven off as booty; and the crops, a part of which had already been laid flat by the autumnal rains, were consumed by the great numbers of horses and men. It seemed certain, therefore, that even if some of the inhabitants had escaped for the moment by hiding, they must die of starvation after the retirement of the troops." (Julius Caesar, *The Conquest of Gaul*). Caesar had now to face a much larger rebellion led by Vercingetorix, leader of the Arverni of central Gallia, who managed to unite the Gauls. He adopted a scorched earth policy against the Romans. Only the Remi and Lingones remained loyal. Caesar was in Cisalpine Gaul when he heard the shocking news.

Opposite: Caesar's conquest of Gaul is one of the great epics of classical history. The Gauls generally outnumbered Caesar's legions and fought with great bravery. However, Celtic resistance was rarely coordinated and the Romans could destroy the Celtic tribes piecemeal. Even Vercingeterix failed to unite the tribes against Rome.

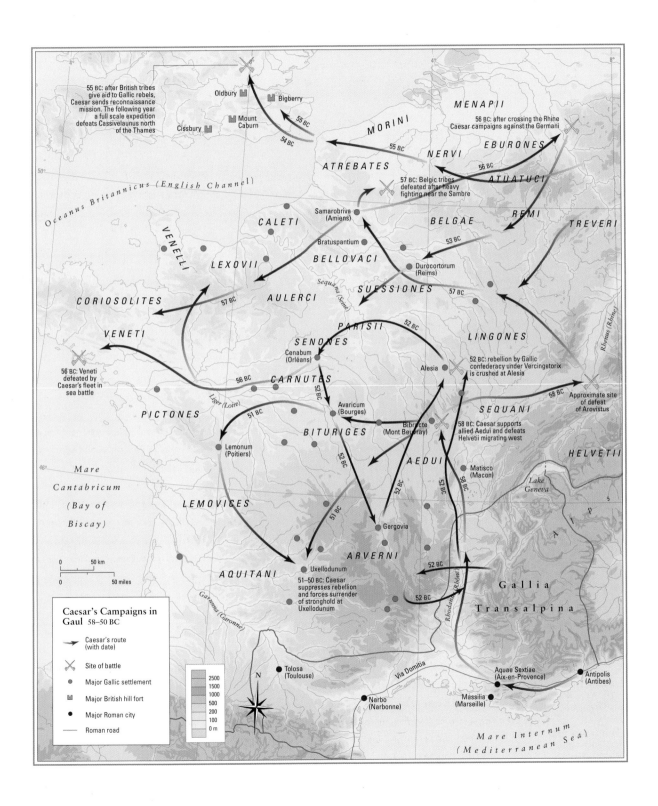

55 BC: after British tribes give aid to Gallic rebels, Caesar sends reconnaissance mission. The following year a full scale expedition defeats Cassivelaunus north of the Thames

56 BC: after crossing the Rhine Caesar campaigns against the Germani

57 BC: Belgic tribes defeated after heavy fighting near the Sambre

56 BC: Veneti defeated by Caesar's fleet in sea battle

52 BC: rebellion by Gallic confederacy under Vercingetorix is crushed at Alesia

58 BC: Caesar supports allied Aedui and defeats Helvetii migrating west

51–50 BC: Caesar suppresses rebellion and forces surrender of stronghold at Uxellodunum

Approximate site of defeat of Arovistus

MENAPII
MORINI
NERVI
EBURONES
ATUATUCI
REMI
TREVERI
ATREBATES
BELGAE
SUESSIONES
CALETI
BELLOVACI
LINGONES
VENELLI
LEXOVII
AULERCI
CORIOSOLITES
PARISII
SEQUANI
VENETI
SENONES
CARNUTES
PICTONES
BITURIGES
AEDUI
HELVETII
LEMOVICES
ARVERNI
AQUITANI
Gallia
Transalpina

Oceanus Britannicus (English Channel)

Mare Cantabricum (Bay of Biscay)

Mare Internum (Mediterranean Sea)

Oldbury
Bigberry
Mount Caburn
Cissbury

Samarobriva (Amiens)
Bratuspantium
Durocortorum (Reims)
Sequana (Seine)
Rhenus (Rhine)
Cenabum (Orléans)
Alesia
Avaricum (Bourges)
Bibracte (Mont Beuvray)
Liger (Loire)
Lemonum (Poitiers)
Matisco (Macon)
Lake Geneva
Gergovia
Uxellodunum
Rhodanus (Rhône)
Garumna (Garonne)
Tolosa (Toulouse)
Via Domitia
Aquae Sextiae (Aix-en-Provence)
Antipolis (Antibes)
Narbo (Narbonne)
Massilia (Marseille)

A L P S

55 BC
54 BC
55 BC
56 BC
57 BC
53 BC
57 BC
52 BC
58 BC
56 BC
51 BC
52 BC
52 BC
51 BC
52 BC
52 BC
58 BC
52 BC

Caesar's Campaigns in Gaul 58–50 BC

→ Caesar's route (with date)
✕ Site of battle
● Major Gallic settlement
🏰 Major British hill fort
● Major Roman city
— Roman road

0   50 km
0   50 miles

2500
1500
1000
500
200
100
0 m

N

SIEGE OF ALESIA

"THE SIEGE WORKS THAT THE ROMANS WERE STARTING TO MAKE HAD A CIRCUMFERENCE OF TEN MILES. EIGHT CAMPS WERE PLACED IN STRATEGIC POSITIONS, LINKED BY FORTIFICATIONS ALONG WHICH TWENTY-THREE REDOUBTS WERE BUILT."
JULIUS CAESAR, THE CONQUEST OF GAUL, VII.69.2

The first incident in Vercingetorix's revolt was the slaughter of Roman citizens, mainly merchants and traders, in Cenabum, the *oppidum* of the Carnutes. This atrocity commenced a series of similar events throughout central Gallia. Simultaneously, Vercingetorix despatched raiders into Gallia Transalpina to hound the Romans and incite other Celtic tribes to rebel in the south. On hearing the news, Caesar traveled to Narbo to set the defense of its province in motion, then journeyed north through the Cévennes mountains via Arverni territory to Vienna (Vienne), where he crossed the Rhône.

Meanwhile, Vercingetorix used his Gallic cavalry to incinerate towns and farms to ensure grain did not reach the Romans. In a momentary lapse, the Gallic leader failed to burn Avaricum (Bourges), the capital of the Bituriges since its inhabitants were sure they could withstand any besieging force. Caesar then split his ten legions into two forces. Four legions were sent north under Titus Labienus to pacify the Senones and Parisi. Caesar led the other six in pursuit of Vercingetorix and set siege lines around Avaricum. The population tried to surrender but Caesar refused and eventually wiped out its population of approximately 40,000 people. Vercingetorix retreated into Arverni territory and made a stand at Gergovia, near Clermont Ferrand. Roman indiscipline led to a severe reverse and Caesar retreated. He joined forces with Labienus, who was returning south along the Seine, having had no success in the north.

The summer of 52 BC saw Vercingetorix mustering a huge cavalry force from all over Gaul to be used to block supplies to the Romans, who circumvented this move by obtaining provisions from Germany and Germanic cavalry. The Celtic horses attacked Caesar's column which formed a square supported by their own cavalry. Finally, the Gauls were scattered and Vercingetorix moved to the *oppidum* of Alésia with some 80,000 men.

Caesar realized that the *oppidum* was too strong to storm and decided to starve it out via siegecraft. Conditions among the besieged and the besiegers deteriorated as food supplies shrunk. The Mandubi, whose *oppidum* Alésia was, decided to push out their women and children to preserve food for the warriors. Caesar left these refugees to starve in the terrain between the wall and the city. The garrison was dismayed but its spirits lifted when a Gallic relief force, some 100,000 strong, arrived commanded by Commius of the Atrebates, Caesar's former ally.

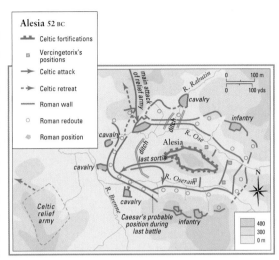

Plan of Alesia, the fortified camp of Vercingetorix, showing the Roman siege walls.

Commius attacked the Roman contravallation while Vercingetorix tried to break out from the *oppidum*. The Romans held both assaults after a day's fighting. A night attack followed two days later, and Caesar was forced to leave part of the wall until Mark Antony turned the tide. An attack from the *oppidum* failed because the Gauls took so long to cross the ditches that they were detected. Next day, another attack was launched by Vercassivellaunus, a cousin of Vercingetorix, using some 60,000 men against the weakest point of the siege lines. The *oppidum*'s force also attacked and the outer lines of fortifications was broken, allowing Gauls to flow into the area between the Roman walls. Labienus was sent to rectify the situation with some 2,500 men. The Gauls were pushed back and the inner line held. Yet the Gallic horde was straining at the breach until Caesar led his cavalry reserve out of the siege lines and threw these 6,000 horsemen against the Gauls' flank. Vercassivellaunus' assault collapsed, with the stranded Gauls inside the two walls being cut down while the Roman cavalry harried the Gallic retreat.

Vercingetorix saw the defeat of the relief force and surrendered. He was finally strangled to death as part of Caesar's triumph in Rome several years later. Those remaining in Alésia and prisoners from the relief force were sold into slavery. Fortunately for them, the Aedui and Arverni were exempted from this fate.

This diplomatic gesture was an attempt to win goodwill, which would help pacify Gaul again. Renewed alliances followed with Gallic tribes and co-operation and trust grew again as the Gallic wars were virtually over. Caesar also subdued the *oppidum* of Uxellodunum under siege.

Caesar's campaigns had savaged Gaul, with an estimated one-third of the population killed or enslaved. The economy took around 50 years to recover. Gauls fled to Britain, where Celts were still free, for a while. Gaul was more populous than Spain and its acquisition meant more lands to tax since there was twice as much land as in Italy. Julius Caesar made so much money he could pay off his debts and buy political services in Rome. Also, he could withdraw legions from Gaul and bring Gallic warriors into auxiliary forces.

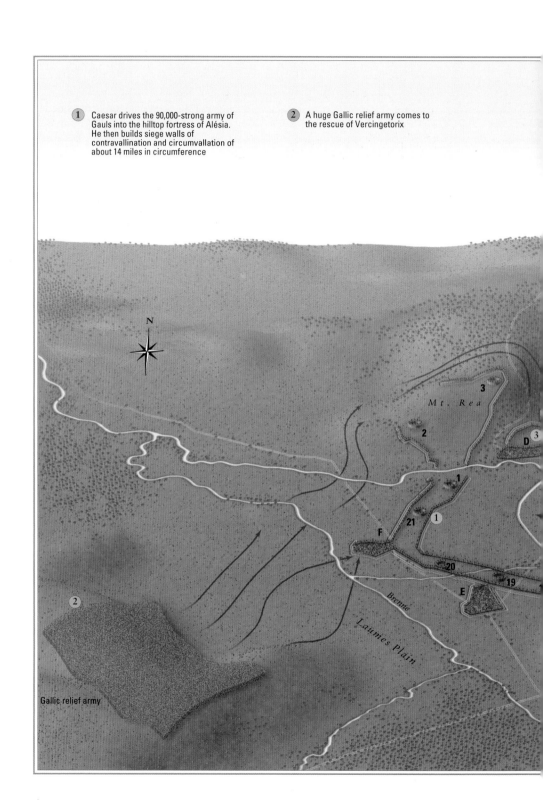

1 Caesar drives the 90,000-strong army of Gauls into the hilltop fortress of Alésia. He then builds siege walls of contravallination and circumvallation of about 14 miles in circumference

2 A huge Gallic relief army comes to the rescue of Vercingetorix

Mt. Rea

Brenne

Laumes Plain

Gallic relief army

At Alesia the Roman army constructed miles of seige walls, completely sealing off the Gauls from re-supply. However, with the arrival of a Gaulish relief force the Romans themselves were beseiged and immediately set about another circitous wall facing outward. Thus they were able to maintain the seige and defeat attempts at relief.

③ Caesar, having collected food and supplies, continues to besiege Alésia, while fighting off relief attempts by Gauls.
Fierce fighting ensues as the Romans repulse the defenders trying to break out and the relieving army trying to break in. The heaviest attacks are on the vulnerable Camp D. On the final day's fighting Caesar leads his reserves in person to smash the Gallic attack

④ Driven to the edge of starvation, Vercingetorix eventually surrenders to Caesar

A B C: infantry camps
D: camp on the hillside
E F G: cavalry camps
H–I: 6-metre ditch
1–21: Roman forts

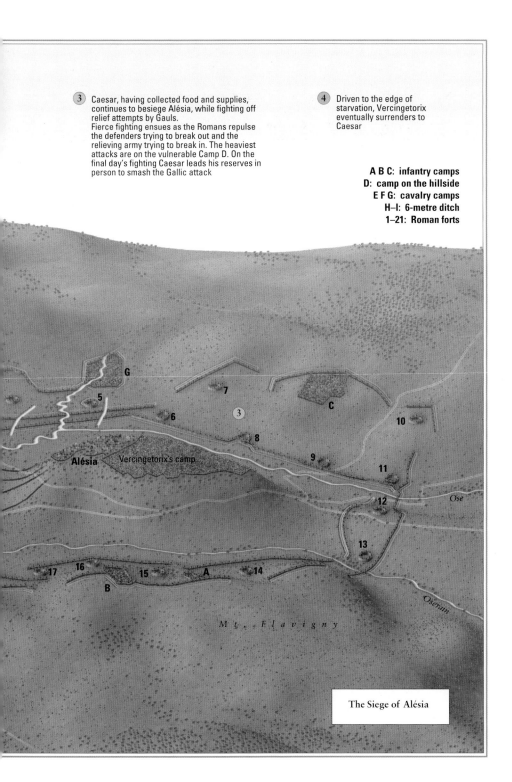

The Siege of Alésia

ROMANIZATION: THE VILLA AT ESTRÉES-SUR-NOYE

ROMAN VILLAS IN CONQUERED TERRITORIES DEMONSTRATED TO CELTIC ELITES THE VIRTUES AND FUNCTIONAL ARCHITECTURE OF ITALY AND INSPIRED HOPE WITHIN THE SUBJUGATED NOBILITY OF ATTAINING ROMAN CITIZENSHIP.

Roman villas were a species of a Roman farming system. After the Carthaginian wars, many peasant soldiers had been away from their land and unable to till it for years. This land was soon bought by wealthy aristocrats, businessmen, and land speculators. There were two major types of villa: the *villa urbana,* which was a country retreat for a town-dweller who sought the peace and tranquillity of the rural scene, and the *villa rustica,* focused on the villa itself but inhabited by servants and slaves, who ran the farm under a manager. Occasionally, the two were combined. The peace and security after the Roman civil wars allowed an upsurge in villa construction, especially from the reign of Augustus. Villas dominated the rural economy in the Po Valley, Campania, and Sicily but were also found in sizeable numbers in Gaul and Britain, where local Gallic elites were encouraged to copy Roman culture in a *civitas* and maybe gain citizenship and senatorial rank. Villas became part of Roman cultural and linguistic assimilation and imperialism as Celts were increasingly Romanized. However, some villas were holiday homes for the wealthy, especially near the Bay of Naples and on the Isle of Capri. The Emperor Hadrian built a pleasure villa of such dimensions at Tivoli that it was a virtual palace. Those villas which have been excavated by archeologists show luxurious conditions, with under-floor heating systems, the hypocaust, mosaic floors, and walls painted with frescoes.

One Gallic villa can be found at Estrées-sur-Noye near Samarobriva (Amiens) in northern France. Aerial photography has revealed 1,000 such villas, many around the Amiens area due to the quality of the soil and climate for agriculture. The villa can be seen in outline with all buildings shown because the remnants of the old stone and mortar original walls have been brought to the surface by

Opposite: Villas all over the empire demonstrated the benefits of civilized Roman life. Many conquered peoples across Gaul and Britain were happy to embrace the new style.

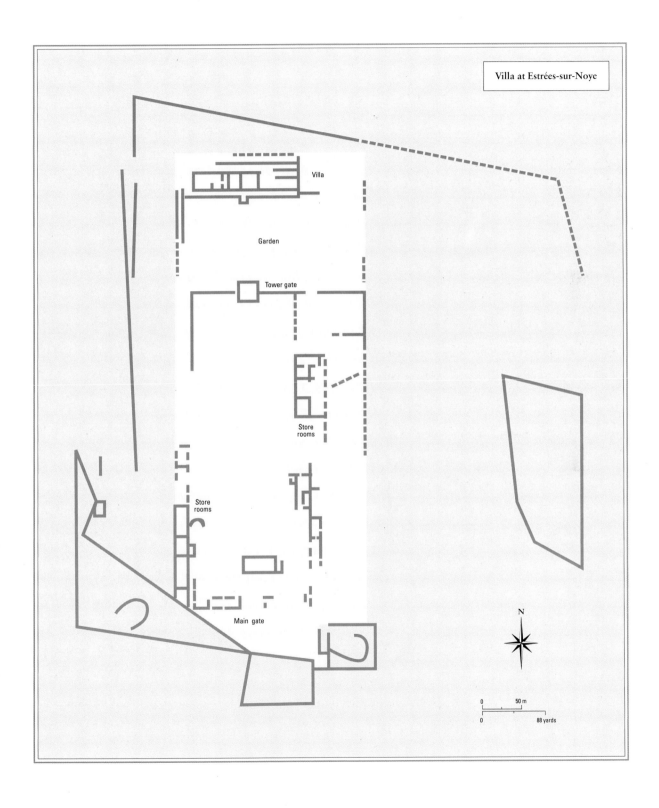

Villa at Estrées-sur-Noye

Villa

Garden

Tower gate

Store
rooms

Store
rooms

Main gate

N

0   50 m

0   88 yards

deep ploughing. The building that belonged to the villa owner is set apart from the main buildings; it is separated by a wall and gateway and possesses its own gardens. What appears to be a manager's house is set inside the major walled area, again with gardens adjacent. Other buildings could be the cottages and dormitories for servants and slaves and other buildings would be barns and storage areas. The totality is enclosed by a security wall.

Such a villa produced cereals in Gaul and Britain, with vineyards in suitable areas, but olives would be grown in much warmer climes. Domesticated animals would include cattle and sheep for milk, butter, cheese, wool, meat, and skins. Bones and horn could be rendered down to produce glue, useful in carpentry. Goats were sometimes reared. Pigs were often used and driven out to forage in woodland, and they provided meat, fat, skins, and bristles. Poultry was common, with ducks, geese, pigeons, and doves producing eggs, meat, feathers, down, and quills. Nothing would be wasted. Motive power for ploughs and carts would be oxen while mules and donkeys would be raised to pull small vehicles and some farm implements or even for riding. Dogs were used as security guards and hunting animals but were also pets.

Villas which existed in Britain can be seen at Fishbourne near Chichester, at Llantwit Major, in Glamorgam, Wales, at Chedworth, near Cheltenham in Gloucestershire, at Lullingstone in Kent and at Brading in the Isle of Wight, among many other placess. Palestine, Malta, Carthage, and Tunisia provide many other fine examples.

Another really interesting example is the *villa rustica* at Montmaurin, not far from Toulouse in the Haut-Garonne in southwest France. This huge villa encompassed 150 rooms and buildings on a two-hectare, nearly five-acre, site. The cultivated area was nearly 3,000 acres and would have needed hundreds of workers. The personal quarters of the owner included a gymnasium, baths, spa, and swimming pool. Found also were six pools made from oyster and mussel shells, the pools originally containing sea water.

Montmaurin was unusual in its size, and its ground plan has shown the many functions this villa performed. There was a wine storage yard where wine amphorae would be buried up to their necks in sand. Normal household requirements have been revealed in the farm kitchen, the wine press, bake-house, vegetable garden, orchard, and an ornamental garden. Other buildings included the artisan workshops for a smithy, pottery, weaving room, and a carpenter's workshop. There would also have been a large threshing floor to deal with cereal grains. The interior of Montmaurin would have involved total luxury for the owner's family, he being really the possessor of a small town. The architecture of large villas required the rooves to drain rainwater into cisterns and pools. A large enterprise required records, and a library would contain papyrus rolls as records and also books, maybe of history and poetry. The private gardens would be laid out formally, including a Roman's favorite plants and shrubs. Favorite flowers included roses, iris, daisy, and oleander. Lilies, violets, anemones and poppies were much liked. Formal structure would be provided by small hedges of box. Cypress trees were desirable for their shape and plane trees might provide shade. In sum, the appeal of the Romanized life-style is recorded as attracting many Celts into a Gallo-Roman blend, separating off the natural Celtic leadership from the mass of its people.

Opposite: The Roman conquest of Gaul, completed by 53 BC, added rich new regions to the empire. Millions of Celtic-speaking Gauls became Roman subjects and witnessed great changes to their land.

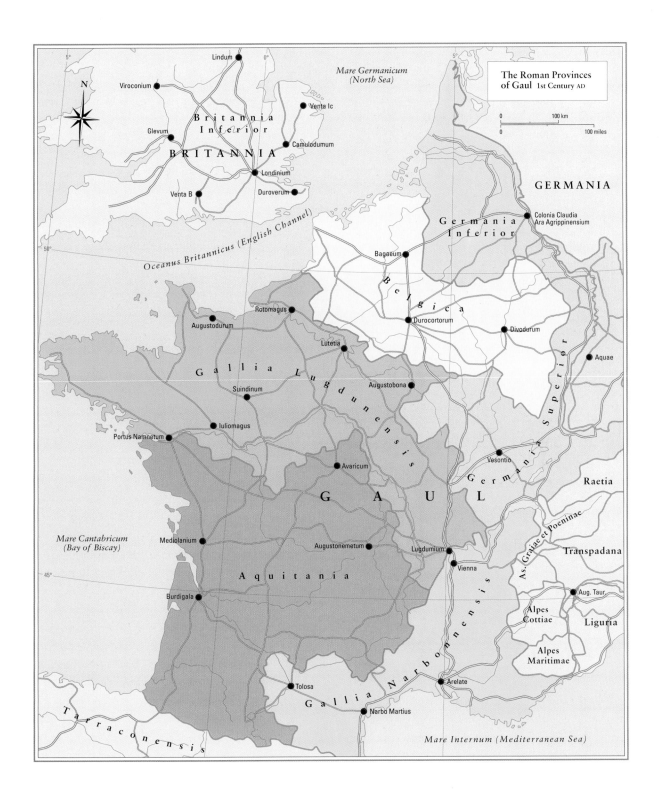

ROMANIZATION: AUGST AND NÎMES

ROMAN CITIES IN OCCUPIED TERRITORIES HELPED

TO INTEGRATE NEW LANDS INTO THE EMPIRE BY PROVIDING

DEFENSIVE FOCAL POINTS AND GARRISONS. THIS WAS DONE IN AN

ATTEMPT TO OVERAWE AND INTIMIDATE THE DEFEATED WHILE

ROMANIZING, ASSIMILATING, AND ERADICATING THE CELTIC

IDENTITY. FOR THE MOST PART, THEY WERE SUCCESSFUL.

The extinction of Celtic sovereignty was achieved not just by military conquest but by establishing small replicas of Mediterranean Rome among vanquished peoples. The wonders of Roman civilization could be offered to the elites of Gaul with the bait of Roman citizenship and the stone trappings of Roman material culture. Acculturation of Gallic elites would guarantee their separation from the mass of poor Celts as these were turned into peasants and serfs or slaves.

Colonia Augusta Rauracorum, east of contemporary Basel, is located near the villages of Augst and Kaiseraugst, just south of the River Rhine. This military settlement was founded by one of Julius Caesar's lieutenants, Lucius Munatius Plancus, after the local Gallic tribe, the Rauraci, were defeated (44 BC). The colony was important in the German wars conducted by Caesar Augustus and by the Flavian emperors. The site occupies a plateau with gently sloping ground on three sides, set just back from the Rhine in between two streams, the Ergolz and Violen, which flow gently into the river. The apex of the triangular plateau points northward to the Rhine, and the tip contains the Roman military camp. Apparently, Augusta Rauricorum comprised part of a triangle of Augustan bases, the others being Augusta Praetoria at the southern end of the St. Bernard Pass at modern Aosta and Augusta Vindelicum, now modern Augsburg. The long base of the triangle stretching from the Rhine to the Danube constituted the frontier against unvanquished Germania.

The city was laid out in a grid pattern, with longitudinal streets parallel to the main street placed at 55-meter intervals. Ten latitudinal streets were superimposed, leading to the creation of city blocks measuring about 50 x 60 meters. The streets were laid on a gravel bed with a gutter on each side, and the important streets had pedestrian walkways which were covered behind rows of columns. Eventually, the colonia's administrative region contained the modern Swiss canton of Basel, the Frick Valley, and the eastern Jura mountain range of the Canton of Solothurn.

Archeological excavations have revealed the richness of monumental Colonia Rauricorum. The theater faces a temple in an architectural unit. The main forum contains the Temple of Jupiter, the basilica, baths, and the Curia, the council house. There is also an amphitheater, and an aqueduct supplied the city with drinking water from the River Liestal. Private commercial buildings have been excavated, including a tavern, bakery, pottery, and tile kiln. In sum, the city offered all the amenities of Rome and comprised an exercise in cultural imperialism. That the city has largely been unexcavated and is the best preserved Roman city north of the Alps means that more data will eventually be collected as inscriptions are found in its environs, including the burial grounds.

Nîmes had been part of the Roman Empire since c. 121 BC and had been exposed to Roman influence probably before that date. Augusta Roracorum was a frontier town; its hinterland was added to the empire by Caesar in around 53BC.

**Romanization:
Augst and Nîmes**

Gaulish Celts

Belgic Celts

Roman province by 58 BC

Conquered by Caesar 58–51 BC

Settlements of Roman army veterans

Greek settlements

Battle site with date

Opposite: Augst, Colonia Rauricorum, developed into a rich city, a cultural center with theaters and bathhouses, all the trappings of a Roman city.

Below: Nimes enjoyed the benefits of Roman engineering, in the construction of a great aqueduct bringing the city a constant water supply from the foothills of the Masif Central.

The city of Colonia Nemauses, modern Nimes, came under Roman rule in the late first century BC and became a colony of Roman citizens under Caesar Augustus. As Octavian, Augustus captured Alexandria during the civil wars following Julius Caesar's murder. Egyptian Greeks were settled at Nemausus, as can be seen in certain coin issues depicting the heads of Augustus and Agrippa, with the reverse side showing a crocodile chained to a palm tree with the legend COL(onia) NEM(ausus). The crocodile is still present in Nimes' coat of arms. A perfectly preserved temple in the forum was dedicated to the princes Gaius and Lucius Caesar, and its classical proportions are those laid down by Vitruvius (fl. 90–20 BC), the classical architect, engineer, and author of a treatise on architectural design. It is now known as the Maison Carrée.

Augustus allowed the town to build city walls, which extended to six kilometres, buttressed by 14 towers with town gates, of which the Porta Augusta and Porte de France remain. The reign of Emperor Claudius witnessed the construction of a famous aqueduct which tapped water from a source near Uzès and transported it for 50 kilometers, with the water level dropping only 17 meters over this distance, an incredible engineering feat. The water certainly fed the town while the baths, pools, and fountains were watered by the sacred spring of the god Nemauses. The remnants of the aqueduct can be seen at the Pont du Gard, which allowed the water to bridge the river. The Romans constructed many aqueducts throughout Europe, giving a fresh supply of water to their towns and cities. In addition, the Romans also built leats, channels underground to supply water to the mines and other forms of industry. This and other innovations in culture and architecture ensured the success of the Roman Empire.

Nîmes Aqueduct
122–124 BC

Massif Central

Uzes — Fontaine d'Eure

Le Pont de Bornegre

Massif Central

Vers

Le Pont Rou

Le Pont de la Sartanette

Collias

Pont du Gard

Remoullins

Massif Central

Sernhac

AQUEDUCT

Gallia Narbonnensis

N

Castellum
Nîmes

0   5 km
0   5 miles

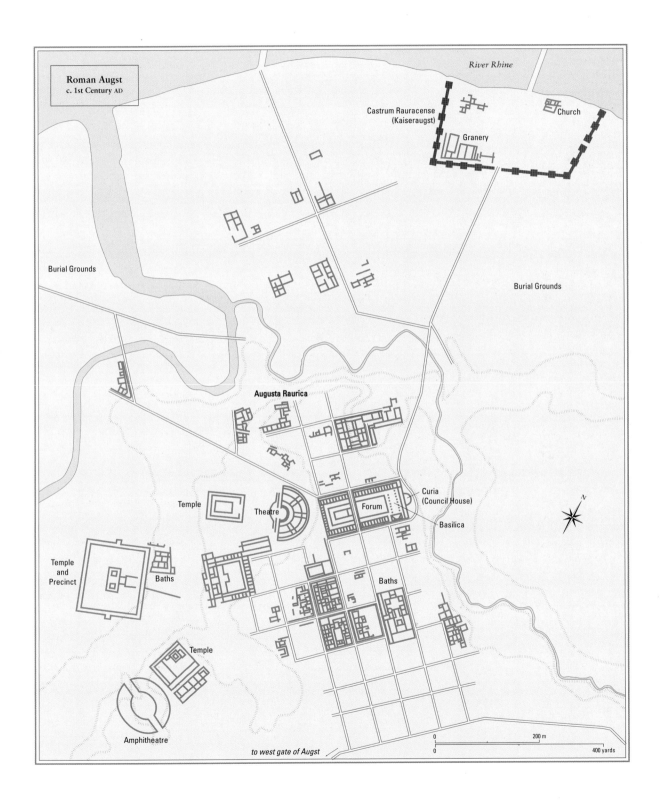

Roman Augst
c. 1st Century AD

River Rhine

Castrum Rauracense
(Kaiseraugst)

Church

Granery

Burial Grounds

Burial Grounds

Augusta Raurica

Temple

Theatre

Curia
(Council House)

Forum

Basilica

Temple
and
Precinct

Baths

Baths

Temple

N

Amphitheatre

to west gate of Augst

0   200 m

0   400 yards

BRITAIN AND GAUL IN THE LATE IRON AGE

THE CENTURY AFTER CAESAR'S INVASION SAW AN EXPANSION OF BRITISH TRADE WITH GAUL AND ROMAN CIVILIZATION. IF A STABLE ROMAN GOVERNMENT WAS ESTABLISHED IN BRITANNIA, THERE WOULD BE GREAT WEALTH AND OPPORTUNITY THERE.

Before the Roman conquest, Iron-Age Britain was linked very closely with Gaul and thus the Roman Empire. Britain supplied minerals such as tin, slaves, and hunting dogs and was renowned for its horses. Southern Britain was the most developed politically, with rulers commanding small areas with a hill-fort for security. Sometimes, chiefs might unite in an alliance for a specific purpose or call themselves by a common name.

Britain and Gaul were linked together by two main communication systems. South-west Britain was tied to Armorica (Brittany) by sea, and a further sea route to the River Garonne led to Roman Toulouse and Narbonne. This latter city was a staging post to the Greek colony at Marseille and Rome itself. An eastern trading system tied south east Britain to Belgic Gaul, eastern Gaul, and south down river valleys to Marseilles. By 100 BC, intense competition to control the trade with Gaul led to infighting among southern rulers, which resulted in the consolidation of larger political units under powerful chiefs.

The seaways were well traveled by a variety of craft. The Massaliote Periplus, a sixth century BC pilotage and trade book, now lost, recorded the trade along the Atlantic coast to Britanny, Britain, and Ireland. It mentions that hide-boats were used at sea. An 18-cm (7-inch) gold model from Broighter, near Limavady in County Derry, may represent this type of vessel. This first-century BC model shows a mast and yard-arm, nine pairs of oars, and a steering oar over the quarter. A log boat from Poole Harbor, Dorset from the third or fourth century BC was 11 meters (36 feet) long and could carry 1.72 tons of cargo and four men in less than 40 cm (16 inches) of water or 18 men in less than 30 cm (1 foot) of water. Sewn plank boats were also used. The Veneti, sea-faring Celts from south

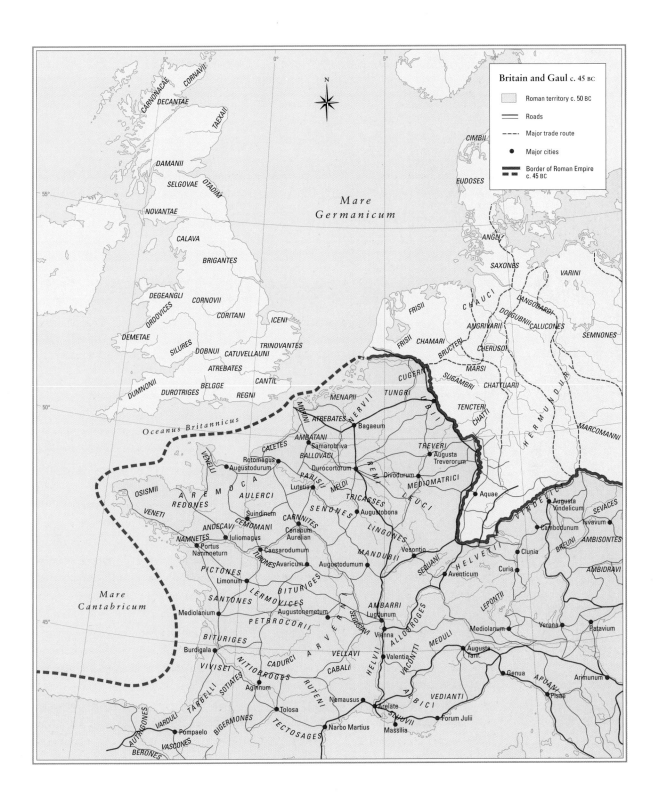

Britain and Gaul c. 45 BC

Roman territory c. 50 BC
Roads
Major trade route
● Major cities
Border of Roman Empire c. 45 BC

CORNONACAE
CORNAVII
DECANTAE
TAEXALI
DAMANII
OTADIM
SELGOVAE
NOVANTAE
CALAVA
BRIGANTES
DEGEANGLI
CORNOVII
ORDOVICES
CORITANI
DEMETAE
ICENI
SILURES
TRINOVANTES
DOBNUI CATUVELLAUNI
ATREBATES
DUMNONII
BELGGE
CANTII
DUROTRIGES
REGNI

Mare Germanicum

CIMBII
EUDOSES
ANGN
SAXONES
VARINI
FRISII
CHAUCI
LANGOBARDI
DOBGUBNII
CALUCONES
SEMNONES
ANGRIVARII
FRISII
CHAMARI
CHERUSCI
MARSI
CUGERI
SUGAMBRI
CHATTUARII
TENCTERI
HERMUNDURI
MARCOMANNI
CHATTI

Oceanus Britannicus

MORINI
MENAPII
TUNGRI
ATREBATES
NERVII
● Bagaeum
TREVERI
● Augusta Treverorum
CALETES
AMBATANI
● Samarobriva
BALLOVACI
Rotomagus ●
Augustodumum ●
Durocortorum
Divodurum ●
MEDIOMATRICI
PARISII
Lutetia ●
MELDI
● Aquae
VENELLI
TRICASSES
LEUCI
OSISMII
SENONES
VINDELICI
REDONES
AREMOCA
AULERCI
Suindinum ●
CARNNITES
● Augustobona
● Augusta Vindelicum
SEVACES
CEMOMANI
Cenabum
LINGONES
Ivavum ●
VENETI
ANDECAVI
Aurelian
Vesontio ●
HELVETI
● Cambodunum
BREUNI
AMBISONTES
NAMNETES
Iuliomagus ●
Caesarodumum ●
MANDUBII
● Clunia
Portus Namnetum ●
TURONES
Avaricum ●
Augustodumum ●
SEQUANI
● Aventicum
Curia ●
AMBIDRAVI
PICTONES
BITURIGES
LEPONTII
Limonum ●
LERMOVICES
AMBARRI
● Lugdunum
Mediolanum ●
Verona ●
Patavium ●
SANTONES
Augustonemetum ●
Vienna ●
ALLOBROGES
MEDULI
Mediolanum ●
PETROCORII
ARVER
VELLAVI
VALCONTII
● Augusta Taur.
BITURIGES
HELVII
Genua ●
APUANI
Arimunum ●
Burdigala ●
CADURCI
CABALI
VEDIANTI
Pisae ●
VIVISEI
NITIOBROGES
RUTENI
Nemausus ●
Arelate ●
ALBICI
VARDULI
TARBELLI
SOTIATES
Aginnum ●
SALUVII
● Forum Julii
AUTRGONES
VASCONES
Pompaelo ●
BIGERMONES
Tolosa ●
TECTOSAGES
Narbo Martius ●
Massilia ●
BERONES

Mare Cantabricum

Brittany constructed oak boats fixed together with iron nails and using leather sails. They controlled the sea routes to Britain.

The development of trade and larger political units was prevalent in the southwest of Britain. Existing hill-forts were refurbished with extra walls and ditches. However, several were abandoned in favor of smaller, easier to defend settlements at river crossings and coastal harbors. The Durotriges' port at Hengistbury Head became very important between 100 to 50 BC. Cornish tin and copper, silver and gold from Wales and the Mendip Hills, as well as freshwater pearls, were accumulated at the port, where they were traded, with Breton Celts receiving pottery, metalwork, and wine in return. Centres such as Danebury, Hod Hill, or Maiden Castle were significant in managing other areas inland and served a commercial function. These well-defended territorial capitals show signs of dense occupation and were prestigious industrial and religious centers. There is evidence that bronze was re-worked on the site.

Meanwhile, the southeast traded raw materials, slaves, and mercenary soldiers to Belgic Gaul. British Celts suffered from Belgic raids in which Belgic leaders could loot and even land-grab territories for themselves. The Belgae extended their control over most of southeast Britain within 50 years, and by AD 25 were reaching to Maiden Castle. Belgic communities in Britain became very important, and these colonies were important in giving aid to their cross-channel kin when the Romans expanded into Gaul.

Julius Caesar reports in his Gallic Wars that King Diviciacus of the Belgic Suessiones, who lived between the Oise and the Marne, ruled extensive lands in Britain as well as northern France. The Belgae introduced the custom of minting coinage, and currency was used where they had influence in Britain: in today's Kent, Essex, the Thames estuary, and parts of Hertfordshire.

Gaul was conquered by the Romans between 58 and 50 BC, bringing the Roman military presence to the Belgic coast. Julius Caesar raided Britain in 55 BC and then invaded with vast numbers of troops in 54 BC, which found it difficult to defeat the British leader, Cassivelaunus, probably from the Catuvellauni, north of the Thames. The Romans made an alliance with the Trinovantes. Trade with Roman Gaul expanded and large numbers of wine amphorae have been unearthed in Essex and Hertfordshire.

Caesar Augustus recognized certain British Celt leaders as client kings: Tincommius of the Atrebates and Tasciovanus of the Catuvellauni. This helped the growth of centralized kingdoms in the southeast of Britain. The west declined in importance because the Veneti fleets had been destroyed by the Romans, who did not engage in much economic activity in Armorica. Society tended to remain with localized political units being still attached to hill-forts. Kings in the southeast built *oppida* as royal centers, some of the most important being at Verlamion (St. Albans), Calleva (Silchester), and Camulodunum (Colchester); these three appear as mint-marks on coins.

Opposite: The 'Limes', Gaul's frontier defense based on the Rhine, was an economy in its own right with its network of garrisons and communities.

The latter was prominent in trade with Gaul and was fought over by the Catuvellauni and the Trinobantes, with the former winning and uniting the two tribes under Cunobelinus, the expansionist Catuvellauni leader. Catuvellauni encroachment on Verica of the Atrebates led to him fleeing to Rome and providing Claudius with an excuse to invade in AD 43.

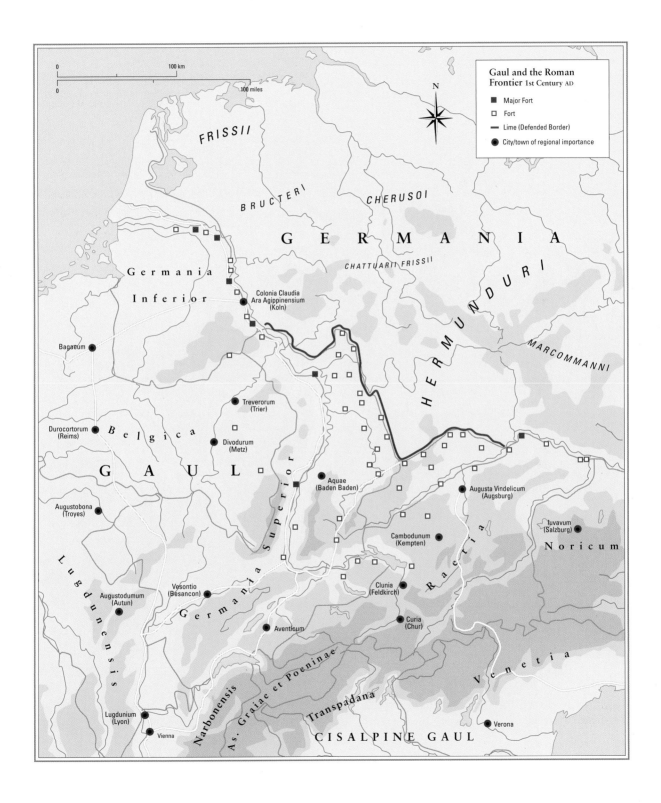

Gaul and the Roman
Frontier 1st Century AD

■ Major Fort
□ Fort
— Lime (Defended Border)
● City/town of regional importance

ROMAN CONQUEST OF BRITAIN

TACITUS STATED THAT SUETONIUS ATTACKED ANGLESEY (MONA) BECAUSE IT WAS THE CENTER OF DRUID RESISTANCE, HAD A LARGE POPULATION, AND WAS A HAVEN FOR REFUGEES; SO HE BUILT A FLEET OF FLAT-BOTTOMED BARGES TO CARRY INFANTRY AND CAVALRY OVER THE MENAI STRAIT.

The Roman invasion of Britain in AD 43 under Aulus Plautius comprised some 40–50,000 men, including four legions (Legio II Augusta, Legio XX Valeria, Legio XIV Gemina and Legio IX Hispana), the remainder being lightly armed cavalry and infantry raised in places like Gaul, Thrace, and Germania. The invasion served a variety of purposes. The Romans landed at Richborough and soon confronted the Celts when attempting to force the Medway. The Britons eventually retreated after a two-day battle and the Romans crossed the Thames. The rest of Briton needed subduing. Legio XX made a base at Colchester while Legio IX and Legio XIV moved into the north and west Midlands. To the south-west Legio II campaigned against the Durotriges in Dorset. Vespasian subdued the Isle of Wight and some 20 hill forts, including the carefully constructed Maiden Castle. Elsewhere, Caratacus fought a guerrilla war for nine years, raiding into the border zone. The Romans felt compelled to advance to the Severn and built new legionary fortresses at Wroxeter (Viroconium) and Gloucester (Glevum). The Roman campaign against the Silures and Ordovices in Wales impinged upon the Brigantes, a powerful tribal confederacy in the north of Britain. The league was split between a major leader, Venutius, who wished to confront Rome, and his wife, Queen Cartimandua, who sought to construct an impregnable personal position within the tribe by seeking a détente with Rome. It was she who captured Caratacus and handed him to the Romans in chains. A divorce soon followed and Cartimandua was forced to seek Roman aid against her ex-husband's revolt against Rome. A second revolt (AD 69) saw the Romans whisking her away to safety. The conquest of the Brigantes began after AD 69 but took years.

Opposite: The island of Britain was invaded during the reign of Emperor Claudius in AD 43. It would take another hundred years to complete the occupation of the island, as far as Hadrian's wall.

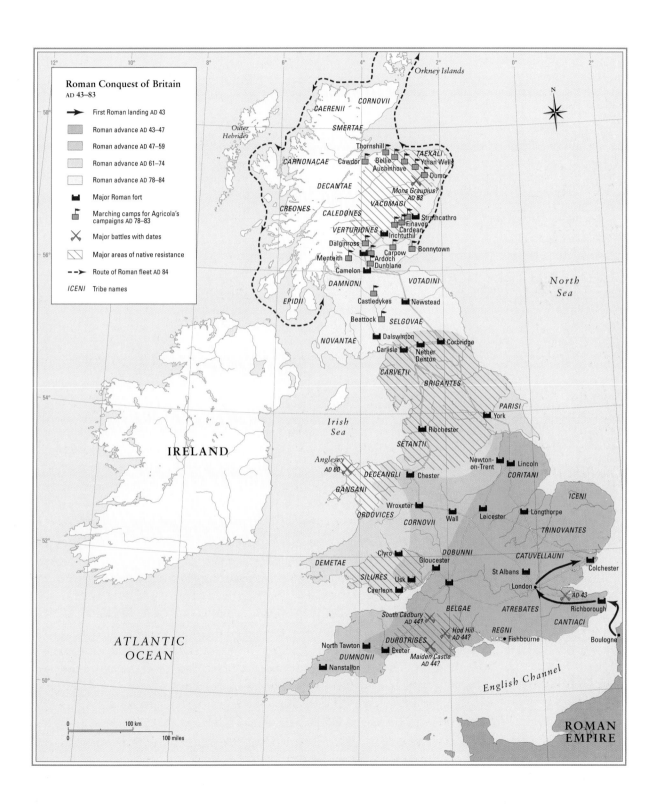

Roman Conquest of Britain
AD 43–83

➤ First Roman landing AD 43

▨ Roman advance AD 43–47

▨ Roman advance AD 47–59

▨ Roman advance AD 61–74

☐ Roman advance AD 78–84

▪ Major Roman fort

▪ Marching camps for Agricola's campaigns AD 78–83

✕ Major battles with dates

▨ Major areas of native resistance

╌╌► Route of Roman fleet AD 84

ICENI Tribe names

Orkney Islands

CAERENII

CORNOVII

SMERTAE

Outer Hebrides

Thornshill

TAEXALI

Cawdor Bellie Ythan Wells
Auchinhove

CARNONACAE

Dumo

DECANTAE

CREONES

Mons Graupius?
AD 83

VACOMAGI

CALEDONES

Strathcathro

VERTURIONES Finavon
Cardean
Inchtuthil

Dalginross

Carpow
Menteith Ardoch
Camelon Dunblane

Bonnytown

DAMNONI

VOTADINI

North Sea

Castledykes

Newstead

Beattock *SELGOVAE*

NOVANTAE

Dalswinton Corbridge
Carlisle Nether
Denton

CARVETII

BRIGANTES

PARISI

Irish Sea

York

IRELAND

Ribchester

SETANTII

Anglesey
AD 60

DECEANGLI Chester

Newton- Lincoln
on-Trent

CORITANI

GANGANI

Wroxeter

ICENI

ORDOVICES

Wall Leicester Longthorpe

CORNOVII

TRINOVANTES

Clyro

DOBUNNI

CATUVELLAUNI

DEMETAE Gloucester

St Albans Colchester

London

AD 43

SILURES Usk

Caerleon

Richborough

CANTIACI

BELGAE *ATREBATES*

REGNI

South Cadbury
AD 44?

Fishbourne Boulogne

Hod Hill
AD 44?

North Tawton

DUROTRIGES

Exeter

ATLANTIC OCEAN

DUMNONII Maiden Castle
AD 44?

Nanstallon

English Channel

ROMAN EMPIRE

0   100 km
0   100 miles

BOUDICCA

" BUT NOW , SHE (BOUDICCA) SAID, IT IS NOT AS A WOMAN
DESCENDED FROM NOBLE ANCESTRY BUT AS ONE OF THE PEOPLE
THAT I AM AVENGING LOST FREEDOM, MY SCOURGED BODY, THE
OUTRAGED CHASTITY OF MY DAUGHTERS.'

TACITUS, *THE ANNALS*, XIV.33-37

The 50s and late 40s saw Roman eyes being turned toward Wales, the base for Caratacus' forays into Roman Britain. The dispossessed heir of the Catuvellauni, Caratacus, incited the Welsh Silures and Ordovices to rebel but was defeated in a set-piece battle, captured (AD 51), and shipped to Rome. Wales remained an area of resistance, especially since Anglesey was the home of the Druids. Roman energies were directed toward its conquest (AD 60), and victory celebrations were marred by news of Boudicca's revolt in the southeast of England.

In East Anglia, there existed the client-state of the Iceni ruled by Prasutagas, whose lands would default to Rome on his death. His wife, Boudicca, contested this inheritance when Roman officials arrived to claim lands and property. Boudicca was flogged and her daughters gang-raped, irrespective of their age. The Iceni exploded in rebellion and were soon joined by the Trinovantes, who deeply resented the existence of Roman colonists at Colchester (Camulodonum). Roman settlements were attacked as the Britons moved toward Colchester, where they butchered 3,000 and besieged a small party who locked themselves in the Temple of Claudius. This was torched and razed to the ground.

The XI Hispania legion sent a relief force of 2,000 men who were slaughtered in an ambush, maybe at Wormingford north of Colchester. With no protection, London was destroyed with the killing of thousands of Romans. Boudicca's march on Verulanium (St. Albans) led to the destruction of that municipality but the inhabitants had already fled. The Roman governor, Suetonius Paulinus, was forced from Anglesey to London but retreated, leaving the city to its fate while he found a site to both resist the Britons and be near communications with Isca Dumnuniorum (Exeter), where the II Augusta legion was stationed but was soon to be summoned as reinforcements.

The Romans and Britons met in battle in the Midlands along Watling Street, possibly at Mancetter in Warwickshire. The Romans found a position with a secure wood to their rear with a defile to the front which would make it difficult for Boudicca to deploy her superior numbers. The Romans numbered 10,000 men, mainly legionaries but supported by several thousand auxiliaries to the front and on the flanks as cavalry. The Romans were divided into three divisions because they could not cover the British front but they were prepared to defend themselves at all points, whether attacked by infantry or by chariots. The Britons drifted into the battle zone in no great order bolstered by their courage and bravado to the extent of bringing their wagon park to the rear, where non-combatants could watch the spectacle.

The British approached the Roman lines in an undisciplined mass, only to be met by a hail of javelins followed by a charge into the British ranks. Close-quarter fighting benefited the Romans with their short thrusting gladius against the long slashing British swords. The battle lasted most of a day, with chariot charges scattering Roman ranks until the drivers were shot down by archers. The melee was an intense, formless swirl of fighters but the Romans maintained their discipline and formations, which more than matched the crazed Celtic attacks. The legionaries' steady advance pressed Boudicca's warriors back against the wagon park where many were cut down, be they men, women, children, or animals.

Roman losses reached the hundreds, but the Britons probably lost at least 8,000, with the dispersal of the rest. Boudicca committed suicide in the pattern of many defeated Celts. Paulinus next devastated the lands of defeated tribes while fortresses and towns were strengthened militarily. His measures were so harsh that he was replaced by the more conciliatory Petronius Turpilianus. Southern Britain now remained peaceful as it was Romanized in administration and trade.

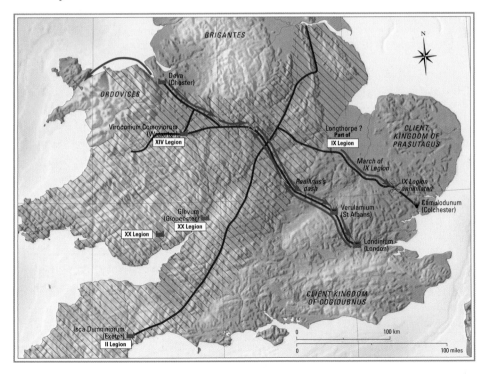

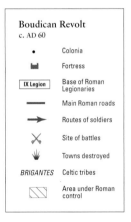

Boudican Revolt
c. AD 60

- • Colonia
- ⌶ Fortress
- [IX Legion] Base of Roman Legionaries
- —— Main Roman roads
- → Routes of soldiers
- ✕ Site of battles
- ⍦ Towns destroyed
- *BRIGANTES* Celtic tribes
- ▨ Area under Roman control

The last serious challenge to Roman rule was led by Boudicca, queen of the Iceni. At first successful, it was ruthlessly suppressed by the battle-hardened Roman legions.

Northern Britain and the Walls

"THE CLYDE AND FORTH... ARE SEPARATED BY ONLY A NARROW NECK OF LAND. THE ISTHMUS WAS NOW FIRMLY HELD BY GARRISONS, AND THE WHOLE EXPANSE OF COUNTRY TO THE SOUTH WAS SAFELY IN OUR HANDS." TACITUS, AGRICOLA, 23

After Agricola's victory at Mons Graupius, the Romans apparently constructed a frontier along the Gask Ridge, a series of glen-blocker forts, and consolidated a Forth-Clyde defensive line, the future site of the Antonine Wall. This occupation of lowland Scotland was brief because the second century witnessed the forts of southern Scotland being destroyed or burnt and a new frontier being built along the Stanegate (c. 105), a road built by Agricola from Carlisle to Corbridge. A new line was built — Hadrian's Wall, running from Bowness on the Solway Firth to Wallsend on the River Tyne. A later fortification, the Antonine Wall, was established from the Firth of Clyde to the Firth of Forth in 142.

The Gask Ridge stands some 70 meters above sea level and is situated between the Highland massif and the rich lands of Fife, comprising part of a corridor northward toward the coastal strip of agricultural land that reaches to the Moray Firth. The Gask frontier includes a line of forts, fortlets, and watch-towers along a military road and might be the earliest Roman lines ever built. Beginning at Glenbank, north of Dunblane, it extends to Bertha, near Perth on the Tay. The fortifications were so close together that they were part of a frontier scheme rather than a signaling system. The Gask lines were abandoned, possibly because of troubles on the Danube in AD 85, which led to the withdrawal of the Legio II Adiutrix and auxiliary units from Britain. Perhaps Britain was regarded as so peripheral that the loss of some border lands was acceptable for the greater good of the empire. Some historians have argued that the Romans normally ruled conquered areas through the original tribal elites, which assumes some type of administrative system upon which to superimpose Roman officials. The Scots had no such system and possibly no tax base, so the north was also considered relatively worthless.

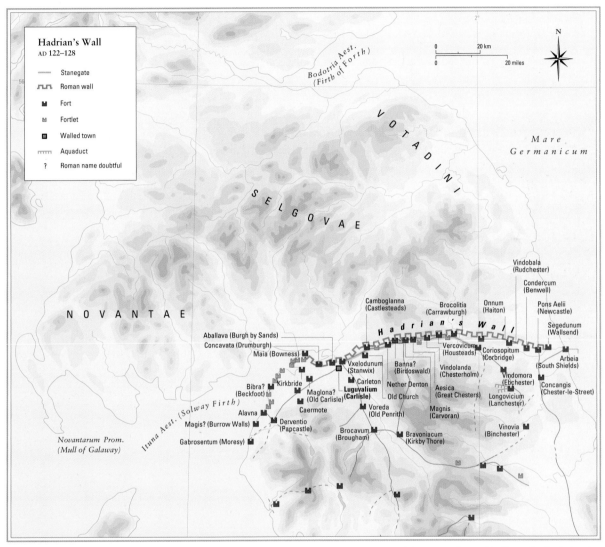

Hadrian's Wall
AD 122–128

- Stanegate
- Roman wall
- Fort
- Fortlet
- Walled town
- Aquaduct
- ? Roman name doubtful

*Bodotria Aest.
(Firth of Forth)*

*Mare
Germanicum*

V O T A D I N I

S E L G O V A E

N O V A N T A E

H a d r i a n ' s   W a l l

Vindobala
(Rudchester)

Condercum
(Benwell)

Camboglanna
(Castlesteads)

Brocolitia
(Carrawburgh)

Onnum
(Haiton)

Pons Aelii
(Newcastle)

Segedunum
(Wallsend)

Aballava (Burgh by Sands)
Concavata (Drumburgh)
Maia (Bowness)

Vercovicium
(Housteads)

Coriosopitum
(Corbridge)

Arbeia
(South Shields)

Vxelodunum
(Stanwix)

Banna?
(Birdoswald)

Vindolanda
(Chesterholm)

Vindomora
(Ebchester)

Concangis
(Chester-le-Street)

Bibra?
(Beckfoot)

Kirkbride

Carleton

Nether Denton

Aesica
(Great Chesters)

Longovicium
(Lanchester)

Maglona?
(Old Carlisle)

**Luguvalium
(Carlisle)**

Old Church

Magnis
(Carvoran)

Caermote

Voreda
(Old Penrith)

Magnis
(Carvoran)

Vinovia
(Binchester)

Alavna

Magis? (Burrow Walls)

Derventio
(Papcastle)

Brocavum
(Brougham)

Bravoniacum
(Kirkby Thore)

Ituna Aest. (Solway Firth)

Gabrosentum (Moresy)

*Novantarum Prom.
(Mull of Galaway)*

0   20 km
0   20 miles

N

The Emperor Hadrian visited Britain in AD 122 and, concerned about imperial frontiers, he ordered a wall built just north of the Stanegate. The wall was some 70 miles long and was ten feet wide, constructed out of stone from Newcastle to the River Irthing, after which a turf wall was built to Bowness-on-Solway. In both sections, the mile-castles were built from turf and timber on the turf wall and elsewhere of stone. Two small turrets were emplaced between each milecastle. The front of the wall was protected by a large ditch except where the wall followed steep cliffs or an escarpment. The wall was eventually narrowed to eight feet for economy and speed of building, which was implemented by detachments from the three British legions. The wall incorporated 15 forts and was further protected to the south by a military zone and an earthwork, the vallum, a ditch between two mounds. The Cumberland coast beyond the wall also had a chain of mile-castles

The Roman Empire deployed a large proportion of its professional army on or close to its frontiers. Strongly built defense works like Hadrian's wall served to demonstrate Rome's resolve to defend and control.

and towers. The wall was intended as an obstacle to the Caledonians and to keep the Brigantes in. Generally, the garrisons were trained to be offensive: rather than defending walls, the Romans would leave them to fight in the open.

In AD 138, Emperor Antoninus Pius re-evaluated the British frontier system and gave a new governor, Quintus Lollius Urbicus, the duty of re-occupying southern Scotland and erecting a new wall across the Forth-Clyde gap. The legions built the wall, which stretched 37 miles with a turf rampart built on stone foundations. Thirteen feet high and 15 feet wide, the wall was fronted by a wide level space, a berm, and a ditch. Nineteen forts were incorporated, being about two miles apart. The wall was designed to control movements and to observe areas northward. It was abandoned around 158 and then re-occupied for a while before a final retreat was made to Hadrian's Wall (c. 163). Further military campaigns north of the walls were carried out by Emperor Septimus Severus and his sons Caracalla and Geta in 208–09 and 210 respectively. Sections of the Antonine Wall were repaired and Severus won several victories over the Caledonii. He took the honorific style Britannicus as if he had conquered Britain, which did not happen.

When evaluating Roman intentions in northern Britain, the Romans never intended to occupy the Highlands, which they could probably have achieved, seeing how the legions had conquered more

A particularly well-preserved section of Hadrian's Wall. The wall was built in what is now northern England under the orders of Emperor Hadrian in AD 122. The wall functioned as a military barrier but it is also thought that the gates served as custom posts for trade routes.

difficult mountain areas elsewhere. However, Scotland was remote, not tied into a market economy, and the cost of the walls impinged upon the imperial budget. The areas south of the walls were more important since they raised corn, but the effort of utilizing the arable land was too great, and so strategic withdrawals were made. In the wider picture, the major threats to the empire lay on the Danube and the Rhine against the Germans, and imperial strategy maintained that no one border area could be safeguarded at the expense of another. A withdrawal to Hadrian's Wall made sense. Also, the Parthians were feared in the east, and two new legions were raised to face that threat. Parts of Hadrian's wall are still standing today, and can be visited. The best-preserved section stretches across a large area of northern England, encompassing the fort at Housesteads. It has now been designated an UNESCO world heritage site.

During the reign of Antonius, a number of wars were fought in northern Britain. This resulted in the building of the Antonine's Wall between the Firth of Clyde and the Firth of Forth.

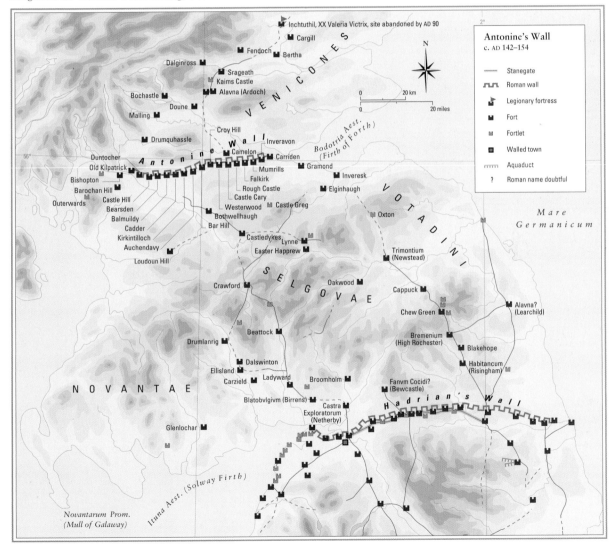

BATTLE OF MONS GRAUPIUS, AD 83

"THE ENEMY'S SLAIN AMOUNTED TO TEN THOUSAND MEN; ON OUR SIDE FELL THREE HUNDRED AND SIXTY, AMONG THEM AULUS ATTICUS... WHOM YOUTHFUL ARDOR AND A SPIRITED HORSE CARRIED INTO THE ENEMY'S LINES."   TACITUS, *AGRICOLA*

Gnaeus Julius Agricola was appointed Governor of Britain in AD 78. Present during Boudicca's revolt and experienced as commander of Legio XX Valeria Vixtrix, Agricola felt that decent treatment would mollify the Britons while a well-administered, prosperous province would give them a stake in the empire. Agricola undertook several campaigns in Britain. His greatest challenge was the wild lands of Scotland. In AD 78, he sought to Romanize the Brigantes, still smarting from Venutius' defeat, and in the next year he advanced north to the Tay estuary while building glen-blocking forts. AD 80 witnessed him consolidating Roman positions along the Forth-Clyde isthmus, using garrisoned positions. This led to his subsequent campaign in south-west Scotland, where he fought several successful battles (AD 81). In AD 82, he advanced north of the Forth engaging the Caledonians, as his biographer and son-in-law, Tacitus, claims. These would most likely have been the Vacomagi and Taexali of Angus and Aberdeenshire. Legio IX Hispana suffered a night attack, being saved by Agricola's mobile forces, but a decisive victory eluded him. In AD 83, Agricola marched northeast. His force comprised detachments from the four legions stationed in Britain together with 8,000 auxiliary infantry and 5,000 auxiliary cavalry. These later included Batavi, Tungri, and British recruits, giving Agricola some 20,000 men. Facing him were a horde of Caledonians, approximately 30,000 men, drawn from a range of Highland tribes under the overall command of Calgacus.

The two armies met in battle at Mons Graupius, as yet an unidentified site. Agricola placed his auxiliary infantry in the front line, backed by a second line, and flanked by the cavalry while the legions were held in reserve as well as guarding his camp. The Highlanders occupied a hillside opposite them, with a horde of chariots running to and fro between the opposing forces. The chariots attacked but were routed by the cavalry. Next the auxiliary infantry advanced up the hill using their shield bosses as weapons as well as the sword. The Caledonians were pushed back up the hill but the Roman momentum faltered in the climb. The main part of the Caledonians were on level ground on top of the hill. When the Romans were held, these Highlanders poured down the slope to outflank and envelop the auxiliary infantry. Agricola ordered in a cavalry reserve, which broke the Caledonians, and then the horsemen turned in on the enemy rear. The Highlanders broke and the cavalry pursuit went on a killing spree until nightfall. The legionaries were not involved. In the battle that followed, the Romans gained the upper hand with their use of cavalry, which broke the Caledonians and allowed the Romans to engage in a slaughter. Roman casualties approximated 1,100 but the Britons lost a reported 10,000.

Despite this victory, the Highlands remained untamed. Ultimately, the Romans abandoned their forts, withdrawing to the River Tweed on the orders of Emperor Domitian. He and Trajan were more concerned with events elsewhere rather than attempting to conquer a remote island. The Romans had to hold the Caledonians at bay, to push them back to the mountains.

The Highlands remained unconquered and intricate defensive systems were emplaced to resist encroachments by a Caledonian and Pictish confederation. Hadrian's Wall and the Antonine Wall were the solutions. This was the only way to bring peace to Britain.

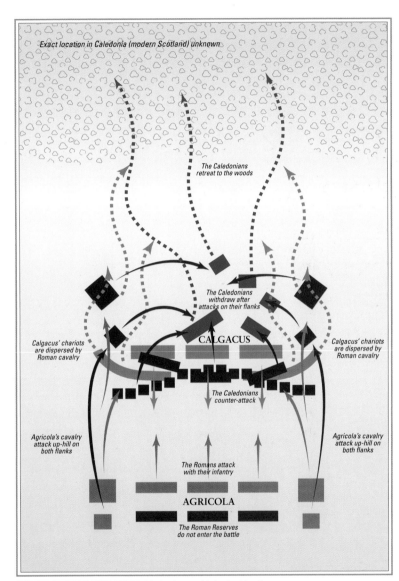

Exact location in Caledonia (modern Scotland) unknown

The Caledonians retreat to the woods

The Caledonians withdraw after attacks on their flanks

Calgacus' chariots are dispersed by Roman cavalry

CALGACUS

Calgacus' chariots are dispersed by Roman cavalry

The Caledonians counter-attack

Agricola's cavalry attack up-hill on both flanks

Agricola's cavalry attack up-hill on both flanks

The Romans attack with their infantry

AGRICOLA

The Roman Reserves do not enter the battle

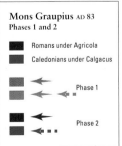

Mons Graupius AD 83
Phases 1 and 2

Romans under Agricola
Caledonians under Calgacus

Phase 1

Phase 2

Under the capable leadership of Gnaeus Julius Agricola, Roman rule expanded northward into the territory dominated by Caledonian tribes. At the battle of Mons Graupius the Roman army won the day, bringing peace to the island of Britain.

ROMAN ADMINISTRATIVE DIVISIONS IN BRITAIN

ROMAN PEACE AND ADMINISTRATION BESTOWED CIVIC
AND POLITICAL INSTITUTIONS WHICH PLANNED TOWNS IN
CHESSBOARD SQUARES FOR COMMUNITIES TO GOVERN UNDER A
PATTERN STANDARDIZED THROUGHOUT THE ROMAN WORLD.

Roman Britain ranked as a consular province, to be ruled by a senator who had held the consulship. As Governor, he was the Emperor's deputy for military and civil affairs. Not only had the Governor to defend the borders but even on campaign civil affairs had to be handled. His brief was to oversee the civil communities, to build and maintain roads, and make the imperial postal system run efficiently. Additionally, he was responsible for military recruitment and ran a legal court of appeal, dealing especially with issues of capital punishment or sentencing people to the mines, a recipe for a tortuous death. As Britain witnessed the foundation of more towns, the governor acted as a virtual circuit judge. In case a governor might misbehave, a procurator was also appointed to be in charge of financial affairs while monitoring the governor's actions.

The system of local government existing in Gaul was transposed to Britain. The Celtic tribes were organized into *civitates*, each *civitas* having a capital town. Civitas capitals were normally built on the site of an old Roman fort which was serviced by a developing community which turned into the capital. Town planning was probably the norm, evidenced by the grid-street patterns. Towns had certain legal rights including the granting of Roman citizenship to the hundred-man council, or *ordo*. In these tribal areas, towns ranked as a *vicus,* which possessed some degree of self-government. The Romans also introduced communities of Roman veterans (*coloniae*) into Britain. These towns of self-governing citizens were partially designed to show the Celtic tribes the virtues of Roman civilization. The three such communities in Britain were founded at Colchester, Lincoln, and Gloucester with municipium being developed too. Each colonia was surrounded by its own territory, and the Roman towns developed a vibrant urban lifestyle.

Opposite: Roads, garrisons, and effective taxation produced a well organized province of the empire, integrated into a greater state that reached from the Atlantic to the deserts of the Middle East.

Roman Administrative
Divisions in Britain

◼ Provincial capital
● Colonia
🏰 Legionary fortress
● Local capital
● Other major town
— Administrative boundaries
(names based on old tribal
areas)

Inchtuthil

Carpow

Antonine Wall

N

Hadrian's Wall

Coriosopitum
(Corbridge)

CARVETII   Liguvalium
(Carlisle)

BRIGANTES

PARISI

Usurium Brigantum
(Aldborough)

EBORACUM
(YORK)

Petuaria
(Brough-on-Humber)

DECEANGLI   Deva
(Chester)

Aquae Amemetiae
(Buxton)

Lindum Colonia
(Lincoln)

Segontium
(Caernarfon)

ORDOVICES

CORNOVII

CORITANI

ICENI

Viroconium
(Wroxeter)

Ratae
Coritanorum
(Leicester)

Venta Icemorum
(Caistor-by-Norwich)

Gariannonum
(Burgh Castle)

DOBUNNI

Durobrivae
(Water Newton)

DEMETAE   Magnis
(Kenchester)

CATUVELLAUNI

TRINOVANTES

Camulodunum
(Colchester)

Moridunum
(Carmarthen)

SILURES   Glevum Colonia
(Gloucester)

Corinium
(Cirencester)

Verulamium
(St Albans)

Caesaromagus
(Chelmsford)

Isca Silvrum
(Caerleon-on-Usk)

Venta Silurum
(Caerwent)

Aquae Sulis
(Bath)

ATREBATES   LONDINIUM
LAUGUSTA
(LONDON)

Calleva
(Silchester)

Durovemum
(Canterbury)

Rutupiae
(Richborough)

BELGAE

REGNENSES

CANTI

Dubrae
(Dover)

DUROTRIGES   Venta Belgarum
(Winchester)

Noviomagus
(Chichester)

Anderida
(Pevensey)

DUMNONII   Lindinis
(Ilchester)

Isca
Dumnoniorum
(Exeter)

Durnovaria
(Dorchester)

ROMANIZED BRITAIN

ROMAN ACTIVITY CAN BE MEASURED BY ROADS BUILT AND MILESTONES FOUND. THE ROMANS CONSTRUCTED 6,000 MILES OF ROADS IN BRITAIN, COMPLETED BY ABOUT AD 340, WHICH ALLOWED FOR TRADE AND MOVEMENT OF THE FOUR LEGIONS STATIONED IN BRITAIN.

The Romanization of Britain followed that in Gaul. The *civitates* and *municipia* of Britain were substantial in comparison with their Mediterranean origins, quality, and architectural proportions. Instead, the system of villas was much more important, especially in the civilian settlements areas south of the Fosse Way, the road linking Exeter (Isca) to Lincoln (Lindum). North of this line, the military were more in evidence, certainly as Hadrian's Wall was approached.

The towns occupied key points where trade routes crossed and served as market places to exchange surplus products such as Cotswold wool, Devon pottery, and jet from the area near Whitby via York. Additionally, markets brought in goods from Europe such as Samian ware pottery, Falernian wine, olives, and olive oil. A coin-based economy led to service businesses in municipal areas such as bakeries, shoe-making, mosaic setting, and interior painting. The Roman taxation system enhanced productivity and generated financial stability, a prerequisite for economic activity. Towns housed temples, *basilicae* and the forum together with temples and public baths with the complete range of rooms from the *frigidarium* to the *caldarium*. Many towns possessed an amphitheater like that at Chester or theaters, and some towns still have the remains of the enclosing walls.

Most people in Britain lived in the countryside, inhabiting the circular wattle and daub houses used traditionally by Iron Age Celts. Others lived in villas and these prosperous farms were home to Romans, wealthy Roman-Britons, Celtic servants, and laborers. Some villas were sumptuous with beautiful mosaics such as the Orpheus mosaic at the Roman villa at Littlecote Manor near Hungerford. Some villas have now been identified as hostelries, sometimes associated with neighboring temples like that of Nodens at Lydney Park in Gloucestershire.

Villas tended to be farms laid out in various patterns following a rectangular style. Prime examples can be visited at Littlecote and at Brading and Newport in the Isle of Wight. Villas included outbuildings such as barns for animals, storage, and servants quarters. Ownership of villas varied with some farm-owners present but those comprising parts of larger estates would be managed by bailiffs. Vectis, the Isle of Wight, owns eight identifiable villas representing all the types among the 700 villas found in Britain. These are found at Brading, Newport, Combley (Arreton), Carisbrooke, Clatterford, possibly Bowcombe, Rock (Brighstone), and Gurnard.

Vectis became a well-populated Romano-Celtic society peaking in prosperity between 250 and 300. The villas practiced mixed faming using crop rotation with green as well as animal manure. Cereal crops such as wheat and barley were grown on the downs and wheat was exported. Meadows were to raise cattle while chicken, geese, goats, and oxen were common. The downs were also used for sheep grazing and for small enclosed fields which can be seen via aerial photographs. The northern part of the island was thick with forest and was used for foraging pigs and hunting, deer, boar, and birds. The sea provided a rich harvest, as it still does. The prosperity of the island partially relied on the easy access to markets with the Solent providing multiple routes to the mainland. Ptolemy dubbed the Solent network as the Magus Portus and anchorages have been found at Yarmouth and Wootton Creek.

The Romans developed British resources such as the lead and silver mines, with occasional gold workings in Wales. Cornish tin was useful for making bronze but was often alloyed with lead to make pewter. The Sussex and Kentish Weald were home to iron smelting as was the Forest of Dean. Trade was extensive and London became an *entrepôt* exporting corn, wool, textiles, and jet, the latter even reaching the Rhineland.

Roman architects and planners achieved exceptional standards, buildings which included central heating, plumbing, and sewerage disposal – very useful in Britain's rainy climate.

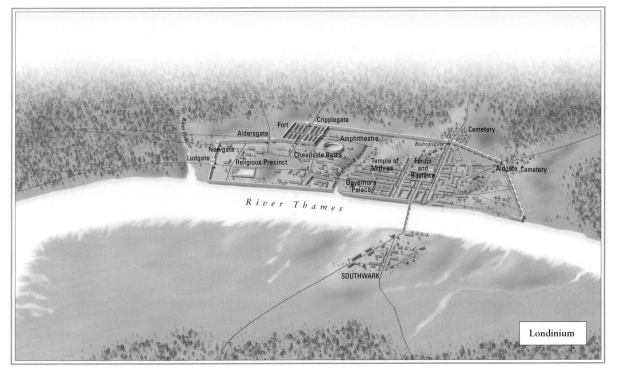

Londinium

AQUAE SULIS AND FISHBOURNE

ROMAN ARCHITECTURE AT BATH AND FISHBOURNE ROMAN
PALACE REVEAL INCREDIBLE BATH SUITES AND THE REMNANTS
OF HYPOCAUST SYSTEMS, TOGETHER WITH BEAUTIFUL MOSAICS
WHICH COULD OFTEN BE FOUND IN ROMAN VILLAS SUCH AS
CHEDWORTH VILLA IN GLOUCESTERSHIRE.

Roman settlements in Britain point to a vibrant energy of the empire and its officials together with the new Romano-British civilization which sprang up. Towns, villas, and palaces exemplify a rich and varied lifestyle providing us with fine examples of Roman Britain.

While the Romans were constructing the Fosse Way, they came upon the Avon Valley and the hot springs at present day Bath. A spa was built, Aquae Sulis, being dedicated to the Roman goddess Minerva and Celtic Sul, the bright one. Founded by the Flavians between AD 60 and 70, the settlement is renowned for its Roman bath system which survives in remarkable condition to this day, being one of the finest examples of its type in Europe. Bath was also a strategic route node since the Fosse Way met the west road from Avonmouth port (Abonae) through Mildenhall and Silchester to London and the southeast road across Wessex to the port at Hamworthy on Poole Harbor.

Silchester (Calleva of the Atrebates), a tribal civitas, was given to Cogidubnus during the Claudian conquest. Originally built of timber, the forum and basilica were reconstructed with stone by the second century. An oval amphitheatre lies outside the town's polygonal defensive walls over 6.3 meters high which enclosed an area of 43 hectares. The grid-street pattern were superimposed on the town after the forum and baths were built because they are not aligned with the grid but with each other. The city contained approximately 180 stone houses but the fringes of the city were occupied with wooden dwellings which were incinerated in a fire in the late third century. It is mentioned by Ptolemy and in the Antonine Itinerary, a classical geographical work. The site of Calleva has produced many inscribed stones, some dedications to one of the three temples. One read "To Julia Augusta, Mother of the Senate and the Encampments, Marcus Sabinus Victor, (dedicates this) by reason of (her virtue)." The town was home to foreign tradesmen and artisans, as evidenced by dedicatory slabs provided by the Guild (Collegium) of Foreigners (Peregrini).

The Roman palace at Fishbourne in Sussex near the main road from Chichester (Noviomagnus) was situated at the head of a creek and was the site of wooden granaries and a naval station, which have been associated with the Claudian conquest, as a supply base. The palace was enlarged during the Flavian period. The palace is linked to King Tiberius Claudius Cogidubnus, a Roman citizen, client-king of the Regni and friend of Claudius. However, another interpretation suggests that it was built for Sallustius Lucullus, a Roman governor of Britain in the late first century. The rectangular palace surrounds a large central courtyard and is itself encircled by formal gardens. The palace is the largest Roman mansion north of the Alps and is comparable in size to large modern palaces, being 150 square meters. The building incorporates and under-floor heating system (hypocaust), a bath-house, and 50 mosaics, being especially known for the Dolphin Mosaic.

Temples have been mentioned several times and religion became important in Britain. The Imperial Cult co-existed with Celtic and Roman gods, the latter often merging with their equivalents. Shrines have been observed to Mars Nodens and the god Faunus, who was given a variety of local names. Eastern cults became important with the worship of Egyptian Isis and the Indo-Iranian Mithras, a god of light, who found adherents in the Roman military. Evidence of his worship has been found at forts on Hadrian's Wall and at Wallbrook, London. Finally, Christianity took root in the fourth century and provided important personages, such as St. Patrick, Pelagius, and St. Alban the martyr.

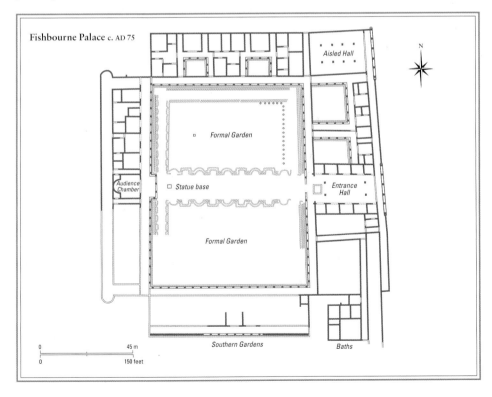

Fishbourne Palace, Roman in all its aspects, was created for a person of Celtic background who enthusiastically embraced the new culture.

Romano-British Defenses and Barbarian Invasions

The military writer Vegetius said the British fleet had some light galleys whose hull, sails, and crew's clothing, and even crews faces, were painted sea-green to make them invisible. The navy called them the painted ones.

The third century saw the Roman Empire being subject to barbarian raids, financial instability owing to inflation, and governmental interference in the provinces. In comparison, Roman Britain remained peaceful, with minor foreign raids, and it was still wealthy. Until the fourth century, Britain's defenses were a barrier to barbarians. Britain's defenses were extensive with Hadrian's Wall and Pennine forts warding off attacks from Scotland. Most urban centers possessed walls and the coasts were studded with forts to deter and counter incursions from Ireland and the Saxons. Unfortunately, Britain faced domestic political problems which probably weakened its security position. In approximately AD 286, Carausius, commander of the British fleet, was accused of various crimes, including peculation, and Rome ordered his death. He reacted by seizing Britain and declaring himself emperor. He invaded Gaul capturing its northern parts but was pushed out by Caesar Constantius. In 367, the Picts, Scots, and Allacotti co-ordinated an onslaught against Britain which captured the Roman commander of the north and killed the Count of the Saxon Shore. The defensive system suffered severe desertions and bandits roamed Britain, although the town walls limited urban damage.

A new barbarian invasion from across the Rhine posed the threat of cutting Britain's links with Rome. The current Emperor Constantine was exchanged for Gratian, and the new emperor crossed to Gaul taking the British garrison with him. Britain was now defenseless, causing the Britons to eject remaining Roman officials and govern for their own sake. Realistically, Britain was alone to face Saxon invasions. In 410, Emperor Honorius, realizing the security situation, informed the British cities that they must carry out their own defense. The same year, Alaric the Visigoth seized and sacked Rome. making the telling point that the Roman West was now the barbarian West.

Opposite: Germanic tribes from the coasts of northern Denmark and Germany had raided Roman Britain for a century or so but from the late 4th century a migration took place that would bring massive changes to the island of Britain. It would remove Celtic speech and culture from most of the island and eventually dominate those who remained.

Roman Britain
4th Century

- ■ Provincial capital
- ● Colonia
- ● Local capital
- ● Other major town
- ● Signal station
- ▬ Fort

Antonine Wall

PICTS

Hadrian's Wall

Coriosopitum
(Corbridge)

Liguvalium
(Carlisle)

Maryport

Britannia
Secunda

Huntcliff
Goldsborough
Ravenscar
Scarborough
Filey

Ravenglass

EBORACUM
(YORK)

SCOTTI

Lancaster

Usurium Brigantum
(Aldborough)

Ribchester

Petuaria
(Brough-on-Humber)

Caer Gybi

Deva
(Chester)

Aquae Amemetiae
(Buxton)

Lindum Colonia
(Lincoln)

Segontium
(Caernarfon)

Flavia Caesariensis

Brancaster

Venta Icemorum
(Caistor-by-Norwich)

Viroconium
(Wroxeter)

Ratae
Coritanorum
(Leicester)

Durobrivae
(Water Newton)

Gariannonum
(Burgh Castle)

Britannia Prima

Magnis
(Kenchester)

Maxima Caesariensis

Walton Castle

ANGLES

Moridunum
(Carmarthen)

Glevum Colonia
(Gloucester)

Corinium
(Cirencester)

Verulamium
(St Albans)

Camulodunum
(Colchester)

Caesaromagus
(Chelmsford)

Isca Silvrum
(Caerleon-on-Usk)

Venta Silurum
(Caerwent)

LONDINIUM
AUGUSTA
(LONDON)

SAXONS

Cardiff

Aquae Sulis
(Bath)

Calleva
(Silchester)

Reculver

Durovemum
(Canterbury)

Rutupiae
(Richborough)

Venta Belgarum
(Winchester)

Dubrae
(Dover)

Lindinis
(Ilchester)

Portchester

Noviomagus
(Chichester)

Lympne

Anderida
(Pevensey)

Isca
Dumnoniorum
(Exeter)

Durnovaria
(Dorchester)

N

BRITANNIA ALONE, AD 410

THE MILDENHALL SILVER DINNER SERVICE, NOW IN THE BRITISH MUSEUM, IS CONSIDERED TO HAVE BEEN BURIED SHORTLY AFTER 367 WHEN THE SAXON SHORE WAS ATTACKED. PRESUMABLY, THE SERVICE'S OWNERS WERE SURPRISED AT THEIR VILLA AND DID NOT LIVE TO DIG IT UP.

The desertion by Rome left Britain to disintegrate into a collection of petty kingdoms ruled by Romanized Celtic leaders. Ranging from the Picts of Scotland through to the Channel was a series of statelets which, from 410, mirrored Christian diocesan districts, probably based upon ancient tribal land holdings. The Celtic successor states faced the Saxon onslaught. The political configuration of Britain showed that it was split into various sub-sections. In Scotland the Picts were dominant until the Scots gained control. Sub-Roman Britain, the remainder of Britain in the south, became united under the High-King, Vortigern (c. 425–55). Sixth century historian Gildas in his On the Ruin and Conquest of Britain (De excidio et conquestu Britanniae) points out that Vortigern invited some Saxons to settle in Britain as mercenaries to replace the Roman forces to confront Jute invaders. Hengist was granted Kent as a foederati but broke his contract and turned Kent into a Saxon kingdom, inherited by his son, Ærc. Other Saxons invaded and the West Saxon, Wessex, kingdom was established.

Elsewhere, the Angles created Bernicia, Lindsey, and Deira and some surged into East Anglia forming the communities of north and south folk in Norfolk and Suffolk. Many Angles streamed into Elmet and founded Mercia leaving the remnant of Elmet the other side of the Trent. The so-called middle Saxons founded Middlesex and eventually captured London. This Anglo-Saxon advance marched ever westward acquiring submissive British subjects or easing out other natives. This left Roman Britain in foreign hands while Scotland, Wales, and Cornwall became the refuge of free Celts. Saxon England saw the larger kingdoms, such as Northumbria, built from Bernicia, Mercia, East Anglia, and Wessex absorbing the smaller Anglo-Saxon kingdoms until Wessex defeated Mercia at Ellendun (825) and became the forerunner of a united England.

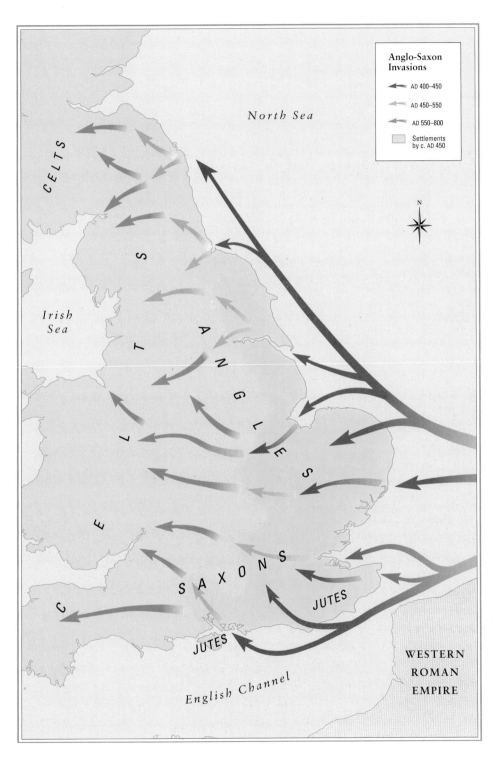

Anglo-Saxon
Invasions

AD 400–450

AD 450–550

AD 550–800

Settlements
by c. AD 450

North Sea

CELTS

*Irish
Sea*

ANGLES

English Channel

SAXONS

JUTES

JUTES

**WESTERN
ROMAN
EMPIRE**

N

Raiding Saxons had appeared
along the east coast of Britain in
the 4th century AD. To combat
this emerging threat the Roman
administration created a chain
of forts from the Wash to
the Channel.

ENEMY AT THE GATES

IN 429, ST. GERMANUS SAID ENGLAND WAS FULL OF TREASURE, FLOCKS AND HERDS AND FOOD, PLUS STRONG CIVIL AND RELIGIOUS INSTITUTIONS. HOWEVER, INVADING ARMIES FROM THE NORTH AND EAST WERE APPROACHING, COMPOSED OF SAXONS, PICTS, AND SCOTS.

Western Europe was an agriculturally rich land, with its interior connected to the seas by broad navigable rivers. Cities grew along these routes and became nodes of trade and communication. The region was well populated as the Romans found when they seized control from its Celtic or Gallic peoples. The Romans imposed law and urban settlement patterns during their occupation but their civilization did not penetrate too deeply. The Celtic tribes were farmers and their villages survived after conquest but were eventually incorporated into the great estates of a provincial Roman or Celtic-Roman aristocracy depending upon how much inter-marriage existed. Celtic status changed as formally free landholders became peasants without freedom and were coerced into paying rents and taxes to the Gallo-Roman elites. Over time, serfdom and slavery became common as the Celts were forced to work the land. When barbarian Germanic tribes were invited into the empire as foederati to defend the frontiers against other barbarians, the newcomers lived amid the Celts bringing new ideas, laws, and a degree of military security against increasing frequent raids.

The peoples outside the Empire lived in settled agricultural villages and had traded with the Romans for years with many surplus young men being recruited into the Roman army. Roman culture was absorbed and Arian Christianity had won many converts. Despite the occasional border raids and counter-raids, the Germanic tribes were not hell bent on expansion but remained content with their artisans producing fine metalwork and iron tools and weapons. The tribes were those who coalesced around successful war leaders and the loyalty felt was strong especially amongst the leaders' hearth warriors or comitatus, who were prepared to fight to the death with their leader. By the time

Opposite: Rome had usually been able to absorb new peoples and integrate them into the empire but from the 4th century the nature of these arrangements changed. Instead newcomers began to rule over the areas they had agreed to defend, forming new power centers. Rome's taxation fell and its ability to pay its armies and control its "citizens" declined.

Eburacum
Deva
Lindum
Angles
Saxons
TEUTONIC PEOPLES
R. Oder
R. Elbe
50°
70°
Glevum
Corinium
ANGLO-SAXONS
by 5th century
loosely held area
given up
CELTIC PEOPLES
Londinium
Rutupiae
Oesoriacum
R. Rhine
FRANKS
Bagacum
Colonia Agrippina
EMPIRE OF
THE HUNS
Mogontiacum
Rotomagus
Remio
Augusta
Treverorum
Agri
Decumates
260 given up
R. Danube
Lauriacum
Vindobona
Carnuntum
ATLANTIC
OCEAN
Lutecia
R. Seine
Argentorate
Augusta
Vindelicum
Cambodunum
Aquincum
OSTROGOTHS
from 454
Turones
R. Loire
Vesontio
Aventicum
Curia
Virunum
Pannonia
by 446 lost to the
Empire of the Huns
Pictavi
Bituriges
BURGUNDIANS
Emona
Mursa
Santones
Lugdunum
Mediolanum
Aquileia
Verona
Siscia
Pannonia
Singidunum
Brigantium
Burdigala
KINGDOM
OF THE
VISIGOTHS
Arverni
Vienna
R. Po
Viminacium
Asturica
Legio
Tolosa
Pollentia
Genoa
Ravenna
Bracara
R. Douro
Clunia
Narbo
Arelate
Florentia
Ancona
Scodra
40°
Salmantica
Caesarea Augusta
Massilia
Rome
Dyrrhacium
Barium
Olisipo
KINGDOM
OF THE
Toletum
Barcino
Tarraco
WESTERN ROMAN EMPIRE
Aleria
Neapolis
R. Tagus
Emerita Augusta
Valentia
Caralis
Codenra
Messina
Tarentum
SUEVES
Hispalis
Panormus
Rhegium
Gades
Carthago
Nova
Icosium
Saldae
Hippo
Regius
Utica
Carthago
Syracuse
Tingis
Malaca
Caesarea
Sitifis
KINGDOM OF THE VANDALS
Hadrumetum
Sala
Auzia
Lambaesis
Constantina
Theveste
Mediterranean Sea
Thaenae
Oea
Sabrata
Leptis Magna
Berenice
30°
Boreum

Enemy at the Gates

*Date of loss of
territory by the
Roman Empire*

475
450
446
431
400

Federates
(allied to Rome)

—— Border of the Western and
Eastern Roman Empire, 450

▨ Anglo-Saxon homeland

➡ Expansion of Anglo-Saxon
settlement

➡ Migration of Ostrogoths

➡ Migration of Visigoths

N

0   200 km
0   200 miles

Opposite: These crosses and a tower are among the ruins left of the medieval monastery of Clonmacnoise. The monastery was founded in 545 by Saint Ciarán and was built in a strategic location, near to the River Shannon, which enabled it to become a bustling center of religion, trade, learning, and craft. However, it was frequently plundered and burned by Vikings, native Irish, and Anglo-Normans until it was finally destroyed and taken over by the English in 1552.

of migrations into the Roman Empire, the enemies at the gates were fairly stable dynastically. When a king died, a tribal assembly would elect the best possible successor from his family, which might not be the eldest son.

In the latter stages of the fourth century the Huns emerged from the steppe, surging westward while conquering one tribe after another. They subordinated the Ostrogoths, who inhabited a kingdom east of the Dniester on the shores of the Black Sea, but the Visigoths, who dwelt in an area from the Dniester to the Danube escaped, begging the Romans for sanctuary on the Roman side of the Danube. The Eastern Emperor Valens allowed them to settle in Moesia (376) maybe because he was an Arian Christian like the Visigoths. More and more Germanic war bands and their families migrated into the empire and often behaved like conquering kings, creating their own power centers, thereby reducing the amount of taxation going to Rome.

The Visigoths were treated by corrupt Roman officials so badly that they rebelled and savaged the Balkans. Valens took the field and lost the battle of Adrianople and his life, being succeeded by Theodosius I. When this emperor died in 395 the empire was split between east and west, each part being given to a son: Arcadius in the East and Honorius in the West. The Visigoths renounced their allegiance to Rome, invaded Greece and migrated to Italy. Other Germans, the Vandals, invaded France (406) and then Spain (409). The Visigoths sacked Rome (410) and traversed the Pyrénées into Spain where they fought the Vandals. The latter, led by Gaiseric, crossed to North Africa (429), defeated the Romans and seized Carthage (439), making it the capital of a Vandal kingdom. They had captured Rome's breadbasket and Vandal pirate fleets raided Sicily, Sardinia, and Corsica. In 455 they entered Rome and sacked it for two weeks before moving to devastate Greece and Dalmatia, which forced the Emperor Zeno to recognize Gaiseric and conclude peace (476).

In Spain, the Visigothic kingdom covered most of the Iberian Peninsula and part of Provence with its capital at Toulouse. Visigoth King Theodoric I died fighting Attila the Hun at Châlons (451) while allied to Rome. A successor, Euric, declared independence from Rome while using aspects of Roman governance and law. He absorbed the Suevi kingdom in northern Portugal (469) but was defeated by the forces of Clovis I, King of the Franks, at Vouillé (507), losing most of Provence and being left with Iberia.

The defeat of Attila freed the Ostrogoths from his rule and they settled in western Hungary and the Balkans of today's Croatia, Slovenia, and Serbia. Emperor Zeno inveigled the tribe into invading Italy where it eventually eradicated Odoacer, the first Barbarian king of Italy, a leader of Heruli foederati. The Ostrogothic King Theodoric used the Roman civil administration and economy while Roman culture influenced the Ostrogoths.

Other Germans settled near Lake Geneva and down the Rhône Valley. These Burgundians existed as a kingdom from 443 to 534, finally being vanquished by the Franks who became Roman allies and established a large kingdom in France and Germany. Gallo-Romans, however, were still able to run their estates and live in an untouched fashion. Taken together with the Anglo-Saxon invasion of Britain, the Celts had been subjugated by both Romans and German tribes and were pushed into the periphery of Europe: Wales, Scotland, Ireland, Kernow (now known as Cornwall), and Armorica (now known as Brittany).

CELTIC BRITAIN

"THEIR HAIR WAS OF GOLD, THEIR CLOTHING WAS OF GOLD AND LIGHT STRIPES BRIGHTENED THEIR CLOAKS. THEIR MILK-WHITE NECKS HAD GOLD COLLARS AROUND THEM, A PAIR OF ALPINE SPEARS GLINTED IN EACH WARRIOR'S HANDS, AND THEIR BODIES WERE PROTECTED BY TALL SHIELDS."   VIRGIL, *AENEID*, VIII. 659.62

Although the Celts were generally crushed by the forces of Germanic tribes and the Romans, nevertheless during the first thousand years of the Common Era, Celtic traditions were woven into early Christian art and became a major component of Christianity, which is enjoying a renaissance commencing in the late second millennium AD. Celtic aestheticism has chiefly developed in Ireland, which never faced Roman rule, and northern Scotland.

Celtic society developed throughout its lifetime, but its organization varied geographically in constant evolution. In Roman Gaul, the Celts organized themselves, and were encouraged by Rome, into a system of urban *oppida* by which each tribe could develop political institutions of a visibly modern limited form of democracy akin to eighteenth-century Britain. The stability achieved allowed the gradual introduction of Roman cultural elements and the cultural imperialism of the Latin language. However, in pagan Ireland, the various tribes were widely dispersed in small settlements in a rural environment with kings as the symbol of unity and the transmitters of ancestral lands and traditions. In comparison with mainland Europe, antiquated social models dominated and the family, clan, and chiefdom, combined with blood-ties and collective ownership of land, survived in Ireland.

Eventually, Christianity reached Ireland, commenced by the mission of St. Patrick who brought with him Latin learning, education, and erudition. Monasteries developed and integrated themselves into the ancient Celtic culture and they acquired wealth, power, and prestige. Christian symbolism digested Celtic La Tène art forms, which stimulated and informed manuscript illumination. The Book of Durrow, reputedly written by St. Columba, comprises four Latin Gospels with translations and commentaries with decorations in gold combining curlicues and inter-twined decorations which influenced the style of Irish

Opposite: The Celtic peoples of Britain now transformed into a Romanized settled society facing a tribal enemy. Angles, Saxons, and others who were semi nomadic, capable of existing in a less organized world, raided and pillaged Romano-Celtic settlements. Some stayed to fight, some fled, and some came to terms with the new people, but the island was changed beyond recognition.

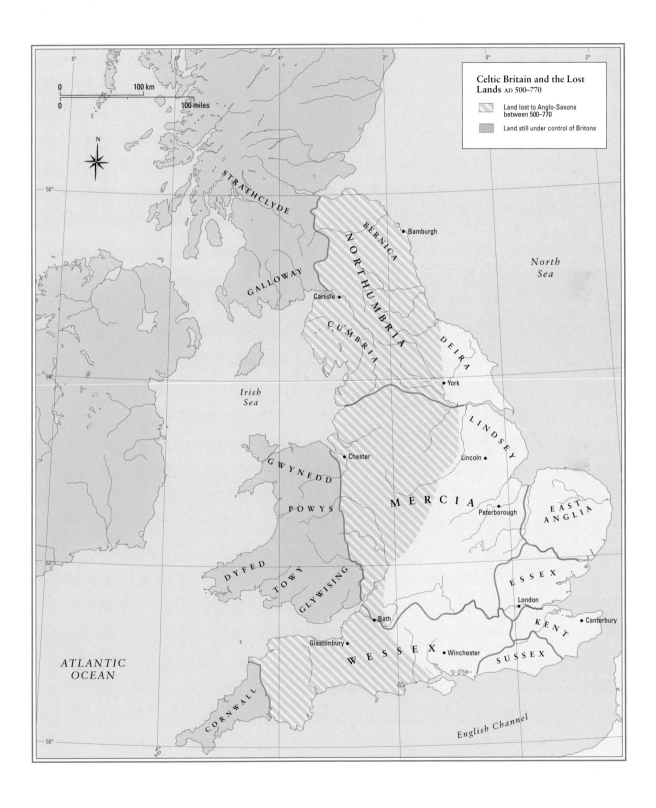

Celtic Britain and the Lost Lands AD 500–770

Land lost to Anglo-Saxons between 500–770

Land still under control of Britons

0   100 km
0   100 miles

N

North
Sea

STRATHCLYDE

GALLOWAY

BERNICA

NORTHUMBRIA

• Bamburgh

Carlisle •

CUMBRIA

DEIRA

• York

Irish
Sea

GWYNEDD

• Chester

LINDSEY

Lincoln •

POWYS

MERCIA

Peterborough •

EAST
ANGLIA

DYFED

TOWY

GLYWISING

• Bath

ESSEX

London •

KENT

• Canterbury

Glastonbury •

WESSEX

• Winchester

SUSSEX

ATLANTIC
OCEAN

CORNWALL

English Channel

56°
54°
52°
50°

8°   2°   0°   2°

and Manx crosses with a circle embracing a central motif. Celtic Christian art absorbed these influences in stately crosses and shrines. Sometimes Norse influences are found, especially in Manx crosses. Many of these developments were suppressed by the monastic orders following the Anglo-Norman invasion when Roman religion imposed its own styles and ideologies. Ultimately, Irish Celtic culture was preserved in literature and its study has a long tradition in universities internationally.

The first known texts originate in the sixth century AD and these comprise brief funerary inscriptions written in Ogham, found in both Ireland and the Isle of Man. Eventually, Latin inscriptions absorbed some Celtic characteristics and grammar. Irish writing style can be seen in a variety of books such as the Life of St. Columba, the Book of Kells, and the Book of Armagh. Texts of law can be recognized, some identifying the rights of women and these Old Irish writings identify the notions and procedures of seventh- and eighth-century law, Brehon Law, while Welsh variants date from the tenth century, as codified by Hywel Dda.

Old poetry and prose were transcribed from their sixth- and seventh-century origins, and the tales of the heroic age depicting the adventures of heroes, their birth and death, journeys to the other world, love affairs, and battles, replicate the ideals held by Celts during the Iron Age. Thus, tales of Cuchulainn are extant in one cycle of work while another genre, the Fenian cycle, directly influenced European ideas during the late Middle Ages. These depict the adventures of the chieftain Finn Mac Cumaill, who protected his lands from foreign raids with great bravery. In Wales, these traditions were subsumed with the Arthurian cycle of legends.

The decline of Celtic languages has been severe but they do continue and are being used as media of education. Also, Celtic culture exists in music in ceilidhs and groups, and Celtic traditions enthused Romantic art in England during Victorian times via Tennyson, the photography of Julia Cameron, and the paintings and art of George Frederick Watts, Sir Edward Coley-Burn Jones, William Morris, John Henry Dearle, and James Archer.

The Celtic tribes that originally occupied Britain included the following:

Atrebates - Silchester, Hants

Belgae - Winchester, Hants

Brigantes - Aldorough, North Yorkshire

Cantiaci - Canterbury, Kent

Carveti - Carlisle, Cumbria

Catuvellauni - St Albans, Hertfordshire

Coritani - Leicester

Cornovii - Wroxeter, Shropshire

Decangi - North Wales

Demetae - Carmarthen, Wales

Iceni - Suffolk

Orodovices - S. Gwynedd, Wales

Parisi - Humberside

Regneses - Sussex

Segontiaci - Essex

Close up of St. Martin's Cross outside Iona Abbey on the island of Iona, on the west coast of Scotland. Founded in 563, the abbey is considered to be one of the oldest and most important religious centers in western Europe. It is believed that the monks of Iona Abbey produced the Book of Kells in the late 700s, an illuminated manuscript famous for its beautiful and decorative calligraphy. The Abbey fell victim to a number of Viking attacks, and in 806 everybody in the abbey was found dead, a supposed Viking massacre.

CELTIC PANTHEON

"THE INLAND CELTS MAKE AN UNUSUAL AND SURPRISING USE OF THEIR TEMPLES... A LOT OF GOLD IS OPENLY DISPLAYED AS OFFERINGS, AND ALTHOUGH THE CELTS HAVE AN EXCESSIVE LOVE OF MONEY, NONE OF THE NATIVES DARES TOUCH IT BECAUSE OF RELIGIOUS FEAR." (DIODORUS SICULUS, *WORLD HISTORY*, V.27)

A coherent picture of Celtic religion and its gods can be gleaned from monuments erected after the Roman conquest, archeological remains, and medieval Irish writings. A constant feature is the importance of natural sites as focal sites for ritual, especially sacred groves, forest clearings, hilltops, and water sources or lakes. Marshes, wells, lakes, and rivers have delivered up votive offerings in the form of weapons, jewellery, coins, potsherds, ritual objects, animal and human bones, and vessels that might have held food offerings. In religion symbols such as decorative skulls have been found in temples and on doorways performing some magic or necromantic purpose. Other religious symbols have been the sun-wheel, the swastika, the triskelli, and spiral; the torque displays authority while animals such as boars, rams, serpents, and mythological creatures possess supernatural meaning. The gods and goddesses who received these gifts are numerous, the following 14 being revered under one name or another throughout the Celtic world. Badhbh was the Irish goddess of wisdom and is linked to Morrigán and Macha as a triad of warrior goddesses, daughters of the mother goddess, Ernmas. The Morrigán was the goddess of prophecy, war, and revenge. This queen of ghosts appears as a hideous fairy to warriors leaving for battle when they are about to be defeated and killed. Associated with these three is Nemain, representing panic and fear. Another god is Cernunnos, shown with horns or antlers, who was probably a fertility god. Taeanis, too, was a god common to Gaul and Britain, being a thunder god. A deity who appealed to both Celt and Roman alike was Epona, a horse goddess. The mother goddess was Dana, her children and their descendants being the people who moved into Ireland, they being known as the Tuatha Dé Danann. Manannán mac Lir was the Irish and Manx god of the sea. Oghmas or Ogmios in Gaul was the god of eloquence.

Opposite: Amorica transformed into Brittany in the 3rd century when the Roman empire was experiencing a major crisis. The population of the region declined, to be replaced by newcomers,; archeological evidence suggests they were from Britain, fleeing the Anglo-Saxons.

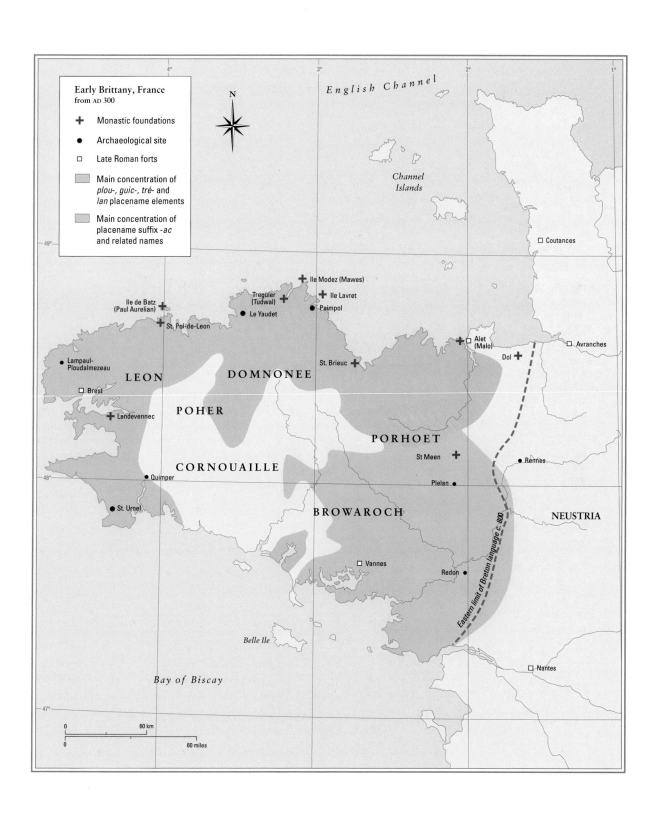

Early Brittany, France
from AD 300

✛ Monastic foundations

● Archaeological site

□ Late Roman forts

Main concentration of
plou-, *guic-*, *tré-* and
lan placename elements

Main concentration of
placename suffix *-ac*
and related names

N

English Channel

*Channel
Islands*

□ Coutances

✛ Ile Modez (Mawes)

Treguier
(Tudwal) ✛ ✛ Ile Lavret
Ile de Batz ✛ ● Paimpol
(Paul Aurelian) ● Le Yaudet
✛ St. Pol-de-Leon ✛ □ Alet
(Malo)
□ Avranches
Dol ✛

● Lampaul-
Ploudalmezeau ✛ St. Brieuc

LEON **DOMNONEE**

□ Brest

POHER
✛ Landevennec

PORHOET
St Meen ✛
● Rennes

CORNOUAILLE

● Quimper ● Plelan

● St. Urnel **BROWAROCH** **NEUSTRIA**

□ Vannes

Redon ●

Eastern limit of Breton language c. 800

Belle Ile

□ Nantes

Bay of Biscay

0   60 km

0   60 miles

DRUIDS

"WE MUST NOT FORGET THE HIGH REGARD IN WHICH THE DRUIDS HOLD THIS PLANT (MISTLETOE). THE DRUIDS (WHICH IS WHAT THEY CALL THEIR MAGICIANS) CONSIDER NOTHING MORE SACRED THAN MISTLETOE AND THE TREE THAT IT GROWS ON, SO LONG AS IT IS AN OAK." PLINY THE ELDER, *NATURAL HISTORY*, XVI.95

Druids were an intellectual elite, privileged not to bear arms, and were highly knowledgeable in literature and poetry, spending some 20 years in their training, memorizing knowledge, sacred rituals, law, and history. Nothing was written down, even though some druids knew the Greek alphabet, with many being literate by the time of Julius Caesar. The druids' training included many stages, such as the study to become a bard in Ireland, for which they learned verse, composition, narrating stories, learning grammar, and *Ogham*.

The druids understood mathematics, studied the heavens, stars, and planets, and claimed they were mediators between men and gods. They approached the gods, ran religious ceremonies, carried out sacrifices, and analyzed omens. They believed and taught that the human soul does not perish with death but migrates from one body to another, or goes to live elsewhere. Believing this, the Celts could conquer the fear of death, acting with fearless ferocity in battle or willingly be sacrificed themselves. In popular imagination, druids are associated with mistletoe, the plant under which people kiss at Christmas. Harvesting mistletoe from only the oak tree, the druids believed this was an endeavor connected with the seasons. Mistletoe was a perennial plant, and as was the soul to the body, so was the mistletoe to the oak, being part of a god incarnate in the plant.

"A priest clad in white climbs the tree, cuts the mistletoe with a golden hook and catches it on a white cloak. Victims are sacrificed with prayers to the god to render this offering propitious to the people who are making it. They believe that mistletoe in a drink confers fertility upon any sterile animal and is an antidote to all poisons." (Pliny the Elder, *Natural History*, XVI.95)

Julius Caesar rendered some detailed observations of the druids, stating that anyone of rank and status in Gaul was either a druid or a member of the nobility. They joined the tribal elites and were free from taxation. Their task was to guard the ancient tribal traditions and administer tribal law, as well as being mediators with the gods. The druids engaged in politics and inter-tribal negotiations and acted as judges when rules, taboos, and laws were broken. "Any individual or tribe failing to accept their award is banned from taking part in a sacrifice – the heaviest punishment that can be inflicted upon a Gaul. (Julius Caesar, *The Conquest of Gaul*, VI, 13)

Caesar also wrote that the druids of Gaul selected one of their number to lead their priestly guild for life and they met annually in a sacred grove of oak trees in the lands of the Carnutes in the center of Gaul. In Galatia, the assembly of the Celts was known as the *drunemeton*, the oak sanctuary. All these meetings were there to argue and decide major matters of note. Possibly, the combined Gaulish decision to unify against Caesar was taken at such a meeting. It was no accident that the Roman destruction of the main druid site on Mona (Anglesey) was a partial trigger in Boudicca's resistance to Rome. The druid sanctuary on Mona was revered by the Celts as the best center for druidical training, a virtual university.

Another sanctuary that Caesar destroyed was in southern Gaul, where an old grove was reputedly covered with human parts and blood. The eradication of such places showed the superiority of Roman arms and gods over the Celts and was designed to overawe and cower the defeated. Celtic sanctuaries can be easily found at La Roquepertuse and Entremont in southern France and at Gournay-sur-Aronde and Ribemont-sur-Ancre in northern France. In sum, the druids were so important that they were actually very dangerous to Rome.

"The vates practiced soothsaying and studied natural philosophy. The bards celebrated the brave deeds of their gods in verse. The druids were concerned with divine worship, the due performances of sacrifices, both private and public, and the interpretation of ritual questions." (Caesar, *The Conquest of Gaul*)

Mistletoe was sacred to the druids and has symbolized a great many things over the centuries to a diverse variety of people. It has also played an important part in our modern culture; kissing under the mistletoe is a classic Christmas tradition in the western world. Mistletoe has even featured in the popular French cartoon, *Asterix*.

Celtic Neo-Paganism

IN SCOTLAND, THE OLD WOMAN OF WINTER, THE CAILLEACH,
IS REBORN AS BRIDE OF THE WHITE WAND, YOUNG MAIDEN OF
SPRING, FRAGILE YET GROWING STRONGER EACH DAY AS THE SUN
REKINDLES ITS FIRE, TURNING SCARCITY INTO ABUNDANCE.

Celtic neo-paganism is a collection of movements that are enthused by the multiplicity of old Celtic gods and religious practices. The groups include a collection of neo-druids who started up during the eighteenth century Romantic period, such are the Ancient Order of Druids (1781) and the Ár nDraíocht Féin (1983). Another identifiable group are New Age Celtic Wicca and the unusual Celtic Neo-Shamanism. Finally, Celtic Reconstructionist Paganism tries to rebuild the historic traditions in as authentic manner as possible, this movement commencing in the mid-1980s.

The Celtic Reconstructionist Pagans (CelticR) operate under the logo of a triskelli with the intent of rebuilding and reviving in a contemporary context the religious, cultural, animist, and multi-deity world of the old Celts, directly echoing Celtic polytheism. The academic appreciation of the past is located within modern Celtic cultures, and new ventures are always based upon an appreciation of the history of the Celts. CelticR audits contemporary society and is prepared to delete those aspects of Celtic culture which would be inappropriate today, such as sacrifice of living beings. Furthermore, slavery and extreme patriarchal power have little place in the modern world. This neo-paganism is a hands-on attempt to achieve a renaissance in Celtic tradition by actively engaging in the study and preservation of the Celtic languages and taking part in Celtic music and dance, especially in the modern ceilidh. Dance groups meet annually in one or other of the Celtic regions, the summer of 2008 witnessing *Yn Chruinnaght* in Ramsey and Peel in the Isle of Man. CelticR live their lives according to certain rituals using purification rites, adding in chants, prayers, and songs from sources such as ancient Irish and Welsh poetry. Community celebrations can include bonfires, songs, dances, divination, and children's games, especially around Halloween and the festivals of Samhain, Imbolc, Beltane, and Lughnasad. CelticR rituals are deeply concerned with the Celtic cosmological triad of Earth, Sea, and Sky, with fire as being the joining force. Celtics are concerned with the inter-play of all aspects of Celtic culture and are specifically interested in religion.

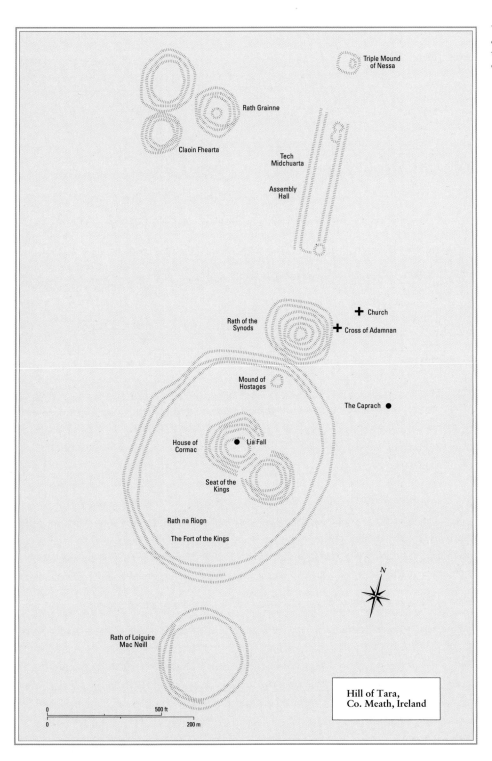

Triple Mound
of Nessa

Rath Grainne

Claoin Fhearta

Tech
Midchuarta

Assembly
Hall

✚ Church
✚ Cross of Adamnan

Rath of the
Synods

Mound of
Hostages

The Caprach ●

House of
Cormac

● Lia Fall

Seat of the
Kings

Rath na Riogn

The Fort of the Kings

Rath of Loiguire
Mac Neill

N

```
0                    500 ft
0              200 m
```

Hill of Tara,
Co. Meath, Ireland

Tara, perhaps the most important cultural site in Ireland, went through many phases of occupation over many centuries.

CUCHULAINN

CUCHULAINN'S MOST FAMOUS EXPLOITS WERE THOSE ACHIEVED
IN THE COURSE OF A CONFLICT DESCRIBED IN THE 20 TALES
IN THE CATTLE RAID OF COOLEY, WHICH IS THE HISTORY OF
THE LONG WAR BETWEEN ULSTER AND THE TWO MUNSTER
KINGDOMS AND THEIR ALLIES, LEINSTER AND CONNAUGHT.

The first century BC saw the construction of many tales of Iron Age Ireland depicting folklore and myths of the past. Some stories were didactic, recounting the exploits of heroes as role models for children and would-be warriors. After the Norse and Hiberno-Norse were defeated, monastic activity in Ireland saw a renaissance in learning and manuscript writing. Old tales were collected and preserved. Two particular manuscripts exciting notice are *The Book of the Dun Cow* and *The Book of Leinster,* which preserves the very earliest remembered stories. Academics have split these sagas into two sets, the Ulster or Red Branch and the later cycle of tales, called the Ossian cycle.

The older Ulster cycle comprises of about one hundred tales of valiant heroes from the kingdom of Ulster in pagan times. Among these offerings are accounts of the warrior Cuchulainn, or Cú Chulainn, especially in *The Cattle Raid of Cooley* and the story of Deirdre. The other branch focuses upon the hero Finn mac Cumhail or MacCool, a mythic chief and poet of the second or third century. These particular stories depict nostalgia for the heroic pre-Christian past. *Táin Bó Cúailgne* (*The Cattle Raid of Cooley*) recounts a long war that the two kingdoms of Munster with the kingdoms of Leinster and Connacht waged against Ulster at the behest of Queen Medb of Connacht. She wished to acquire herds of cattle and the fabled Brown Bull of Cooley. Historians who think that Tara was part of Connacht at this time would see the war as a duel to establish the high king of Ireland. In the story, Medh invades Ulster when its defenders, the Red Branch of Ulster, the defense militia or knightly order, are inflicted by a god-given malaise which paralyzed the warriors in winter. Only Cuchulainn is unaffected, a consequence of his father being Lug, a solar king. This hero faces the invaders and duels with one enemy each day, killing him, in a campaign lasting three months. He then combats groups of warriors and slaughters them.

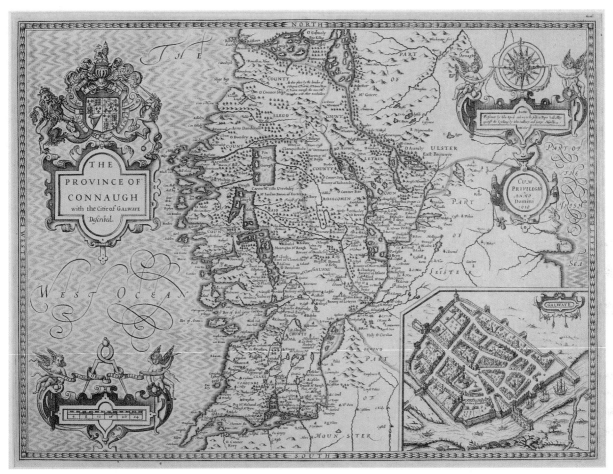

An ancient map depicting the Province of Connaught, known as Connacht, a western province of Ireland. Queen Medb is Queen of Connacht in Ulster mythology.

He is helped by magic learned from the witch, Scatbach, who lived in Scotland, and by Lug, who uses potions and magic herbs to heal his wounds and strengthen him. Morrigan, goddess of war, also uses witchcraft on his behalf before she turns against him later. In another tale, Cuchulain acts out the Aryan myth by killing his son, Conlach, conceived by the witch Aiffe, who sends her son to duel with his father. Cuchulainn is horrified at his actions and falls into madness and is an unhappy man for the rest of his life. The hero's career has seen him kill so many men in duels that he is pursued by the hatred of his victims' parents and sons. He is eventually lured by three witches to the Plain of Muirthemne by which time he has lost his own magic and his supernatural spear. He is attacked on all sides and is killed but as he dies his sword fell and severed the hand of the enemy who had come to decapitate him for a trophy of war.

In legend, Cuchulainn personifies the forces of heat and light while his enemies are dark or come from the night. The horses drawing his chariot are black and one white, his body warmth makes water boil and snow melt. He is also the myth of the tribal man who exalts heroism as a social function. Later, Christian versions of his death have Cuchulainn going to his last battle with the voices of angels ringing in his ears, after which he confesses his sins and receives the offer of salvation from the true faith.

The Mabinogion

THE LITERARY MASTERPIECE, THE *MABINOGION*, IS BASED ON HISTORICAL CHARACTERS AND INCIDENTS IN THE DARK AGES OF WALES, EMBELLISHED WITH SUPERNATURAL AND FOLKLORE ELEMENTS ECHOING PRIMORDIAL CELTIC MYTHOLOGY AND FOLKLORE, INCLUDING ANCIENT GODS AND GODDESSES.

The *Mabinogion* is a collection of eleven tales drawn from medieval Welsh manuscripts. These stories were conserved in two books called the *White Book of Rhydderch* and the *Red Book of Hergest*. Modern scholarship suggests that they were written between 1060 and 1425. However, some of the stories pre-date the manuscripts, deriving from an oral tradition which includes magic and supernatural elements in the tales. The title of the collection comes from the word '*mab*' which means 'boyhood' or 'youth' but now means 'tale' in common parlance.

The first four heroic tales concern a main character, Pryderi, who holds the series together. The first story, *Pwyll, Prince of Dyfed*, recounts Pryderi's parents, his birth, fostering, acquisition of a kingdom, and wedding while the second, *Branwen, Daughter of Llyr*, concerns Branwen's marriage to the King of Ireland, in which Pryderi plays little part. The third tale, *Manawyddan, son of Llyr*, sees the hero imprisoned by witchcraft and his release. The final story, *Math, son of Mathonwy*, tells of Pryderi's conflict with *Math and Gwydion*, and his death in battle. The stories comprise several themes: fall and redemption, loyalty, marriage, love, fidelity, the wronged wife, and incest. They are located in a weird and enchanted landscape on the coasts of north and south Wales and are replete with magic, white horses, giants, beautiful women, and heroic warriors.

All of the stories in the *Mabinogion* were collected and translated into English in a famous edition by Lady Charlotte Guest in the mid-nineteenth century.

The other tales, outside the first cycle of four, comprise a collection of native stories and some Arthurian romances. The first group are: *The Dream of Macsen Wledig*, based on the legend of Roman Emperor Magnus Maximus; *Llud and Llefelys* which includes fairy tale pieces; *Culhwch and Olwen*, the earliest known Arthurian romance in Welsh; *The Dream of Rhonaby*, a humorous recounting of Britain's heroic past; and *The Tale of Taliesin*, a twelfth story included in some versions of the *Mabinogion*.

The three Arthurian romances are Welsh versions of Arthurian stories whose subject matter also appears in the works of Chrétien de Troyes (c. 1135-1183). They also include material not in the writings of the French poet who was concerned with Camelot as a center of romantic love where knights worshipped their ladies and engaged in audacious quests in a world filled with magic and make-believe. These three stories are: *Owain, or the Lady of the Fountain*; *Peredur, son of Efrawg*, and *Geraint and Enid*.

The Dream of Macsen Wledig is a good example of how history and legend are intermingled. Roman Emperor Macsen was out hunting when he lay down to have a siesta, enjoying a dream which took him to a distant island. He crossed the island an saw another separated by a strait. This other island had a castle which he entered and found the daughter of the owner. He fell in love with her but his reverie was shattered by the noise of the hunt. His romantic bewitchment caused him to neglect the empire to such an extent that his advisers said he should send out searchers to find this castle, which they did. She refused to go to Rome, so Macsen traveled to Anglesey to see his Elen. He married her and constructed three castles as her morning-gift: Caernarfon, Caerleon, and Carmarthen.

Seven years later, a usurper arose in Rome, so Macsen returned with his legions and Elen's brothers and their warrior bands. The Britons retook Rome after which some went home while others remained on mainland Europe and founded Brittany. Thus, this Emperor Magnus Maximus was actually the man who left England, taking Roman troops and native auxiliaries with him, to kill and usurp the real Emperor Gratian. He then marched on Rome, was defeated and beheaded. Elen or Helen was really Emperor Constantine the Great's mother, who was translated into Maximus' wife. The link is that Constantine was another British-grown emperor. Hence, the original story is a historical conflation with Helen being a lowly born woman coming from present-day Turkey.

The *Mabinogion*'s British mythology sees life as only being secure in a tribal stronghold. Leave its walls and the world of nature took over with tales recounting magical happenings when out hunting. Talking animals and birds are featured and Celtic divinities are translated into forces of nature. It is now thought that the stories or myths have a religious purpose providing mystical explanations of religion's mysteries or rites. Thus a tale describing a visit to the other world could be a rite of passage when one passed from childhood to adulthood thus dressing up a ritual period of absence from the tribal stronghold. Therefore, the *Mabinogion* requires analysis from alternative perspectives.

These unique stories weave together fact and fiction, history and fantasy. The tales are filled with Welsh lineages and place-names, as well as references to real historical events. Yet there is always, beneath it all, a sense of the mythical. This mixture of the real and the fantastic has comed to be seen as the main feature of Celtic literature. Despite having roots in Wales and Brittany, the influence of these tales has spread far and wide.

Lady Charlotte Guest writies in her introduction that Celtic tales are the source of much of the Romance tradition prevalent in Europe. The *Mabinogian*, she writes, "has strong claims to be considered the cradle of European Romance" and that "it is remarkable that when the chief romances are examined, the name of the heroes and their scenes of action are to be found in Celtic, and those of persons and places famous in the traditions of Wales and Brittany."

TRISTAN AND ISEULT

TRISTAN AND ISEULT'S ILLICIT LOVE AND THE POLITICAL

CONFLICTS SURROUNDING THEIR AFFAIR MIRROR THOSE OF

LANCELOT AND GUINEVERE IN ARTHURIAN LEGENDS. THE TALE

HAS GIVEN RISE TO WAGNER'S OPERA, *TRISTAN UND ISOLDE*, AND

AN ARYAN FILM MADE BY JEAN COCTEAU AND JEAN DELANNOY.

Sometime between 1155 and 1170 witnessed the writing of the earliest surviving version of the popular romance, *Tristan*. The two French poets responsible were Thomas of Britain and Béroul, and their sources can be traced back to Celtic romances. Another later tradition of the tales emerged from the *Prose Tristan* (c. 1240), which differs from earlier variants, becoming the source for Sir Thomas Malory's *Le Morte d'Arthur* (c. 1469). Here the theme of noble characters torn by the conflicting demands of passionate love and feudal and moral duty is fully elaborated. Is a contemporary take on older, more earthy roots fitted in with the society of romantic courtly love and its culture of *troubadours* and *trouvères*. One composer, Marie de France, constructed several *chansons de geste* from a cycle of old Celtic Breton tales, the *Breton Lais*. Countess Beatrice of Dia (died c. 1175) wrote wholeheartedly of romance, secrecy, unrequited love, and adultery, the very themes of Tristan and Iseult's story.

Tristan, the nephew of King Mark of Cornwall, was a renowned warrior who fought a duel with the Irish knight Morholt, fighting Viking-style alone on an islet, before a sword blow splits Morholt's helmet and skull. This hero is then sent to bring his uncle's bride, the Princess Iseult, from Ireland. On board ship they accidentally drink a love potion intended to ensure the happiness of the married couple. The two fall in love and cannot bear life apart from each other. The lovers resort to dishonorable tricks and stratagems to conceal their love from the elderly and jealous King Mark. The normal moral standards of life in feudal society are turned on their heads. The two lovers feel freed from all responsibility. Tristan and Iseult are admired for their goodness and loyalty to each other in maintaining an adulterous love which leads them to lie and plot the deaths of those who would betray their secret. The barons who reveal their adulterous passion to the king are condemned as envious, spiteful, and wicked men. In Béroul's version, the love philter wears off and the couple are free to end their affair. Another version has King Mark killing Tristan with a poisoned lance.

The more romantic tale sees the personalities in the love triangle struggling with their love for each other, which situation is resolved when Mark gets proof of the pair's guilt and decides to punish them for their affair, which was also treason. The relationship endangered the Cornish kingdom, which needed a legitimate heir. Tristan was to be hanged and Iseult tried by ordeal and then imprisoned in a leper colony. However, Tristan escapes, rescues Iseult, and the two hide in the forest of Morrois where Mark eventually finds them. The affair is ended when Tristan agrees to exile while Iseult returns to her husband. Tristan travels to Brittany where he marries Iseult of the White Hands, daughter of King Hoel of Brittany and sister of Sir Kahedin.

Thomas of Britain's romance sees Tristan dying a hero's death. He is wounded by a poisoned lance while rescuing a maiden from six evil knights. Tristan asked Kahedin to find Mark's Iseult because she can heal his wound. His brother-in-law is asked to come back with his ship, showing white sails if Iseult is with him and black sails if not. Iseult of the White Hands, consumed with jealousy, lies to Tristan about the color of the sails and Tristan dies in anguish believing that Iseult does not love him. Iseult sees his body and collapses over his corpse and expires.

Some tales have the two lovers buried in adjacent graves. A honeysuckle grows from one and a hazel from the other with their branches intertwining. Despite three severe prunings, the merging keeps occurring and the one joined tree is allowed to remain.

An illuminated manuscript depicting Tristan and Iseult as they embark on their journey from Ireland to Cornwall, England. The earliest version of this popular romance was written sometime between 1155 and 1170. The adulterous love affair between the Cornish knight and Irish princess has inspired countless works of art, operas, and films and is possibly even the source of the legend of Sir Lancelot and Guinevere.

TINTAGEL

"UTHER... YOU SHALL BE KING OF ALL BRITAIN. FOR THE STAR, AND THE FIERY DRAGON UNDER IT, SIGNIFIES YOURSELF, AND THE RAY EXTENDING TOWARD THE GALLIC COAST PORTENDS THAT YOU SHALL HAVE A MOST POTENT SON ..." (GEOFFREY OF MONMOUTH, *THE HISTORY OF THE KINGS OF BRITAIN*, VII. 15)

Tintagel is invariably associated in people's minds with the Arthurian cycle of stories, being first recounted in Geoffrey of Monmouth's *History of the Kings of Britain*. Uther Pendragon became king when his brother died and a dragon-shaped comet lit the skies. As high king, Uther fought Saxon and Irish invaders in the north and Angles in Bernicia and fought with the King of Strathclyde against the Scots. When he returned to Caer-Lundein (London), he received Gorlois, Duke of Cornwall, with his beautiful wife, Igraine, with whom Uther immediately fell in love. He invited Gorlois back to the court later but the duke refused, knowing what was on Uther's mind. The high-king was determined to have Igraine and invaded Cornwall, where Gorlois placed Igraine in the impregnable Tintagel while he held another fortress at Dimilioc. Uther persuaded his magician, Merlin, to shape-shift him to look like Gorlois. This disguise enabled him to enter Tintagel and seduce Igraine, who conceived Arthur that night. Gorlois died in battle at Dimilioc and Uther married Igraine. Part of the deal struck with Merlin was that Arthur was given to the seer at birth to be raised in secret.

In more acceptable traditions, most of Tintagel castle was constructed by Prince Richard, Earl of Cornwall in the 1230s but tradition stated that an earlier fortress was built by Earl Reginald about 1141 and that he was brother to Geoffrey's patron, Robert, Earl of Gloucester. Thus a manufactured court history to curry favor might have been on the cards. However, Geoffrey's work might have preceded the foundation because Reginald wanted to bathe in a fabled heritage by founding the castle on a literary work.

Archeological digs under Radford in the 1930s showed that there was Dark Age occupation around Tintagel Castle. Over 20 rectangular stone buildings were excavated on the terraces on the eastern slope of Tintagel promontory and on the plateau around the Castle Chapel, dedicated to St. Juliot, a

Cornish saint. Later excavations re-dated these buildings to the medieval period but the castle chapel revealed earlier foundations. 1985 witnessed a fire on the island and a new survey with its aerial map showed up nearly 50 more buildings, with many on the plateau. Very narrow trenches have been sunk to uncover that less substantial stone structures were covered by those found by Radford. Radford's archeological interpretation claimed his finds as the cells and outbuildings of a Dark Age monastery. More recent interpretations claim that the expensive pottery found at the site, with some from the eastern Mediterranean, demonstrates the residence of a high-status chief or king who was involved in, or the recipient of, international trading commodities. A main feasting hall may well lie under the medieval castle since foundations were constantly re-used. The chapel was dedicated to a saint who was the son of King Brychan of Brycheiniog, suggesting a royal fortress. If this was a residence of a king of Dumnonia, one should remember that Arthur was alleged to come from that dynasty.

Tintagel Castle on the north coast of Cornwall in southern England, was a fortified site that is the focal point for many Celtic tales, including associations with King Arthur.

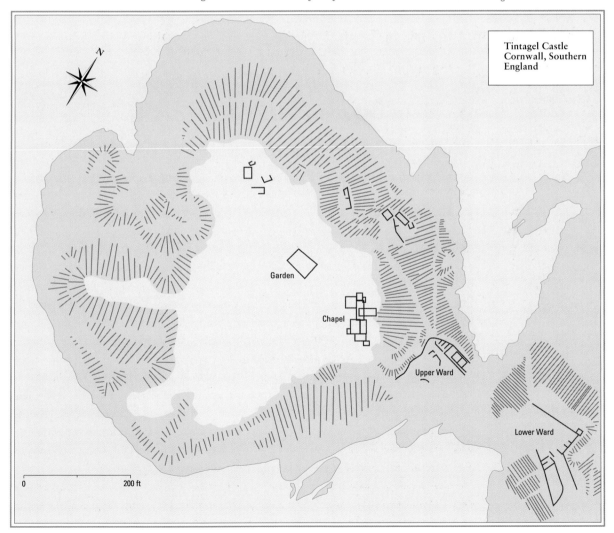

**Tintagel Castle
Cornwall, Southern
England**

Garden

Chapel

Upper Ward

Lower Ward

N

0   200 ft

LEPRECHAUN

"LAY YOUR EAR CLOSE TO THE HILL,

DO YOU NOT CATCH THE TINY CLAMOR,

BUSY CLICK OF AN ELFIN HAMMER,

VOICE OF THE LEPRACHAUN SINGING SHRILL

AS HE MERRILY PLIES HIS TRADE?"   (WILLIAM ALLINGHAM)

The leprechaun is a key feature in much Irish literature and oral tradition but it is just one of a series of creatures of faerie. This example of the little people has suffered from commercial exploitation and has been depicted in art as less fairy than a little old man guarding a hidden treasure while dressed stereotypically in seventeenth or eighteenth century clothes. A factor that obscures the nature of a leprechaun is the multiplicity of alternative parallel or regional names for the creature. Alternate names are lochramán, luchragán, luprecan, and lurikeen, among others.

A very early reference to the leprechaun is a water sprite, a luchorpán, which is mentioned in an eighth century text, The Adventure of Fergus Son of Léte (*Echtra Fergusa maic Léti*). This tale has Fergus sleeping in his chariot by the sea when the water sprites lift him up, take his sword away, and transport him over the water. He awakes and grabs three of them, who promise to teach him their swimming techniques if he lets them go. Thus this faerie creature is aquatic or amphibious.

There are two other little people which tend to be confused with the leprechaun. The first is the *cluricaune,* who drinks, smokes, and lurks in cellars and comes from a later tradition, otherwise there would be no tobacco, and second is the *fear dearg*. This Red Man with his macabre sense of humor likes gruesome jokes and laughs in your ear like a dead man. The true leprechaun of old Irish tradition is grim, dour, saturnine, and is ugly and stunted with a face like a dried up apricot. He may be argumentative, whining, drunken, or foul-mouthed. He is known as a fairy cobbler, the leprechaun's name perhaps deriving from the Irish *leath bhrógan*, meaning shoe-maker. Traditionally, if captured by a human being and asked where his gold is hidden, the gold will become the human's provided he keeps the leprechaun in sight. However, in this genre, the leprechaun always distracts the human by working on his greed.

Other depictions of the fairy see him sitting on a toadstool, with a red beard, a green hat and a suit. This could be a borrowing from European folklore, such as the German *kobold,* who helps with household chores or causes mischief or lives in mines like the Cornish knocker. The Scots brownie (*brùnadh*) is a similar household figure, possibly brought by Scots settlers to Ulster.

The tale of *Jack and the Cluricaune* is a traditional depiction of a leprechaun. Jack captures him and demands his gold because he is courting Peggy and needs money to prove to her father that he is a suitable son-in-law. Jack kept the little creature in his hands and in sight all the time. He was directed into the middle of a bog to a bouchlawn plant and was told to dig there. The elf pretended to use Peggy's voice projecting it behind Jack, who spun round finding no girl and turning bachk saw the leprechaun had gone. However, he knew the position of the gold and marked it carefully with his garter. Jack then went off to find a spade but on his return found the entire nine acre bog covered in bouchlawns, each with a garter making them. Jack, learned from his mistake, worked hard, saved his money, and eventually married Peggy rather than trying to be too clever. The story of *Bridget and the Lurikeen* follows the same pattern, with the leprechaun distracting Bridget so she takes her eyes off the fellow, allowing him to escape. Like the Cornish piskey, the leprechaun is said to have ridden farmer's animals, especially dogs, like horses until they became exhausted.

Yeats collected together folktales and described the leprechaun thus:

"He is something of a dandy, and dresses in a red coat with seven rows of buttons, seven buttons on each row, and wears a pointed hat, upon whose pointed end he is wont in the north-eastern countries, according to McNally, to spin like a top when the fit seizes him."

Another key Irish fairy creature is the Banshee or Bean Sidhe. Legend claims that an early race in Ireland was the Tuatha Dé Danann, which hid underground when attacked by enemy tribes. The Tuatha then took a new name from the many mounds where they were thought to be hiding; the name was Aes Sidhe, the Race of Mounds. This invisible world's name was abbreviated to Sidhe or Shee, as it is pronounced. The Banshee or fairy woman, a descendant and a queen of the Tuatha, is only seen before someone dies, presaging death by wailing. The queens of the underworld, the Shee, are best exemplified by Áine.

The Irish merman is known as the merrow or silkie. Good or bad weather, the male merrow sits on a rock, scanning the sea for cases of brandy lost from wrecked ships. He is a friendly fellow with a red nose (from drinking too much brandy). He is a bringer of good luck, and wears a red cocked hat, has a green body, and green hair and teeth. He has the eyes of a pig, scaly legs, and arms like fins. The female merrow is much more sinister, luring men with her beauty to their deaths on the rocks by causing storms. The Selkies are seals during the day but beautiful men and women by night.

The Lian Shee, or love fairy, is extremely dangerous. She seeks the love of mortal men, and they must consent or they become her slave. Her lovers usually die young, having withered away with love, or having passed through death to enjoy her in the fairy land of Tir-na-n-Og.

When a mother finds a foul mouthed, ill-tempered, yellow-faced little man in their baby's cradle, if she is wise she knows that the baby has been traded by the fairies for this changeling. These changelings have enormous appetites, and after a year or so, their hands become like claws, and they grow a full set of teeth.

MANX FAIRIES AND CORNISH PIXIES

"WHEN I TALKED WITH HER IN HER NEAT COTTAGE AT NEWLYN, MISS MARY ANN CHIRGWIN TOLD ME THIS: 'THE OLD PEOPLE USED TO SAY THE PISKIES WERE APPARITIONS OF THE DEAD COME BACK IN THE FORM OF LITTLE PEOPLE ...'"

As you drive from Douglas to Castletown on the A5 in the parish of Malew, you cross the Fairy Bridge in Ballalonna Glen. It is bad luck not to wish the fairies 'good day' at this point. This fairy belief was very prevalent in years past when every hill, glen, cave, river, and mound had its fairy inhabitant. The true Manxman never uses the word 'fairy' but speaks of the Little People (*Mooinjer veggey*) or 'Themselves' of the Little Boys or Little Fellas (*Guillyn veggey*). The older generation held fairies in dread for the fear of being waylaid and taken along dark roads and paths to make the Manx lose their sense of direction, unable to find their way.

There existed a fear of the fairies calling you by name and, if answered, they had you in their power. Yet the fairies were supposed to be normally only inches tall and nothing big to fear. There was a belief that at Keeill Moirrey (St. Mary's Church), near Glen Meay, a tiny old woman wearing a red cloak is occasionally seen coming over a mountain there toward the keeill ringing a bell, just when church service begins. Keeill Moirrey was originally a sixth-century Celtic cell. The belief in fairies extends even further to the realm of gods. A prayer used two hundred years ago was purely pagan when old Manx people still considered Manannan, the Tuatha Dé Danann god, in his status as Lord of the Sea.

Manannan beg mac y Keirr, fer vane yn Ellan,
Bannee shin as nyn maatey, mie goll magh
As cheet stiagh ny share lesh bio as marroo 'yn vaatey.'

[Little Manannan son of Llyr, who blest our island,

Bless us and our boat, well going out
And better coming in with living and (fish) in the boat.]

Cornwall is replete with legends of giants and fairies, with the pixies (piskies) and knockers also being well reported. Knockers are mine-spirits who warn miners of impending danger. These 'little people' might be pre-Brythonic inhabitants of the land who taught mining to the Celts. Custom has Cornish miners leaving the last pieces of the pasties to feed the knockers. Tradition holds that knockers can move from mine to mine. When an American mine was sealed off in 1956, people of Cornish descent petitioned the owners to unseal the mine to set the knockers free so they could enter other mines. The mine owners agreed.

Piskeys are said by some to be giant-size gods of pagan Cornwall but were shrunk in size after being sprinkled with Holy Water. They are supposed to be mischievous but helpful and might do a household's tasks at night when everyone was asleep or thresh a farmer's corn by moonlight. However, they might ride a horse to distraction after making stirrups from a plaited mane. Like the Manx fairies, they could cause a wayfarer to be piskey-led into losing all sense of time and place. However, it was not unknown for the Cornish to believe in some malevolent piskeys who would rain down curses upon people, who would then go to the wells to be blessed by saints to remove the curses.

Cornish folklore is very extensive and includes legends of the dead. Fishermen once thought that the dead in the sea will be heard if a drowning was about to occur. Strangely, a Cornish woman went to a clergyman to have him exorcise the spirit of her dead sister who came to her in the shape of a bee. Miners were wont to think that white moths are spirits. Whatever the beliefs in Cornwall, it is certainly true that there has been a long tradition of believing in fairy creatures who could help or hinder mankind.

A Cornish mine. Cornish folklore describes knockers, mine-spirits who look out for their miners. The name of these "little people" stems from the legend that they would knock on the wall of the mine, pre-empting a collapse, and saving the miners from a suffocating end.

The Buggane of St Trinians

IN MANX MYTHOLOGY, BUGGANES WERE GIANT OGRES COVERED IN BLACK HAIR WITH LONG FANGS AND CLAWS WHO LIVED UNDERGROUND BENEATH PLACES LIKE CHURCHES. THEY COULD ALSO BE SHAPE-SHIFTERS, WATER SPRITES WHO COULD TAKE THE FORM OF A COW OR HORSE BUT OCCASIONALLY THE DEFORMED HUMAN FORM OF AN OGRE OR BOGLE.

In Celtic myth, especially Manx, a buggane is a spirit, an ogre which burrows underground and often lies beneath a ruined building such as a church. It is huge with fangsand cloven feet and is covered from head to foot with hair.

In the church Barony of St. Ninian's in Marown, some lands were granted to the Priory of Whithorn in Galloway. St. Trinian's is a church standing on the lands of the barony and it has remained unfinished ,without a roof, standing by Greeba Hill. The Manx call the church *Keeill Brisht*, the Broken Church. Each time worshippers sought to build a roof, the Buggane crawled out of a hole in the church floor and, roaring, would destroy the roof in a mess of splintered timber and slates. Perhaps a howling storm brought down the roof but the populace feared evil. Nevertheless, another attempt was made, and a new roof was constructed, but every time it was destroyed.

Near Greeba lived a brave tailor who said he would spend the first night under the church roof and would make a pair of breeches while he was there. To fulfil his wager, Timothy the Tailor, entered the church near dusk with his cloth, needle and thread, thimble, and scissors. He sat cross-legged and cut the cloth to a pattern and commenced sewing by the light of a pair of candles, totally unconscious of the moving shadows made as he moved to and from with his needle. He was more interested in finishing the breeches, getting out, and collecting the money in the wager. As the wind rose outside, keening the while, the branches of trees scratched the walls and twigs beat on the windows. Timothy just sat there intent on his work, his courage swelling while thinking that the Buggane did not exist.

Suddenly, the floor moved, a hole appeared in the stone and a huge head was thrust through with shaggy black hair, long fangs, eyes like burning bonfires, with an ugly, red mouth screaming, "What are you doing here? Do you see my big head?"

"I see," said Timothy. Then, the Buggane's massive shoulders heaved through the floor and it waved a large, hairy fist at the tailor.

"Do you see this big body of mine and my long arms?" The Buggane's whole leathery black body appeared with its hands ending in long, sharp talons. "Do you see my claws?" shrieked the beast.

"I see, I see," said Timothy while sewing some more stitches.

The Buggane thumped his foot on the floor. "Do you see my cloven foot? Do you see my big fists?"

Timothy finished his last two stitches, cut the thread and legged it down the aisle and out the door, running as fast as his feet would carry him.

The Buggane's screaming laughter rent the air as the spirit-beast shambled down the road after Timothy who was sprinting full of fear. The tailor knew that a way down the Douglas road was via Marown Church and that he could seek sanctuary in the hallowed ground of the churchyard. Timothy leapt over the church wall, leaving the Buggane outside screaming with rage since it was powerless to enter. The ogre was so incensed with rage it tore off its head with its two hands and lobbed it over the wall, where it just missed Timothy as it exploded on hitting the ground. Then the Buggane vanished and was never seen again. The tailor was unhurt and collected his winnings from his friends. As for the Church of St. Trinian's, it remains in the shadow of Greeba Mountain, without a roof lest the Buggane re-appear, the Broken Church, *Keeill Brisht*.

Another Buggane was thought to live on the steep slopes of the mountain known as Slieau Whallian, where his screams could be sometimes heard. Another such fiend was supposed to frequent the Gob-ny-scuit, "mouth of the spout", a small waterfall in the parish of Maughold, where his wailings could be heard. This last Buggane was never in fact a spirit at all. A Manxman with a scientifically trained and inquiring mind visited the waterfall and examined the rock over which the water fell and found that the wailing noises only occurred when the wind blew from a certain point. Further investigation found a narrow cleft in the rock below the waterfall through which the wind blew, causing the sound.

As well as the buggane, there is a catalogue of other magical beasts, some of which are unique to the Isle of Man. There are tales of giants, witches and mermaids, but the more interesting tales are those about uniquely Manx inventions. The moddey dhoo (pronounced mawthey doo), a black dog that haunts Peel Castle, the tarroo ushtey, a supernatural bull that appears near water, and the phynnodderee, a fairy who fell in love with a human girl and was punished by being turned into a satyr-like creature are three good examples. The tales of monsters usually do not end well. By the end of the story either the humans in the tale, the monster, or both, come to an unhappy end. In the story of the moddey dhoo (literally "black dog" in English), the guard who in a fit of bravado follows it down a dark passageway returns pale faced with horror and speaks not a word before dying three days later. The common threads that run through these stories are usually some sort of warning not to interfere or become involved with the supernatural if you can possibly help it.

KELPIE

THE SUPERNATURAL SHAPE-SHIFTING WATER-HORSE HAUNTED
THE RIVERS AND STREAMS OF SCOTLAND. IT DISGUISED ITSELF AS
A PEACEFUL, BEAUTIFUL HORSE TO ENTICE THE WEARY TRAVELER.
ANY RIDER WOULD INCUR DROWNING AS THE HORSE PLUNGED
INTO WATERY DEPTHS.

The Celts honored and propitiated river deities, and the remnants of their beliefs can be found in folklore with a fascination for the indwelling spirits of rivers. In Lancashire, folk memory states that the River Ribble at the stepping-stones at Brungerley requires a life every seven years to appease the anger of the river spirit. The mythical Jenny Greenteeth, an old woman with long, green fangs, lurks under river weeds to catch unwary children. The name is also used to describe 'duckweed', which forms a dangerous layer over the surface of the water. The story came about as a way to keep children away from the danger.

The River Conon in old Ross-shire was notorious when in winter flood. It was apparently haunted by a beautiful woman dressed in green who would leap out of the river and entice travelers into the treacherous water. Every stretch of the river has a story of a waterwraith, undine, or kelpie, the horse shape of a water sprite.

A famous water creature is the Loch Ness monster, which is recorded in Adomnan's *Life of Columba*, written in the seventh century. St. Columba saw a man who had been grabbed and bitten by a water beast in the River Ness and was being buried on the bank by members of the local community. Despite this disaster and danger, St. Columba requested one of his entourage to swim to the opposite bank and return with a boat that was moored there. A man, Lugne mocu-Min, dived into the river and started swimming. His plunge alerted the monster, which was resting in the depths. Disturbed, it surged to the surface and lunged at Lugne. The monster was open-mouthed and roaring, striking terror into everyone except St. Columba. He made the sign of the cross and ordered the beast back to its lair. The beast obeyed the command, fleeing into the depths and it has not been seen since, or not very often.

Opposite: The Kelpie legends are closely associated with the Gaelic-speaking peoples of the Scottish highlands and islands.

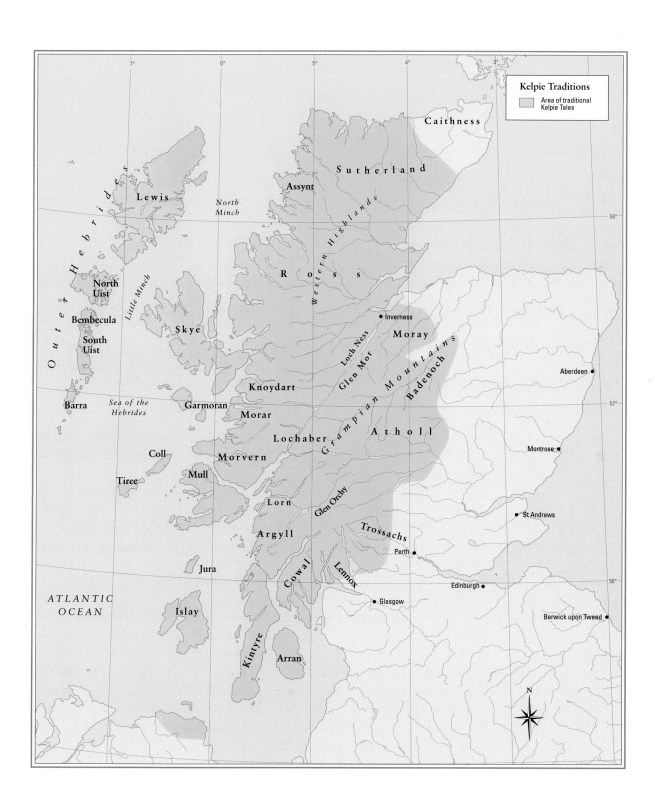

Kelpie Traditions

Area of traditional
Kelpie Tales

Caithness

Sutherland

Assynt

*North
Minch*

Lewis

Outer Hebrides

R o s s

Western Highlands

North
Uist

Little Minch

Bembecula

South
Uist

Skye

• Inverness

Moray

Loch Ness

Glen Mor

Grampian Mountains

Badenoch

Aberdeen •

Knoydart

Barra

*Sea of the
Hebrides*

Garmoran

Morar

Atholl

Coll

Lochaber

Morvern

Montrose •

Tiree

Mull

Lorn

Glen Orchy

St Andrews •

Trossachs

Argyll

Perth •

Jura

Cowal

Lennox

ATLANTIC
OCEAN

Edinburgh •

Islay

• Glasgow

Berwick upon Tweed •

Kintyre

Arran

N

KING GRADLON AND DAHUT

PRINCESS DAHUT IS AKIN TO THE FEROCIOUS SPRITE, THE KORRIGAN, WITH ITS FLASHING EYES AND RED HAIR WHO KILLS MEN WHO FALL IN LOVE WITH THE PRINCESS OR DRUIDESS SHAPE IT MIGHT ADOPT. THEY ACT LIKE SIRENS AND MERMAIDS, LURING MEN TO DEATH OR THEY LURK BY DOLMENS AWAITING PASSERS BY.

The Dark Ages and myth often merge to create legends of beauty and mystery. One tale recounts how King Gradlon of Cornouaille built the fabled city of Ys. Sources suggest that several Gradlons did exist between the fifth and ninth centuries. Apparently, this Gradlon was king of a region settled by Britons from Cornwall (Kernow) in what is sometimes known as Cornovia. He gained much wealth from raiding and making war with his ships against countries of the north, presumably the warrior Irish, Scots, and Picts. On campaign, Gradlon met Malgven, Queen of the North, who incited him to kill her aged husband before eloping with him and bearing his daughter, Dahut, while at sea. Malgven requested Gradlon to leave her on an island but said Dahut would have her features so that he would not forget her.

Gradlon built the city of Ys, which legends locate in Douarnenez Bay. Evidently, Dahut (aka Ahès) asked this, as she loved the sea. Ys or Is was built below sea level and, at high tide, the water level flowed into the city. Another source claims that Ys had existed for 2,000 years on dry land but the sea level had risen over time with the same threat of inundation. A dike was constructed to keep the sea out at high tide but at low tide gates in the dike were unlocked to allow the sea and ships to enter the port of Ys. The king kept the only key.

Dahut had an evil reputation, being dissolute, and turned the city into a place of sin marked by her orgies and her custom of killing her lovers the morning after a night of passion. Each man was given a magic mask on his arrival at her palace, a mask making him invisible. However, when a lover left Dahut, the enchanted mask would tighten and strangle him. The corpses allegedly were seized by a shade who flung the body on his horse like a sack of corn, after which the shade rode to a high precipice and threw the cadaver into the sea. Such was the corruption in the city that St. Winwaloe, patron of Gradlon, known as St. Guénole (c. 460–532), warned of God's anger but was paid no attention by Dahut and the inhabitants. All they wanted to do was drink and engage in wanton pleasures.

One day, a gaily dressed knight arrived at Ys and Dahut invited him at night to her room. A storm was raging with the waves smashing against the dike's gate. Dahut was asked by the knight to prove her love by creeping into her father's chamber to steal the key around his neck. The knight, the devil in disguise, or Dahut herself, according to another version of the myth, opened the gate at the height of the storm and at high tide. Waves poured in and smashed Ys. King Gradlon mounted his magic horse, Morvarc'h (sea-horse in Breton), given to him by Malgven, placing Dahut behind him.

The tale next has two versions. One says that St. Winwaloe begged Gradlon to push off the demon sitting on the horse's crupper. Another account says the celestial voice of the red-headed Malgven prayed for him to do likewise to save himself. He shoved Dahut off his steed and she vanished forever to become a mermaid or morgen, known as Marie-Morgane, whose incredible beauty still entices sailors to the bottom of the sea. These tragedies will not stop until a Good Friday mass is celebrated in the churches of the drowned city of Ys. Morgens are a distinctive feature of Breton mythology.

Gradlon traveled to Quimper, which became his new capital where his statue stands between the spires of the Cathedral of Saint Corentin. Stories say that the bells of the churches of Ys can still be heard during calm seas. Another tale says that the legend is an allegory of the victory of Christianity, since St. Winwaloe converted Gradlon and the inundation of Ys was the Lord's vengeance against the druidical leanings of Dahut and the populace. This theme is partially reinforced by the account claiming that Gradlon oversaw the burial of the last Druid in Brittany. After witnessing this event, he built a chapel in the pagan's sacred grove.

The legend of Dahut is closely related to the Korrigan of Breton legend, a fairy or dwarf-like spirit. The name is derived from Korr dwarf, that is, "small dwarf." Other names are *kornanden, ozigan, nozigan, torrigan, viltans, poulpikan,* and *paotred ar sabad*. Korrigans have beautiful hair and flashing eyes. They are often described as significant figures amongst the Celts: princesses or druidesses who refused to convert to Christianity when the apostles came to convert Brittany and have a hatred for priests, churches, and the Virgin Mary. They are able to predict the future, change shape, and move at lightening speed. In a similar way to sirens and mermaids, they sing and comb their long hair, and they haunt fountains and wells. They make men fall in love with them and then kill them. They deceive unwary mortals who see them dancing or looking for treasure, and often steal human children, swapping them for changelings.

One Breton poem, Ar-Rannou, tells of 9 korrigan, who "dance, with flowers in their hair, and robes of white wool, around the fountain, by the light of the full moon."

Another Breton legend concerns the Ankou, a personification of death. Anatole le Braz, who collected legends in the nineteenth century, writies of the Ankou: "The Ankou is the henchman of Death. The last dead of the year, in each parish, becomes the Ankou of the parish for the following year. When there has been, in a year, more death than usual, one says about the Ankou: *War me fe, heman zo eun Anko drouk.* ('on my faith, this one is a nasty Ankou')." Other spirits of Breton mythology include the Bugul Noz, a creature of incredible ugliness who wanders in the forest, and the cannard noz, three old washerwomen,who go to the water's edge to wash shrouds for those who are about to die.

Mermaids

CORNWALL IS "PRE-EMINENTLY THE REGION OF DREAM AND MYSTERY. THE GHOSTLY BIRDS, THE PALL-LIKE SEA, THE FROTHY WIND, THE ETERNAL SOLILOQUY OF THE WATERS, THE BLOOM OF DARK PURPLE CAST … AN ATMOSPHERE LIKE THE TWILIGHT OF A NIGHT VISION." (THOMAS HARDY, *A PAIR OF BLUE EYES*, 1873)

The people of Cornwall, England, have reveled in tales of little people, spirits in the mines, and also in legends of the sea. Everywhere in Cornwall is close to the sea, which has provided a livelihood through fishing and a medium of transport with other coastal Celts over the millennia. The herring runs have always been important, but sometimes the fruitful sea has demanded a price, with terrible storms taking boats and their crews. December 1981 witnessed the lifeboat Solomon Browne attempting to rescue crew and passengers from the Dublin-registered Union Star. Crewed entirely of men from the small fishing village of Mousehole, the village suffered disaster when all the crew were taken by the sea.

The village of Zennor, once the home of D. H. Lawrence and his German wife, is the abode of a famous legend or myth that is similar to Breton coastal tales. The fisher folk of the village would go to the church, St. Senara's, to give thanks for their catch and their safety and to pray for a rich sea harvest next day. Part of the religious ritual involved the choir singing at Evensong. The final hymn was always sung by Matthew Trewhella, variously described as the churchwarden's or squire's son. This handsome young man had such a wonderful voice that it carried from the church right down to the sea.

One evening Matthew's voice reached a mermaid, named Morveren, one of the daughters of Llyr, king of the sea. She emerged from the sea to sit on a rock, the better to hear the voice which moved her. The wind-borne hymn ended as the wind dropped, leaving Morveren to slip back into the waves and swim home. Next evening she returned and swam closer to the shore and listened again to Matthew's voice. Eventually, she reached the moored fishing boats, pulling herself out of the water so she could see the origin of the music. She wanted to go to the church but feared to be stranded by an ebbing tide. She explained to Llyr that she must see the owner of the voice. The king told her that it was man-music and to hear was enough because sea people should remain in their own environment and not go on land.

Morveren was fascinated by Matthew and longed to see him, loving his voice. The king realized his daughter could not be constrained and gave her a dress so she could hide her tail when she pulled herself up to the church. Swimming to land, the mermaid hauled herself up a path to the church, peering in to fall in love with Matthew. She constantly repeated this performance, always leaving to in order not to be caught by the tide stranding her.

One evening, Morveren was so enraptured by the singing that she sighed. Matthew heard the sound, turning to see Morveren as her head scarf slipped revealing her shining wet hair. Matthew stopped singing, staring at her, as he was bewitched by her beauty. She attempted to get away fast as she felt herself dehydrating, having been out of water too long. Matthew chased after her, soon reaching and catching her as she fell being tangled in the dress. Matthew beseeched her not to leave but she told him she was a sea-creature and would die on land. He saw her fish tail protruding from her dress and realized she was a mermaid. He said he would go with her and carried her to the sea shore. His mother and the fishermen chased after the two but Matthew walked into the water and the waves covered them as Morveren took Matthew to the land of Llyr. He learned the songs of the sea and the fishermen could tell by his songs, as they reached land, whether the sea would be rough or safe for fishing. Or maybe the voices of the waves always carry a message to those who understand.

Kynance Cove, an inlet on the Lizard Peninsula in southwest Cornwall. The dramatic combination of rugged cliffs and turquoise sea inspired a great deal of the folklore amongst the local people. Various legends of the sea and tales of beautiful mermaids have been recounted over the years.

Arthurian Legends

THE SEMI-LEGENDARY, MYTHIC KING OF BRITAIN, ARTHUR, PERHAPS A FORM OF ROMAN ARTORIUS, OR EVEN CELTIC ARTOS VIROS, BEAR-MAN, HAS BEEN IDENTIFIED WITH CELTIC KING RIOTHAMUS AND HAS CONNECTIONS WITH THE SERBIAN PRINCE MARCO AND THE RUSSIAN ILYA MUSOMYETS.

The stories of King Arthur, Queen Guinevere, the Knights of the Round Table, the courageous knight Lancelot, the wizard or druid Merlin, and the castle of Camelot are the very stuff of medieval legends and the tales of troubadors in the medieval strongholds of courtly love and romance. The tales of Wales and Brittany all include some reference to a mythical figure who is assumed to be some past great king or warlord who held an enemy at bay. There have been continuous debates as to whether Arthur is a real historical character or someone in fiction.

To some, Arthur is a real Celtic or Romano-British hero, a petty king or general in the western part of Britain who led a fierce and determined resistance against Anglo-Saxon invaders. He is judged to have been the leader of Romano-Celtic forces who won a key victory over the Saxon invaders at Mount Badon, which set back the enemy advances for several years. Yet if scholars of the Dark Ages are asked about his identity, there will be no agreement nor will any evidence be uncovered. Supporters of the warlord scenario claim that there are so few documents about the Dark Ages that a man like Arthur could have flourished and we would be none the wiser. He has been located in most parts of sixth century British-Celtic Britain, from the Scottish lowlands and the Pennines to Wales and Cornwall. Other candidates include Artorius, or the Roman Lucius Artorius Castus, and Artur, a historical figure, who was the son of Gaelic king Aidan Mac Gabrain of Argyll; he might have been a military figure.

The first literary reference to Arthur is in the Welsh, possibly sixth-century, *Y Gododdin,* and he was undoubtedly a character featuring orally in the tales of the bards whose stories were passed on for generations. Other Arthurian writers include Geoffrey of Monmouth, Chretien de Troyes and Brut. Eventually, Sir William Malory's *Le Morte d'Arthur* created a definitive version of the legends.

Opposite: King Arthur, a legendary British leader, might be based on a Roman-British war lord who fought the Angles and Saxons as well as any other raiders who attempted to despoil peaceful Britain.

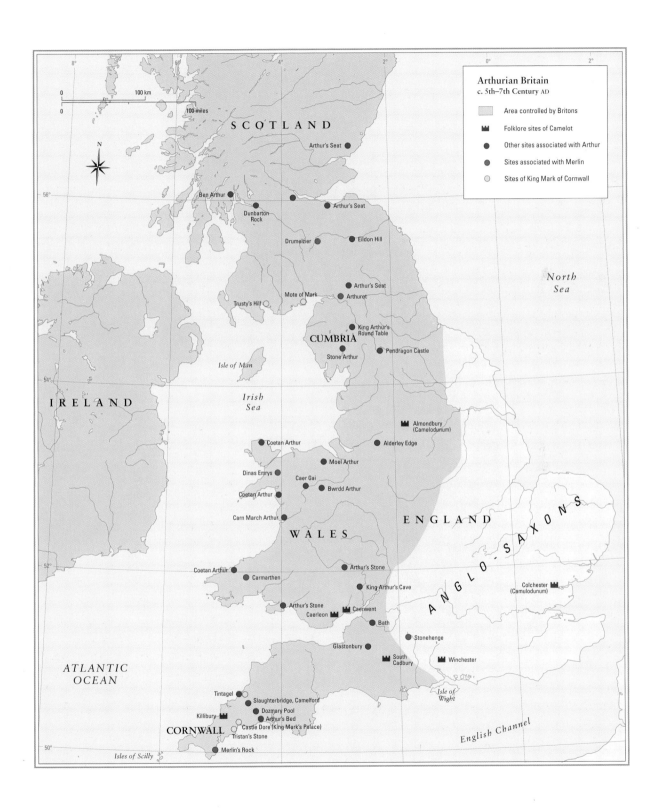

Arthurian Britain
c. 5th–7th Century AD

Area controlled by Britons
Folklore sites of Camelot
Other sites associated with Arthur
Sites associated with Merlin
Sites of King Mark of Cornwall

SCOTLAND

Arthur's Seat

Ben Arthur

Arthur's Seat

Dunbarton Rock

Drumelzier   Eildon Hill

North Sea

Trusty's Hill   Mote of Mark   Arthur's Seat
                                      Arthuret

CUMBRIA   King Arthur's Round Table

Stone Arthur   Pendragon Castle

Isle of Man

IRELAND

Irish Sea

Almondbury (Camelodunum)

Coetan Arthur   Alderley Edge

Dinas Emrys   Moel Arthur

Caer Gai
Coetan Arthur   Bwrdd Arthur

Carn March Arthur

ENGLAND   ANGLO-SAXONS

WALES

Coetan Arthur   Arthur's Stone

Carmarthen   King Arthur's Cave   Colchester (Camulodunum)

Arthur's Stone
Caerleon   Caerwent

Bath

Stonehenge

Glastonbury

South Cadbury   Winchester

ATLANTIC OCEAN

Isle of Wight

Tintagel
Slaughterbridge, Camelford
Killibury   Dozmary Pool
              Arthur's Bed
CORNWALL   Castle Dore (King Mark's Palace)
Tristan's Stone

English Channel

Isles of Scilly   Merlin's Rock

0   100 km
0   100 miles

N

8°   4°   2°   0°   2°

56°

54°

52°

50°

TRISKELLI

"THE THREE-BRANCHED GYRATORY MOTIF FROM THE INSIGNIA OF THE ISLE OF MAN MIGHT BE A VERY ANCIENT CELTIC DESIGN, BUT IT IS NOT UNIQUELY CELTIC ... THE VARIOUS VERSIONS OF THE TERM ITSELF... COME FROM AN ANCIENT GREEK ROOT, TRISKELÊS [THREE-LEGGED]." (VENCESLAS KRUTA, *CELTS*, 2004)

The triskelli, triskele, or triskelion is a design comprising three interlocking spirals, or three bent human legs, bent at the knee and joined at the crotch. It symbolizes the pantheon of Celtic gods: Daghad, Ogme, and Lugh or the cycle of life representing the child, the adult, and the old. It denotes the symbols of the main elements in Celtic life: air, water, and fire, with the earth being formed in the center. The symbols are ancient and even predate the Celts. The Irish passage tomb at Newgrange, in County Meath, is a superb example of Neolithic architecture and is decorated with triskelli spirals on the passage wall as you look from the central chamber toward the entrance.

The symbol has been used in many parts of the prehistoric and ancient world and has been found on sixteenth-century gold Mycenaean cups, on Babylonian pottery, and on coins from Lycia, Pamphylia, and Pisidia. The legged version has been discovered in the Khwaresm satrapy of the Archaemenid dynasty in Persia and also on a silver coin minted in the Indian Mauryan empire.

In particular, triskelli symbols can be found on coinage from the Danube region with Vindelici gold staters and similarly from Gaul's Bituriges. The Teutones minted electrum staters while the Cotini punched a tetradrachm, all with spirals. A silver disc, part of horse harness, decorated with embossed human faces and with a central triskelli, was found in Manerbio, Brescia, dating from the second century BC. Other spiral examples have been unearthed in the Celtiberian *oppida* of Lansbrica and Coeliobriga. An archeologist can search for the symbol throughout Celtic Europe and find a gold stater of Vercingetorix's Arverni tribe existing amid the legs of a five-legged horse. The Petrocorii of French Périgord issued triskelli coins, as did the British Atrebates and Corieltauvi and the Bohemian Boii.

The Manx flag displays armored and spurred conjoined legs while the Sicilian trinacria shows a

Medusa head in the center. However, the Celtic version was firmly based on the cycle of life, which became displaced by a Christian meaning after pagan times, representing the Holy Trinity. In Brittany, the triskelle is used alongside the ermine in the flag of the Duchy of Britanny, dating from 1316, and in the traditional Breton flag, the *Gwenn Ha Du* (the black and white). Another type of triskelli is used by the Bretons in an interlaced form representing the Trinity in the daughter, the mother, and grandmother or God, Jesus, and the Holy Spirit.

One example of a developed triskelle in early Celtic Christian design is the four-man swastika at Meigle, in Perthshire, Scotland, while other spiral designs relate to a three-rayed swastika, which represents a "motionless mover", most high God around whom all things revolve. A design of this nature can be found in the *Book of Durrow*, a seventh-century illuminated manuscript from the abbey of that name. Similar designs may be found on the Nigg Cross in Ross-shire, Scotland.

The symbol has now been taken over by silver smiths using stylized triskelli and placed on Manx sovereigns in a very linear fashion. New Celtic pagans interested in druids and the notion of Celtic angels are using the symbol in their recreation of the past, where various trilogies are considered in an alternative cosmology and religion. The image in various forms has been utilized by disparate organizations such as the Afrikaner Weerstandsbeweging, the extreme right-wing South African neo-fascist group and it has also been incorporated in the roundel of the Irish Airs Corps. Interestingly, the triskelli may be found in certain Philippine university fraternities and sororities and comprises part of the logo for the United States Department of Transportation.

The flag of the Isle of Man features the armored triskelli, three bent legs interlocked at the crotch circulating in a spiral motion. It is an ancient motif, symbolizing the three Celtic gods, the cycle of life, and the key elements in Celtic life.

Surviving Cults

"IN SCOTLAND, WALES AND IRELAND, BONFIRES, KNOWN AS THE BELTANE FIRES, WERE FORMERLY KINDLED WITH GREAT CEREMONY ON THE FIRST OF MAY, AND THE TRACES OF HUMAN SACRIFICE AT THEM WERE PARTICULARLY CLEAR AND UNEQUIVOCAL." (SIR JAMES GEORGE FRASER, *THE ILLUSTRATED GOLDEN BOUGH*, 1978)

Celtic paganism has left strong traces in many places. Christian chapels and keeills have been sited on Druid sanctuaries, and many miraculous fountains and wells are the objects of pilgrimages and votive offerings, such as the Madron Well in Cornwall. Water sources were venerated by the Celts for their religious powers and sacred wells and springs continue to be visited in Christian times as a font of spiritual healing, often being dedicated to Celtic saints. Contemporary well-dressing in Derbyshire, England, undoubtedly has an origin in this belief system. Trees decorated with rags are a common feature in Ireland and might be echoed in the modern Christian Christmas tree. The construction of corn dollies might also be an old aspect of an agricultural practice after a successful harvest. More obviously, survivals of old rites are found in festivities associated with Beltane (1 May), Midsummer Day (24 June), and Samhain (1 November), now turned by the Christian church into All Saints' day rather than being a cult of the night and the dead.

Beltane was an open-air festival, with fires being lit on hills and promontories and modern day bonfires and Beltane cake being used in many rural communities. The festival began during the pastoral season, when flocks and herds of cattle were taken from winter pastures and led to summer pastures and mountain and hill grazing. The celebration was a symbol of the importance of cattle to the Celts and they were sometimes driven between two fires to purify them. Today, young people often dance at Beltane and enjoy this tradition. Those who seek to recreate Celtic culture are symbolized by the Edinburgh Beltane Society, which lights a fire annually on Calton Hill. Upward of 12,000 people join in. This society also celebrates other Celtic festivals, as its website informs. Some people still put out their house fires and relight them from the community Beltane fire while others visit wells and springs.

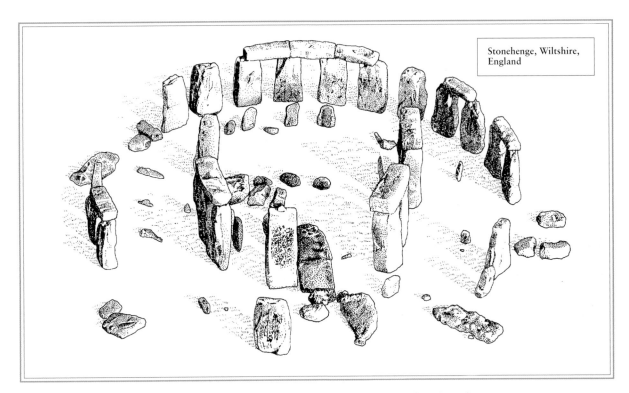

Stonehenge, Wiltshire, England

Midsummer Eve and Midsummer Day, the summer solstice, witness the lighting of bonfires; this custom is not just Celtic but occurs among the inhabitants of Morocco and Algeria too. Midsummer Day was not so important to Celts as Beltane and Samhain, but neo-pagans and neo-Druids try to recreate Druid rituals at the solstice at Stonehenge in England, seemingly oblivious to the fact that it is a Neolithic monument pre-dating druidic practice.

Samhain and Halloween, the previous day, are both Celtic in origin and are the days when Celts observed their New Year's Day, which represented the last harvest of the year when cattle would be slaughtered and stored for winter. Like Beltane, the community fires would be lit and the flame transferred to individual dwellings. According to Celtic belief, the spiritual boundaries between the living and the dead would nearly disappear and the spirits of the other world could join the communities. People would sometimes set a place with food to encourage their ancestors to visit. Ancestor commemoration is important to Celtic re-constructionists but for most modern observers food and dance are more appropriate.

The importance of the day can also be seen in agricultural hiring and firing because New Year's Day on 1 November was when land tenure ended and when menservants re-commenced their service. Another custom from 31 October or Samhain's eve is the Halloween lighting of candles inside pumpkins or rutabaga (swede and turnip). These lanterns refer back to the Celtic belief that the spirit and power of a person reside in the head, so the lanterns can drive off evil spirits, a modern version of recreational head-hunting. This candle might also be a beacon to a spirit who wants to find its way home. Halloween, originally a Celtic festival, is now observed around the world.

Stonehenge in England has become the focus of the summer solstice celebrations for neo-pagans and neo-Druids.

Contemporary Celtic Christianity

"WHEN... THE CELTIC CHURCH CEASED TO EXIST, WE LOST A FORM OF INDIVIDUAL CHRISTIANITY WHICH, THROUGH ITS DRUIDIC ROOTS, WAS TRULY LINKED TO THE PERENNIAL PHILOSOPHY OF HUMANITY." (S. TOULSON, *THE CELTIC ALTERNATIVE*, 1987)

The old Celtic Church was characterized by the widespread extent and power of the monastic foundations in Ireland. The end of the sixth century saw the individual personality and local traditions of these institutions clinging fervently to their identity in the face of attacks by Rome and Canterbury to bring them into conformity and under the authority of continental Church customs. The Synod of Whitby in 664, hosted by St. Hilda, saw the defeat of the Celtic Church, a turning point which greatly influenced British Christianity.

The Celtic Community of Christ (CCC), founded in 2006, believe that Celtic Christianity was as pure and serene as that of the age of saints and could hardly be equaled and never repeated. The Celtic variant of Christianity had its own innate spirituality and a serene inner life. The CCC is an independent component of the Catholic Church and believes in Jesus Christ and the teachings and writings of the apostles. The CCC is led by a presiding bishop and assisted by a chancellor bishop. Each diocese is headed by a bishop who has judicial autonomy within and for his own diocese. Each person has their personal duty through prayer and study to arrive at a personal understanding of the Truth revealed in Christ's teachings and then act upon it in their own and the community's lives. The CCC thus totally rejects the dogma of the infallibility of the Bishop of Rome, the Pope. The CCC welcomes all people into its midst irrespective of previous religious affiliation. The CCC states very clearly that it is neither Roman Catholic nor Protestant but Celtic. This church wishes to emulate the ancient Celtic Church by acting like old Celtic missionaries, who preached a duty of care in small communities, winning people over with a strong sense of pastoral care. Instead of wooing people away from the worship of trees, water, and pagan gods, the CCC wishes to win people away from the worship of power, money, and greed.

Opposite: The first Christian missionaries may have come from Gaul in the 4th and 5th centuries. Ireland became the first country outside the Roman Empire to be converted.

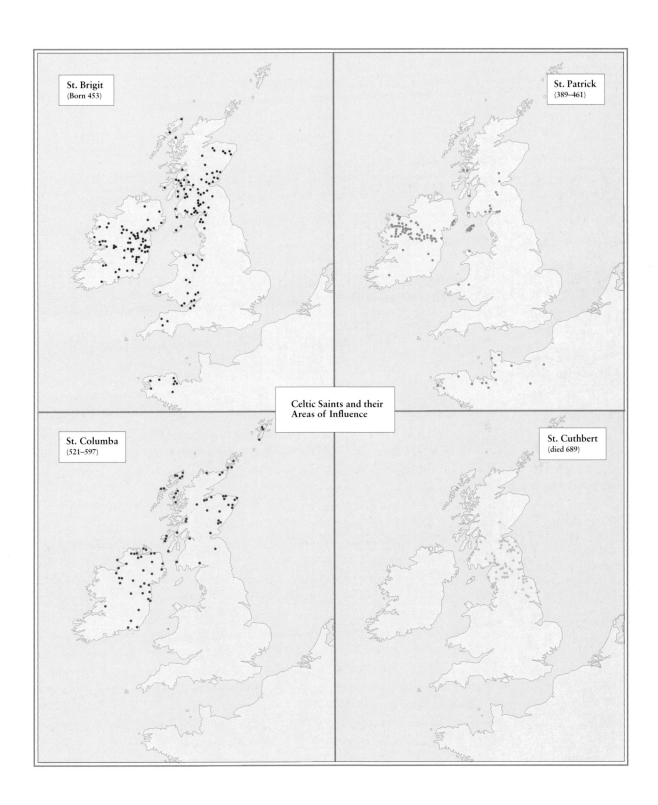

St. Brigit
(Born 453)

St. Patrick
(389–461)

Celtic Saints and their
Areas of Influence

St. Columba
(521–597)

St. Cuthbert
(died 689)

Voyages of St Brendan

"IN THE ISLAND THEY FOUND MANY FLOCKS OF SHEEP, ALL PURE WHITE, SO NUMEROUS AS TO HIDE THE FACE OF THE LAND. THEN THE SAINT DIRECTED THE BRETHREN TO TAKE FROM THE FLOCKS WHAT WAS NEEDED FOR THE FESTIVAL; AND THEY CAUGHT ONE SHEEP ..."

NAVIGATIO SANCTI BRENDANI ABBATIS, IX

St. Brendan of Clonfert (c. 484-c. 577), also known as the "Navigator" or the "Voyager" was renowned for his piety, his spreading of Christianity, and his voyages. He was born near the lakes of Killarney in Ciarraighe Luachra in County Kerry., in Munster province. He was baptized at Tubrid by St. Erc and educated by him. Tradition has him variously studying under the auspices of St. Ita and St. Enda, being eventually ordained by St. Erc in 512. During this period the Irish Church was organized around a series of monasteries. On becoming abbot, Brendan helped build monastic cells at Ardfert, then established a monastery there and others at Inishdadroum in County Clare, Annadown in County Galway, and Clonfert in Galway too.

Brendan was a proven and successful traveler. Ancient manuscripts refer to his journeys. He sailed several times along the west coast of Ireland and sailed to the Western Isles of the Scots coast to confer with St. Columba, who founded the monastery at Iona. Evidence suggests that he journeyed to Wales, Brittany, the Orkneys and Shetlands, and even Faroe Island. Thus St. Brendan was used to the waves and had the courage to sail them. The description of one voyage in particular is recounted in *The Voyage of St. Brendan the Abbot* (*Navigatio Sanctii Brendani Abbatis*). The manuscript states that St. Brendan sailed into the Atlantic, with fourteen monks, one being the future St. Malo, in search of a wonderful land in the West over the ocean. Brendan was encouraged to build a boat from a framework of wood covered with ox-hides and sail in search of the land. This Brendan did, after which he and his crew set forth, and later the adventures were recorded. Various landfalls were made at the Island of Sheep, and on the back of a whale, thought to be an island until a cooking fire brought it out of sleep. The *Navigatio* records finding a huge column of crystal floating in the sea, a sea monster breathing fire from its nostrils, an island where the crew were showered by hot rocks, and a place where Irish monks were living under a rule of silence and then finding the wonderful land. The tale has been criticized as lacking truth, a mere fantasy taking elements from several Irish voyage stories (*imram*). However, some historians have argued the possibility of the adventure, with the Sheep Island being the Faroes, the crystal an iceberg, the molten rocks being the slag from an Icelandic volcano, and the aggressive sea monster as a belligerent whale, killer whale, or walrus. The silent community of monks were a possibility because Irish monks were prone to travel and settle on far islands, and the Norse, on discovering Iceland, were reported to have found monks there.

The well-known traveller Tim Severin put the possibility of the voyage to the test by building a sea-going vessel from wood and hides using old records and methods to guide him. His *The Brendan Voyage* describes how he and a few companions used this boat to travel from Ireland to the Hebrides, the Faroes, Reykjavik in Iceland and then used the Greenland current to travel southward, making a landfall in Newfoundland, the journey taking over a year. During the trip Severin encountered icebergs, whales, and porpoises, which suggest that the *Navigatio* could be factual. Whatever the case, the impact of the voyage, alleged or actual, was that Brendan's fame increased, with masses of pilgrims and students visiting him at Ardfert with religious foundations built to accommodate the crowds. Since then, St. Brendan has become the Patron Saint of sailors and travelers.

St. Brendan's voyages included visits to Scotland, Wales, and Brittany as well as a legendary voyage to the far west via the Faroes and Iceland.

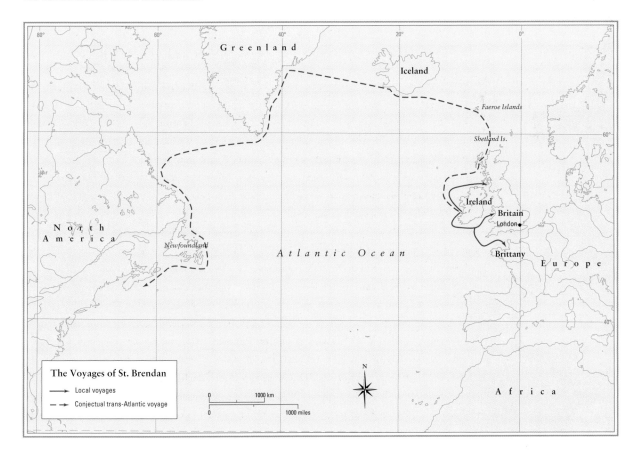

The Voyages of St. Brendan

→ Local voyages

--→ Conjectural trans-Atlantic voyage

THE EARLY IRISH

IRELAND HAS PROVIDED SOME TRULY WONDERFUL SPECIMENS OF
LA TÈNE-STYLE ARTWORK, SIMILAR TO THE CELTIC ART OF CENTRAL
EUROPE, INCLUDING CAREFULLY MADE WAR TRUMPETS, GOLD
TORQUES, DECORATED BRONZE SWORD SCABBARDS, AND HORSE
HARNESS BITS, SUGGESTING A HORSE-RIDING NOBILITY.

The first Celtic peoples arrived in Ireland in the second half of the first millennium BC during the Iron Age. There is no evidence of the Halstatt Celts in Ireland but artifacts made following the La Tène style have been found mainly in the north and west of Ireland. Amongst these finds are the Turoe Stone, war trumpets, gold torques, horse bits, and sword scabbards. Thus evidence suggests that the Irish Celts possessed a warrior society similar to Celts in Europe.

When Christianity arrived in Ireland during the fifth century, literacy was introduced with the teaching of Latin. This cultural borrowing from the Roman world saw the development of the Ogham script, comprising notches carved in stone based upon letters of the Latin alphabet, producing the earliest written Irish. Old tales and oral histories were committed to writing, and it is possible to build a picture of the political realities in Irish history.

By the seventh century AD, the dominant Érainn people of Munster were being pressured and overshadowed by the linked dynasties known as the Eóganachta. Their legends claim that these people were Irish colonists returning from Britain. Their capital was at Cashel, which is reputedly a word borrowed from the Latin "castellum." The Eógonachta expanded their territories at the expense of the over-kingdom of Laigin (Leinster). The latter's border rested on the Barrow in the west, and the kingdom ranged north to the Boyne. However, by the sixth century, the border was thrust back to the Liffey, and was governed by two distinct dynasties: the Uí Dúnlainge, based at Kildare, and the Uí Chennselaig, centred on Ferns.

The Uí Néill squeezed the Laigin in Meath, and Connacht became subject to the power of two dynasties: the Uí Briúin and the Uí Fiachrach. Connacht was named after and mythical figure

Opposite: By 300 BC the style of art practiced by the Celtic peoples of Europe, called La Tène, had become established in the northern half of Ireland. However, when this influence arrived, it contributed to the creation of the early "Irish."

Conn of the Hundred Battles, ancestor of the Uí Néill. This clan ruled in northwest Ireland and is known as the Northern Uí Néill, with a base at Ailech, whereas the southern variant controlled the midlands. The most important symbolic and ritual site, Tara, was seized from the Laigen by the southern Uí Néill, whose over-king took the style of King of Tara, which eventually came to be linked to the high-kingship of all Ireland. The Northern Uí Néill exerted pressure elsewhere against the Ulaid, helped by the subject Airgialla. The Ulaid were pushed east of the Bann and their most important dynasty, the Dál Fiatach, ruled the Mourne Mountains from Downpatrick.

The power struggles in Ireland might partly explain the colonizing movements led by the Irish in Britain. The fourth and fifth centuries observed a large Irish colony being formed in south-west Wales by the Déisi from the Munster coast. North Wales was also home to another, less important Irish colony ruled by the Laigin, who left their name on the Lleyn Peninsula. The Cornish peninsula became home to yet another Irish colony, led by the Uí Liatháin from the eastern part of County Cork. The most important Irish colony was led by the Dál Riata of Antrim in northern Ireland, who settled in Scotland to create a state

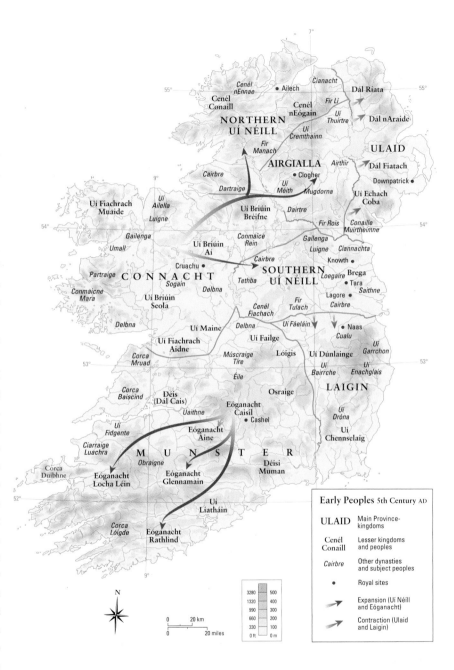

known as Dál Riata there in Argyll and the Hebrides. This colony eventually exerted power over the Picts and was instrumental in creating the Kingdom of a United Scotland, begun by Kenneth MacAlpine. The Romans eventually called Ireland Scotia, rather than Hibernia, and the Irish Scoti; hence the name became applied to all of Scotland.

St Paul's Epistle to the Galatians

"NOW THE WORKS OF THE FLESH ARE MANIFEST, WHICH
ARE THESE; ADULTERY, FORNICATION, UNCLEANNESS,
LASCIVIOUSNESS, IDOLATRY, WITCHCRAFT, HATRED, VARIANCE,
EMULATIONS, WRATH, STRIFE, SEDITIONS, HERESIES, ENVYINGS,
MURDERS, DRUNKENNESS, REVELINGS, AND SUCH LIKE ..." (THE
EPISTLE OF PAUL *THE APOSTLE TO THE GALATIANS* 5: 19-21)

Before St. Paul went on his missionary journeys, the Celtic Galatians, who had been invaded by the Roman Empire in 25 BC and turned into a Roman province, not only venerated the Roman emperor but practiced a type of Romano-Celtic polytheism. During his missionary journeys Paul was welcomed by the Galatians, and the inhabitants of Lystra tried to sacrifice to him, thinking that he and Barnabas were the gods Hermes and Zeus, after Paul performed a miracle by healing a man who had been crippled from birth and who had never walked (Acts 14:8).

Paul wrote his letter hoping to counteract the influence of a few Jewish Christians who attempted to persuade the Galatians that they must be circumcized and obey the Mosaic Law to be perfect Christians. They had thus criticized Paul for not having taught the full perfection of Christianity. Paul's letter falls into three sections. The first two chapters state that he is an apostle neither through men nor through the teaching of any man but from Christ himself and that the gospel, or good news, he taught was in harmony with the teaching of the great apostles who had given him the right hand of friendship. Chapters three and four explain the pointlessness and inefficacy of circumcision and the Mosaic law and that redemption was owed to Christ alone. Here, he appealed to the experience of the Galatian converts and provided proofs from Holy Scripture. The final two chapters saw Paul appealing to the Galatians that although they were free from Mosaic Law, they were not free to indulge in crimes, for criminal activity would ban them from attaining the Kingdom of God. To him circumcision was pointless since there was no virtue in cutting flesh. Otherwise the more you cut, the more perfect you would become – so why not castrate yourself? The epistle is important because Paul avowed that faith was a gift of God but also that faith was of no avail because it works by charity (Galatians 5: 6). He pointed out that a good life was necessary for salvation.

St. Paul's travels and preachings had taken him through Galatia on several occasions. The region still retained notable Celtic characteristics.

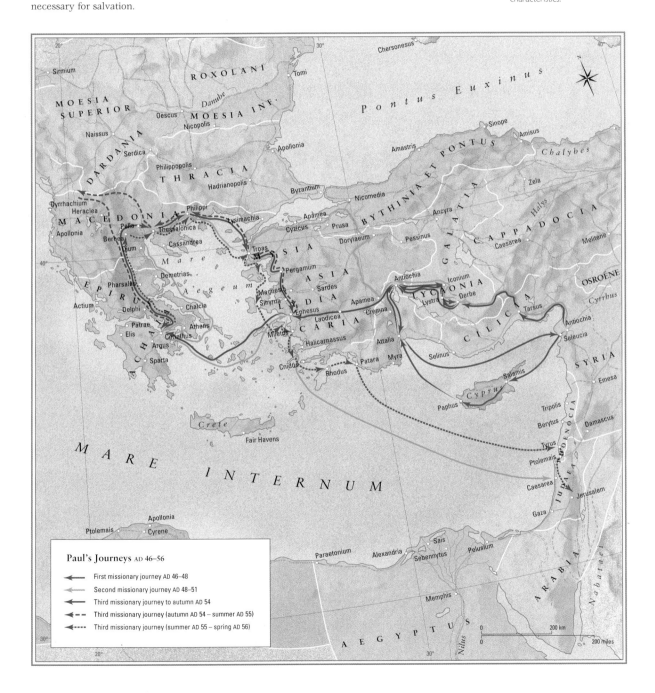

Paul's Journeys AD 46–56

First missionary journey AD 46–48
Second missionary journey AD 48–51
Third missionary journey to autumn AD 54
Third missionary journey (autumn AD 54 – summer AD 55)
Third missionary journey (summer AD 55 – spring AD 56)

Irish Monasticism

"BUT AFTER I REACHED IRELAND, I USED TO PASTURE THE FLOCK
EACH DAY AND I USED TO PRAY MANY TIMES A DAY. MORE AND
MORE DID THE LOVE OF GOD, AND MY FEAR OF HIM AND MY
FAITH INCREASE, AND MY SPIRIT WAS MOVED ... THE SPIRIT WAS
BURNING IN ME AT THAT TIME." ST. PATRICK, *CONFESSIO*, 16

Christianity had arrived in Ireland by the fifth century and maybe earlier. The first bishop, Palladius, was appointed by the Pope in 431. By the sixth century, the most significant churches were controlled by a monastic hierarchy. The early monasteries were not merely religious institutions but the hub of economic activity. The early monastery of Nendrum was founded on Mahee Island in Lough Strangford, County Down, and was accessible only via a causeway. Excavations there have found workshop-style building, a possible school, as well as homes, a church, and the remnants of a tower. Sometimes groups of monasteries were linked together if thought to have a common founder. These clusters were known as a parucha, and the most important was that at Armagh, which proclaimed its pre-eminence, citing its presumed association with St. Patrick as legitimacy.

The stimulus and drive behind this monasticism came from Britain. St. Enda founded the church on Inis Mór, the largest of the Aran Islands, in Galway Bay. He originated in Whithorn, in Galloway, Scotland, where he had studied with St. Ninian. The Welsh St. David and St. Cadoc inspired others like St. Máedóc of Ferns and St. Finnian of Clonard. The latter schooled men who themselves became significant monastery founders. Among them were Brendan (Clonfert), Ciarán (Clonmacnoise), Colum Cille, and Columba (Durrow, Derry and Iona). Convents of nuns were also established, noticeably St. Brigit's at Kildare. Some monks preferred the life of a hermit or wished to find a haven from world affairs like the island of Sceilg Mhicil off Kerry. The development of knowledge and the love of Christianity drove some monks to evangelize overseas in Scotland, East Anglia, Northumbria, in Picardy and Belgium, and in Germany. Scholarship was so brilliant that Irish monastic scholars during this golden age of Celtic Christianity were welcomed as teachers in European courts.

Opposite: By the 7th century Ireland's monastic schools were beginning to produce great scholars and holy men whose work was comparable with that emmanating anywhere in Christendom.

The monastic movement generated great monasteries like those already mentioned. They were great ecclesiastical centers, civitates, or cities, as they were dubbed. The abbots came from the aristocracy and the wealthy elites of society. Patronage was important and some monasteries became big land-holders, wielding much influence. Some monasteries became increasingly secularized and some wealthy abbots married into the highest ranks of the aristocracy. Like later Renaissance princes, they funded works of art, and Ireland witnessed a flowering of calligraphy with the beautiful Irish script and metal work such as the Tara brooch based on La Tène stylistic elements using animal heads and gold and silver intaglio. Book illumination, such as in the Book of Kells, reached the highest standards, as did the metalwork in the Armagh and Derrynaflan chalices. Under church auspices, the Irish high crosses were erected throughout the land. Iona and Armagh were the major ecclesiastical power houses in the Irish Celtic world with a widespread influence. The ninth abbot of Iona, Adomnán, proclaimed his "Law of Innocents", which was enacted by all the kings in Ireland and Dalriada and by the king of the Picts. The law excluded women and children from battle and protected them and clerics from violence. At this time, it was not uncommon for women warriors to die in battle, as Boudicca's daughters did in Britain.

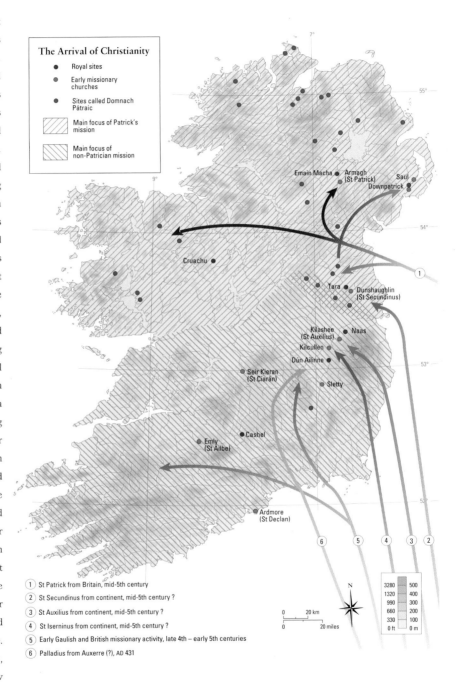

The Arrival of Christianity

- ● Royal sites
- ● Early missionary churches
- ● Sites called Domnach Pátraic
- ▨ Main focus of Patrick's mission
- ▨ Main focus of non-Patrician mission

① St Patrick from Britain, mid-5th century
② St Secundinus from continent, mid-5th century ?
③ St Auxilius from continent, mid-5th century ?
④ St Iserninus from continent, mid-5th century ?
⑤ Early Gaulish and British missionary activity, late 4th – early 5th centuries
⑥ Palladius from Auxerre (?), AD 431

0   20 km
0   20 miles

3280	500
1320	400
990	300
660	200
330	100
0 ft	0 m

Map labels: Emain Macha, Armagh (St Patrick), Saul, Downpatrick, Cruachu, Tara, Dunshaughlin (St Secundinus), Kilashee (St Auxilius), Naas, Kilcullen, Dún Ailinne, Seir Kieran (St Ciarán), Sletty, Cashel, Emly (St Ailbe), Ardmore (St Declan)

Irish Churchmen and Scholars in Europe

"This first proof of miraculous power... let this divine miracle, worked by our Columba, shine as a light in the beginning of this book ..." Adomnán of Iona,

The Life of Columba

The sixth century saw Irish monks reaching out into the wider world from their penitential environment on the rocky islets off the coast from Scelih Mhicil to Aran and Rathlin. In 563 Colum Cille (Columba) traveled to the lonely Hebridean island of Iona, and from there he and his followers evangelized among the Picts and Scots, converting many. His Ionian monastery eventually became the ecclesiastical capital of the Scots kingdom of Dál Riata. The Iona monks spread the faith throughout Scotland and then took Christianity into the Anglo-Saxon kingdom of Northumbria. Here, Aidan led a band of monks from Iona to Lindisfarne, where he became its first bishop. The Venerable Bede (c.673-735) wrote the history of this energetic character, who was helped in his work through friendship with local kings and because he learned English. Lindisfarne became a center of knowledge and a training ground in ecclesiastical matters. This Irish movement of "pilgrims for Christ" (peregrini pro Christo) was continued by Fursa, who preached in East Anglia after being given a monastic site in the fortress of Cnobesburh (Burgh Castle, Suffolk). Fursa then moved to France and established a monastery at Lagny gifted to him by Erchinoald, mayor of the palace of Frankish Nuestria. Fursa's death in 649-50 at Mézerolles set in train a competition for the corpse of this saintly man. Erchinoald acquired the body and interred it at Péronne, where his tomb became a focus of pilgrimage. Fursa's brothers, Faelán and Ultan, were exiled from Cnobesburh in 650 by King Penda of Mercia; they visited their brother's grave and became abbots of Péronne in turn. This abbey introduced the cult of St. Patrick, which was being established by the religious center at Armagh. Péronne became a sanctuary for Irish monastic recruits, a staging place for pilgrims en route to Rome or the Holy Land, and a place where penitents could retire.

Fursa's younger brother, Faelán, also fled East Anglia with his community from Cnobesburh and journeyed to Nivelles, where there was a famous convent under Itta, widow of Pipin I, mayor of the palace of Austrasia. This Benedictine convent was eventually governed by Itta's daughter, Gertrude. Together, the two women helped Faelán establish a monastery at Fosses in about 651.

Many Irish pilgrims traveled to France, and Brittany abounds with a number of Irish saints: Briac, Maudez, Ninnoc, and Ronán. However, the first well-recorded Irish monk in France was Columban, who trained under Comgall in the monastery at Bangor. This Spartan monastery comprised a collection of round wooden huts enclosed by a palisade with some communal buildings. The days would be spent in frequent periods of prayer interspersed with laboring in the fields. Forms of mortification were common, but the monastery was a happy milieu in which Scriptures and Latin were taught and perhaps even some Greek. Columban is thought to have left Bangor in 591 for France, where he founded a monastery at Annegray in a disused Roman fort destroyed in the past by Attila the Hun. A ruined temple to Diana was repaired and used as a church. The numbers of monks increased so rapidly that another monastery was established eight miles away in another former Roman fort at Luxovium (Luxeuil). Eventually, a third foundation was opened at Fontaine, three miles from Luxeuil. The Columban rule was strict, with severe penances and confessions twice a day. Columban's Penetential became an agent for changing penitential discipline in the Church in Western Europe, a system which also offered restitution and hope.

Columban refused to condone or countenance the sinful life of Thierry, King of Burgundy, and the king's mother, Brunhilde, induced him to expel the Irish and British monks from Luxeuil. These ecclesiastical refugees found their way to Bregenz on Lake Konstanz. A three-year trip to Switzerland was marred by a disagreement with Gall, his colleague of twenty years, who refused to cross the Alps. Columban decreed that Gall was never to celebrate mass while he lived. Another account states that Gall was too ill to travel. He died as a hermit on the River Steinach, where an abbey was raised in his name after his death. Columban journeyed to Italy, where he established his final monastery at Bobbio, and he died there in 615. Eventually, the daughter houses of Luxeuil embraced the Benedictine Order, as did Luxeuil and Bobbio.

France benefited from the mother house at Luxeuil because it trained so many Frankish people, who became the founders of monasteries all over France. The impact of St. Columban and the Irish was enormous in developing the spread of Christianity.

The Luxeuil school also had an impact elsewhere. St. Amand, educated at Luxeuil, preached in Belgium. An aristocrat, Richerius, joined the clerical life and founded a monastery at St. Riquier in Ponthieu. St. Fara of Meaux founded a convent, eventually called Faramoutiers. Luxeuil was also behind Rebais, Jumièges, and Corbie. Other Irish founders were those who stayed in France after Columban's expulsion. Such were Deicolus of Lure and Roiun of Beaulieu in the Argonne. Additional developments lay in the reclusive hands of Fiachra, who established a hostel for Irish pilgrims and established a garden to grow food for them. He later became the patron saint of gardeners. Other hermits were Kilian, who dwelt at Aubigny near Arras, and Gobán, who settled about 20 kilometers west of Laon.

Irish missionaries entered Germany for certain in the late seventh century with St. Kilian. He was martyred with two companions, Totnan and Kolonat, in Würzburg in 689. These "Apostles of Franconia" were placed in Würzburg's first cathedral in 752 and became a center of pilgrimage. Another martyr-missionary was Bishop Marin, who was murdered at Wilparting. The eighth century saw many apparent

Opposite: A trickle of Irish missionary activity became a flood, taking their Christian preaching from what became Scotland to central Europe and even to places a few hundred miles from Rome itself.

Below: Traveling from Iona, Scotland Saint Aidan led a group of monks to Lindisfarne, also known as Holy Island, a small island off the northeast coast of England. After founding the monastery in AD 635, Aidan became the first bishop of Lindisfarne, and the Holy Island went on to become an important religious center.

Irish missionaries near Munich. St. Korbinian of Freising was a missionary around 715. Fergil or Virgil of Salzburg moved from Ireland to Francia in about 753, after which he was sent on a mission to Duke Odo of Bavaria. He was appointed Bishop of Salzburg. Elsewhere, in Germany, St Fintan of Rheinau spent twenty-five years near the Falls of Schaffhausen in the Rhine region, dying there about 878. Irish monks were also important in the Benedictine transformation. Places where they worked were Metz, Cologne, and Waulsort. This Irish Benedictine "Schottenklöster" developed Irish communities at Trier and Mainz, with penitents dwelling in Fulda, Paderborn, and Regensburg. The Irish Benedictines of Vienna even managed to found a monastery at Kiev, but the Mongol invasions of 1241 caused them to withdraw.

Oher Irish exports to Europe were scholars, many of whom left Ireland as monasteries were attacked by Vikings. Their learning earned them positions as masters in the schools of the Carolingian empire. Dicuil or Dungals wrote texts on geography, grammar, and astronomy, most notably writing Liber de Mensura Orbis Terrae. Others were knowledgeable as poets, philosophers, philologists, lexicographers, and biblical commentators. Although some stayed in Aachen, the Carolingian capital, most moved west to the Episcopal sees of Laon, Soissons, Rheims, Cambrai, and Liège. The pinnacle of Irish scholastic achievement lay in the hands of Sedulius Scottus of Liège and Johannes Scottus Eriugena in Laon. Sedulius wrote works on grammar, philosophy, and theology as well as penning over 80 known poems in Latin. Some are humorous — asking a bishop for more food and drink — or are lyrical about death.

"Of mirth-provoking sap I too have need,

Some beer, or Bacchus' gift, or perhaps some mead,

And then there's meat, produce of earth and sky,

And I have none, but ask the reason why."

Erugenia was an accomplished philosopher and theologian discussing such matters as predestination. He claimed that philosophy was a science in De Divisione Naturae. In sum, Irish monks and scholars made a major contribution to the development of Christianity and to learning in Europe, carrying the monastic golden age's fruits into the ignorance of Europe.

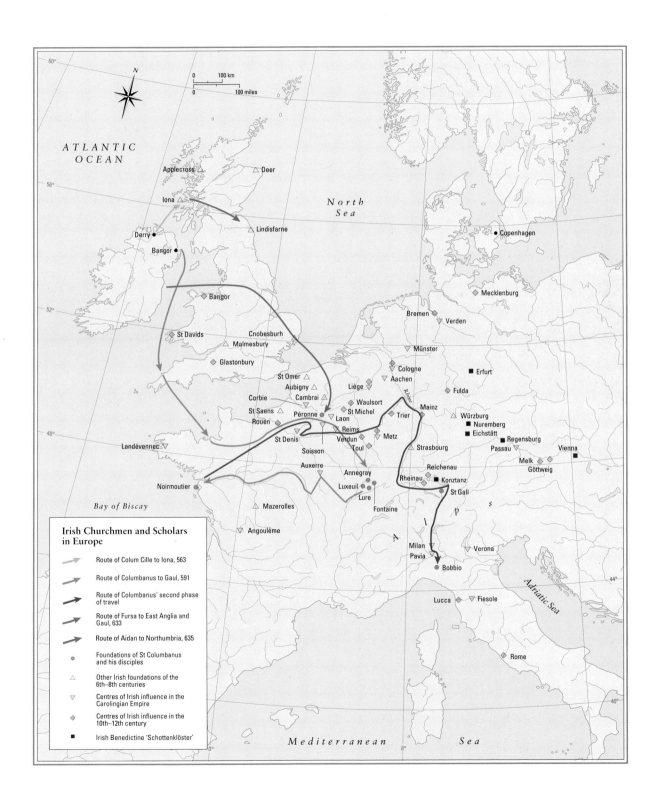

ATLANTIC
OCEAN

North
Sea

Bay of Biscay

Mediterranean   Sea

Adriatic
Sea

**Irish Churchmen and Scholars
in Europe**

Route of Colum Cille to Iona, 563

Route of Columbanus to Gaul, 591

Route of Columbanus' second phase
of travel

Route of Fursa to East Anglia and
Gaul, 633

Route of Aidan to Northumbria, 635

● Foundations of St Columbanus
and his disciples

△ Other Irish foundations of the
6th–8th centuries

▽ Centres of Irish influence in the
Carolingian Empire

◆ Centres of Irish influence in the
10th–12th century

■ Irish Benedictine 'Schottenklöster'

Applecross
△ Deer
Iona △
△ Lindisfarne
Derry ●
Bangor ●
● Copenhagen
◆ Mecklenburg
◆ Bangor
Bremen ▽ Verden
St Davids
Cnobesburh
△ Malmesbury
▽ Münster
◆ Glastonbury
St Omer △
Cologne ▽
◆ Erfurt
Aubigny △
▽ Aachen
Liège ▽
Corbie
Cambrai △
◆ Fulda
St Saens △
◆ Waulsort
Mainz ■
Rouen ◇
Péronne ●
St Michel ▽
Trier ▽
Würzburg ▽
Landévennec ▽
St Denis ▽
Laon
Reims ▽
■ Nuremberg
Verdun ▽
Metz ▽
■ Eichstätt
Soisson
Toul ▽
Strasbourg ▽
Regensburg ◆
Auxerre
Passau ◆ Vienna ■
Annegray ●
Reichenau ◆
Melk ◆
Noirmoutier ●
Luxeuil ●
Rheinau ◆
Konztanz ■
Göttweig
Lure ●
St Gall ■
Fontaine
△ Mazerolles
△ Angoulème
Milan ●
▽ Verona
Pavia
● Bobbio
Lucca ● ▽ Fiesole
● Rome

Rhine

0   100 km
0   100 miles

N

The Irish Sea in the Viking Age, 800–1170

The Vikings treated the Irish Sea like a Norse lake, raiding the coastal regions before settling in the cities. They were successful in establishing a state comprising the Western Isles and the Isle of Man.

The Norse and Danes turned the Irish Sea into a virtual Viking lake for nearly 400 years between 800 and 1170. Their military prowess and economic strength allowed them to take control of trade routes and create mini-states around the sea's littoral. 837 witnessed two Viking fleets raiding on the rivers Boyne and Liffey, resulting in the eventual establishment of fortified encampments at Annagasan in contemporary County Louth and Dublin (841). Olof the White, from the Norwegian line of Vestfold kings, founded a dynasty of kings which utilized Dublin as a base to control all the Norse colonists on the Irish coast.

Olof subjugated the Norse colonists of the Hebrides and Galloway while conducting ranging raids in Scotland and Ireland. A companion war leader of Olof was Ivar the Boneless, who was co-leader of the great army that invaded England in 865 and conquered York and parts of Northumbria in 866. The Vikings encircled the Irish Sea by the tenth century, when Norse migrants surged into northwest England and colonized the territory between the Wirral and Galloway. Large numbers of settlements in Cumbria and Westmoreland meant that a Viking land bridge stretched across the whole of northern England from the Irish Sea to the North Sea.

In Scotland, the Norse first raided Iona in 795 to loot the monastery at Colmcille. It was sacked a further four times. The early raids were eventually transformed into building settlements on the islands and along the Galloway coast to the Moray Firth. In Orkney and the Shetlands, the Celts were subordinated and absorbed, and 99 per cent of place names are of Norse origin. However, in the Hebrides and southwest, the subordinate Celts inter-married with the Norse to produce an ethnic fusion, called by the Irish, the Gall-Gaedhil or foreign Gaels; this is the source of the region of Galloway. Celtic influence

Opposite: The Irish Sea in the 9th century was a Viking sea. Sea lanes carried trade and shiploads of armed men intent on exploitation and adventure.

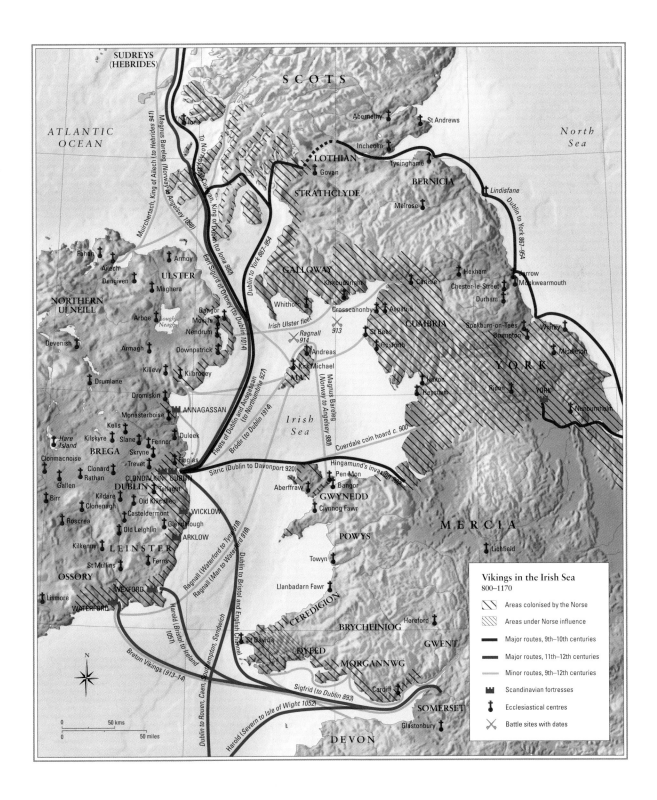

SUDREYS
(HEBRIDES)

SCOTS

ATLANTIC
OCEAN

North
Sea

Iona

Magnus Bareleg (Norway to Hebrides 941)

Muirchertach, King of Ailech (to Angelsey 1088)

To Norway via Gut

Earl Sigurd of Orkney (to Iona 980)

an, King of Dublin (to Iona 980)

Dublin to York 867–954

Abernethy

St Andrews

Inchcolm

Tyninghame

LOTHIAN

Govan

BERNICIA

Lindisfane

STRATHCLYDE

Melrose

Dublin to York 867–954

GALLOWAY

Fanat

Armoy

Ailech

ULSTER

Dungiven

Maghera

NORTHERN
UI NEILL

Arboe

Lough
Neagh

Bangor

Movilla

Nendrum

Devenish

Armagh

Downpatrick

Kirkcudbright

Whithorn

Crosscanonby

Irish Ulster fleet

Ragnall
914

913

Aspatria

St Bees

CUMBRIA

Hexham

Carlisle

Chester-le-Street

Durham

Jarrow

Monkwearmouth

Sockburn-on-Tees

Brompton

Whitby

Gosforth

Andreas

Middleton

YORK

Killevy

Kilbroney

Kirk Michael

MAN

Drumlane

Dromiskin

Fleets of Dublin and Annagassan

Brodir (to Dublin 1014)

Irish
Sea

Magnus Bareleg (Norway to Angelsey 980)

Heton

Heysham

Ripon

YORK

Nunburnholm

Monasterboise

ANNAGASSAN

Kells

Hare
Island

Kilskyre

Slane

Duleek

Fennor

BREGA

Skryne

Trevet

Finglas

Clonmacnoise

Clonard

Rathan

CLONDALKIN

DUBLIN

Gallen

Kildare

DUBLIN

Talaght

Cuerdale coin hoard c. 900

Sitric (Dublin to Davonport 920)

Hingamund's invasion 902

Pen Mon

Bangor

Aberffraw

GWYNEDD

Birr

Clonenagh

Old Kilcullen

Casteldermont

WICKLOW

Clynnog Fawr

Roscrea

Old Leighlin

Glendalough

ARKLOW

POWYS

Lichfield

Kilkenny

LEINSTER

Ferns

Towyn

St Mullins

OSSORY

Llanbadarn Fawr

CEREDIGION

Lismore

WEXFORD

WATERFORD

Ragnall (Waterford to Tyne 918)

Ragnall (Man to Waterford 916)

Dublin to Bristol and English Channel

Harold (Bristol to Ireland 1051)

Dublin to Rouen, Caen, Southampton, Sandwich

Breton Vikings (913–14)

St David's

DYFED

Hereford

BRYCHEINIOG

MORGANNWG

GWENT

Sigfrid (to Dublin 893)

Cardiff

Harold (Severn to Isle of Wight 1052)

SOMERSET

Glastonbury

DEVON

N

0   50 kms
0   50 miles

Vikings in the Irish Sea
800–1170

⬛ Areas colonised by the Norse

▨ Areas under Norse influence

━━ Major routes, 9th–10th centuries

━━ Major routes, 11th–12th centuries

━━ Minor routes, 9th–12th centuries

♜ Scandinavian fortresses

♰ Ecclesiastical centres

⚔ Battle sites with dates

meant that Celtic Christianity spread among the Norse by 900. A Viking saga recounts how Ketil Flatnose became the first Norse ruler of the Hebrides in the ninth century, from approximately 840 to 880. By the end of the century the Vestfold kings had gained sovereignty over the Orkneys, creating an earldom there. They also claimed dominion over the Hebrides but failed to assert their control for 200 years. The Orkney earldom rapidly assumed authority over the Norse areas of Scotland by the rule of Sigurd Hlodvirsson the Stout (c. 985-1014), whose mother was supposed to be the daughter of Irish king Cerball mac Dúnlainge of Osraige.

The Norse impacted upon the power relationships between the four ethnic group inhabiting Scotland. These were the Picts of the Highlands, the Scots of Dalriada, the Britons of Strathclyde, and the Anglo-Saxons of Northumbria. All were subject to Viking attacks, and the Picts are last mentioned in an Irish source in the early tenth century. The Scots suffered the least and swiftly overran the Picts in 844 under Kenneth MacAlpine (c.843-858), who established a dynasty that conquered the Britons in the 920s and Lothian in 973, leading to the creation of the kingdom of Scotland. This unification process also meant that Scots Gaelic spread to be come the major language in Scotland by the twelfth century.

Elsewhere, York became a major commercial center, and still retains Viking street names such as Goodhamgate and Swinegate; "gate" comes from "gade", meaning "street." The monk William of Malmesbury (c. 1080/94-1143) recorded that ships from Scandinavia, Ireland, and Germania traded there. In the Irish Sea, Dublin was a fortified staging post, providing protection and sanctuary to Viking merchants and raiders who sailed the Atlantic route, which connected to Francia and the Mediterranean. The Norse only controlled the coastal margins of south-ast Ireland rather than a large settled hinterland as in England around York. The Vikings of Dublin and York constantly sought to co-operate with each other but communications were difficult. An overland route was opened up by Hingamund's attack on the Wirral in 902 and King Sitric's rape of Davenport in Cheshire in 920. The so-called Chester route marched from the Wirral to York by way of Ribblesdale and Wharfdale but another ran from Carlisle to York along the old Roman road. These trans-Pennine ways were dangerous, and merchants would be forced to leave their ships beached while moving overland.

A preferred route between the two Viking capitals was a voyage to the firths of the Forth and Clyde. Evidence suggests that there was a portage across Kintyre and elsewhere. The bond between York and Dublin grew stronger, and soldiers from one went to the other. Relationships with Scots rulers became frequent as interests were gradually held in common. The Scots helped Guthfrith's invasion of Northumbria in 927 but he was driven from York that year by Athelstan of Wessex. Olaf Guthfrithson made himself leader of the Dublin and Irish Norse and asserted his father's claims over York, and he allied with Scots and Strathclyde Britons, an alliance which met defeat at Brunanburh in 937. This victory failed to outlast Athelstan's reign.

In 954, York passed backward and forward, with the last Viking ruler being Erik Bloodaxe, who struggled with Dublin's King Olaf Sihtricson and English King Eadred for control of the city. The Northumbrians ejected him and he was killed in an ambush, with Stainmore being butchered with his entourage. This Danish weakness in England probably allowed Dublin to expand its influence, mint its own coinage, and expand its own merchant class. Viking influence grew in the Isle of Man, as attested by the major Viking finds there. Burial mounds include that of longships at Knock y Doonee and Balladoole, and other mounds at Cronk ny Arrey Lhaa, Jurby, and Knock-y-Dowan. Norse crosses can also be found at Andreas, Braddan, Jurby, Maughold, and Kirk Michael, showing a spiritual change to Christianity and wealth in commissioning such objects. Likewise, crosses can be found at Gosforth in England.

Dublin began to re-orient its trade, as did Norse Wexford and Waterford. Ships sailed to Caen and Rouen in France and to Southampton, the Isle of Wight, and Sandwich. Commerce with Bristol was especially important, as were staging posts on the Welsh coast at Haroldston, Skomer, and Flat Holm. Dublin changed in other ways as Christianity took hold, with King Olof Cuaran making pilgrimage to Iona in 980. Dublin possessed a Norse bishop and diocese and kept its Norse flavor and culture until the Anglo-Norman invasion in 1169. Other Norse bishoprics were created at Waterford and Limerick, and Dublin was elevated to an archbishopric in 1152. Dublin was reduced in status by the battle of Clontarf in 1014. Thereafter, it became a desirable grant in the contest for dominance among the various provincial kings, no one being as strong as the dead high-king Brian Boru. By the time of the Anglo-Norman invasion, the coastal Irish towns were inhabited by hybrid Hiberno-Norse, whose monopoly of trade in the Irish Sea was an affront to the rising Angevin state in England and France. The Bristol trade was a magnet pulling Strongbow's adventurers into Ireland and the chaos among contesting kings was a devil's brew attracting intervention in Ireland. Ultimately, Angevin King Henry II invaded Ireland to prevent Strongbow establishing a personal principality. He gave Bristol traders concessions in Dublin as a reward for their aid in his royal venture.

Rathlin Island is situated off the coast of County Antrim in Northern Ireland. In 795 the island witnessed the first Viking raid on Ireland, and many invasions followed as the Vikings gained control of, and eventually settled in, Dublin.

VIKING WARS IN IRELAND

AFTER THE VIKINGS ESTABLISHED THEMSELVES IN IRELAND, THEY
INTER-MARRIED WITH THE LOCAL POPULATION, CREATING A
NEW ETHNIC GROUP, THE HIBERNO-NORSE. THEY JOINED IN THE
COMPETITIVE WARS BETWEEN IRISH KINGS BUT THEIR POWER
WEAKENED AS IRISH KINGS IMPROVED THEIR WEAPONRY.

The eighth century witnessed Viking bands sailing from Scandinavia to trade and plunder western Europe, voyage across the Atlantic, enter the Mediterranean, and traverse Russia via its river system. Some raided for plunder while others eventually tried to settle, with great success, in the British Isles and Normandy. Evidence suggests that the first Viking attack on Ireland occurred in 795 when Norsemen attacked several island monasteries off the Irish littoral, such as Rathlin, Inishmurray, and Inishbofin. These raids started in the northern and western coasts but by 824 Sceilg Mhicil in the southwest had been attacked.

The raids, confined to the immediate coastal hinterland, generally robbed Irish churches because they were the focal points of communities and the center of economic activity. Church precious metal-ware, stored goods and food, and slaves were taken. Eventually, the Norse began moving inland on waterways like the Shannon, looting the monastery at Clonmacnoise (836), and then into Lough Erne. The winter of 840-41 saw them wintering on Lough Neagh while some established a camp at Dublin which became the major base for operations in Ireland. The Dublin camp was built on the estuary which entered the Liffey, and by the tenth century it was an important slave market and commercial and manufacturing center.

Initially, the Vikings were Norse but 851 saw the Danes in control of Dublin until ejected by Olof the White from the Vestfold kingly line. The Norse were sucked into Irish local politics, becoming allies of neighbors or just fighting them for survival. Olof's death saw Ivar the Boneless succeeding to the Dublin kingdom in 873 and then political life destabilized. Opportunities for raiding were developing elsewhere and many Norse raided England or Francia while some traveled to Iceland to settle there, with others using the island as a base for eastwardsjourneys to Greenland and the Americas. The notion

Opposite: The Norse raiders, "Vikings", created new settlements along the coast of eastern Ireland. From these bases they fought the local chieftains and intermarried with Irish women, creating a new ethnicity. These "new" people went to sea, taking their raiding to Britain and beyond.

that the Vikings were always victorious is incorrect. The Irish kings learned how to fight the Norse and inflicted defeats on them at Downpatrick (811), Waterford (860), and Youghal (866). Also, some parts of Ireland were relatively free from Norse incursions, notably the interiors of Munster and Leinster, Connacht, and west Ulster.

The period between 874 and 914 witnessed relative peace in Ireland, and with so many Vikings fighting in western Europe, the Dublin Vikings were quite weak and were ousted in 902. The Norse were soon back though and built substantial settlements not just in Dublin but at Wexford, Waterford, and Limerick. 914 saw a large Viking fleet arriving at Waterford. More Norse arrived and, in 915, they attacked Munster and Leinster, looting the monasteries of Cork, Lismore, and Aghaboe.

Niall Glúndub, high king of the Uí Néill led an Irish counter-offensive in 917 without much success and was then defeated and killed by the Vikings in a battle of Dublin (919). Raids were conducted along Irish rivers such as the Shannon, and one occasion saw inter-community Viking strife when Olof Sihtricsson, king of Dublin, destroyed a Limerick Viking ship force near Lough Ree in 937. Viking raids from the Hebrides were a constant series of pinpricks. The Irish were not slow to learn improved sailing from the Norse, and fleets were built in the north. Muirchertach, king of the northern Uí Néill, devastated the Hebrides in 941.

Viking success was not long-lasting. They made no great or lasting territorial conquests but probably weakened Irish kingdoms in their immediate vicinity. The Norse towns fought among themselves, and Dublin Vikings were often intent on securing York (Jorvik) in England for themselves, thereby not concentrating on their Irish interests. Only Irish disunity allowed the small, hemmed-in Norse communities to survive. Despite raids on monasteries, no major monastery ceased functioning. In fact, Christianity converted many Vikings and repeated inter-marriage created the Hiberno-Norse, who spoke Gaelic rather than Norse.

The Viking Wars

⬛ Dublin Vikings active, 917–1014

⬜ Viking settlement

▲ Viking encampment

★ Viking raids and battles, 795–835

★ Viking raids and battles, 836–902

➡ Vikings inward

·➤ Vikings outward

1 First Viking raid, 795
2 To York, 920–940
3 To Scotland, 866–870
4 Dublin taken, 841
5 Danes arrive, 851 and 875
6 To Scotland, 918

THE AGE OF BRIAN BORU

"HIS REIGN ... WAS ONE FULL OF BATTLES, WARS, COMBATS, PLUNDERING, RAVAGING, UNQUIET. BUT AT ITS CONCLUSION, THIS REIGN ... BECAME BRIGHT, PLACID, HAPPY, PEACEFUL, PROSPEROUS, WEALTHY AND RICH, WITH FESTIVE GIVING OF BANQUETS AND LAYING OF FOUNDATIONS." COGADH GAEDHEL RE GALLAIBH

In 976, Brian Boru became king, a man admired in the sagas and destined to become an icon of modern Irish nationalism. Brian swiftly gained control of all Munster, pushing the previous Eóganachta hegemon into the background after he defeated them in the Battle of Belech Lechta (978). His ambition was to become high king of Ireland and thus he posed a threat to the Uí Néill high king, Máel Sechnaill. Eventually, through a series of campaigns, Brian won the submission of the Uí Néill high king and established his position in a number of campaigns in the north. He soon gained the title, "Emperor of the Irish," Imperator Scotorum, a term used in a note inscribed in the Book of Armagh. A period of relative peace followed.

The year 1013 witnessed Dublin and Leinster rebelling, and Brian spent the latter part of the year trying to crush them. Despite reinforcements, the rebels were defeated at the battle of Clontarf, where Brian Boru was killed. This inter-Irish battle using Norse allies as makeweights set a pattern for Irish history until the arrival of the invading Anglo-Normans under Strongbow. Many provincial kings contended for the status of high king but none could retain that position. The power struggles were fueled by a burgeoning population producing more manpower, and an improvement in weapons technology meant that separate kings sought to move out of their traditional landholdings and conquer extra land and people in a process of internal colonization and seizing extra kingly titles. In this tense period, Diarmait Mac Murchada of Leinster sought foreign allies and, in 1169, three shiploads of soldiers under Robert fitz Stephen from England arrived at Bannow Bay followed by two more ship-loads under Maurice Prendergast, of Flemish descent yet residing in Pembrokeshire. The Anglo-Norman invasion had commenced.

Opposite: Brian Boru rose to power, overcoming rivals to become king of Munster. He later emerged as a high king in 1002. He styled himself as "Emperor of the Irish." Brian's greatest victory was at Clontarf in 1014, where he defeated a Viking army. However, Brian himself was slain.

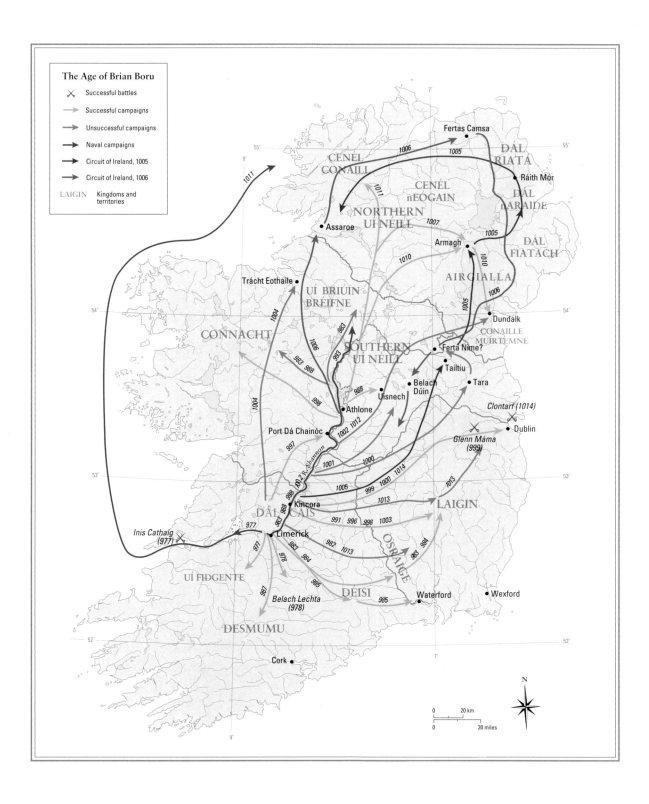

The Age of Brian Boru

✕   Successful battles

→   Successful campaigns

→   Unsuccessful campaigns

→   Naval campaigns

→   Circuit of Ireland, 1005

→   Circuit of Ireland, 1006

LAIGIN   Kingdoms and territories

GODRED CROVAN, KING OF MAN

"...THOSE THAT WERE LEFT BEGGED GODRED WITH PITIFUL CRIES TO SPARE THEM THEIR LIVES. MOVED WITH COMPASSION... HE CALLED OFF HIS ARMY..." ON THE BATTLE OF SKYHILL, CHRONICA REGUM MANNIAE ET INSULARUM

Norsemen began raiding the coast of Ireland and the Isle of Man during the late eighth century. The Isle of Man and its now mixed Celtic and Norse population became a desirable territory in Norse chieftains' power struggles. Eventually, Earl Thorfinn the Mighty of Orkney (1014–64) added the island to his possessions: Orkneys, Shetlands, Caithness and Ross, and maybe lands in Ireland and Galloway too. After Thorfinn died, the Orkney earldom lost control of the isles.

Enter Godred Crovan (1079–95). He was raised for some years in Man but his main home was probably in Islay. He fought under Harold Hardrada of Norway against Harold of England at Stamford Bridge (1066) and fled to to the Isle of Man after that Viking defeat. He vanished from history and then reappeared leading two failed invasions attempts on the Isle of Man but the Manx defeated him. *The Chronicles of Man and the Isles,* recorded by the Cistercian monks, have Godred returning to the island three times. He beached his ships at Ramsey and hid 300 men in the woods on Skyhill. When the Manx attacked his invasion force, the hidden warriors ambushed the Manx rear, causing them to flee until entrapped by the River Sulby. Their lives were spared and Godred ruled until his death in 1095 while his descendants ruled until 1265. This first Manx king united the Hebrides and the Isle of Man. In order to control his far-flung possessions, Godred designed an administrative system of government with his kingdom having 32 representatives drawn from the 32 major islands in his realm, with 16 being apportioned to Man. Known as Keys, they met at an annual parliament at Tynwald or Thingvöllr (meeting place). Over time, the kingdom was shorn of its possessions but refused to dimish the number of Keys, which remain at 24. The term "Keys" probably originates in the Manx Gaelic *Yn Kiare-as-feed* (The Four and Twenty), being contracted into Keys. Hence Tynwald is the oldest parliament in the world.

Opposite: Godred Croven created a well-administered state, based on the island archipelago of the Hebrides, administrated from the Isle of Man.

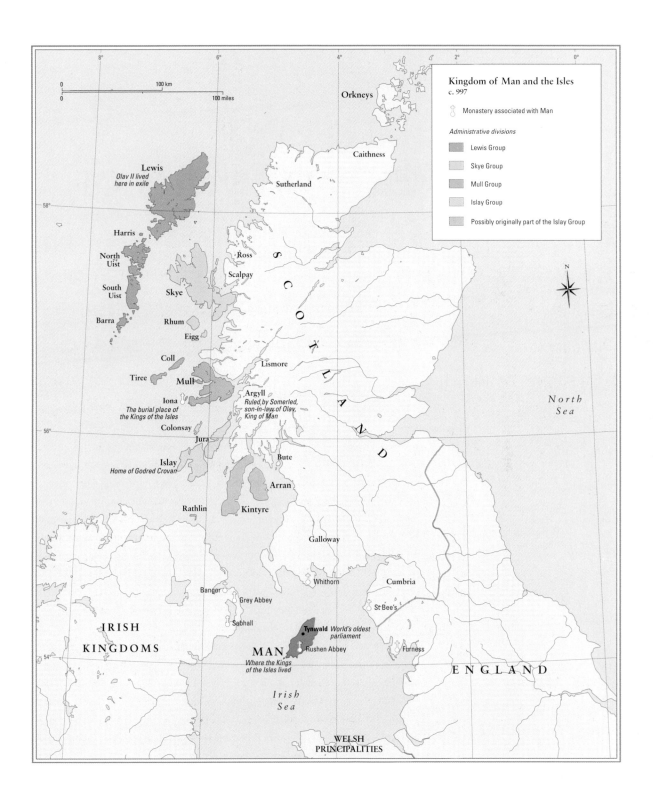

Orkneys

Caithness

Sutherland

Lewis
*Olav II lived
here in exile*

Harris

North
Uist

Ross

Scalpay

South
Uist

Skye

Barra

Rhum

Eigg

Coll

Lismore

Tiree

Mull

Iona
*The burial place of
the Kings of the Isles*

Argyll
*Ruled by Somerled,
son-in-law of Olav,
King of Man*

Colonsay

Jura

Bute

Islay
Home of Godred Crovan

Arran

Rathlin

Kintyre

Galloway

Whithorn

Cumbria

Bangor

Grey Abbey

St Bee's

Sabhall

Tynwald *World's oldest
parliament*

MAN
*Where the Kings
of the Isles lived*

Rushen Abbey

Furness

**IRISH
KINGDOMS**

ENGLAND

*Irish
Sea*

**WELSH
PRINCIPALITIES**

*North
Sea*

S C O T L A N D

0   100 km
0   100 miles

Kingdom of Man and the Isles
c. 997

✝ Monastery associated with Man

Administrative divisions

Lewis Group

Skye Group

Mull Group

Islay Group

Possibly originally part of the Islay Group

N

Anglo-Norman Invasion

THE ANGLO-NORMANS INTERVENED IN IRISH POLITICS UNDER THE COMMAND OF RICHARD FITZGILBERT, STRONGBOW, WHOSE MILITARY SUCCESS CAUSED KING HENRY II TO INTERFERE LEST STRONGBOW ESTABLISH A KINGDOM IN IRELAND. HE SWORE HOMAGE TO THE KING IN RETURN FOR LEINSTER WHILE HENRY ADDED IRELAND TO HIS VAST LANDS.

After Diarmit MacMurchada, King of Leinster, was expelled from Ireland, he sought to return with foreign knights, allowed by Henry II of England after Diarmit acknowledged Henry as his lord. The year 1171 witnessed Henry's intervention in Irish affairs by preventing an independent Irish-Norman kingdom being established by Richard (Strongbow) âFitzGilbert de Clare, Earl of Pembroke, who was helping Diarmit. Strongbow had seized the Kingdom of Làeinster, plus the towns of Waterford, Wexford, and Dublin and part of the Kingdom of Meath. Henry II landed with his army at Waterford, causing Strongbow to offer to hold Leinster as a fief. The kingdom was formally granted to him in return for homage, fealty, and the service of a hundred knights while the king kept the city and Kingdom of Dublin and all seaports and fortresses. Meath was given to Hugh de Lacy, who had accompanied Henry II's army to Ireland. While traversing Munster to Dublin, the English King received submission and hostages, as well as promises of tribute, from seven Irish Kings. A church synod recognized his overlordship, a logical reaction since Pope Adrian IV, an Englishman, had granted Henry II and his successors the right to rule over Ireland.

Now that military conquest had finished, the invaders pursued economic exploitation. The Anglo-Normans invested heavily in imported agricultural systems, based upon the famed English manor with its mixture of arable and pastoral farming. Anglo-Norman economic development resulted in increased commercial activity, as evidenced by new towns. Rural woodlands were cleared, arable lands opened up, and crop rotation introduced, leading to increased volumes of domestic and foreign trade.

Opposite: The aggressive Anglo-Norman state wasted no time in exploiting any weakness in the Welsh principalities. With the decline of Gwyned the power to resist declined, and the Anglo-Normans advanced.

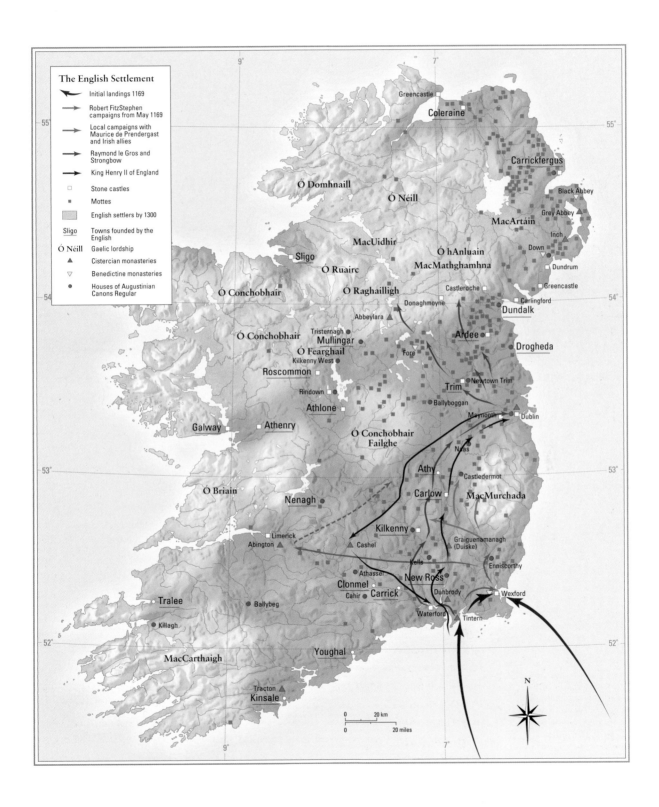

The English Settlement

Initial landings 1169

Robert FitzStephen campaigns from May 1169

Local campaigns with Maurice de Prendergast and Irish allies

Raymond le Gros and Strongbow

King Henry II of England

□ Stone castles

■ Mottes

English settlers by 1300

Sligo — Towns founded by the English

Ó Néill — Gaelic lordship

▲ Cistercian monasteries

▽ Benedictine monasteries

● Houses of Augustinian Canons Regular

Greencastle

Coleraine

Carrickfergus

Black Abbey

Grey Abbey

Inch

MacArtain

Down

Ó Domhnaill

Ó Néill

Dundrum

MacUidhir

Ó hAnluain

MacMathghamhna

Greencastle

Ó Ruairc

Castleroche

Carlingford

Sligo

Donaghmoyne

Dundalk

Ó Conchobhair

Ó Raghailligh

Abbeylara

Ardee

Drogheda

Tristernagh

Ó Conchobhair

Mullingar

Fore

Ó Fearghail

Kilkenny West

Newtown Trim

Trim

Roscommon

Ballyboggan

Rindown

Maynooth

Dublin

Athlone

Galway

Athenry

Ó Conchobhair Failghe

Naas

Athy

Castledermot

Ó Briain

Carlow

MacMurchada

Nenagh

Kilkenny

Graiguenamanagh
(Duiske)

Limerick

Abington

Cashel

Enniscorthy

Kells

Athassel

New Ross

Clonmel

Carrick

Dunbrody

Wexford

Tralee

Cahir

Waterford

Tintern

Ballybeg

Killagh

MacCarthaigh

Youghal

Tracton

Kinsale

N

0   20 km

0   20 miles

IRISH RESISTANCE

THE ANGLO-NORMAN CONTROL OF IRELAND WAS CHALLENGED
BY BRIAN O'NEILL, RECOGNIZED AS HIGH KING OF IRELAND BY
IMPORTANT REMAINING IRISH RULERS. THIS RESISTANCE TO THE
ENGLISH WAS ENDED AT THE BATTLE OF DOWN (1260), AFTER WHICH
O'NEILL'S HEAD WAS DISPLAYED AT THE TOWER OF LONDON.

The failure of Rory O'Connor to resist Strongbow after he captured Dublin and the loss of his army together with the submission of Irish Kings and Church to Henry II did not mean that Irish resistance had ended. However, savage reprisals ensued against armed resistance. This intimidation helped diminish raids against new towns and settlements. O'Rourke, King of Bréifne, was treacherously murdered by de Lacy on his way to negotiations in 1172. His head and decapitated body were placed on display at various places on the walls of Dublin. Thu, kings who survived the initial Anglo-Norman military juggernaut knew that they had to work with the new power to survive and to think about consolidating their local interests rather than anything else.

Anglo-Norman rule involved the foundation of new towns, with streets laid out in grid patterns with narrow fronted plots and long narrow pieces of land held in burgage tenure. The maximization of frontages implied a desire to turn the new towns into successful commercial centers. Many people came to settle in the towns, from Bristol but elsewhere in England and Wales too, with some from as far afield as France and Flanders. The most successful towns generated the wealth needed by the lords to build vastly improved castles.

Accommodation did not last. The thirteenth century saw uncoordinated English territorial advances, despite the promises of English kings that this would not happen. By the 1250s, the Irish reacted, and in 1258 the chief Irish kings challenged Anglo-Norman rule by acclaiming Brian O'Neill as high king of Ireland. In 1260, his forces were defeated by the English at the Battle of Down, O'Neill's head being sent to publicly decorate the Tower of London as a warning.

Another aspect of Anglo-Norman rule commenced when King John visited Ireland in 1210, establishing

Opposite: Dunluce Castle, County Antim, Ireland. This 13th-century stronghold was established by Richard de Burgh, Earl of Ulster. Located on the edge of a basalt outcropping and surrounded by terrifyingly steep cliffs on either side, it was only accessible via a bridge connecting it to the mainland. It would have presented a formidable defense against invaders.

a civil government independent of the feudal lords, which became fully organized during the thirteenth century. 1200 had witnessed the creation of an Irish exchequer followed by a chancery in 1232. Ireland was divided into counties for administrative reasons while English law was introduced, and attempts were made to diminish the feudal liberties of the Anglo-Norman lords, liberties being lands held in the personal control of aristocratic families and the Church. Parliament commenced; 1297 saw peers and prelates joining county representatives and in 1350 towns also sent members. However, this institution only represented the Anglo-Irish; the native Irish, especially in Ulster under the O'Neills and O'Donnells, and southwest Munster under the MacCarthys, were unrepresented. However, the Irish chieftains were viewed by John as an interest group which he could use, like the Church and town burgesses, to threaten the great feudal barons with their large liberties, such as Trim.

The English colonists failed to settle in large numbers outside the towns, and the Anglo-Normans could not eradicate the most powerful Irish Kings, meaning that the complete conquest of Ireland was intensely problematic. Nevertheless, Anglo-Norman ambitions could not be extinguished so easily, and the late 1230s saw a large-scale invasion of Connacht, resulting in the creation of English colonies in places as remote as Mayo. This new expansion could not continue because many able Anglo-Norman leaders in the 1240s left no sons to inherit their territorial dreams. Additionally, the MacMurroughs of the Wicklow Mountains, from the 1270s, attacked the suburbs of Dublin, the center of English royal government in Ireland. The 1297 parliament reported that some settlers were beginning to lose their own culture and take on that of the native Irish.

A particular military development in Ireland was the creation of mercenary bands of kerns, a form of bare-footed light infantry who hired themselves out to Irish and Anglo-Norman lords. Retinues on either side became more alike, and during times of peace the kerns roamed the countryside causing much tension. Their existence helped to fuel the prevalent skirmishing between the Irish and the invaders. When these fighters began to disappear, Ireland was being introduced to troops from the Western Isles of Scotland. These were the famous Scots galloglass (gall-ó-glaigh), foreign warriors. In 1259, Aed O'Connor, son of the King of Connacht, married the daughter of Dougal MacRory, Lord of the Hebrides. Her dowry included 160 gallowglass led by her uncle. Such warriors strengthened the Irish lords by reducing English military superiority. A move was set in train that every Irish lord, big or small, wanted a war-band, which was paid for by the bands milking any agricultural surplus. Anarchy became endemic and the economy was seriously weakened.

Colonial weakness was seriously revealed and Ireland was threatened by Edward Bruce, brother of King Robert I of Scotland, who invaded Ulster in 1315, joining the O'Neills in an attempt to drive out the English migrants. Despite failing to win unanimous Irish support, Bruce managed to defeat English forces several times and nearly achieved the capture of Dublin. The Scots threat was finally ended with the defeat and death of Bruce at Forbart near Dundalk in 1318 by John de Bermingham.

During the Bruce wars, a decisive battle occurred at Athenry in August 1316. This comprised a war within a war since Felim O'Connor wanted to make himself supreme king of Connacht and kick out the Anglo-Normans to win back lands lost in 1232. He was joined by the Kings of Meath, Bréifne, Annelly, Leney, Ui Maine, Ui Tiachrach Muaidhe, and Munster. Some 20,000 men faced the Connacht Normans and their main leaders, Richard de Burgh, Earl of Ulster, and Lord Bermingham of Athenry. The Irish reputedly suffered 10,000 casualties, mown down by archers and armored might, including five kings killed, leaving Connacht firmly in Norman hands.

The Bruce invasion and defeat revealed the latent strength of the English presence. The settlers were united against the Bruce onslaught despite Bruce's bullying tactics to loosen their allegiance to the English King. The settlers regarded themselves as superior to the "barbarian" Irish. Facing this conquering self-esteem, the Irish waited for further opportunities to improve their condition. English control was further augmented by the creation of three new Anglo-Irish earldoms: Kildare, given to the head of the Leinster Fitzgeralds; Ormonde, granted to the head of the Butlers, who held lands around Tipperary; and Desmond, gifted to the head of the Munster Fitzgeralds.

The Irish economy was weakened by the Bruce wars, famine in 1315-17, and the arrival of the Black Death in 1348-49. Absentee landlords, the nobility torn by increasing numbers of feuds, and large numbers of peasants returning to England enabled the Irish to begin re-conquering frontier settlements. So worried were the English that Edward III's son, Lionel, Duke of Clarence, viceroy from 1361 to 1367, passed the Statutes of Kilkenny. The English were forbidden to speak Irish, marry Irish, or foster children with Irish families. Irish outside the obedient Pale were dubbed enemies holding land through usurpation. Other statutes forbade the use of March or Brehon law, wearing Irish clothes, using Irish hair styles, and selling to the Irish food or horses in time of war and weapons in times of peace. In reality, the Irish were feared with their attacks against a beleaguered English outpost of civilization bought off by heavy ransom.

Upper Lake Glendlough is located within the Wicklow mountain range in County Wicklow, Ireland. The MacMurroughs of the Wicklow Mountains were members of the Irish Resistance who attacked the English government in Dublin around 1270.

GAELIC REVIVAL

GAELIC CULTURE SURVIVED THE BLACK DEATH, WHICH HIT
DUBLIN AND THE SOUTHEAST PORTS IN 1348. FAMINE AND WAR,
TOO, COULD NOT PREVENT A RENAISSANCE IN IRISH LEARNING,
WITH WELL-EDUCATED FAMILIES IMMERSING THEMSELVES IN
MEDICINE, LAW, POETRY, MUSIC, HISTORY, AND GENEALOGY.

The power of the English in Ireland became more muted as many of their original leaders died, sometimes without sons or any issue. Estates were divided among daughters whose husbands had interests other than Ireland. The Bruce wars had weakened the Irish economy, which became a burden to the English crown. Famine in 1315-17 and the Black Death in 1348-49 damaged Ireland further. The population shrank and marginal land went out of cultivation. Many colonists returned to England and much land lay to waste. English defensiveness responded to a resurgent Gaelic culture seeking to recoup its losses since 1170. By the end of the thirteenth century, the educated Gaelic families commenced a cultural journey producing poetry, legal commentaries, translations of European medical treatises, and works of genealogy and Irish history. Aristocratic patronage saw the production of great books like the *Leabhar Breac* or the *Yellow Book of Tara*. In some ways, the Irish revival was nostalgic, seeking to provide links with the archaic past and its continuity with the present. Gaelic culture became so strong that it appealed to leading Anglo-Norman families like the de Burghs, Butlers, and Fitzgeralds.

The years 1360 to 1369 witnessed the English crown pouring time and money into Ireland, yet the Irish chieftains maintained virtually independent Gaelic areas. The Wars of the Roses in England saw English rule being confined to the Pale. During the later part of the Wars of the Roses, the earls of Kildare rose to prominence and ruled Ireland until broken by King Henry VIII in 1534. Eventually parliament decreed that the government of Ireland was inferior to England's and that all royal ordinances were to be obeyed. The Earl of Kildare remained a powerful nobleman who could generate strong rule and efficient government while being limited by law.

Opposite: The cataclysms of the Black Death brought massive changes to Ireland. Those English colonists who survived the disease returned to England. A resurgent Gaelic culture emerged which sought to recoup its losses.

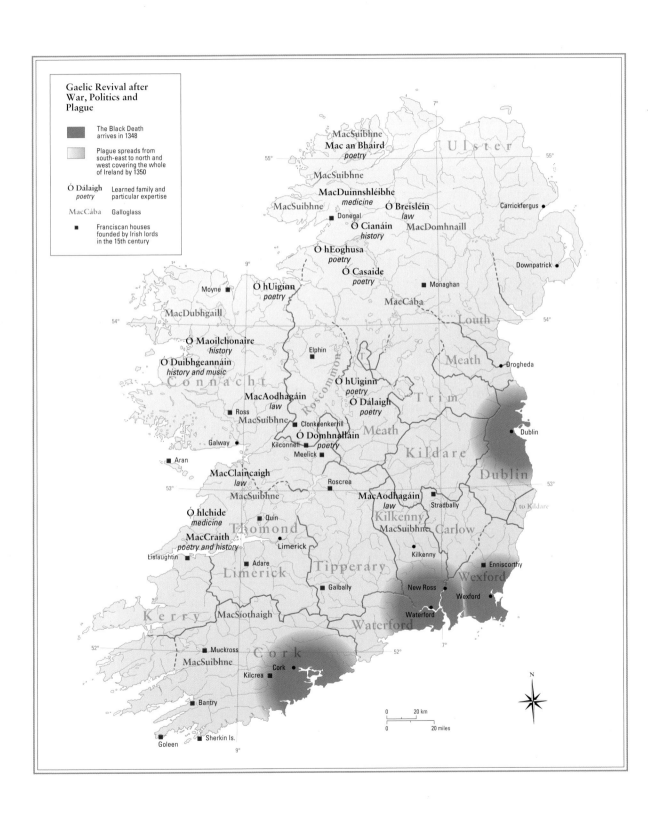

Gaelic Revival after
War, Politics and
Plague

The Black Death
arrives in 1348

Plague spreads from
south-east to north and
west covering the whole
of Ireland by 1350

Ó Dálaigh   Learned family and
poetry   particular expertise

MacCába   Galloglass

■ Franciscan houses
   founded by Irish lords
   in the 15th century

MacSuibhne
Mac an Bhaird
poetry

Ulster

55°

MacSuibhne

MacDuinnshléibhe
medicine

MacSuibhne   Ó Breisléin
law

Carrickfergus ●

■ Donegal
Ó Cianáin
history   MacDomhnaill

Downpatrick ●

Ó hEoghusa
poetry

Ó Casaide
poetry

Moyne ■   Ó hUiginn
poetry

Monaghan ■

MacCába

MacDubhgaill

Louth

54°

Ó Maoilchonaire
history

Connacht

Elphin ●

Meath

Drogheda ●

Ó Duibhgeannáin
history and music

Ó hUiginn
poetry

Trim

Ross ■

MacAodhagáin
law
MacSuibhne

Roscommon

Ó Dálaigh
poetry

Clonkeenkerrill ●
Ó Domhnalláin
poetry

Meath

Kildare

Dublin ●

Galway ●   Kilconnell ●
Meelick ■

Dublin

Aran ■

MacClaincaigh
law

Roscrea ●

53°

to Kildare

MacSuibhne

MacAodhagáin
law

Stradbally ■

Kilkenny

Ó hIchIde
medicine

Quin ■

Thomond

Carlow

MacSuibhne

MacCraith
poetry and history

Limerick ●

Kilkenny ●

Enniscorthy ●

Lislaughtin ■

Adare ■

Limerick   Tipperary

New Ross ●   Wexford
Wexford ●

Galbally ●

Kerry   MacSiothaigh

Waterford ●

Waterford

52°

7°

Muckross ■

Cork

52°

MacSuibhne
Kilcrea ■

Cork ●

■ Bantry

N

Goleen ■   ● Sherkin Is.

0   20 km

0   20 miles

TUDOR AND STUART IRELAND

ELIZABETHAN RULE IN IRELAND CREATED SOME SPANISH HEARTS
AS THE IRISH SAW A RELIGIOUS SAVIOR IN KING PHILIP OF SPAIN.
HOWEVER, THE DASHING OF THE ARMADA ON THE IRISH COAST
DURING SEVERE STORMS SAW THE DEATH OF SOME 10,000 SPANIARDS
BY DROWNING OR MURDER AS THEY STRUGGLED ASHORE.

Henry VIII exported the Reformation into Ireland in 1537, accompanied by the dissolution of the monasteries with the usual destruction of church architecture, images, and relics. He attempted to placate the Irish with a new status under their customary laws. English courts observed Irish rights and peace was enjoyed. Elizabeth and the first Stuart king, James I (1603-25) advanced the power of the Anglican Church in Ireland. The Church of England absorbed all the assets of the Church of the Pale and was allowed to digest the possessions of the Celtic Church as well. The Reformation impacted upon the Church of the Pale but the Roman Catholic faith, which imbued the Celtic Church, retained the loyalty of nearly all the Celtic population of Ireland, including those Irish in the Pale. The Anglican Church was used by the English as one more political tool to serve the interests of the English rulers in Dublin Castle. James I decreed that English law was the only law of the land, thus eradicating the independence of the Irish lords.

Civil War broke out in England in 1642, and Charles desired peace in Ireland so he could use Irish forces against his enemies in England. An Irish peace was reached in 1643 between the confederates and the Earl of Ormond, the Lord Lieutenant in Dublin. A peace was signed in 1646 but a Papal Nuncio, Giovanni Rinuccini, claimed that there were not enough guarantees for the Roman Catholic Church. After the execution of Charles I in 1649, an alliance was formed between the confederates and the Dublin government against the English Parliamentarians which turned the Irish civil war into a theater of the English Civil War. An English army had already landed in Ireland, and it met an Irish army at Rathmines (Baggot Rath) in August 1649. The Irish lost half of their force dead or as prisoners. 1649 also witnessed Cromwell landing in Ireland.

Opposite: The idea of protectant "plantations" of English and Scots settlers in Ireland did not generate the numbers originally hoped for. The outcome left a lasting mark on Irish history, especially in Ulster.

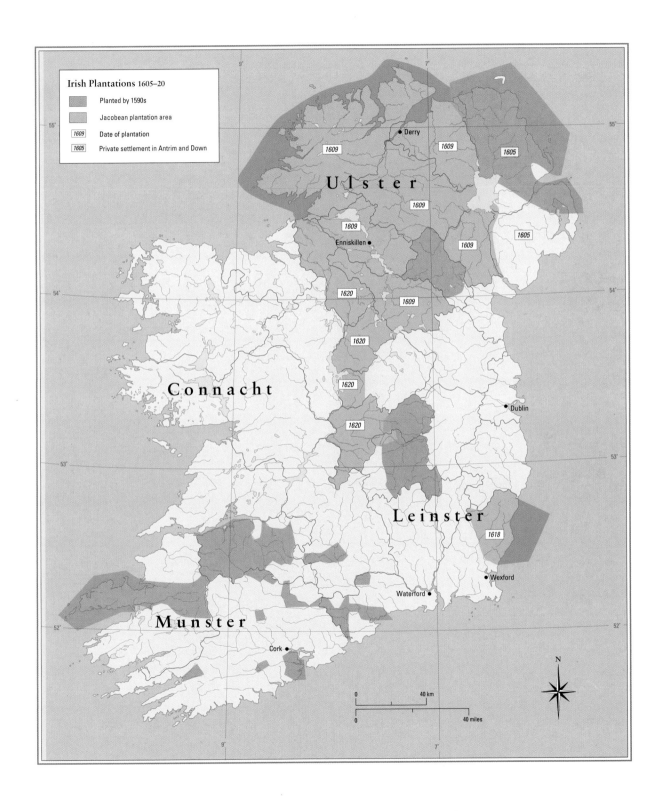

Irish Plantations 1605–20

Planted by 1590s

Jacobean plantation area

1609 Date of plantation

1605 Private settlement in Antrim and Down

Ulster

Connacht

Leinster

Munster

Derry

Enniskillen

Dublin

Wexford

Waterford

Cork

1609
1609
1605
1609
1605
1609
1609
1620
1609
1620
1620
1620
1618

N

0   40 km

0   40 miles

CROMWELL IN IRELAND

ROYALISTS IN DROGHEDA (1649) TOOK SHELTER IN ST. PETER'S CHURCH. ON REFUSING TO SURRENDER, CHURCH FURNITURE WAS PILED AGAINST THE WOODEN STEEPLE AND SET ALIGHT, BURNING THE DEFENDERS ALIVE. THOSE IN OTHER TOWERS WERE STARVED OUT, WITH ONE IN TEN BEING SHOT WHILE OTHER SURVIVORS WERE SENT TO SERVITUDE IN THE WEST INDIES.

When Cromwell arrived in Ireland with 3,000 Ironsides, he was confronted by the broken remnants of the Earl of Ormonde's royalist army, so recently defeated at Rathmines by General Michael Jones. Cromwell's men were well disciplined on the battlefield but gained an infamous reputation, as did Cromwell, for their brutal behavior. Cromwell, sometimes known as God's executioner, commenced his campaign by the siege of Drogheda accompanied by 12,000 soldiers of the New Model Army. He needed a swift victory to improve public morale after the shock execution of Charles I. Hence he was determined to break Drogheda's 3,000-strong garrison of English royalists and Irish Catholics.

The Parliamentarians asked Sir Arthur Aston, the Drogheda commander, to surrender but he refused. On 11 September, Cromwell's troops attacked the town and breached the flimsy medieval wall with artillery, storming the town and slaughtering soldiers and civilians. According to the usages of war at the time, such a massacre was an acceptable outcome in Europe, as attested by the devastation and loss of human life during the Thirty Years' War. Yet Cromwell's actions proved abhorrent in Europe. The brutality might have been occasioned by the considerable losses the besiegers suffered in the attack but this does not explain the death of Aston's last three hundred troops, who surrendered at Millmount fort. They were just slaughtered. Cromwell maintained that his action was just vengeance for the butchery meted out to Protestant settlers in 1641. He claimed that the events at Drogheda were "a righteous judgement of God upon these barbarous wretches, who have imbrued their hands in so much innocent blood." The

Opposite: In August 1649 a tough, battle-hardened army arrived in Ireland commanded by the ruthless parliamentary general Oliver Cromwell. He quickly subdued and gained control of eastern Ireland. In 1650 he left for Scotland, leaving further operations to his commander, Henry Ireton, to complete his plan.

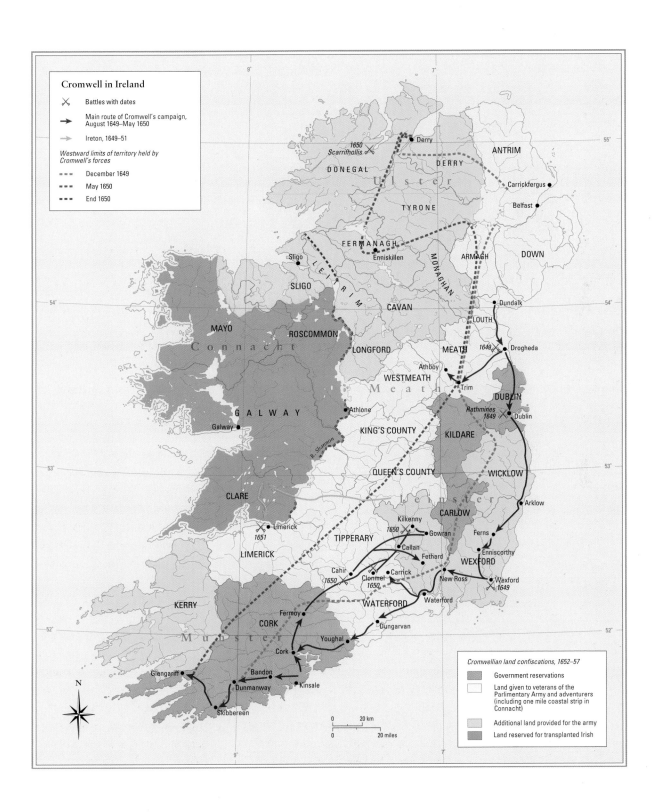

Cromwell in Ireland

✕ Battles with dates

➡ Main route of Cromwell's campaign,
August 1649–May 1650

➡ Ireton, 1649–51

*Westward limits of territory held by
Cromwell's forces*

- - - December 1649

- - - May 1650

- - - End 1650

Cromwellian land confiscations, 1652–57

▨ Government reservations

☐ Land given to veterans of the
Parliamentary Army and adventurers
(including one mile coastal strip in
Connacht)

▨ Additional land provided for the army

▨ Land reserved for transplanted Irish

0   20 km
0   20 miles

savagery might have been an attempted psychological blow against the insurgents, persuading them to give up lest they suffer a similar fate. Cromwell hoped his policy would "prevent the effusion of blood for the future." In fact, Irish resistance stiffened and hatred grew so strong that the war continued for another four years. The fact that approximately 3,500 people were killed exacerbated the hostility, especially with reports of soldiers firing into houses. Also a captured officer was killed in cold blood in front of Cromwell. Other Irish towns learned how to fight the Ironsides.

Cromwell now headed south and took Wexford by escalade. The Parliamentarian troops went berserk, indulging in the butchery of 2,000 people before taking New Ross and compelling the surrender of Cork, Youghal, and Kinsale. However, Waterford survived for some while but Cromwell managed to capture Kilkenny and Clonmel, with heavy losses, before he returned to England in 1650. Left behind to complete the conquest of Ireland was Henry Ireton, his son-in-law, a more moderate and just man. At the siege of Limerick in 1651, a Colonel Tothill was accused of executing or murdering troops who had surrendered to a junior officer. The Colonel was stripped of his command but Ireton thought this punishment "fell short of the justice of God required therein to the acquitting of the army from the guilt of so foul a sin." He informed the royalists of the court martial and freed other prisoners without ransom or any form of exchange.

Ireton's mopping up task proved to be less than easy. Ormond had the undefeated Army of the North commanded by Bishop MacMahon. He met an English force commanded by Sir Charles Coote. Combat commenced at Scarrifhollis (Letterkenny) on 21 June 1650. Coote's force lost about a hundred men but an English officer on the Irish side reckoned that fifteen hundred Irish died fighting. A number given quarter were dragged before Coote and "were shott or hacked down by his Orders: for his Officers and private soldiers...had more Mercy than he had." In sum, 2,000-3,000 Irish perished, including most of the officers, without which an effective fighting force would take too long to rebuild. Bishop MacMahon was hanged and quartered, with his head impaled on the gate of Londonderry. During the siege of Limerick, an Irish relief force numbering some 3,500 to 5,000 men commanded by Viscount Muskerry were confronted by a smaller English force under Lord Broghill at Knockbrack (Knocknaclashy) on 25 July 1651. The Irish were defeated but the English sustained approximately the same number of casualties. The relief of Limerick failed and the city was taken in October 1651. Galway surrendered in May 1652, after which Irish resistance folded. Some Irish officers surrendered and negotiated their release, with recruiting rights to take service overseas as mercenaries, creating the Wild Geese. Others suffered transportation to the West Indies and a harsh life and probable death from disease and fever. The remaining centers of opposition in Ulster and Connacht fell in 1652 ,finalizing the Cromwellian conquest.

The Cromwellian administration imposed upon Ireland involved two major strands: religious persecution and land confiscation. Firstly, a set of parliamentary commissioners were despatched to Ireland to eradicate Roman Catholicism and introduce a puritan church. Catholic priests were tracked down and killed, imprisoned, or exiled. However, persecution of the faith served to strengthen it and priests continued their ministry. The remnants of the Irish army were encouraged to seek service overseas and many went to France and Spain. Known as 'tories", some disbanded soldiers turned to theft and banditry, generally against settlers.

The second policy comprised an ultra-large plantation. A 1652 Act of Settlement listed those Irish who were to lose their lands or part thereof for their complicity in the rebellion. Those who were entitled to retain their estates were to be sent west of the Shannon and compensated with sequestered lands. Their old lands would be distributed in any way the English parliament deemed fit, much going to the army. Connacht was thus to be a reservation, a ghetto. The plan was hard to implement, but thousands were transported while the landless generally remained to serve the new owners.

The impact of these harsh measures was to increase the number of Protestants in Ireland and the quantity of land in their possession. This rural land revolution was mirrored by similar confiscations in the towns, where the Roman Catholic presence was virtually eliminated, making towns and their trade Protestant possessions. Irish land-holdings were reduced from sixty to twenty percent and Roman Catholics lost many political and commercial opportunities, a situation that was not redeemed by the restored King Charles II (1660).

On 30 January 1661, Cromwell's corpse was disinterred from Westminster Abbey and hanged from a gibbet at Tyburn while his head was impaled on a spike in public view for the next 20 years.

In Ireland, Oliver Cromwell and his army of Ironsides gained a reputation for their brutal behavior both on and off the battlefield. Religious faith was persecuted, as Cromwellian law sought to eliminate Roman Catholicism. In addition to this, land was confiscated and redistributed at the whim of the English. Cromwell died at Whitehall on Friday, September 3, 1658.

WILLIAM III AND IRELAND

THE BLOODY BATTLE OF AUGHRIM (1691) BROKE THE JACOBITE ARMY IN IRELAND, WITH ITS SURVIVORS LEAVING IRELAND TO JOIN THE SERVICE OF FRANCE AND SPAIN. GALWAY AND LIMERICK SURRENDERED, AND WILLIAM III SECURED HIS GRIP ON THE THREE KINGDOMS OF ENGLAND, SCOTLAND, AND IRELAND.

Charles II was succeeded by his brother, James II, who despatched the Irish Catholic, the Earl of Tyrconnell, to Ireland, where he placed Catholics in important posts, especially the army. He also planned to overturn the Cromwellian land settlement, thus causing consternation among Protestants, who feared the intentions of their Roman Catholic king. Many fled to Holland to invite William of Orange, James' son-in-law, to take the crown. William landed at Torbay in 1688, establishing what historians call the Glorious Revolution.

In Ireland, Protestants in Derry raised militias and closed the gates against any new king's garrison. In 1689, James landed in Ireland and besieged Derry, which was filled with refugees. The city held out until relief ships broke through the siege lines. Shortly afterwards, William landed at Carrickfergus to campaign against James, who was sponsored by William's enemy, Louis XIV of France. James retreated to Dublin and decided to hold the line of the River Boyne. William advanced with his English, Dutch, Danish, Swiss, German, and French Huguenot troops. During the subsequent battle William's well-disciplined Dutch Guards cracked one Irish attack with platoon volleys, which the Irish could not fight with mere pikes and matchlocks. The Jacobite army eventually retreated, protected by a skilled French rearguard, which ensured that three- quarters of the Jacobite army survived. James II fled the battlefield to Dublin, taking a ship from there to France.

After James left and the French withdrew their troops, the Irish field army located itself west of the Shannon. The Irish possessed some 20,000 troops commanded by the French Marquis de St. Ruth. William's Dutch general, Baron de Ginkel, was ordered to cross the Shannon, crush this army, and seize the remaining two Jacobite ports of Galway and Limerick. Ginkel forced the Shannon after taking

Athlone, marching on until he found the Jacobites at Aughrim. Battle followed on July 12, 1691. The Irish fought bravely, sometimes suicidal with clubbed muskets, but St. Ruth lost his head to a cannonball ,causing his lifeguards to flee followed by other Irish cavalry. The Irish were crushed, losing nearly 8,000 men. Galway and Limerick fell, leaving William in control of Ireland with Irish hopes shattered for the moment. After the Treaty of Limerick, General Patrick Sarsfield sailed for France with 12,000 Irish troops to really establish the Wild Geese.

Protestant power in Ireland was now assured and reinforced, with the Protestant minority dominating politics, society, and economic life. Despite the Treaty of Limerick guaranteeing Roman Catholics the right to practice their faith, the treaty was ignored. About one million more acres were sequestered from the defeated Irish, leaving them owning only about one-seventh of the land. Land-holdings were further reduced during the eighteenth century, and members of the Irish Parliament, an increasingly powerful institution, were compelled to take an anti-papal oath, which meant that Roman Catholics were precluded from taking their seats, thereby diminishing Catholic power again.

The penal laws were extremely harsh. Catholics could not bear arms or send their children overseas for an education, and their clergy were banned from Ireland. The Irish were prevented from owning more land and could not buy any from Protestants, and land leases were for a limited tenure. Catholics could not make wills, and property was to be divided among all sons of a deceased person. However, if the eldest accepted the Church of Ireland, an Anglican institution, then primogeniture could work. Catholic schools were disallowed and, in 1728, the Catholics were disenfranchised. The Ulster Presbyterians were also barred by a sacramental test from public office and a military career. However, fears about the Protestant dissenters were assuaged when the Ulster Presbyterians supported the Crown against new Jacobite rebellions.

On July 11, 1690 the army of William of Orange, some 35,000 to 40,000 strong, attacked the forces of James II. The infantry struggled indecisively. William's more numerous cavalry began an envelopment. James was unable to counter and after savage fighting was forced to flee the field.

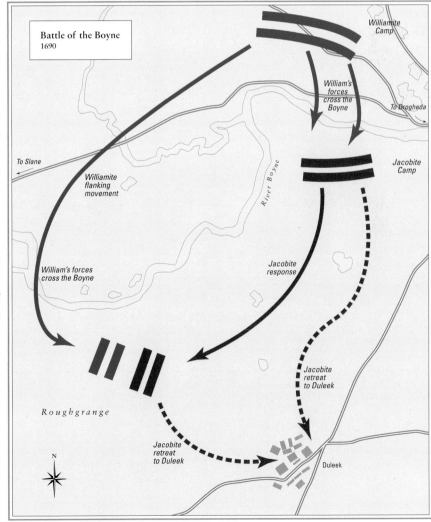

Battle of the Boyne
1690

Williamite Camp

William's forces cross the Boyne

To Drogheda

To Slane

Williamite flanking movement

River Boyne

Jacobite Camp

William's forces cross the Boyne

Jacobite response

Jacobite retreat to Duleek

Roughgrange

N

Jacobite retreat to Duleek

Duleek

REBELLION, 1790S

THE 1798 REBELLION ENTIRELY DISCREDITED THE SEMI-INDEPENDENT GOVERNMENT IN DUBLIN. THE ACT OF UNION WAS PASSED ON JANUARY 1, 1801, DESTROYING THE REBELLION, BUT THE FAILURE TO DELIVER CATHOLIC EMANCIPATION ENSURED THE CONTINUATION OF SECTARIAN DIVISIONS UNTIL IRELAND GAINED FULL INDEPENDENCE.

By the 1790s, Ireland was riven by sectarian loyalties driven by penal laws, which fueled political sentiments among Catholics. Armagh witnessed Catholic vigilantism, with the birth of the Catholic Defenders protecting Catholics against Protestant violence. A growing population increased land hunger. Meanwhile, some Protestants and Presbyterians enjoyed a more philosophical view about events. They looked to the American War of Independence and the French Revolution as inspirations behind a campaign to reform the representative system. They built an organization known as the United Irishmen in 1791, led by the charismatic Wolfe Tone. He visualized an Ireland where Catholics, Protestants, and dissenters unified and destroyed links with England. He also dreamed of complete Catholic emancipation.

Catholics were given the franchise in 1793, but this originated with Westminster rather than pressure from the United Irishmen. After war broke between England and Revolutionary France, the French sent an invasion force to Bantry Bay, but bad weather (December 1796) prevented a landing. Given a breathing space, the Protestant-controlled Irish Parliament armed paramilitary groups to coerce the United Irishmen with torture and bullying. Some rebels fought back but they were suppressed in Dublin, Meath, and Kildare while incurring heavy casualties (1798).

Elsewhere, County Wexford saw United Irishmen victorious in several large skirmishes, but an Ulster rising was crushed at Antrim and Ballynahinch. General Lake was reinforced by British troops and continued advancing in a concentric ark on Wexford. The insurgents' army was divided into

Opposite: William of Orange landed at Torbay, England in 1688, establishing the 'Glorious Revolution'. This would have profound effects on Ireland. In the following year William and his multi-ethnic protest army landed in Ireland, ready for battle.

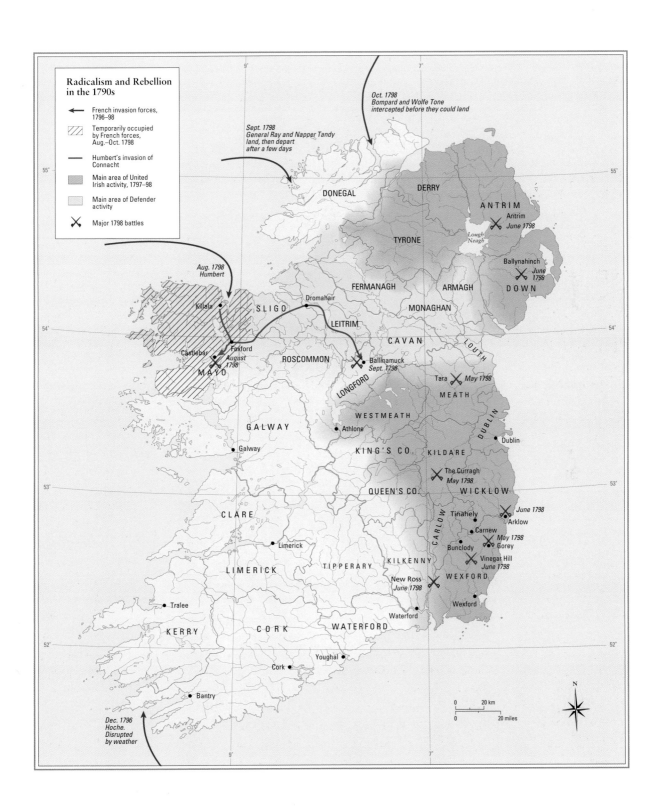

Radicalism and Rebellion in the 1790s

→ French invasion forces, 1796–98

▨ Temporarily occupied by French forces, Aug.–Oct. 1798

— Humbert's invasion of Connacht

■ Main area of United Irish activity, 1797–98

▨ Main area of Defender activity

✕ Major 1798 battles

Oct. 1798
Bompard and Wolfe Tone intercepted before they could land

Sept. 1798
General Ray and Napper Tandy land, then depart after a few days

DONEGAL

DERRY

ANTRIM
Antrim
June 1798

TYRONE

Lough Neagh

Ballynahinch
June 1798

DOWN

Aug. 1798
Humbert

FERMANAGH

ARMAGH

MONAGHAN

Killala

Dromahair

SLIGO

LEITRIM

CAVAN

LOUTH

Castlebar

Foxford
August 1798

Ballinamuck
Sept. 1798

Tara   May 1798

MEATH

MAYO

ROSCOMMON

LONGFORD

WESTMEATH

DUBLIN

GALWAY

Athlone

KING'S CO.

KILDARE

Dublin

Galway

QUEEN'S CO.

The Curragh
May 1798

WICKLOW

CLARE

CARLOW

Tinahely

June 1798
Arklow

Limerick

Carnew
May 1798

LIMERICK

TIPPERARY

KILKENNY

Bunclody

Gorey

Vinegar Hill
June 1798

New Ross
June 1798

WEXFORD

LIMERICK

Tralee

KERRY

CORK

WATERFORD

Waterford

Wexford

Youghal

Cork

Bantry

Dec. 1796
Hoche.
Disrupted by weather

0   20 km
0   20 miles

N

northern and southern armies, which failed to join up, and Lake's force confronted the northern army at Vinegar Hill (June 21, 1798). The British advanced, protected by hedges and fences, and brought light field artillery into play while facing some 15,000 United Irishmen. The insurgents were compressed on Vinegar Hill, an easy target for artillery. A British victory ensued and the Irish dispersed, several hundred falling to British cavalry. Total Irish casualties are unknown. Some went home while others were pursued by flying columns, which destroyed the last insurgent formation at Ballyboghil (14 July).

Some 1,000 French, commanded by Humbert, landed at Kilala in August 1798. They enjoyed a victory at Castlebar but failed to generate a rebellion in Connacht. He was chased by other British troops which brought him to bay at Ballinamuck on 8 September. The French troops were outmaneuvered and surrendered while their Irish allies were shot and rode down. Those that were captured were hanged. Another French incursion was attempted at Lough Swilly. Admiral Bompart left Brest with a squadron of ten vessels carrying 2,800 men and stores. They were attacked, losing seven ships captured. The victorious Admiral Warren found Wolfe Tone on a French vessel, but he cut his own throat before they were able to put him on trial for treason.

The British troops used in Ireland were a mixture of Irish militia battalions with Protestant officers and Catholic soldiers, Irish Protestant Yeomanry, Fencibles (a sort of home guard), and some regulars. In combination, they engaged in random butchery to the consternation of the English generals Cornwallis and Moore, thereby causing even more bitter resentment among Catholics.

The outcomes of the 1798 rebellion were a discredited Irish Parliament, and the rebels were proven to lack real unity. The Irish Catholic middle classes were striving to be heard and had failed in pushing the Westminster government into making wide-ranging reforms. The pressure on the land remained while rents and tithes increased and wages fell. Resentment remained among ordinary people because at least 20,000 had died in the rebellion, too many to be militia murders. Then came the 1801 Act of Union, which wrote out the Irish Parliament and failed to provide Catholic emancipation. Prime Minister Pitt of England was prevented from delivering this owing to pressure from Protestants in both kingdoms. The difficult struggle for emancipation was to continue under the leadership of Daniel O'Connell.

Irish Free State

THE NEW STATE REMAINED A BRITISH DOMINION AND
ATTEMPTED TO AUGMENT ITS POWERS OVER TIME. THE BRITISH
KING WAS "BY THE GRACE OF GOD, OF GREAT BRITAIN, OF
IRELAND, AND THE BRITISH DOMINIONS BEYOND THE SEAS KING,
DEFENDER OF THE FAITH, EMPEROR OF INDIA." HOWEVER, HIS
POWERS WERE EVENTUALLY GIVEN TO THE IRISH PRESIDENT.

T he nineteenth century witnessed variable fortunes for the Irish people. Roman Catholicism became stronger with a greater provision of priests and nuns. Churches were refurbished or built anew and growing wealth allowed the Church to take responsibility for schools, orphanages, hospitals, and other institutions, providing social cement and making religion an even more important part of national identity. However, economically, Ireland felt the competition of mechanized industry in England; it severely damaged cottage industries of spinning linen in Leinster,and parts of Connacht and Ulster. Industry in Ireland was very limited, impacting upon economic development.

Another feature of the nineteenth century was the growth of emigration. In 1841–45, some 65,000 Irish emigrated annually to the Americas, providing a total of nearly a million people between 1815 and 1845. Half a million migrants reached Britain, to work in the industrial sector or as seasonal migrants while approximately 65,000 were shipped to the penal settlement in Australia. So Ireland was exporting people and also produced an annual food surplus, which was also exported. However, a deadly import arrived in 1845 in the form of a fungal disease which infected the potato crop, the staple Irish food. The blight spread for four years ,causing malnutrition and starvation leading to the deaths of a million, which devastated the rural areas.

The famine incited Irish men and women to migrate, particularly women. The population entered a period of decline, with people moving to the cities of the American eastern seaboard. The population was also affected by the fall in the marriage rate, yet the birth rate remained above the European average. The

Opposite: Having prevailed in the Civil War, the Cumann na nGaedheal government embarked on a program to promote stability and growth in the new-born state.

The Anti-Treaty Vote in
the General Election 1923

- - - Proposed change of border

*Percentage of first-preference
votes for Sinn Féin (anti-Treaty)*

31 or over
21 to 30
14 to 20

0   20 km
0   20 miles

1 January 1923: establishment
   of Garda training camp
2 March 1924: army 'mutiny'
3 1926: establishment of state
   power company
4 May 1926: public launch of
   Fianna Fáil
5 July 1927: assassination of
   Kevin O'Higgins
6 August 1927: entry of Fianna Fáil
   into Dáil
7 Establishment of state
   broadcasting system: 1926 Dublin,
   1927 Cork, 1932 Athlone
8 July 1929: opening of Shannon
   hydroelectric scheme
9 1931: IRA Wolfe Tone commemoration
   prohibited

decline in people and migration was fueled by economic change, as land was no longer divided amongs all issue but was inherited by one person alone. Small-holdings were consolidated, leading to dairy farming, which caused agricultural workers to be cast off to seek work in cities or abroad. Subsistence farming turned into producing an agricultural surplus with the growth of commercial farming. The economy was aided by improvement in communication, allowing a surplus of goods to be exported internally or sold in Britain.

Politically, the Irish responded to the nineteenth century with a renaissance of nationalism. The Gaelic League tried to defend its language in the face of the increasing use of English while Young Ireland instigated a failed rebellion in 1848 in Tipperary. The Irish Republican Brotherhood, the Fenians, were another revolutionary group, who wanted to create an independent Irish republic. Their insurrection in 1867 failed but their bombings in mainland Britain highlighted the Irish issue, to be investigated by William Gladstone, the prime minister of Britain. In Parliament, Protestant Charles Stewart Parnell operated the Irish Parliamentary Party while in 1905 Sinn Féin was founded, with demands for independence. Gladstone attempted on two occasions to pass a Home Rule Bill, in 1885 and 1893, but was defeated by the Conservatives and the Unionists.

The Great War of 1914–18 prevented an act of Parliament from being implemented. However, several counties of Ulster were outside Ireland, these being counties with large Protestant populations. In Ulster, militants of a sectarian nature formed the Ulster Volunteer Force, which confronted the National Volunteers. The years of war witnessed the 1916 Easter Rising, led by radical nationalists in Dublin. Its failure was followed by a bloody aftermath, with Ireland under martial law and the execution of dissidents. Nationalism was strengthened by the rhetoric of Patrick Pearce, the failed leader, and by the execution of James Connolly, a wounded rebel who was shot tied to a chair. The Volunteer movement became designated the Irish Republican Army while Sinn Féin became extremely radical.

The IRA undertook a guerrilla war against the , who retaliated by using special militias known as the Black and Tans. The 1918 British election had seen Sinn Féin members elected to Parliament, but they refused to sit, instead forming their own assembly in Ireland. In December 1920, Ireland was partitioned, with six counties in Ulster remaining as British political divisions, but with the south being left to its own devices. On December 6, 1921, the 26 counties of the south became known as the Irish Free State, with the Dáil as its parliament, the country having dominion status, like Canada, and remaining within the British Commonwealth.

Éamon de Valera and his Sinn Féin did not accept the situation, and a civil war ensued with guerrilla warfare and the killings of leaders on both sides, including the charismatic Michael Collins. A ceasefire was made in 1923 and elections were held for the Dáil. In 1923, the Irish Free State joined the League of Nations and the 1931 British Statute of Westminster stated the British government would not overturn legislation passed in its dominions' legislatures. De Valera ended his boycott of the Dáil and entered it leading his new party, Fianna Fáil.

De Valera's work led to a new constitution in 1937, approved by referendum. A new state came into being, Éire. This term applied to all Ireland but common parlance saw it as an expression of the 26 counties. The country was ruled by a president as head ofs, *Uachtarán na hÉireann*, with the prime minister known as *An Taoiseach*.

DUBLIN TODAY

VOTED THE FRIENDLIEST CITY IN EUROPE, DUBLIN IS A MODERN,
THRIVING MULTI-CULTURAL CITY, FULL OF HISTORICAL
ARCHITECTURE AND HOME TO WRITERS AND ARTISTS OF
INTERNATIONAL STANDING AS WELL AS MAJOR INTERNATIONAL
CORPORATIONS, FINANCIAL SERVICES, AND BANKING.

Home to famous literary figures, persecuted religious minorities, and a now multicultural society, Dublin (*Baile Átha Cliath*, Town of the Ford of the Hurdles) is a thriving contemporary city basing its economy on service industries and tourism. The city possesses a rich history which has left its mark, particularly in its educational buildings and the Georgian town houses, such as those in Merrion and Fitzwilliam Squares.

Dublin is a partial enigma. Developed during the Protestant Ascendancy, the city reigned over persecuted, disenfranchised Roman Catholics for years. Yet two persecuted religious minorities found a refuge and home there. When Louis XIV of France revoked the Edict of Nantes (1685), ushering in the attempted forced conversion of a million Protestant Huguenots, some 200,000 fled France. They sought sanctuary in Protestant countries but others joined their religious kin in Dublin, which had received French Protestants since 1630. These skilled foreigners boosted the local economy, as they did everywhere they settled in Europe, being noted for their textile weaving and design and their gold and silver smithing. The Huguenots' increasing wealth helped finance Dublin's architectural magnificence and contributed to its commercial expansion. The second persecuted migrants were Jews, arriving from Spain and Portugal in the eighteenth century, followed by a relative flood in the late nineteenth century after the Russian pogroms. Most Jews became members of the professional middle classes and now number nearly two thousand, with several prominent in politics. Today, many members of the European Union have sought employment in Dublin, including some 50,000 Poles. Multiculturalism can also be observed in the range of cuisines offered by restaurants, from traditional to Indian and Thai food, and the Dun Laoghaire festival of world cultures.

Dublin hosts many institutions of higher education, symbolizing the rich cultural life of the city, particularly its literary activities. Found there are University College, Dublin City University, Dublin Institute of Technology, and the world-renowned Trinity College, founded by Queen Elizabeth I and custodian of the *Book of Kells*. Trinity alumni have included Jonathan Swift, Oliver Goldsmith, Oscar Wilde, and Samuel Becket. Edmund Burke, educated at Trinity, so criticized the French Revolution that his ideas and political philosophy became the rock upon which British political conservatism has been built. The city houses several internationally famed libraries as well as a series of museums. These include the Natural History Museum, the James Joyce Museum, the Irish-Jewish Museum, and the Bram Stoker Dracula Experience. The classic cultural experience is rounded off by the various art galleries.

Ireland has traditionally been a land of scholastic achievement, as evidenced by the Celtic Church's golden age. More recently, Dublin has given birth to numerous writers, playwrights, and poets.George Bernard Shaw, at one time a Fabian socialist, was arguably the best playwright since Shakespeare, with his *Pygmalion* being turned into the stage play and film, *My Fair Lady*. W.B. Yeats, a brilliant poet, is known for his peculiar mysticism and his brief dalliance with the dream of a new fascist reality. The list goes on, with Brendan Behan and the more recent prolific woman writer, Maeve Binchy.

Modern Ireland: a view over the River Liffey, with the Four Courts in the background. Dublin is now a thriving capital city and a popular tourist destination. Crowds are attracted to the city's rich history, impressive cultural life, and the lively nightlife.

WALES AND SCOTLAND

ENGLAND'S NEIGHBORS SUFFERED FROM THE NORMAN CONQUERORS, WHO SOUGHT TO EXPLOIT THE MILITARY POTENTIAL OF ENGLAND. ENDLESS WARFARE ENSUED OWING TO ENGLAND'S MUCH LARGER POPULATION, EXCEPT WHEN ANARCHY PREVAILED DURING THE CIVIL WAR BETWEEN STEPHEN AND MATILDA.

Norman relations with Scotland fluctuated between violence and friendship. English and Norman influence penetrated Scotland by stealth. Malcolm III's second wife was Margaret, the sister of Edgar Atheling; three of her six sons ascended the Scots throne. After Malcom III was succeeded by his brother Donald Ban, Margaret's son, Edgar, ousted him with the aid of a Norman army. The development of the Scottish Church by David I saw the growth of territorial dioceses, grants of land to new religious orders, including the Cistercians, Tironensians, and Premonstratensians whose mother houses were in France, and the abbots and bishops bore Norman names, although these tended to disappear in the next century.

Compared with Scotland, Norman relationships with Wales were turbulent. Wales had been an anarchic mass of petty kingdom but by the time of the Conquest, four major kingdoms emerged: Gwynedd in the northwest, Powys in the northeast, Deheubarth (Dyfed) in the southwest and Glywysing (Morgannwg) in the south. The size and influence of these kingdoms changed over time but these four were the core leaders of Welsh resistance. After Gruffudd ap Llywelyn became the first ruler of all Wales using Viking and English mercenaries, an English army was despatched to Wales, defeating and killing Gruffud in 1063. Thereafter, north Welsh kings were appointed by the English, then the Normans, although the nature of the overlordship was scarcely defined. Norman control rested in the lowlands. The resilience of the Welsh princes, the mountainous terrain suited to guerrilla warfare, and the Welsh longbow prevented any rapid conquest. By the end of the twelfth century, the Normans were resident in south Wales, taking tribute from the local populations but also bringing English and Norman settlers into the south in Glamorgan, Gwent, the Gower peninsula, and Pembroke.

Opposite: After consolidating their hold on England, the Normans looked for new opportunities. This led to the establishment of military lordships on the eastern border of Wales and into south Wales itself. In Scotland, Norman lords were invited to establish "modern" lordships, largely in the Scottish lowlands.

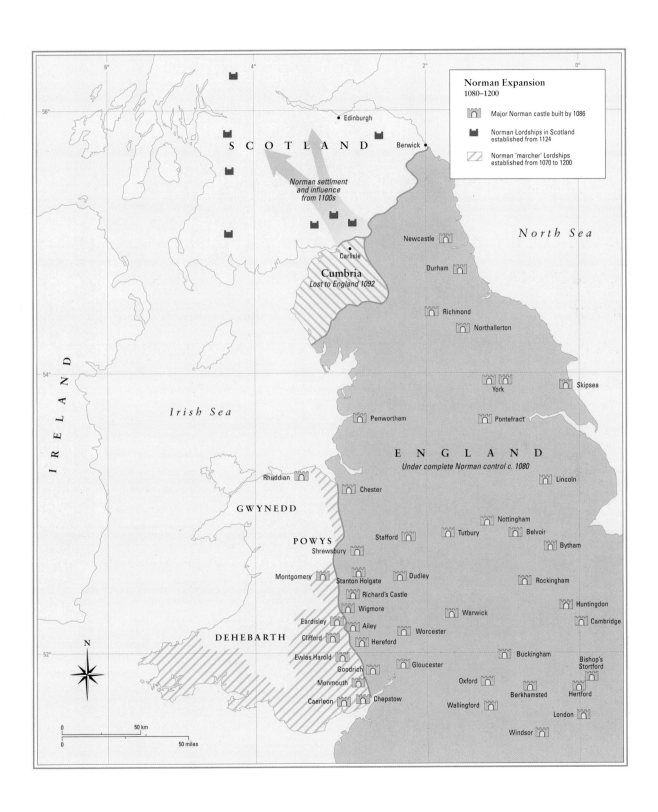

Norman Expansion
1080–1200

Major Norman castle built by 1086

Norman Lordships in Scotland
established from 1124

Norman 'marcher' Lordships
established from 1070 to 1200

6° 4° 2° 0°

56°

• Edinburgh

SCOTLAND Berwick •

North Sea

Norman settlment
and influence
from 1100s

• Carlisle

Cumbria
Lost to England 1092

Newcastle

Durham

Richmond

Northallerton

54°

Irish Sea

York   Skipsea

Penwortham   Pontefract

E N G L A N D
Under complete Norman control c. 1080

I R E L A N D

Rhuddian   Chester   Lincoln

GWYNEDD

Nottingham

POWYS   Stafford   Tutbury   Belvoir
Shrewsbury

Montgomery   Stanton Holgate   Dudley   Rockingham   Bytham

Richard's Castle

Wigmore   Warwick   Huntingdon

Eardisley   Ailey   Worcester   Cambridge

52°   Clifford   Hereford

DEHEBARTH   Ewlas Harold   Buckingham   Bishop's
                Goodrich   Gloucester   Stortford

N   Monmouth   Oxford   Berkhamsted   Hertford

Caerleon   Chepstow   Wallingford   London

Windsor

0   50 km

0   50 miles

CELTIC SCOTLAND

AETHELFRITH OF BERNICIA CUT TO PIECES THE ARMY OF AEDAN
MAC GABHRAN, FIRST KING OF THE IRISH SCOTS OF DALRIADA, AT
DEGSASTAN (603). THIS ACTION STOPPED ALL FURTHER DALRIADAN
ATTEMPTS AT WAR AGAINST THE ENGLISH, LEAVING AETHELFRITH
OF NORTHUMBRIA OVER-KING.

The Gaelic Irish colonizers from Dál Riada in Antrim were the driving force in unifying the different Gaelic speakers of Scotland. The earliest native inhabitants of Britain north of the Clyde-Forth diagonal line were the Picts, whom the Irish Scotti displaced in Argyll, Arran, and Bute. The Scotti split into three separate tribes in these coastal regions. The colonizers brought Christian missionaries with their families and fighters. The Picts were eventually converted and gradually absorbed Scottish influences in art and sculpture. Scotland, south of the Clyde-Forth diagonal, was home to the British kingdoms of Strathclyde and the Gododdin of Lothian, heirs of the Votadini. Southern Lothian came under attack from the Angles of Berenicia and was absorbed into Northumbria. Despite being defeated, the Angles held Lothian until the ninth century, allowing their language to permeate the area. The Forth continued to be the border between the Picts and the Angles.

A balance of power was established between the Scots, Picts, British, and English by the eighth century, and then the Vikings arrived. By the mid-ninth century, Scandinavian colonists had occupied the Orkneys, Shetlands, Caithness, Sutherland, and the west coast down to Islay. Large numbers of Norse colonizers inter-married with local women producing a Gallo-Norse population, especially in Orkney and Caithness, which were considered in the Icelandic sagas to be part of Scandinavia. While the Danes were causing chaos in England, the mac Alpines expanded into Lothian, Strathclyde, and Cumbria. By 1018, after Malcolm mac Alpine defeated the Northumbrians and pushed the Scottish border to the Tweed, Scotland was divided into several political entities. The Norse occupied the Hebrides and west coast islands down into Galloway, the Scots created a kingdom across central Scotland, and Moray was run by a separate dynasty, its most memorable king being Macbeth.

Scotland, as it would eventually be called, was a meeting of Geals, Picts, Britons, and Angles. Celtic Gaelic would become the speech of the highlands and islands. English or the Scots dialect of it would become the speech of the lowlands, east, and borders. It was brought into the country by Germanic Angles of the southeast.

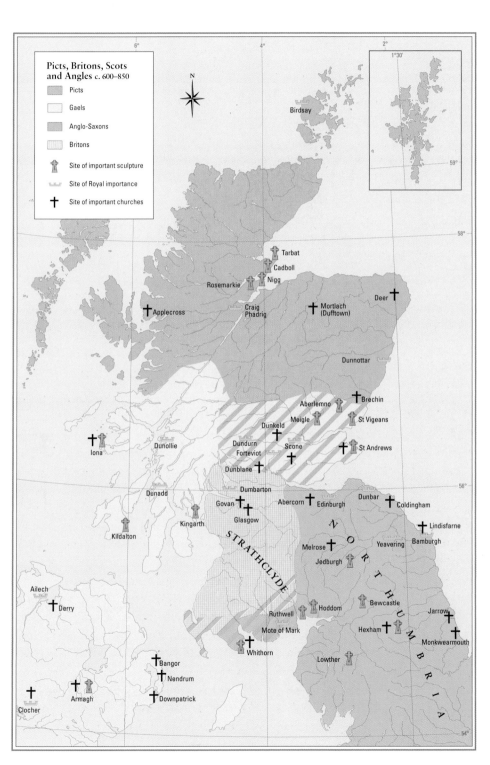

Picts, Britons, Scots and Angles c. 600–850

- Picts
- Gaels
- Anglo-Saxons
- Britons
- Site of important sculpture
- Site of Royal importance
- Site of important churches

N

1°30'

59°

58°

Birdsay

Tarbat
Cadboll
Nigg
Rosemarkie

Deer

Applecross

Craig
Phadrig

Mortlach
(Dufftown)

Dunnottar

Aberlemno
Meigle
Brechin
St Vigeans

Dunkeld

Iona

Dunollie

Dundurn
Forteviot
Scone
St Andrews

Dunblane

Dunadd

Dumbarton

Govan
Glasgow

Abercorn
Edinburgh

Dunbar
Coldingham

Kingarth

Kildalton

STRATHCLYDE

Lindisfarne
Bamburgh

Melrose

N O R T H U M B R I A

Yeavering

Jedburgh

Ailech

Derry

Hoddom
Ruthwell

Bewcastle

Jarrow

Mote of Mark

Hexham

Monkwearmouth

Whithorn

Lowther

Bangor
Nendrum

Clocher
Armagh
Downpatrick

6°

4°

2°

56°

54°

SCOTLAND'S WARS WITH ENGLAND

KING EDWARD I OF ENGLAND DISPLAYED GREAT AMBITION IN SEEKING TO UNIFY BRITAIN BY INTERFERING IN THE AFFAIRS OF SCOTLAND AND WALES, LEAVING BOTH COUNTRIES DEVASTATED, ESPECIALLY THE SCOTS BORDERS.

The years following the creation of Scotland saw a consolidation of kingship, although son did not necessarily follow father. Various cultures vied with each other in court: Celtic, Norse, and Norman. In 1286, Alexander III of Scotland died, leaving Margaret, the Maid of Norway, as his heir. Edward I of England desired this queen of Scotland to marry his son, Edward of Caernarvon, but the premature death of Margaret destroyed this notion of a peaceful and prosperous union. The competitors for the throne all swore an oath of fealty to Edward, who selected John Balliol from their midst to be King. This futile man became Edward's puppet, whose task was to turn Scotland into a client state serving England's interests. Eventually, Balliol tired of this humiliation and renounced his fealty. Edward stormed north and captured Berwick-on-Tweed. A war of independence soon broke out because 1297 witnessed an insurrection throughout Scotland except Lothian. William Wallace killed the entire English garrison at Lanark and soon became the leader of a small, mobile strike force which roamed the country attacking isolated outposts. English officials were kidnapped and the tax collectors found their task impossible. Hostilities culminated in the battle of Falkirk (1298), which Edward won. Edward advanced into Scotland, burning and killing as he went, so that many Scots lords sought peace terms. Wallace became isolated, eventually being betrayed in 1305. He was hanged, drawn, and quartered, his head being impaled in London with the rest of his body being distributed between Perth, Berwick, Stirling, and Newcastle. Scots politics were soon turned inside out. Exiled King John, Balliol's chief supporter, John Comyn of Badenoch, Red Comyn, was murdered by Robert the Bruce, Earl of Carrick. Balliol's supporters, hitherto Scots patriots, turned against Bruce by joining the English, whereas Bruce, who had helped the English hunt down Wallace, became the icon of the fight for Scots independence.

Opposite: Scotland's wars with England always involved the smaller states struggling with the expansionist desires of the more powerful England.

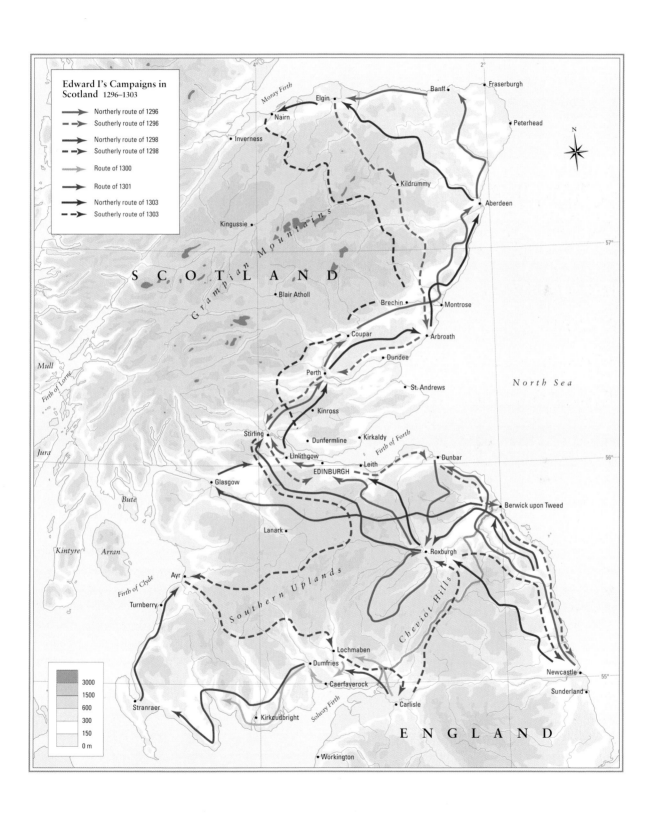

Edward I's Campaigns in
Scotland 1296–1303

→ Northerly route of 1296
⇢ Southerly route of 1296
→ Northerly route of 1298
⇢ Southerly route of 1298
→ Route of 1300
→ Route of 1301
→ Northerly route of 1303
⇢ Southerly route of 1303

Bannockburn and Robert the Bruce

The English defeat saw serious losses among knights and squires. Over 500 English elite soldiers were ransomed.

Robert the Bruce was crowned king of Scotland in March 1306. Meanwhile, Edward I had died in July 1307, leaving the throne to his lazy, shiftless son, Edward II. At this point, Scots castles were still mainly in English hands, and a determined English campaign could have unseated Bruce, who was still opposed by many Scots. Edward II vacillated, allowing Robert and his brother to win the southwest, leaving only a few castles in English control. By the end of 1308, Bruce ruled most of Scotland. Bruce now raided England, savaging Coquetdale and Redesdale, even threatening Durham. The Northumbrians paid Bruce £2,000 not to damage their county further. In 1313, raids surged into Tyndale, Durham was marauded, and Hartlepool looted. This time, Bruce was given £10,000 to leave. Elsewhere, Dundee Castle was taken and all the English castles in the southwest. However, the key castle at Stirling remained under the command of English Sir Thomas Mowbray, who promised to surrender the castle if he was not relieved by June 1314.

Edward II was now stirred into activity, deploying a large invasion force which marched virtually unopposed from Wark to Stirling, where Bruce was waiting. The Scots comprised some 5,000 men in pike-carrying schiltrons with a few archers and 500 cavalry. Thousands of poorly armed peasants waited nearby to help out if the Scots were to win the battle. In the fighting that ensued the English suffered heavy losses. The Bruce now launched raids into England, incinerating Appleby and Durham and looting Hartlepool again. Many other towns suffered in his path of destruction. In September 1327, Edward II was murdered at Berkely Castle, the crown being taken by the young Edward III. He wished to stop the constant destruction in the north of England and recognized Robert the Bruce as the king of Scotland. On March 1, 1323, the thirteen year truce was agreed. In 1329, Robert died of leprosy.

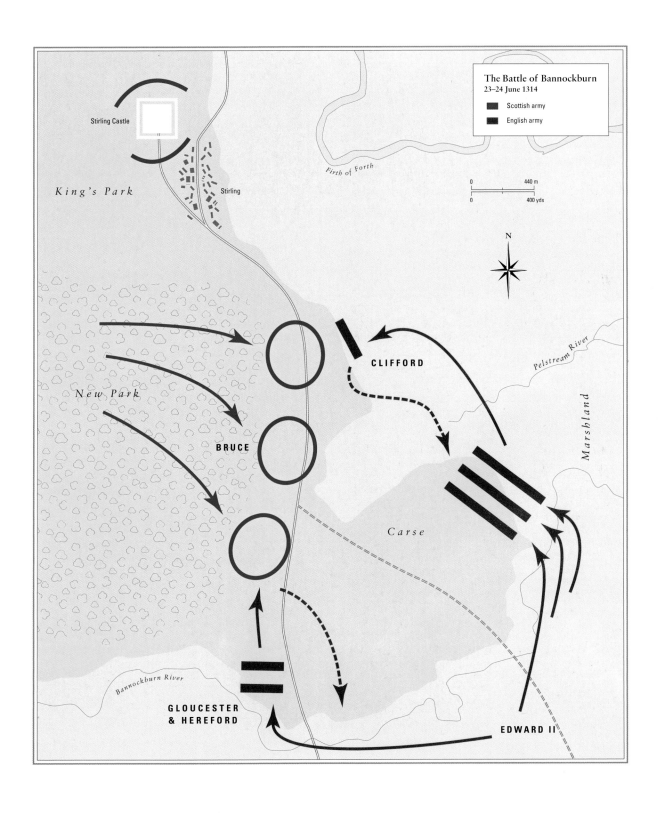

Stirling Castle

King's Park

Stirling

Firth of Forth

The Battle of Bannockburn
23–24 June 1314

Scottish army

English army

0   440 m

0   400 yds

N

CLIFFORD

Pelstream River

New Park

Marshland

BRUCE

Carse

Bannockburn River

GLOUCESTER
& HEREFORD

EDWARD II

NEVILLE'S CROSS

THE NEW ENGLISH TACTIC OF MIXING ARCHERS AND MEN-AT-ARMS CAUSED THE SLAUGHTER OF UNARMORED CLANSMEN AND THE CAPTURE OF KING DAVID II. THE HARDY SCOTS, HOWEVER, CONTINUED TO FIGHT UNTIL A TRUCE WAS MADE IN 1356.

Opposite: At the Battle of Neville's Cross, both armies arranged themselves in three lines of battle, both adopting a defensive posture. This stalemate, which favored the outnumbered English, lasted until the afternoon, when English longbowmen stepped forward and opened fire, forcing the Scots to attack. The Scottish army's inferior position resulted in their formations becoming disorganized as they advanced. This allowed the outnumbered English to deal more easily with the Scottish attack. It became clear that the battle was not going well for the Scots, and two key commanders fled the field, leaving King David II to face the English alone. He was captured in the late afternoon as the rest of his army fled.

During the Hundred Years' War, King Philip VI of France was apprehensive that King Edward III of England would break the Truce of Malestroit and resume hostilities. The Frenchman appealed for Scots aid in invading northern England to take pressure off France, which awaited an attack in unprepared northern France. In 1346, the English mustered their forces in southern England prior to crossing the Channel. In October 1346, King David II of Scotland marched south across the Tweed with some 12,000 men. The Scots targets were Durham and Yorkshire, the first being reached on October 16, when the Scots made camp at Beaurepaire.

The Scots attack had been anticipated by Edward III, who had excluded the northern Border lords from his invasion muster. A heavy mist obscured the English advance, which bumped into the Scots unit. This armored surprise left 250 Scots dead while the English occupied a narrow ridge near Neville's Cross near Durham. The battle was described thus in the Lanerost Chronicle: William Zouche, the fighting prelate of York "ordered that no man should spare a Scot and he himself rode against them with such a staff (mace) that without confession he absolved many Scots of all future trouble in this world. Then amid the blare of trumpets, the clash of sword on shield, the hurtling of arrows, you might hear the wailing of the wounded. Arms were broken, heads shattered, many lay dead upon the field." The Scots had not learned the lessons of Dupplin Moor and the Battle of Halidon Hill. A brave charge was no match for the mixed force of archers and knights. Kind David was captured and languished in the Tower of London.

Neville's Cross severely weakened Scots independence, and losses in battle included the leading officers of state. That Edward III was distracted by affairs in France meant that Scotland became less important and survived. Another distraction for Europe was the Black Death.

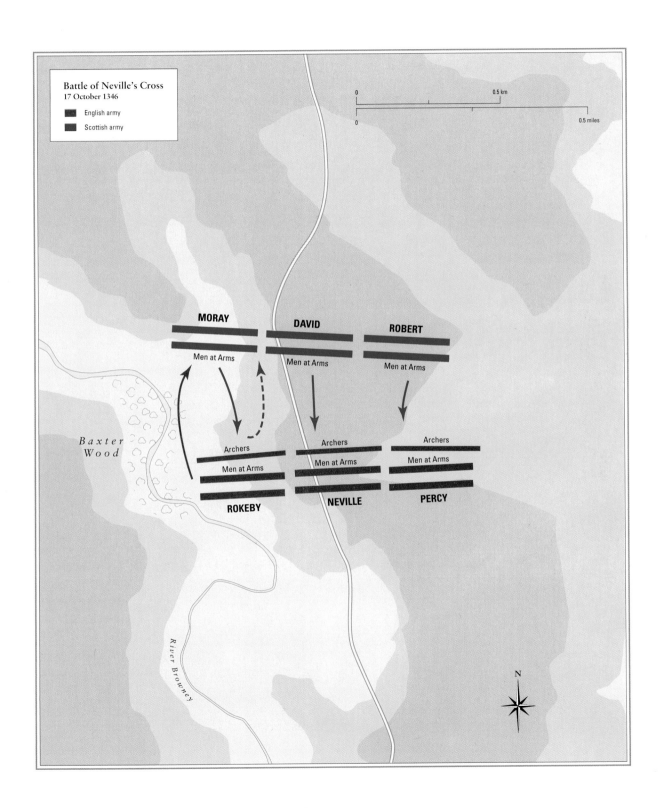

Battle of Neville's Cross
17 October 1346

English army
Scottish army

MORAY

DAVID

ROBERT

Men at Arms

Men at Arms

Men at Arms

Baxter
Wood

Archers

Archers

Archers

Men at Arms

Men at Arms

Men at Arms

ROKEBY

NEVILLE

PERCY

River Browney

N

STEWART RULE

THE SCOTS ENDED THE WAR OF INDEPENDENCE BY DEFEATING
HENRY PERCY'S ARMY BUT THEIR LEADER DOUGLAS MET THREE
SPEARS SIMULTANEOUSLY. "... THE ONE STRUCK HIM ON THE
SHOULDER, ANOTHER ON THE BREAST AND THE STROKE GLINTED
DOWN TO HIS BELLY, AND THE THIRD STRUCK HIM IN THE
THIGH." *FROISSART IN BRITAIN*, P. 148

D avid II's eleven years in captivity allowed Robert the Stewart to keep burning the fires of independence; and the king was released in 1357. The death of Edward III (1377) provided Scotland with an occasion to cease paying David's ransom and for eradicating English garrisons still holding Lochmaben and Teviotdale. The new English king, Richard II, was so involved in domestic and international affairs that the Scots invaded the north of England, defeating an English army led by Henry Percy at Otterburn (1388). The resulting truce lasted until the death of Richard II (1400).

Meanwhile, David's death in 1371 passed the crown to Robert II (1371-90), son of Robert I's daughter, Marjory. Neither he nor his son, Robert III (1390-1406), were strong kings, and considerable political instability occurred in wrangles with the great nobility. The latter sent his son, James, for safety to France. He feared for his life, potentially threatened by his dissident younger brother, Robert, Duke of Albany. However, James was captured at sea in 1406 and returned, ransomed, to Scotland in 1424.

James I (1406-37) sought to reduce the Albany's power and that of the Douglas family. Accordingly, Murdac of Albany was executed, which subdued other lords. Domestically, James attempted to instigate an English-style parliament but failed to elevate Scotland out of its traditional feudal court. However, he did manage to establish the University of St. Andrews in 1414, a training ground for a clergy which could be used in the state bureaucracy. In 1437, James was murdered by Walter Stewart in thr Earl of Atholl's plot to grab the throne. He and other conspirators were executed.

Now Scotland entered a period when all king's commenced their reign as a minor, which left them

Opposite: The Stewart's great struggle in state building was that Scotland itself was barely a state. Powerful lords ruled in the highlands and islands, in the south equally independent powerful border lords controlled the frontier with England. Both these power centers eyed the new Stewart hierarchy with circumspection.

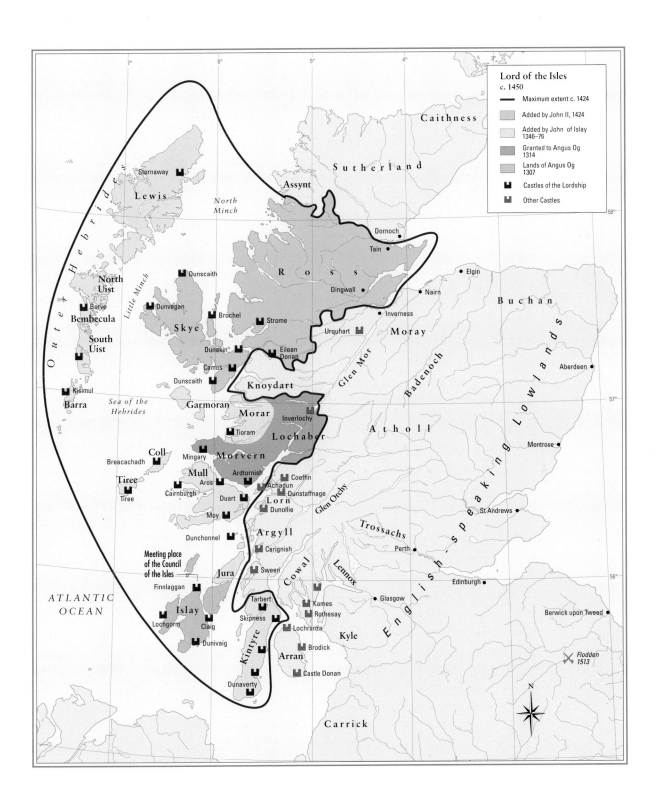

Lord of the Isles
c. 1450

—— Maximum extent c. 1424

Added by John II, 1424

Added by John of Islay 1346–76

Granted to Angus Og 1314

Lands of Angus Og 1307

Castles of the Lordship

Other Castles

Caithness

Sutherland

Assynt

Lewis

North Minch

Stornaway

Dornoch

Tain

R o s s

Elgin

Dingwall

Nairn

Dunscaith

North Uist

Borve

Dunvegan

Little Minch

Brochel

Skye

Strome

Inverness

Urquhart

Moray

Buchan

Badenoch

Glen Mor

Bembecula

South Uist

Dunakin

Camus

Eilean Donan

Dunscaith

Knoydart

Kisimul

Barra

Sea of the Hebrides

Garmoran

Morar

Inverlochy

Aberdeen

Atholl

Tioram

Lochaber

Coll

Breacachadh

Mingary

Morvern

Ardtornish

Coeffin

Montrose

Tiree

Tiree

Mull

Aros

Cairnburgh

Duart

Achadun

Dunstaffnage

Lorn

Dunollie

Glen Orchy

St Andrews

Moy

Dunchonnel

Argyll

Trossachs

Perth

Meeting place of the Council of the Isles

Carignish

Cowal

Lennox

Finnlaggan

Jura

Sween

Edinburgh

ATLANTIC OCEAN

Islay

Lochgorm

Claig

Tarbert

Skipness

Kames

Rothesay

Glasgow

Berwick upon Tweed

Lochranza

Kyle

Dunivaig

Kintyre

Brodick

Arran

Flodden 1513

Dunaverty

Castle Donan

Carrick

E n g l i s h   s p e a k i n g   L o w l a n d s

O u t e r   H e b r i d e s

N

at the mercy of lords competing for power, such as the Chrichton and Livingstone families, who sought to control James II (1437-60). He continued his father's work against the nobility, personally stabbing to death the 8th Earl of Douglas and attainting the lands of the 9th earl. The year1451 saw the foundation of the University of Glasgow, but the king could not carry out many policies because he was killed by an exploding cannon while besieging Roxburgh Castle, a fortress still in English hands. James III (1460-88) expanded Scotland's borders, to absorb the Orkneys and Shetlands and to seriously curb the power of the Lord of the Isles. He had married Margaret, daughter of the King of Norway and Denmark, and she brought the islands as a pledge for her dowry. When the money failed to arrive, James foreclosed on the debt. However, this king, too, was murdered, maybe because he attempted good relations with England ,thereby upsetting the militantly patriotic nobles. His son, the Duke of Rothesay, led rebels against the King at Sauchieburn. The King fled, fell off his horse, and was borne unconscious to a watermill, where an un-named person stabbed him.

To picture fifteenth-century Scotland as a violent and dangerous place would be incorrect. Monasteries, cathedrals, and colleges were built and the economy was expanding. Literature flourished in Latin and Scots but also in Gaelic. Edinburgh was increasingly used as a capital. These developments continued into the reigns of the next two kings with the writings of Robert Henryson and William Dunbar.

James IV (1488-1513) fell foul of a dangerous international situation. In 1513, King Henry VIII of England invaded France, and James determined to help his ally by invading England. With French finance and munitions, James engaged an English army at Flodden (September 9, 1513). The English victory, proving the superiority of bill over pike, was a terrible tragedy for the Scots. Some 10–12,000 were killed, including their king, several earls, and the French ambassador. The lament, *Flowers of the Forest,* captures the memory of the losses that day. James V (1413-42) was only two when he became king, which led to another period of strife between competing lords who shared different views of foreign policy, whether pro-English or pro-French. His sad experiences, the loss of all his baby sons, and a minor defeat by the English at Solway Moss, together with the death of his first wife, the daughter of the King of France, may have contributed to his death. He left an heir in Mary Queen of Scots, daughter of Mary of Guise, his second wife. By the Treaty of Greenwich (1543), Queen Mary (1542-67) was to marry Edward, son of Henry VIII. The Scots refused to hand over the baby to England whose raids became severe in retaliation. Scotland was defeated at Pinkie (September 1547), causing the Scots to send Mary to France. French troops helped expel the English but gained a hold over the country while Mary married the French dauphin in 1558. Returning to Scotland on her husband's death (1561), Mary went through a series of husbands, bore a son, was forced to abdicate, and fled to England (1568), where she was held under arrest until she was executed by Queen Elizabeth in 1587. During this period, Protestantism and the preaching of John Knox split Scotland into two religions, and in 1560 the Scots parliament broke with Rome.

James VI (1567-1625) steered a clever passage between religious reform and the Church, but finally ratified the break with the Pope and acknowledged the new church with its synods and General Assembly. Parliament became more democratic and the legal system ran evenly, although local justice remained in the hands of landowners. In 1603, Queen Elizabeth I died and, as her legal heir, James became James I of England in a personal union of two crowns.

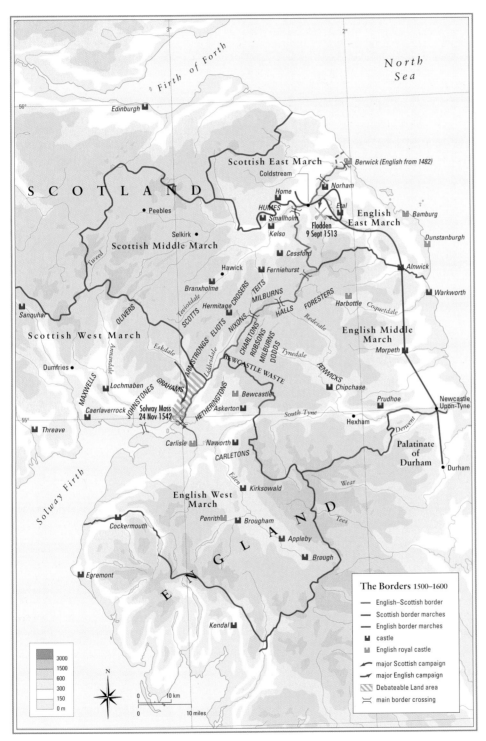

The Scottish border country in some ways was similar to the Highlands and was dominated by fiercely independent-minded border lords. Controlling them and gaining ascendancy over them, was a key requirement for the new Stewart kings.

Firth of Forth

North Sea

56°

Edinburgh

S C O T L A N D

3°

2°

Scottish East March

Coldstream

Berwick (English from 1482)

Norham

Home

• Peebles

HUMES

Smallholm

Kelso

Etal

English East March

Bamburg

Flodden
9 Sept 1513

Dunstanburgh

Selkirk •

Scottish Middle March

Cessford

Hawick •

Ferniehurst

Alnwick

Branxholme

Hermitage

TEITS

CROSERS

MILBURNS

Warkworth

Tweed

Teviotdale

SCOTTS

ELIOTS

NIXONS

HALLS

FORESTERS

Harbottle *Coquetdale*

English Middle March

OLIVERS

Sanquhar

Scottish West March

Eskdale

ARMSTRONGS

Liddesdale

CHARLTONS

ROBSONS

MILBURNS

DODDS

Redesale

Tynedale

Morpeth

Dumfries •

BEWCASTLE WASTE

FENWICKS

Chipchase

55°

Lochmaben

MAXWELLS

JOHNSTONES

GRAHAMS

HETHERINGTONS

Askerton

Bewcastle

Prudhoe

Newcastle Upon-Tyne

Caerlaverrock

Solway Moss
24 Nov 1542

South Tyne

Hexham

Derwent

Threave

Carlisle

Naworth

Palatinate of Durham

CARLETONS

Eden

Wear

Durham

Kirksowald

English West March

Tees

Cockermouth

Penrith

Brougham

Solway Firth

E N G L A N D

Appleby

Brough

Egremont

Kendal

The Borders 1500–1600

— English–Scottish border
— Scottish border marches
— English border marches
🏰 castle
🏰 English royal castle
⚔ major Scottish campaign
⚔ major English campaign
▨ Debateable Land area
⋈ main border crossing

3000
1500
600
300
150
0 m

N

0 ___ 10 km

0 ___ 10 miles

SCOTLAND AND THE CIVIL WAR

THE MARQUESS OF MONTROSE COMMENCED A YEAR OF VICTORIES IN 1644. USING IRISH INFANTRY, HIGHLANDERS, AND LORD GORDON'S CAVALRY, HE ENJOYED SUCCESS AS AT KILSYTH (1645). HIS CAMPAIGNS FAILED TO PREVENT THE SCOTS ARMY WINNING THE WAR FOR PARLIAMENT AT MARSTON MOOR.

Charles I was crowned in Scotland in 1633 using an Anglican service, which upset the Kirk. His attempt to force a new liturgy and set of church rules by decree caused many of the Scots aristocracy to confront Charles by establishing a provisional government and signing a National Covenant (1638). To bring these recalcitrant lords to heel, Charles planned a three-pronged strategy to win over Scotland. He would invade Scotland from the south while the Marquis of Hamilton landed on the east coast. Elsewhere, the Earl of Antrim would land his Irish soldiers on the west coast. The whole plan collapsed. The Scots invaded England, brushed aside an English force at Newburn, and occupied Newcastle. One Covenanter officer, the Earl of Montrose, changed sides, joining King Charles. Montrose ran circles around the opposition, making a series of successful raids: He was joined by Lord Gordon, a renegade Covenanter who brought him regular infantry and cavalry. When the last Covenanter army in Scotland was broken, Montrose was temporarily in control of Scotland.

Glasgow was occupied by the royalists, and Montrose called a Parliament. Montrose's victories kept alive Royalist morale in England, causing King Charles to want to join him after the defeat at the battle of Naseby. However, Montrose was suffering from desertion, and David Leslie with his Scots army in England was pursuing the King north from Naseby. The superiority in Leslie's numbers and cavalry allowed an outflanking movement which defeated Montrose's men. Montrose had lost considerable numbers of men but, more importantly, he no longer appeared invincible. He took his remaining men into the Highlands to wage guerrilla warfare. Montrose continued his campaign and was defeated by Colonel Strachan at Carbisdale in April 1650. On the run, he was betrayed and carted through the streets of Edinburgh. He was hung, drawn, and quartered on May 21, 1650 at Mercat Cross.

Opposite: The civil wars in Scotland (1639-50) began as a result of Charles I's alienation of the ruling elite. The Scots gentry decided against royal authority, signing the "National Covenant" in 1638.

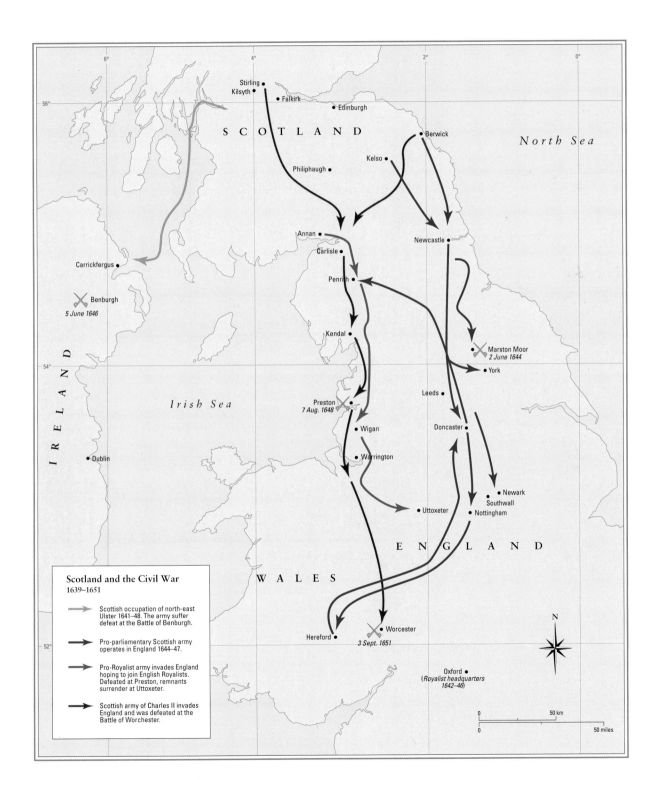

N

Scotland and the Civil War
1639–1651

➤ Scottish occupation of north-east
Ulster 1641–48. The army suffer
defeat at the Battle of Benburgh.

➤ Pro-parliamentary Scottish army
operates in England 1644–47.

➤ Pro-Royalist army invades England
hoping to join English Royalists.
Defeated at Preston, remnants
surrender at Uttoxeter.

➤ Scottish army of Charles II invades
England and was defeated at the
Battle of Worcester.

Stirling
Kilsyth
Falkirk
Edinburgh
S C O T L A N D
Berwick
North Sea
Kelso
Philiphaugh
Annan
Newcastle
Carrickfergus
Carlisle
Benburgh
5 June 1646
Penrith
Kendal
Marston Moor
2 June 1644
York
I R E L A N D
Irish Sea
Leeds
Preston
7 Aug. 1648
Wigan
Doncaster
Warrington
Dublin
Newark
Southwall
Uttoxeter
Nottingham
E N G L A N D
W A L E S
Hereford
Worcester
3 Sept. 1651
Oxford
(Royalist headquarters
1642–46)

0   50 km
0   50 miles

CROMWELL AND SCOTLAND

AFTER LESLIE'S SCOTS WERE DEFEATED AT DUNBAR WITH 3,000
DEAD AND 10,000 CAPTURED, A SCOTS PREACHER COMPLAINED
THAT CROMWELL WAS WORSE THAN THE DEVIL: "FOR THE
SCRIPTURE SAID, RESIST THE DEVIL AND HE WILL FLIE FROM YOU
— BUT RESIST OLIVER AND HE WILL FLIE IN YOUR FACE."

The execution of Charles I had tremendous repercussions in Scotland, which objected to the English killing the Scots king. Accordingly, angry Scots nationalist Kirkmen pronounced Charles II King in February 1649. After Montrose was crushed, the king agreed to Presbyterian conditions and constraints and signed the Covenant, while the Scots mustered an army of 5,440 cavalry and 13,400 foot. To counter this peculiar alliance between the monarch and its former ally, the English Council of State assembled an army of 16,000 soldiers at Newcastle, commanded by Oliver Cromwell.

The Scots responded by pursuing a scorched earth policy in the lowlands. The English army slogged its way by the eastern route to the Scots' capital but realized that combat against entrenchments, peat-bogs, and stone walls would disrupt the troops and incur large losses. English morale was low. The Scots came down from the hills at Dunbar, but were taken in the flank by a cavalry charge. The Scots suffered a few hundred killed, with a 1,000 wounded and 5,000 being made prisoners, and marched south. After more skirmishes, the Scots were left with two alternatives: either continue the conflict in Fife or invade England and draw Cromwell away from Scotland. Charles II attempted a Royalist uprising in England but the Royalists were doomed to failure. He fled and made his way abroad to France, leaving Scotland to the mercies of the English. Many Scots prisoners were subsequently killed by disease while a multitude ended as forced labor in the sugar fields of Barbados. The war in Scotland ended with the sack of Dundee. The country was placed under military occupation, with outposts sealing off the Highlands. Cromwell's government in Scotland brought in judges less susceptible to corruption by letting off suspected family members and the Scots Council of State was backed by an English army. The occupation was fairly peaceful, with some landowners making their peace with England.

Opposite: Scots resistance to the new reality after the execution of the king in 1649 was effectively destroyed by Cromwell's invasion and victory at Dunbar. After the destruction of the last Scots army at Worcester in 1651, Scotland was effectively under the control of Cromwell's New Model Army.

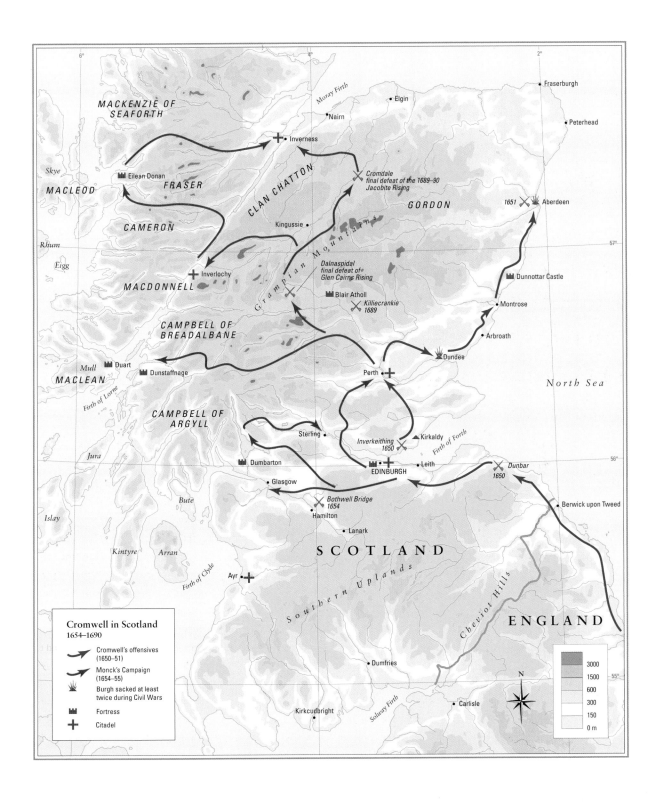

MACKENZIE OF
SEAFORTH

Skye

MACLEOD

FRASER

Eilean Donan

CAMERON

Rhum

Eigg

MACDONNELL

Inverlochy

Mull

MACLEAN

CAMPBELL OF
BREADALBANE

Duart

Dunstaffnage

CAMPBELL OF
ARGYLL

Jura

Islay

Kintyre

Arran

Bute

Firth of Clyde

Dumbarton

Glasgow

Sterling

Ayr

Hamilton

Lanark

Moray Firth

Inverness

CLAN CHATTON

Kingussie

Grampian Mountains

Nairn

Elgin

Cromdale
final defeat of the 1689–90
Jacobite Rising

GORDON

Dalnaspidal
final defeat of
Glen Cairns Rising

Blair Atholl

Killiecrankie
1689

Perth

Inverkeithing
1650

Kirkaldy

Firth of Forth

EDINBURGH

Leith

Fraserburgh

Peterhead

1651 Aberdeen

Dunnottar Castle

Montrose

Arbroath

Dundee

North Sea

Dunbar
1650

Berwick upon Tweed

Bothwell Bridge
1654

SCOTLAND

Southern Uplands

Dumfries

Cheviot Hills

ENGLAND

Kirkcudbright

Solway Firth

Carlisle

N

Cromwell in Scotland
1654–1690

⟶ Cromwell's offensives
   (1650–51)

⟶ Monck's Campaign
   (1654–55)

✸ Burgh sacked at least
   twice during Civil Wars

♜ Fortress

✝ Citadel

	3000
	1500
	600
	300
	150
	0 m

6°

4°

2°

57°

56°

55°

JACOBITE REBELLIONS

"WHEN JOHNNIE COPE TAE DUNBAR CAME, THEY SPIERED AT HIM,

"WHERE'S A' YOUR MEN?"

"THE DEIL CONFOUND ME GIN I KEN, FOR I LEFT THEM A THIS

MORNING."

"HEY JOHNNIE COPE ARE YOU WAUKING YET, OR ARE YOUR DRUMS

A BEATING YET?"   (TRADITIONAL)

King Charles II died in 1685, being followed by his avowedly Roman Catholic brother, James II, who operated through Catholic officers and bureaucrats whom he had appointed. That James' wife gave birth to a son was one blow too many for Protestants, determined to fight Popery. William of Orange of the United Provinces was invited to be king, and he landed in Torbay on November 5, 1688. James fled England.

The impact upon Scotland was immediate. The Presbyterian dominance in the Convention of Scottish Estates guaranteed William's rule south of the Tay, where Viscount Dundee raised troops on behalf of James. The Scots government army was directed toward Dundee, to generate a battle between mutually hostile clansmen. A Highland charge hit the government troops before they had time to fit plug bayonets, tearing a large hole in their ranks. Many fled and ultimately only three forces stood firm, including Hastings' regiment, the only English one on the battlefield. Dundee was shot and killed by those searching the corpses after the conflict. Killiekrankie showed that when some government troops stood firm, their volley fire was damaging since a third of the Jacobites were lost. With Dundee killed, the Jacobites had no real leader remaining.

The Jacobites felt unable to seek militarily outside the mountains and, under Alexander Cannon marched toward Braemar to threaten Aberdeen. Meanwhile, the Earl of Angus had been ordered to defend Dunkeld with his regiment of Camerons. The clansmen from Atholl saw the opportunity of attacking Angus and harming an old enemy, which might have seemed more important than supporting

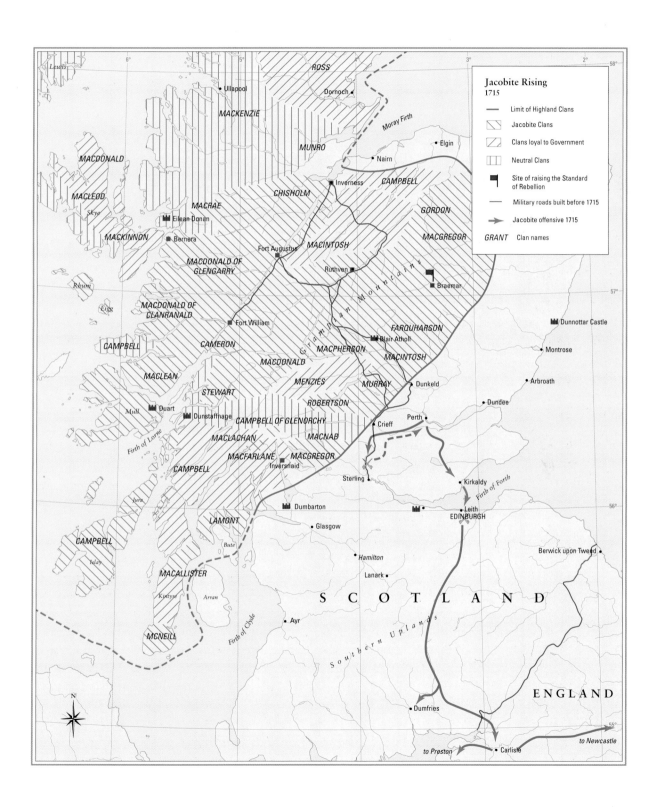

Jacobite Rising
1715

— Limit of Highland Clans

⬛ Jacobite Clans

⬛ Clans loyal to Government

⬛ Neutral Clans

⬛ Site of raising the Standard of Rebellion

— Military roads built before 1715

➡ Jacobite offensive 1715

GRANT   Clan names

the Jacobite cause. The small force, 800 men, faced some 4,000 Highlanders but were well able to defend Dunkeld Cathedral and its grounds, surrounded by walls. The attackers lost some 300 dead before leaving the assault, whereas the Camerons incurred 50 casualties. Cannon was proved to be an inadequate leader, even with an overpowering force, and lost his military credibility. This first Jacobite war ended in one more engagement, at the Haughs of Cromdale in May 1690. It was clear that the Jacobites were beaten.

The heirless King William and Queen Mary, and likewise Queen Anne, passed the English crown to George I from Hanover in 1714. This Protestant succession was seen as the way James II's son, Prince James Edward Stuart, could be deprived of any succession. A civil war erupted between supporters of the Old Pretender and the new monarchy. In England, MP Thomas Forster raised a Northumbrian force joined by 1,500 Scots. The rebels advanced on Preston, where they met an English force with a superiority of three to two. The town suffered damage during the fight. The Jacobites were finally trapped and they surrendered rather than be massacred, as was threatened (November 12-14, 1715). The English Jacobite Earl of Drinkwater was tried and executed.

The next scene of the conflict was at Sheriffmuir, on November 13, 1715. On November 10, James Erskine, Earl of Mar, marched an army of some 6,000 men to join Jacobite forces south of the border, which enlarged his force. The Duke of Argyll had the thankless task of opposing him with a smaller force of 3,500, most of George I's troops being abroad. Outnumbered nearly three to one, Hanoverians faced Mar at Sheriffmuir when 2,000 men on the Jacobite right flank charged, receiving a volley killing their leader. They charged again with the sword and broke the Hanoverian's left wing but were slowed down by Argyll's cavalry. The other flank saw Argyll's dragoons charging Mar's left flank, pushing it back two miles. Eventually, Argyll collected the remnants of his forces but Mar did not press home an attack with his remaining men because they were worn out. Although Argyll lost nearly three times as many men as his foe, Mar's indecision demonstrated his incompetence as a leader and the 1715 uprising began to fizzle out. The Jacobite cause was now crushed for 30 years.

While Britain was engaged with France during the War of the Austrian Succession (1740-48), the Old Pretender's son, Bonnie Prince Charlie, landed at Arsaig in Scotland, but the chieftains of Skye refused to support him. Nevertheless, he raised 2,500 clansmen and occupied Edinburgh and defeated General Sir John Cope. Prince Charlie next led 5,500 Jacobites into England. Marching down the west coast, they reached Derby on December 4 . Advised to retreat owing to the lack of French support, the Scots retreated, fighting a small rearguard action at Clifton (December 18). Had the Scots pushed on, the opposing forces were scarcely larger than their own, with London virtually open.

Meanwhile, the Hanoverians reoccupied Edinburgh. A penultimate battle occurred at Falkirk (January 17, 1746). Here, Generals Hawley and Huske faced Prince Charles and Lord Murray. After overwhelming a cavalry attack, the Highlanders charged Hawley's infantry whose left wing regiments fled before contact. The Scots pursued, leaving Hawley's right wing standing firm which mounted a counterattack. The Hanoverians then retreated with Burrell's Grenadiers covering the rear until they reached Linlithgow. Although technically defeated at Falkirk, the Hanoverians were soon able to reform themselves while Moray withdrew his force into the Highlands.

Opposite: In 1745 a new Jacobite rebellion was organized, led by the young pretender, Bonny Prince Charles. Supported by only a tiny minority, his army still managed to seize Edinburgh without any serious fighting. The army marched south, winning a minor victory at Prestonpans and eventually reaching Derby, where they turned north and retreated back to Scotland. The Bonny Prince's army was eventually obliterated by the government army at the battle of Culloden in 1746.

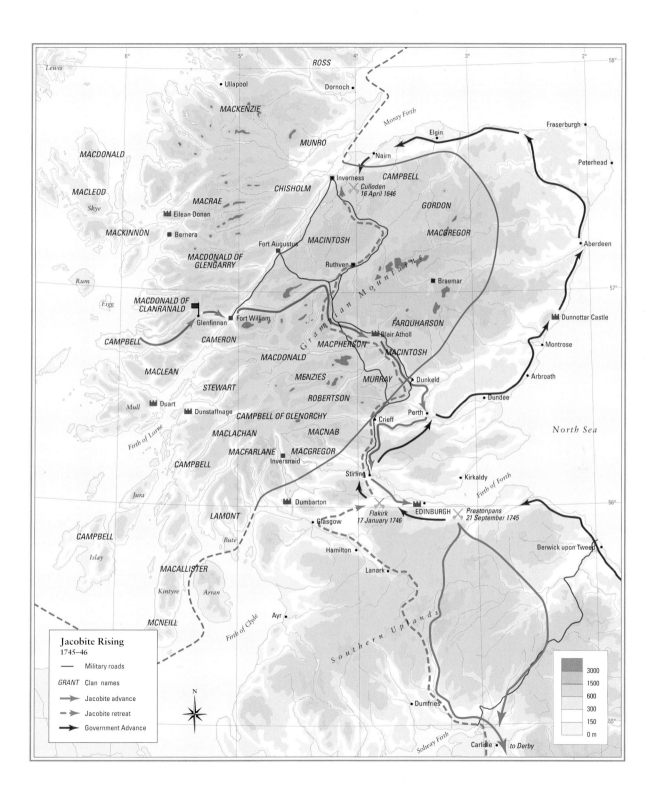

Lewis

6°

ROSS

Ullapool •

Dornoch •

5°

MACKENZIE

4°

Moray Firth

Elgin •

Fraserburgh •

3°

58°

2°

Peterhead •

MACDONALD

MUNRO

Nairn •

MACLEOD

Skye

MACRAE

CHISHOLM

Eilean Donan

Inverness
Culloden
16 April 1646

CAMPBELL

GORDON

MACKINNON

Bernera •

MACDONALD OF
GLENGARRY

Fort Augustus

MACINTOSH

MACGREGOR

Aberdeen •

Ruthven •

Rum

57°

Braemar ■

Eigg

MACDONALD OF
CLANRANALD

Glenfinnan

Fort William

FARQUHARSON

Dunnottar Castle

CAMPBELL

CAMERON

Blair Atholl

MACPHERSON

MACINTOSH

Montrose •

MACDONALD

MACLEAN

STEWART

MENZIES

MURRAY

Dunkeld

Arbroath •

ROBERTSON

Perth

Dundee •

Mull

Duart

Dunstaffnage

CAMPBELL OF GLENORCHY

Crieff •

North Sea

MACLACHAN

MACNAB

Firth of Lorne

MACFARLANE

MACGREGOR

Jura

Inversnaid ■

Stirling

Kirkaldy •

LAMONT

Dumbarton

Firth of Forth

CAMPBELL

Bute

Glasgow •

Flakirk
17 January 1746

EDINBURGH

Prestonpans
21 September 1745

56°

Berwick upon Tweed •

Islay

Hamilton •

CAMPBELL

MACALLISTER

Lanark •

Kintyre

Arran

MCNEILL

Firth of Clyde

Ayr •

Southern Uplands

Jacobite Rising
1745–46

Military roads

GRANT Clan names

Jacobite advance

Jacobite retreat

Government Advance

N

Dumfries •

Solway Firth

Carlisle •

to Derby

55°

3000
1500
600
300
150
0 m

CULLODEN

"THE PRETENDER'S SON, IT IS SAID, LAY AT LORD LOVAT'S HOUSE AT AIRD THE NIGHT AFTER THE ACTION. BRIGADIER MORDAUNT IS DETACHED WITH 900 VOLUNTEERS THIS MORNING INTO FRAZIER'S COUNTRY, TO ATTACK ALL THE REBELS HE MIGHT FIND THERE..." *GENTLEMEN'S MAGAZINE*, 1746

The final fling in the Jacobite rebellion took place at Culloden on April 16, 1746. After Falkirk, the Duke of Cumberland, with over 8,000 men, pursued the Highlanders toward Aberdeen. Prince Charles was forced to give battle. The battle took place near Culloden Park estate on Drummosie Moor, leaving the Jacobites to attempt a night march and attack while the enemy slept on Cumberland's twenty-fifth birthday. After fierce fighting during which the government used bayonets to force a Scots retreat after hordes of men charged at them, the cavalry were eventually turned loose to hack down any retreating enemy while the infantry killed wounded Scots. Ripped by case shot, the Scots reached the enemy line, to receive volleys of musket fire. When they hit the battalions on Cumberland's left, they pushed them back with the Hanoverians retreating using the bayonet. Those Scots who pushed through gaps in the line were met by flanking fire from Wolfe's battalion and Campbell Highlanders. Reportedly, the end of the battle saw government bayonets bloodied to the muzzles of their muskets. The Scots were forced to surrender. Only 154 Scots were taken prisoner with the 222 French-Irish unit while some 1,500 were killed. The Hanoverian losses were reported as 320 dead and wounded, nearly half from Barrel's battalion. Elsewhere, Prince Charles had been ushered away rather than exposing his body while trying to rally his men. He fled, followed by Scots Lord Ellcho yelling, "Run, you cowardly Italian," referring to his early years in Rome and Bologna. He returned to Italy, ending up as so debauched a drunk that his erstwhile allies repudiated him as a possible heir to the Scots and English thrones. Meanwhile, the remnants of the Highland army mustered at Strathspey, causing Cumberland to invade the Highlands and exact reprisals against its inhabitants. One hundred and twenty were executed and 1000 transported to the Americas. Culloden ensured the Jacobite cause was dealt a very decisive defeat.

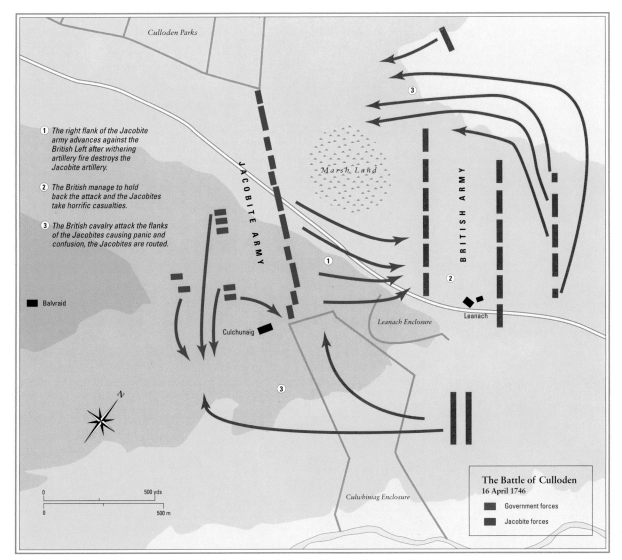

1 The right flank of the Jacobite
army advances against the
British Left after withering
artillery fire destroys the
Jacobite artillery.

2 The British manage to hold
back the attack and the Jacobites
take horrific casualties.

3 The British cavalry attack the flanks
of the Jacobites causing panic and
confusion, the Jacobites are routed.

Culloden Parks

JACOBITE ARMY

Marsh Land

BRITISH ARMY

■ Balvraid

Culchunaig

Leanach Enclosure

Leanach

Culwhiniag Enclosure

The Battle of Culloden
16 April 1746

■ Government forces

■ Jacobite forces

0   500 yds
0   500 m

Cumberland sent his troops throughout the Highlands in punitive seaches, burning homes and crops, leading to the devastation of the southern Highlands. New laws banned Highlanders from owning weapons, wearing traditional dress, or playing the bagpipes. Jacobitism lost its leadership. Clan chiefs in exile had to wait a generation before they could return home to buy back their sequestered estates. These lands had been placed in the hands of Lowland gentry, who tried to modernize them. Eventually, clan chief was transformed to land owner, leading the way to the Highland clearances. The Highlands were traditionally overburdened with men of fighting age who owed their loyalty to their chief. As chiefly interests became associated with the economic development of lands, that surplus population, dependent on loot from war, became a nuisance to be cleared away. Tenants became sucked into the cash nexus where tradition was destroyed by a new capitalist economy supplanting a medieval society.

Above: After making a night march to catch the government army by surprise, the Jacobites found their enemy ready for battle. When drawn into line of battle, the tired Highlanders withstood concentrated cannon fire then charged: the feared highland charge. They were repulsed and finally routed by cavalry charges, leaving some 1,000 dead on the battlefield.

HIGHLAND CLEARANCES

"THE HABITS, EMPLOYMENTS, AND CUSTOMS OF THE HIGHLANDER SEEM TO FIT HIM FOR THE AMERICAN FOREST, WHICH HE PENETRATES WITHOUT FEELING THE GLOOM AND MELANCHOLY EXPERIENCED BY THOSE WHO HAVE BEEN BROUGHT UP IN TOWNS..." DR. GESNER, LETTER DATED AUGUST 19, 1842

After 1745, with the gradual commercialization of agriculture in Scotland, landowners in the north of the country increasingly introduced the Cheviot breed of sheep onto to their land because it produced more and better wool than native breeds. As winter set in, the sheep tended to move toward the sheltered valleys, where small townships existed which were an obstacle to grazing sheep. Landowners therefore found ways to clear families off their land because the sheep produced more wealth than did rents.

A particularly avaricious landowner was Elizabeth Gordon, Countess of Sutherland, who owned two-thirds of the land in Sutherland in Scotland. The Sutherland clearances epitomize the worst excesses of the general clearance process. Between 1807 and 1821, half the population of Sutherland, some 10,000 people were evicted. The Highlanders were treated extremely harshly in other ways. Some landowners used soldiers and baton-wielding police against those resisting eviction. The Church also failed the people, ministers often being the mouthpieces of the landlords, telling the people not to be law-breakers. However, some caring ministers broke away from the Church of Scotland, founding the Free Church in 1843. Overall, hundreds of clearances occurred from Shetland to Arran and from the Hebrides to Aberdeenshire. One avenue open to the evicted was emigration to the Americas, and during the clearances approximately 100,000 left. The conditions of passage could be dire with filth and disease breaking out in a cramped deck space; cholera, smallpox, typhoid, and dysentery were normal. Despite the clearances, the Highland population increased and severe famine broke out.

Many young men joined the British army, where they could wear Highland attire with pride. Scots regiments have since enjoyed a reputation for good discipline and fighting ability.

Opposite: After the '45 rebellion, clan chiefs rejected their traditional role and began to see themselves as landowners with profit as their priority. Sheep and deerstalking became more profitable than people.

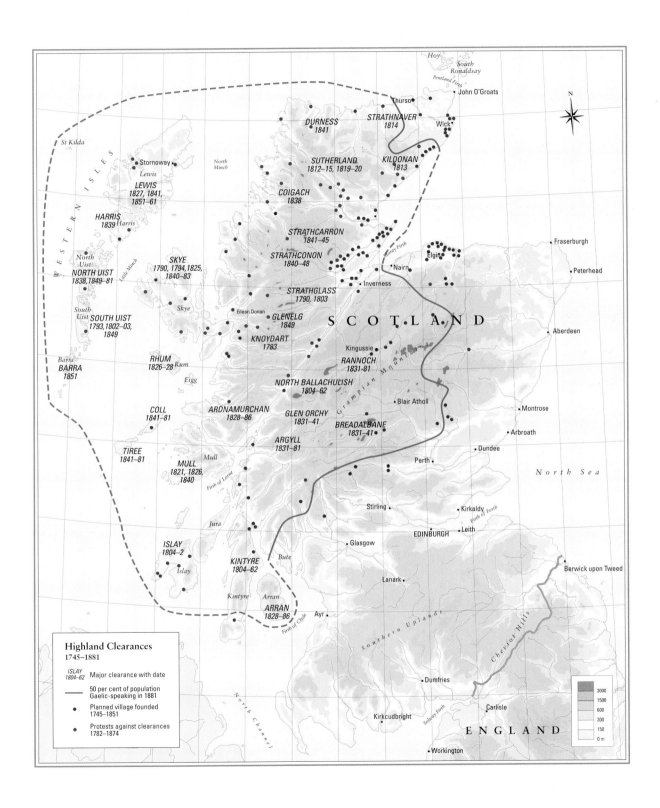

Hoy
South
Ronaldsay
Pentland Firth
John O'Groats
Thurso
DURNESS
1841
STRATHNAVER
1814
Wick
St Kilda
Stornoway
Lewis
North
Minch
SUTHERLAND
1812–15, 1819–20
KILDONAN
1813
LEWIS
1827, 1841,
1851–61
COIGACH
1838
HARRIS
1839 *Harris*
WESTERN ISLES
*North
Uist*
Little Minch
STRATHCARRON
1841–45
Fraserburgh
SKYE
1790, 1794, 1825,
1840–83
STRATHCONON
1840–48
Elgin
NORTH UIST
1838, 1849–81
Moray Firth
Nairn
Peterhead
Skye
Inverness
STRATHGLASS
1790, 1803
Eilean Donan
*South
Uist*
SOUTH UIST
1793, 1802–03,
1849
GLENELG
1849
S C O T L A N D
Barra
KNOYDART
1783
Aberdeen
BARRA
1851
RHUM
1826–28 *Rum*
Kingussie
RANNOCH
1831–81
Grampian Mountains
Eigg
NORTH BALLACHULISH
1804–62
COLL
1841–81
ARDNAMURCHAN
1828–86
GLEN ORCHY
1831–41
Blair Atholl
Montrose
TIREE
1841–81
BREADALBANE
1831–41
Arbroath
Mull
ARGYLL
1831–81
Dundee
MULL
1821, 1826,
1840
Firth of Lorn
Perth
North   Sea
Jura
Stirling
Kirkaldy
Firth of Forth
ISLAY
1804–2
Bute
Leith
EDINBURGH
Islay
KINTYRE
1804–62
Glasgow
Berwick upon Tweed
Kintyre *Arran*
Lanark
ARRAN
1828–86
Ayr
Firth of Clyde
Southern Uplands
Cheviot Hills

Highland Clearances
1745–1881

*ISLAY
1804–62*   Major clearance with date

———   50 per cent of population
Gaelic-speaking in 1881

●   Planned village founded
1745–1851

●   Protests against clearances
1782–1874

*North
Channel*
Dumfries
Carlisle
Kirkcudbright
Solway Firth
E N G L A N D

3000
1500
600
300
150
0 m

Workington

THE BIRTH OF WALES

"HAPPY THEY, THE CYMRY, WHEN THEY SAY,

THE TRINITY DELIVERED US FROM TIME FORMER TROUBLE.

LET NOT DYVED OR GLYWYSSYG TREMBLE."

(PROPHECY OF PRYDEIN THE GREAT, BOOK OF TALIESIN, VI. III)

P rior to the birth of Wales, Roman Wales experienced two styles of rule: the south saw the growth of a typical Mediterranean-style culture while the north was more a military zone with roads and forts speaking of a military occupation. A community was established at Carmarthen, Maridunum, and gold was mined in the area. A major legionary fort was constructed at Isca Silurum, Caerleon, and included a large amphitheater.

The north observed the creation of Caernarfon, Segontium. As well as gold, Wales produced copper, especially in the old druid island of Anglesey. Here, there is arguably a villa in the well-preserved ruins of a defended hut group at Din Lligwy. Roman culture, the growth of a southern villa system, and the growth of Christianity, demonstrated an important cultural mix which allowed the local Celtic Brythonic language to become permeated with Latin terminology. Hence, Welsh consciousness included a Roman cultural heritage bolstered by a Latin-using Christian church, helping construct an identity determined to resist the invading Germanic tribes materializing after the Roman withdrawal from Britain in 410.

Opposite: The national flag of Wales consists of the red dragon on a white and green field. Although only granted official status in 1959, the red dragon has been associated with Wales for centuries. The most famous legend regarding the red dragon is the prophecy of Merlin. A long fight took place between a white dragon and a red dragon, and the red dragon eventually emerged as the victor.

The Saxons at anchor on the sea always
The Cymry venerable until doomsday shall be supreme
They will not seek books nor be covetous of poets
The presage of the Isle will be no other than this.'
The Omen of Prydein the Great, Book of Taliesin VI

The years following the Roman exodus are poorly recorded in history. The early incoherent narrative

of Gildas and those writing long after events like Bede and Nennius might be misleading, and the *Anglo-Saxon Chronicle* and the *Pictish List of Kings* have their own political agendas. However, it seems that the Romano-Celtic Britons, led by a legendary leader, sometimes called Arthur, or by Ambrosius Aurelianus as recorded by Gildas, defeated the Saxons at Mount Badon (c. 516).

This victory was overturned c. 577 when the West Saxons were victorious at Dyrham, leading to the loss of Gloucester, Cirencester, and Bath, which pushed the Britons firmly backward toward Wales. Now a wedge was driven between the Britons of Wales and Cornwall, which opened up the Severn river valley to Saxon settlement.

In Wales, Brythonic leaders were unable to continue Roman modes of governance and established a number of small kingdoms in the hill and mountain country. Gwynedd, Powys, and Dyfed and Seisyllg, Morgannwg, and Gwent became the heirs of Romano-Britain. These states protected the Celtic heritage, resolutely fighting the Anglo-Saxon kingdoms of Mercia and Northumbria in England. The constant warfare eventually fixed a border between Wales and England, which roughly stands today.

Gwynedd was established by the legendary warrior, Cunedda, a Gododdin leader, who led the Votadini from north of the Tyne to north Wales, his former lands falling to the Angles of Bernicia, as recorded in Aneirin's poem *Y Cododdin*. In the seventh century, Powys, based on the old tribal area of the Cornovii, stopped further Mercian encroachments, causing Aethelbald of Mercia to defend his recently acquired Brythoic territories by building a border earthwork known as Wat's Dyke.

At one stage, Powys included Wroxeter, Roman Viriconium, in Shropshire, an area lost in skirmishes as occurred elsewhere along the border. The later Mercian King Offa developed this earth rampart into Offa's Dyke, which is, in some places, 65 feet wide (including its ditches) and eight feet high, and runs for 185 miles.

Southwestern Wales was subject to an Irish colony which established the Kingdom of Dyfed, and Irish influence apparently spread to Ceredigion, Ystrad Tywi, and Brycheiniog. To the southeast were born Glywysig and Gwent, which eventually united for a while to form Morgannwg; today the area is known as Glamorgan.

The Brythonic Celtic language eventually developed into what is now known as Welsh, which was a barrier to communication between Britons and Saxons, who shared little interaction except border raiding. The Irish were much more important to the Welsh for cultural interaction, especially with the common link of Christianity.

Wales has recently had a rebirth. The Welsh have always considered themselves as having a unique identity, seperate to the rest of the UK. In recent years, there has been a major national revival, with the Welsh looking back to their Celtic origins, and a push to preserve their unique language.

The flag of Wales incorporates the red dragon (Y Ddraig Goch) of Prince Cadwalader along with the Tudor colors of green and white. It was used by Henry VII at the battle of Bosworth in 1485 after which it was carried in state to St. Paul's Cathedral. The red dragon was then included in the Tudors' royal arms to signify their Welsh descent. It was officially recognized as the Welsh national flag in 1959.

Hen Wlad fy Nhadu (Land of My Fathers) is the national anthem of Wales. It is sung at sports events and days of national importance. St David's Day, March 1, is the national day. The daffodil is also associated with Wales, being a national emblem.

Opposite: As Angles and Saxons pushed further westward, the main stronghold of independent Britons were the hills and vales that would become Wales.

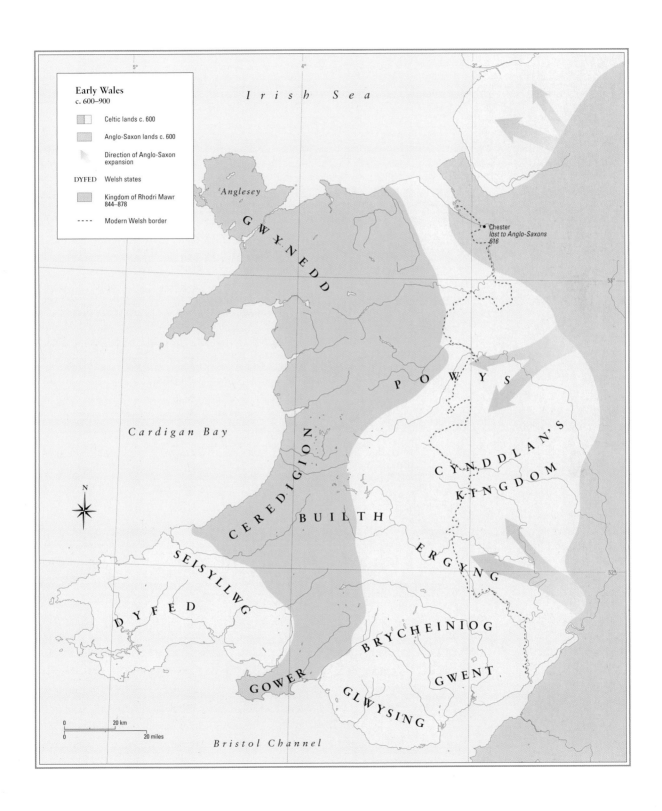

Early Wales
c. 600–900

- Celtic lands c. 600
- Anglo-Saxon lands c. 600
- Direction of Anglo-Saxon expansion
- DYFED Welsh states
- Kingdom of Rhodri Mawr 844–878
- - - - Modern Welsh border

Irish Sea

Anglesey

GWYNEDD

Chester
lost to Anglo-Saxons
616

POWYS

Cardigan Bay

CEREDIGION

CYNDDLAN'S
KINGDOM

BUILTH

ERGYNG

N

SEISYLLWG

DYFED

BRYCHEINIOG

GOWER

GWENT

GLWYSING

0   20 km
0   20 miles

Bristol Channel

WELSH PRINCIPALITIES

THE BRITONS OF WALES OFTEN ALLIED WITH DANISH VIKINGS
TO SUCCESSFULLY COMBAT THE ANGLO-SAXONS. GRUFFYDD AP
LLYWELYN, KING OF WALES, ALLIED WITH NORWEGIAN VIKINGS.
THIS ENSURED THE SAXONS NEVER CONQUERED CELTIC WALES
AND GAVE WALES PEACE FROM INVASION FOR DECADES.

The various Welsh successor states were continuously engaged in attempts at unification, but only those states with extensive lowlands that could be exploited agriculturally. Thus the four corners of Wales were potential nuclei for a greater kingdom: Gwynedd, Dyfed (Deheubarth), Glywysing (Glamorgan), and Powys. Despite the size and power of these lands fluctuating, their princes remained the major leaders of the Welsh resistance to Anglo-Saxon or English incursions from the seventh century through the Norman conquest to the Statute of Rhuddlan in 1284.

The first noticeable leader to attempt unification was Rhodri Mawr (c. 820-878). He inherited his kingdom from his father in 844, then, in 855, inherited Powys from his uncle, finally acquiring Seisyllwg when its prince died by virtue of marrying his sister, Angharad (872). Rhodri was remembered not just for his territorial expansion but because he fought off Viking attacks. His sons founded three separate dynasties: Aberffraw for Gwynedd; Dinefwr for Deheubarth; and Mathrafal for Powys. All of them sought to dominate each other.

The Welsh princes often used English mercenaries in their expansionist policies, and the weaker principalities sought aid by entering into allegiance with the English Kingdom of Wessex, eventually expressed in terms of homage and fealty. Anarawd, a son of Rhodri, submitted to Alfred, even though he had been powerful enough to inflict a defeat upon Aethelred of Mercia on the River Conwy in 881. One important Welsh King at this time was Rhodri's grandson, Hywel ap Cadell (Hywel Dda, the 'Good', c. 880–950), who started ruling in Seisllwyg and Dyfed, transforming them into Deheubarth. He usurped the principalities of Gwynedd and Powys, ruling Wales from Prestatyn to Pembroke. Hywel enjoyed good relations with Athelstan of Wessex, accepting the status of a sub-king, undoubtedly recognizing the

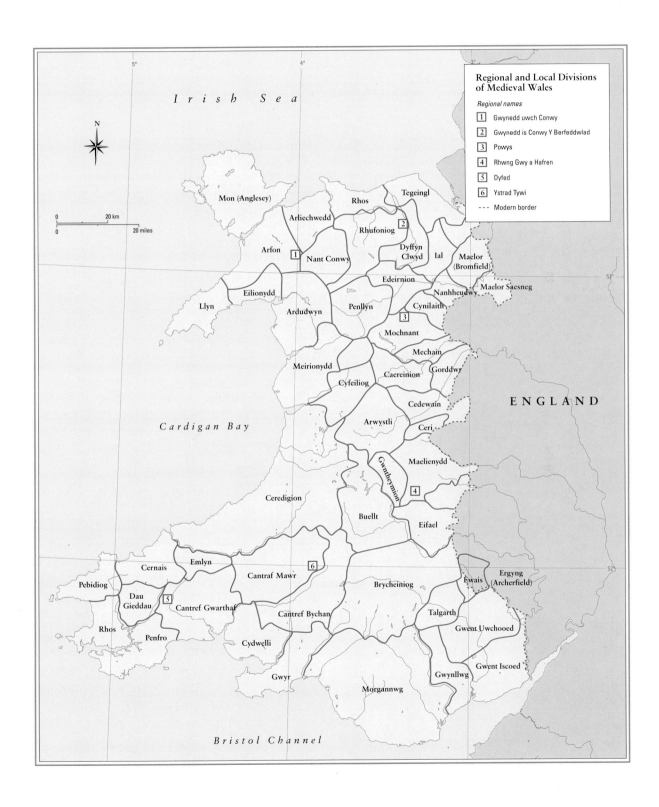

Regional and Local Divisions
of Medieval Wales

Regional names

1 Gwynedd uwch Conwy

2 Gwynedd is Conwy Y Berfeddwlad

3 Powys

4 Rhwng Gwy a Hafren

5 Dyfed

6 Ystrad Tywi

--- Modern border

Irish Sea

Mon (Anglesey)

Rhos

Arliechwedd

Tegeingl

Rhufoniog

Arfon

1 Nant Conwy

Dyffyn
Clwyd

Ial

Maelor
(Bromfield)

Edeirnion

Maelor Saesneg

Eilionydd

Nanhheudwy

Llyn

Ardudwyn

Penllyn

Cynilaith

3

Mochnant

Mechain

Meirionydd

Gorddwr

Cyfeiliog

Caereinion

Cedewain

Arwystli

Ceri

Gwnthermion

Maelienydd

ENGLAND

Cardigan Bay

Ceredigion

4

Buellt

Eifael

Cernais

Emlyn

Cantraf Mawr

6

Pebidiog

Brycheiniog

Ewais

Ergyng
(Archerfield)

Dau
Gieddau

5

Cantref Gwarthaf

Cantref Bychan

Talgarth

Rhos

Penfro

Gwent Uwchooed

Cydwelli

Gwynllwg

Gwent Iscoed

Gwyr

Morgannwg

Bristol Channel

N

0   20 km

0   20 miles

realities of power. He was allowed to mint his own coinage in English Chester and is renowned for his pilgrimage to Rome and enacting the Law Codes, blessed by the Pope, which endured well after his death when his dominion was split between three sons.

Maredudd ap Owain (d. 999), a grandson of Hywel Dda brought Deheubarth and Gwynedd together and managed to increase his realm further. However, his reign witnessed extensive Viking raids, especially on Anglesey, and his death opened Wales to Viking and English intervention. Another prince who commenced his power play from Deheubarth and Gwynedd was Gruffudd ap Llywelyn (c. 1007-63). His career saw him defeating Mercians at Rhyd y Groes near Welshpool and seizing Deheubarth from Hywel ap Edwin, but then he was driven out of his lands by Gruffyd ap Rhydderch of Gwent. The latter was killed by his rival who allied himself with Ælfgar of East Anglia, who had lost his earldom to Harold Godwinson and family. Gruffydd ap Llewelyn became so powerful that he grabbed Morgannwg and Gwent and went on to defeat an English army near Glasbury and takk some English territory too. He now claimed the title of Prince of Wales, acknowledged by the English. Gruffydd was now so dangerous that Harold Godwinson gained approval from Edward the Confessor to attack Wales (1062). Two years later Gruffydd was killed by the son of Iago ap Idwal, who Gruffydd had killed while uniting Wales.

Gruffydd's realm was now divided into the traditional kingdoms, with the kings being appointed by the English, such as Bleddyn ap Cynfyn in Gwynedd and his brother, Rhiwallon, in Powys. English influence was soon superseded by the Normans once King Harold Godwinson was killed by the Norman, William the Conqueror in 1066. The Normans established the three Marcher earldoms of Chester, Shrewsbury, and Hereford and these were used as staging posts for raids into Wales. However, the only lasting penetration into Wales under William I was along the south principality of Gwent, where some Norman settlement occurred. Also, Rhys ap Tewdwr of Deheubarth made a pact with William providing him with power and authority in his own lands and possible influence in areas far outside Norman control. After Rhys' death, the Normans invaded nearly all of south Wales and founded the lordships in the areas of Cardigan, Pembroke, Brecon, and Glamorgan.

When Belddyn ap Cynfyn of Gwynedd and Powys died in 1075, he was succeeded by Gruffydd ap Cynan, whose mother was of the Viking Dublin royalty, the Hiberno-Norse descended from Sigtrygg Silkbeard. Claimant to Gwynedd, once ruled by his grandfather, Gruffydd made several attempts on the throne, using Danish and Irish troops in his second attempt, which failed leaving him eventually a prisoner of Earl Hugh of Chester. Gruffydd escaped and assumed control of Gwynedd when a Norwegian fleet under King Magnus III defeated the Normans at Anglesey. Negotiations with Henry I of England saw his already substantial kingdom extended to Ll n, Eifionydd, Ardudwy, and Arllechwedd.

Homage was paid to King Henry after a Norman attack but this did not prevent Gruffydd expanding eastward and southward, his sons leading his troops. The cantrefs of Rhos and Rhufoniog were seized in 1118, Meirionnydd grabbed from Powys in 1123, and Dyffryn Clywd in 1124. His sons, Owain and Cadwaladr, allied with Deheubarth, defeated the Normans at Crud Mawr near Cardigan in 1136, and acquired Ceredigion as the prize. Aged 82 years, he died in 1137 and was buried in Bangor Cathedral, which he had helped rebuild. Gruffydd laid the basis for the work of his son Owain and his great-grandson Llywelyn the Great.

Dolbadarn Castle in Gwynedd, north Wales. The castle was built by Llywelyn the Great and is strategically positioned at the foot of Mount Snowdon. This meant that any invading troops were denied access to the heart of Snowdonia. It is reputed that Llwelyn ap Gruffudd used the castle's tower to imprison his brother, Owain ap Gruffud, as they struggled to gain control of Gynwedd in the 1250s.

LLYWELYN THE GREAT

LLYWELLYN FAWR, THE GREAT, PRINCE OF GWYNEDD, BECAME A MAJOR FIGURE IN ENGLISH POLITICS AND RULED OVER A DOMINATED RATHER THAN UNITED WALES UNTIL HIS DEATH IN 1240.

P olitical leadership in Wales devolved upon Llywelyn ap Iowerth, aka Llewelyn Fawr, "the Great," (11731240), Prince of Gwynedd. Unlike his predecessors, Llywelyn managed to hold Gwynedd together. Maybe he was aided by having lived in England as a ward of King John, whose daughter, Joan, he married. 1201 witnessed a treaty whereby Gwynedd swore fealty and did homage to John as his liege lord. The treaty divided loyalties and allowed John to attack Gwynedd's sovereignty and so spread the germs of future conflict within Gwynedd and in its external relations. The family association was finally ruptured when John led two expeditions into Gwynedd (1211); the first failed while the second achieved some success. The English plunged into the depths of Gwynedd; Joan interceded for terms, which involved ceding all Gwynedd east of the River Conwy. Llywelyn also had to agree that if he were to die without a legitimate heir, all his land would go to the king. John hoped to reinforce his dominance by castle building in Wales. However, this plan was abandoned in the face of political pressures in England when the baronage forced John to sign the Magna Carta in 1215.

With other Welsh princes, Llywelyn used this opportunity to take back their lands. Llywelyn also gained when his son Gruffydd was returned after having been a hostage since 1211. Gwynedd now led all the independent princes of Wales. In 1216, the lesser princes gave their homage to Llywelyn again but Gwenwynwyn, who had had his Powys lands restored by John, reneged and returned to John and lost his lands to Llywelyn for the second time. When John died, Llywelyn concluded the Treaty of Worcester (1218) with the new King, Henry III, which confirmed the former in all his Welsh lands.

Llywelyn died in 1240, along with his united Wales. A power struggle occurred between his son and heir, Dafydd and his half-brother Gruffudd. In February 1246, Dafydd died and the Welsh princelings submitted to the English. By the Treaty of Woodstock (1247), Dafydd's heirs, Owain and Llywelyn ap Gruffudd, also submitted and Henry reclaimed homages and services of all barons and nobles in Wales while Gwynedd was divided between the heirs. Wales now reverted to a collection of petty statelets.

Opposite: Facing attacks from land-hungry Norman warlords, Llwelyn the Great took advantage of civil war among his enemies. He launched effective campaigns which kept his enemies on the defensive and allowed him and his successors to create an effective Welsh state.

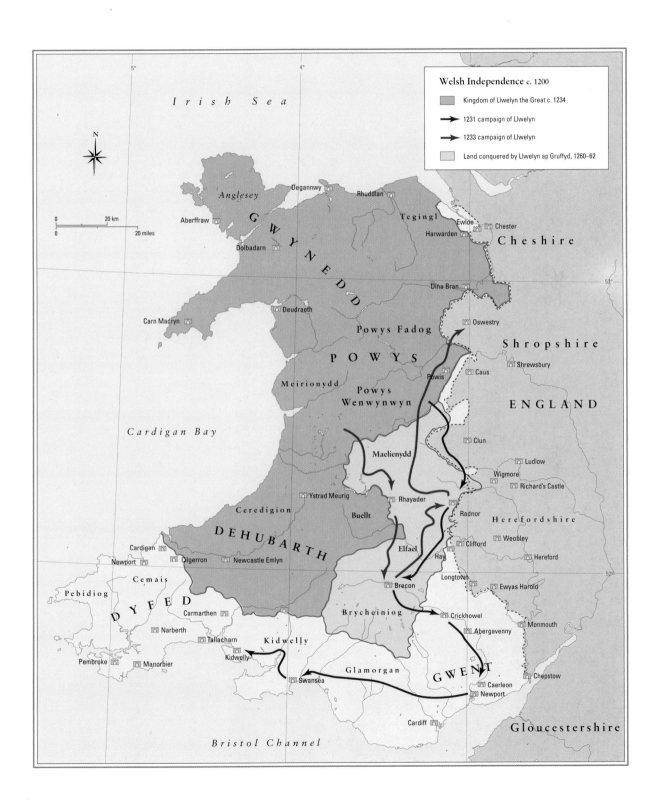

Welsh Independence c. 1200

Kingdom of Llwelyn the Great c. 1234

1231 campaign of Llwelyn

1233 campaign of Llwelyn

Land conquered by Llwelyn ap Gruffyd, 1260–62

Irish Sea

N

0   20 km
0   20 miles

Anglesey

Degannwy

Rhuddlan

Tegingl

Ewloe   Chester

Aberffraw

Harwarden

C h e s h i r e

Dolbadarn

G W Y N E D D

Dina Bran

Deudraeth

Oswestry

Carn Madryn

Powys Fadog

S h r o p s h i r e

Shrewsbury

P O W Y S

Powis   Caus

Meirionydd

Powys
Wenwynwyn

E N G L A N D

Clun

Cardigan Bay

Maelienydd

Ludlow

Wigmore

Richard's Castle

Ystrad Meurig

Rhayader

C e r e d i g i o n

Buellt

Radnor

H e r e f o r d s h i r e

D E H U B A R T H

Elfael

Weobley

Cardigan

Clifford

Hereford

Newport   Cilgerron   Newcastle Emlyn

Hay

C e m a i s

Elfael

Longtown

Brecon

Ewyas Harold

Pebidiog

D Y F E D

Carmarthen

B r y c h e i n i o g

Crickhowel   Monmouth

Narberth

Abergavenny

Tallacharn

K i d w e l l y

Pembroke   Manorbier

Kidwelly

Glamorgan

G W E N T

Chepstow

Swansea

Caerleon

Newport

Cardiff

G l o u c e s t e r s h i r e

Bristol Channel

CASTLES IN WALES: CHEPSTOW

WELSH CASTLES ARE OFTEN FORGOTTEN BUT MANY WERE BUILT. CHEPSTOW IS ONE OF THE MOST SIGNIFICANT. BUILT ON A CLIFF-TOP SITE, IT OCCUPIED A STRATEGIC POSITION ON THE RIVER WYE. THE CASTLE IS STILL STANDING TODAY.

A leading supporter of William the Conqueror in his quest for the English throne was William fitz Osbern, who provided ships packed with his own men for the invasion. As a reward, William made fitz Osbern Earl of Hereford and gave him sundry other lands in adjacent areas, including the town of Chepstow. Before his death in battle in 1071, the earl founded the castle and a Benedictine priory within the town.

The castle at Chepstow was one of a series of castles built or refurbished by William. Richard's Castle, Wigmore, Clifford, and Ewyas Harold in Herefordshire and Monmouth secured the southern March while the Earl of Chester constructed a similar line of castles to control the central and northern Marches. Chepstow was built of stone from the outset, with local quarries supplying material. Roman finds in the walls suggest that remnants of the Roman settlement at Caerwent were used in the construction.

Chepstow was carefully selected for military purposes: to act strategically by controlling a communication point on the River Wye and tactically, since it took clever advantage of the cliff-top site on the west bank of a loop in the river, a few miles from its junction with the River Severn estuary. The castle was easily defensible and dominated a route across the border from the Severn crossing at Gloucester into the Welsh southern march. On the Welsh side of the Wye, the castle acted as a forward base and staging post for fitz Osbern's raids into Gwent. The town was the old Kingdom of Gwent's port and trading center, its very name meaning "trading place." Possibly, the castle was desired by William I to overawe Rhys ap Tewdwr, the local Welsh King.

Chepstow Castle took advantage of the river cliffs and a steep valley of the Dell as natural defenses, and a rock-cut ditch of the upper bailey helped enclose an area about 340 feet long and approximately

65 feet wide. A great Norman tower, a hall-keep, overlooks the defenses, with a blind wall facing landward and a row of windows open to the north over the River Wye. The barbican was added in the early thirteenth century to protect the potentially weak west end of the castle. It comprised a powerful outer ward, separated from the upper bailey by a rock-cut ditch and drawbridge. Chepstow Castle and fitz Osbern lands were forfeited when Earl William's son plotted against the king. The castle remained in royal hands until granted by Henry I to Walter fitz Richard of Clare, known as Stongbow and ultimate ruler of conquered Leinster in Ireland. His heiress, daughter Isabel, was a royal ward, married to the paladin William Marshall, who took her father's title as Earl of Pembroke.

The Marshall family developed the castle into a magnificent double-bailey, curtain-walled edifice, still in good condition today. Earl Roger Bigod of Norfolk, is reputed to have enclosed Chepstow town with a wall and certainly built luxurious private accommodation within the castle. Ultimately, Chepstow did not suffer violence in the Middle Ages, and when the conquest of Wales was attempted by Edward I, he built a series of new castles to surround northern Wales, leaving Chepstow to its own peaceful devices.

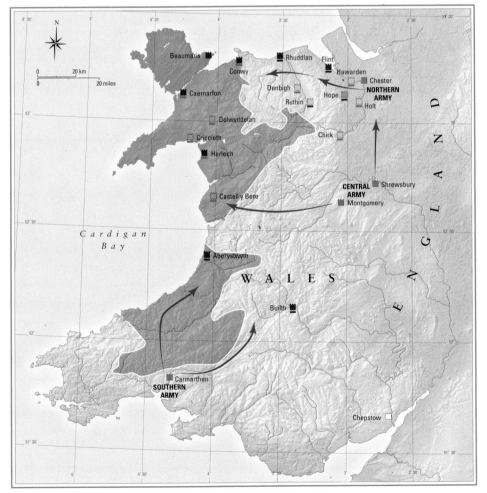

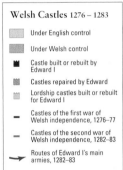

Welsh Castles 1276 – 1283

Under English control

Under Welsh control

Castle built or rebuilt by Edward I

Castles repaired by Edward

Lordship castles built or rebuilt for Edward I

Castles of the first war of Welsh independence, 1276–77

Castles of the second war of Welsh independence, 1282–83

Routes of Edward I's main armies, 1282–83

Chepstow Castle's strategic position on the border of Wales continued to influence the political and military situation for over 400 years.

WALES AND THE ANGLO-NORMAN CONQUEST

EDWARD I OVERAWED AND INTIMIDATED THE SUBJUGATED WELSH BY ENCLOSING THE WELSH HEARTLAND IN A RING OF IRON AND STONE IN THE FORM OF GARRISONED CASTLES. ENGLISH PLANTATION TOWNS COMPLETED THE WELSH DEFEAT.

In 1255, Llywelyn ap Gruffudd overcame his brother Owain in battle and became the sole ruler of Gwynedd. He then spread his power through Wales, and the Treaty of Montgomery (1267), asserted his status as overlord of all Wales. However, matters changed when Edward I succeeded to the English throne in 1272. Llywelyn ignored summons to court on several occasions, refusing on somewhat debateable grounds. Edward retaliated by seizing Eleanor de Montfort traveling to Wales to marry Llywelyn and by declaring the Welshman a rebel.

Edward conducted two campaigns against the Welsh. Edward's first campaign used forces on land and by sea employing a triple pincer movement on Gwynedd. The result was the submission of Llywelyn in the face of English might. The 1277 Treaty of Aberconwy fined Llywelyn £50,000 while the Welsh prince was coerced to London to pay homage, accompanied by hostages from the Welsh leading families, and reinstatement of his brother Owain after keeping him in prison for 20 years. The English built rapidly; by 1282, Gwynedd was circumscribed by an arc of castles. The English presence in Wales involved brutality, the ignoring of Welsh law, and the excessive use of privileges by English merchants in the new boroughs surrounding the new castles. Despite a national uprising, Edward crushed any bid for independence. The English crossed the Conwy, seized Anglesey and finally overpowered Snowdonia. Dafydd was captured and hanged, drawn, and quartered in 1283. Subjugation commenced. Castle building began on a grand scale with the rapid construction of Conwy, Harlech, and Caernarfon while Hope was refurbished and smaller castles begun at Holt, Ruthin and Denbigh. Anglesey was adorned with Beaumaris. In 1301, Edward invested his son, Edward of Caernarfon, with the title of Prince of Wales, since held by the eldest son of the reigning English monarch, the current honor being held by Prince Charles.

Opposite: Llywelyn's state was eventually weakened by internal disunity. It was not long before English aggression took advantage.

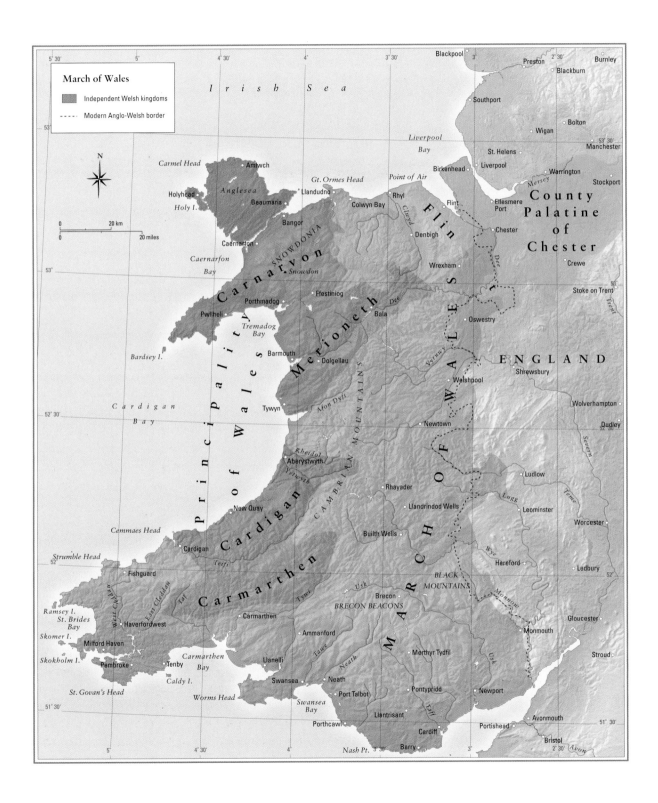

March of Wales

Independent Welsh kingdoms

---- Modern Anglo-Welsh border

Irish Sea

N

0   20 km

0   20 miles

Blackpool

Preston   Burnley

Southport   Blackburn

Carmel Head

Amlwch

Gt. Ormes Head

Point of Air

Liverpool Bay

Wigan   Bolton

St. Helens   Manchester

Liverpool

Holyhead

Anglesea

Beaumaris

Llandudno

Colwyn Bay

Rhyl

Flint

Birkenhead

Warrington

Stockport

Holy I.

Bangor

Denbigh

Ellesmere Port

Chester

Crewe

County Palatine of Chester

Caernarfon

SNOWDONIA

Flint

Caernarfon Bay

Snowdon

Wrexham

Stoke on Trent

Carnarvon

Porthmadog

Ffestiniog

Bala

Oswestry

Pwllheli

Dee

Merioneth

Tremadog Bay

Barmouth

Dolgellau

Welshpool

Shrewsbury

ENGLAND

Bardsey I.

Vyrnwy

MARCH OF WALES

Wolverhampton

Cardigan Bay

Tywyn

Afon Dyfi

Newtown

Dudley

Principality

of Wales

Rheidol

Aberystwyth

Ystwyth

CAMBRIAN MOUNTAINS

Rhayader

Ludlow

Lugg

Leominster

Teme

Worcester

New Quay

Cardigan

Llandrindod Wells

Cemmaes Head

Builth Wells

Hereford

Strumble Head

Cardigan

Teifi

Wye

Ledbury

Fishguard

Carmarthen

BLACK MOUNTAINS

Ramsey I.
St. Brides Bay

East Cleddau

Taf

Tywi

Usk

Brecon

BRECON BEACONS

Monnow

Gloucester

Skomer I.

Haverfordwest

Carmarthen

Ammanford

Monmouth

Stroud

Milford Haven

West Cleddau

Llanelli

Tawe

Merthyr Tydfil

Usk

Skokholm I.

Pembroke

Tenby

Neath

Newport

Carmarthen Bay

Swansea

Neath

Pontypridd

St. Govan's Head

Caldy I.

Port Talbot

Taff

Avonmouth

Worms Head

Llantrisant

Portishead

Porthcawl

Cardiff

Bristol

Swansea Bay

Nash Pt.

Barry

Avon

CISTERCIANS IN WALES: TINTERN

THE MONASTIC CISTERCIANS BUILT ABBEYS IN REMOTE REGIONS AND OPENED UP MUCH NEW LAND. THEIR ESTATES WERE AT THE FOREFRONT OF AGRICULTURAL INNOVATION AND PRODUCED GREAT WEALTH.

The origins of the Cistercian order of monks lay with St. Benedict of Nursia, who lived in the monastery of Monte Cassino in Italy. This baton was passed to Abbot Robert of Molesme, who desired to return to a purer form of monastic life and religious observance. He established a new monastery at Cîteaux, where the new monastery's third abbot, Stephen Harding, instated on the spiritual ideals of the Cistercian order in *Carta Caritatis*, the *Charter of Charity*. The Cistercians insisted uncompromisingly on poverty and situated their abbeys in remote spots away from towns and men. The monks espoused the virtue of manual labor, and, eschewing tithes and rents, relied on intensive cultivation of agricultural land to provide the necessities of life.

Walter fitz Richard of Clare, Lord of Chepstow, decided to introduce them to Chepstow at Tintern in the Wye Valley. Like other abbeys, Tintern acquired land which was farmed by lay brethren, the *converse*, who established outlying farms known as granges. The monks improved the land by felling timber and draining marshes on the Monmouthshire levels. The monks were successful in establishing a balanced agricultural set of holdings. A second founder of Tintern was Roger Bigod, Earl of Norfolk, who became heavily involved in the abbey's building program, especially the abbey church. Later, Tintern acquired tithes, against the Rule, from the church at Lydd in Kent in 1326-27.

The foundation of Cistercian abbeys was very important in newly acquired lands. The monks helped develop local economies by expanding agriculture by virtue of using marginal land. Hence the monks brought a political benefit to Anglo-Normans in a hostile land. Tintern was one of a network of Welsh Cistercian abbeys bringing development, religious civilization, and medical aid (through its infirmary) to local populations. A process of socialization was on the march.

Opposite: The formation of a Cistercian abbey at Tintern introduced a new economy into the region, exploiting marginal lands previously ignored as unproductive.

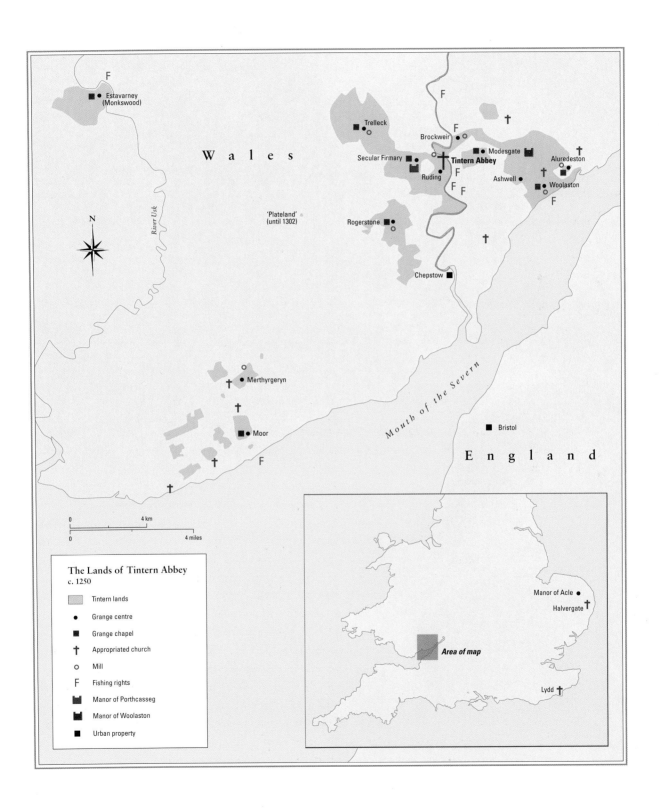

F
Estavarney
(Monkswood)

W a l e s

Trelleck
Brockweir
F
Modesgate
Secular Firmary
Aluredeston
Tintern Abbey
Ruding
F
Ashwell
Woolaston
F F
F

River Usk

N

'Plateland'
(until 1302)

Rogerstone

Chepstow

Merthyrgeryn

Mouth of the Severn

Bristol

Moor

E n g l a n d

F

0   4 km
0   4 miles

The Lands of Tintern Abbey
c. 1250

- ▨ Tintern lands
- ● Grange centre
- ■ Grange chapel
- † Appropriated church
- ○ Mill
- F Fishing rights
- ▰ Manor of Porthcasseg
- ▰ Manor of Woolaston
- ■ Urban property

Area of map

Manor of Acle
Halvergate

Lydd

OWAIN GLYNDWR'S REVOLT

GLYNDWR'S UPRISING WAS IN RESPONSE TO THE DEATH OF KING RICHARD II, WHO HAD PROMOTED WELSH INTERESTS. KING HENRY IV ATTEMPTED TO REPEAL HIS PREDECESSOR'S WELSH POLICIES, CAUSING THE WELSH TO FEEL UNCERTAIN ABOUT THEIR FUTURE. THIS LED TO WIDESPREAD RESENTMENT AND REVOLT.

After Llywelyn's death, Wales was quiescent except for the brief revolt in 1294-95 of Madog ap Llywelyn. The fourteenth century saw an identity of interest develop between elite Welshmen and the English crown. Richard II, who had several Welshmen in his entourage, was deposed in 1399 by Henry Bolingbroke, who proclaimed himself King Henry IV but who lacked the Welsh sympathies of Richard. In addition, Wales did feel certain pressures such as the plague, which affected the labor market at a time when the country was making a difficult transition from the medieval and feudal past to a more capitalist economy.

Owain Glyndwr raised a national rebellion which drew strength from all society. Owain, who had gained military experience as Bolingbroke's squire, was proclaimed Prince of Wales (1400) and soon gained a victory over the English at Mynydd Hyddgen. In retaliation, Henry occupied the Cistercian Abbey of Strata Florida, dispossessing the monks and turning it into a military base. Owain visualized Wales as a sovereign state with its own legislature, Church, and universities and a return to the customary law of Hywel Dda. English resistance was severely limited to a few small localities. Owain was in touch with leading Englishmen, as he was with France and Brittany. Eventually, the English won a number of encounters. English-controlled castles were used to obstruct trade and build an economic blockade so that parcels of Wales could be broken in detail. The Welsh lords began to surrender. The Welsh prince was now a fugitive and operated as a guerrilla leader, finally vanishing from sight in 1412. Next year, new King Henry V chose to appease the Welsh, with Welsh leaders being pardoned, and the rebellion fizzled out. No one knows what happened to Glyndwr although speculation suggests he lived in the home of his daughter, Alys, in disguise as a Franciscan monk. Owain has become a romanticized hero figure.

Opposite: After Edmond's conquest, English rule did not sit well with many Welsh lords. By 1400, an accumulation of grievences boiled over into open rebellion.

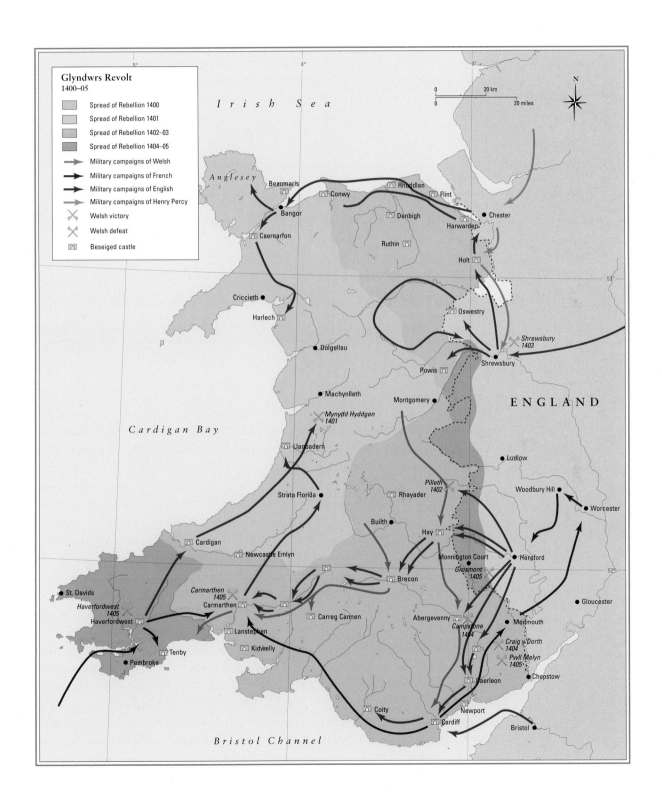

Glyndwrs Revolt
1400–05

Spread of Rebellion 1400
Spread of Rebellion 1401
Spread of Rebellion 1402–03
Spread of Rebellion 1404–05

Military campaigns of Welsh
Military campaigns of French
Military campaigns of English
Military campaigns of Henry Percy
Welsh victory
Welsh defeat
Beseiged castle

Irish Sea

Anglesey

Beaumaris

Conwy
Rhuddlan
Flint
Chester

Bangor

Denbigh
Harwarden

Caernarfon

Ruthin

Holt

Criccieth

Oswestry

Harlech

Dolgellau

Shrewsbury 1403

Powis

Shrewsbury

Cardigan Bay

Machynlleth

Montgomery

E N G L A N D

Mynydd Hyddgen 1401

Ludlow

Llanbadarn

Pilleth 1402

Rhayader

Woodbury Hill

Worcester

Strata Florida

Builth

Hay

Cardigan

Newcastle Emlyn

Monnington Court

Hereford

Grosmont 1405

Brecon

St. Davids

Haverfordwest 1405
Haverfordwest

Carmarthen 1405
Carmarthen

Carreg Cannen

Abergavenny

Campstone 1404

Monmouth

Gloucester

Craig y Dorth 1404

Lanstephen

Kidwelly

Pwll Melyn 1405

Chepstow

Tenby

Pembroke

Caerleon

Coity

Newport

Cardiff

Bristol

Bristol Channel

N

0   20 km
0   20 miles

WALES AND THE ACT OF UNION, 1536

THE ACT OF UNION WAS PASSED BY AN ENGLISH PARLIAMENT WITH NO WELSH REPRESENTATIVE. THE WELSH COUNTIES WERE UNDER ENGLISH LAW WITH ENGLISH THE FIRST LANGUAGE, BUT THEY DID OBTAIN REPRESENTATION AT WESTMINSTER.

During the fifteenth century, despite penal legislation, the Welsh gentry managed to consolidate compact freehold estates and achieve public office, but they resented having second-rank status in their own country. They wanted equality with the English and hoped for much when Henry Tudor, a Welshman, secured the throne on Bosworth Field, thereby ending the Wars of the Roses. However, nothing really changed; this Henry VII was no savior. Matters changed when Henry VIII ascended the throne (1509). Henry desired to unify his country, and Thomas Cromwell was requested to find a solution to unify Wales within itself and make Wales part of England in a legal sense. Cromwell's policy of harmonization swept away the Marcher lordships and established the final borders of Wales. Justices of the peace ran the law and the Marcher lordships lost the power to try serious criminal cases. Wales was now able to send elected members to the English parliament at Westminster, so Welshman achieved equal political and legal status. The acts passed between 1536–43 secured Henry's designs but the official language was to be English. The laws pleased many of the Welsh gentry. Order, stability, and prosperity began to develop although Anglicization was never complete. The gentry themselves did not all forget their roots and bards. Some immersed themselves in Celtic learning and literature while the peasantry lived in their valleys occupied in subsistence agriculture. The Protestant Reformation failed to take root, and evangelists of whatever faith wasted their time. Only when the New Testament and Prayer Book were published in Welsh in 1567 and the Bible in 1588 did the Reformation trickle into the valleys. The Welsh were the only Celtic nation to enjoy the Bible in their vernacular, and this ensured the survival of Welsh in its literary form. Learned Welshmen began to take notice of their history and Welsh antiquities, thus conserving the Welsh heritage for future nationalism.

Opposite: The Act of Union in 1536 saw the land of Wales reorganized into English-style counties, each with its own sheriff, in line with the legal and administrative system of England.

N

The Act of the Union
1536

ANGLESEY

● Bangor

Denbigh ●   FLINT

CAERNARFONSHIRE

● Caernarfon

DENBIGHSHIRE

0   20 km
0   20 miles

53°

MERIONETHSHIRE

POWYS
MONTGOMERYSHIRE

ENGLAND

RADNORSHIRE

CARDIGANSHIRE

52°

BRECKNOCKSHIRE

● St. Davids

CARMARTHENSHIRE

Brecon ●

PEMBROKESHIRE

● Carmarthen

MONMOUTHSHIRE

● Pembroke

GLAMORGANSHIRE

Swansea ●

Cardiff ●

5°   4°   3°

Welsh and Scottish Industry

WELSH AND SCOTTISH INDUSTRIALISATION LED TO A GROWTH IN WEALTH. THIS PROGRESS AIDED THE GROWTH OF THE BRITISH EMPIRE AND SAW THE MIGRATION OF WELSH MINERS AND THE SCOTS FROM THE HIGHLANDS INTO URBAN SQUALOR.

After union with England, Wales was virtually an economic backwater, lacking in industry and with activity concentrated upon the agrarian sector based upon hill farming and sheep rearing. Wales was virtually divided into north and south economically, with the north linked to English economics via Wrexham, Chester, and Liverpool and the south tied to the markets of Bristol. The vast central area was linked to the droving markets, as cattle were driven to the Midlands and London.

Other industries were cottage-based woollens, occasional coal mining, and smelting in the northeast and the southwest of the south Wales coalfield. Such industry as there was served the agrarian sector but showed promise for a future large-scale development. Investment possibilities grew in the mid-eighteenth century as English capitalists invested in the iron-producing regions of south Wales, noticeably at the Dowlais Works (1759) and Cyfartha (1765) in Merthyr. By the 1840s, iron works were evident across the north of the coalfield from Ystalyfera to Blaenavon. South Wales was instrumental in meeting the needs of war in the eighteenth and nineteenth centuries and then providing materials for the railroad boom.

South Wales also witnessed the smelting of copper, brought in from Anglesey and Wales, and all was based upon the need for people who migrated in from central Wales, Pembroke, and England. Much later, coal was mined for sale, leading to the development of the village ribbon development in the valleys. South Wales also needed a communication system to meet new economic demands. A coastal trade had always existed; it was overtaken in some ways by turnpike roads following old droving routes both north and south of the coalfield. Canals were built to link individual valleys to ports such as Kidwelly, Swansea, Neath, Cardiff, and Newport. By the 1840s, the ports were overtaken by railway development, which proved more convenient when moving coal to London.

Opposite: Industrialization and urbanization in Scotland was largely confined to the central lowlands and the east coast.

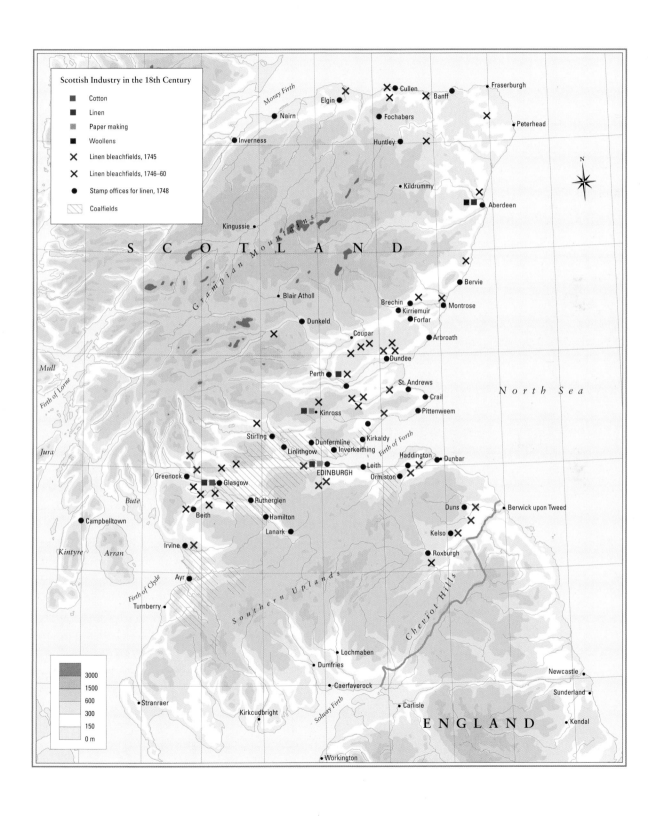

Scottish Industry in the 18th Century

■ Cotton
■ Linen
■ Paper making
■ Woollens
✕ Linen bleachfields, 1745
✕ Linen bleachfields, 1746–60
● Stamp offices for linen, 1748
▨ Coalfields

SCOTLAND

Moray Firth
Cullen
Elgin
Banff
Fraserburgh
Nairn
Fochabers
Peterhead
Inverness
Huntley
Kildrummy
Aberdeen
Kingussie
Grampian Mountains
Blair Atholl
Bervie
Dunkeld
Brechin
Montrose
Kirriemuir
Forfar
Coupar
Arbroath
Dundee
Perth
St. Andrews
Crail
Pittenweem
Kinross
Stirling
Kirkaldy
Dunfermline
Firth of Forth
Linlithgow
Inverkeithing
Haddington
Dunbar
EDINBURGH
Leith
Ormiston
Greenock
Glasgow
Duns
Berwick upon Tweed
Rutherglen
Bute
Beith
Kelso
Campbelltown
Hamilton
Lanark
Roxburgh
Irvine
Kintyre
Arran
Ayr
Turnberry
Firth of Clyde
Southern Uplands
Cheviot Hills
Lochmaben
Dumfries
Newcastle
Caerfaverock
Sunderland
Stranraer
Carlisle
Kirkcudbright
Kendal
Solway Firth
ENGLAND
Workington

Mull
Firth of Lorne
Jura

North Sea

N

3000
1500
600
300
150
0 m

Northeast Wales saw the development of a swathe of ironworks in Flint together with large-scale coal mining. Lead mining occurred nearby and in Cardiganshire. Copper was excavated in Anglesey and slate quarrying grew as a response to house building, especially in the quarters for industrial workers in British towns and cities as well as in Wales. Overall, industrialization transformed the demographics of Wales, emptying out the central regions into the urban industrial towns, but the admixture of migrant labor from Ireland and England did not destroy the use of Welsh nor was Welsh culture undermined. Nonconformist religion remained strong as did music in choirs and bands. A later development in the nineteenth century was the serious growth of Welsh rugby football. 1881 saw 11 rugby clubs forming the Welsh Rugby Football Union and the selection of a team to play England.

Before union with England, Scotland's economy incorporated the early linen and flax industries with a considerable degree of woollens which were exported south. English capital ensured that many border areas contributed to the cottage outworkers of the northern English woollen industry. Some coal was dug and lead smelted with the beginnings of a glass and papermaking industry. Overall, Scotland was rural with a pastoral economy with very small pockets of industry; however, the potential existed for a surge in new industrial endeavor and a rapid rate of industrialization.

The economy started to perform with trade based in Glasgow importing American tobacco until the Revolution. An explosion in the linen industry followed, with production in 1748–52 being double the level in 1728-32. The black cattle droving trade continued, being fueled by cattle ranching in the highlands. The production of fine threads and linens fueled the textile industry in Glasgow and Paisley and was aided by considerable investment from Spitalfields. The lowlands became a hive of new banking activity, which aided trade as banknotes in circulation increased 15-fold in the mid-eighteenth century and lines of credit were advanced.

After 1863, water-powered cotton-spinning came in and compensated for the decline in the tobacco industry, but the roots of the cotton industry lay in the original flax, linen, and silk trades. Commencing in a wide geographical spread, spinning became heavily concentrated in the Glasgow and Paisley region. A real industrial breakthrough happened when the hot-blast furnace process was introduced into iron foundries; west-central Scotland became the lowest-cost pig-iron producing region in the United Kingdom. By 1849, Scotland's share of British output had risen significantly, from five to twenty-five per cent.

The production of iron led to the growth of the Clydeside shipbuilding industry. Wooden ships had been built previously but this trade declined. The new material ensured that by 1850, the Clyde produced 66 percent of the tonnage of iron vessels in Britain. In sum, the central Lowlands became the industrial heartland of Scotland, and its expansion sucked in many of the dispossessed from the Highland clearances. The highlands remained a region with the highest proportion of males engaged in agriculture and were similar to the English counties of Bedfordshire, Hertfordshire, and Rutland.

By 1851, Scotland was probably more industrialized than the rest of Britain, yet wage levels were lower although some trades did well, such as carpenters in Glasgow. On the other hand, rural poverty existed in the Western Highlands and Islands and the 1846 potato blight caused hardship as elsewhere. Urban and rural malnutrition and disease had social implications, as did a huge increase in emigration, which affected industry.

Opposite: The main areas of industry in Wales were concentrated initially in the north east. Later, as the south Wales coalfields developed, population and industry was concentrated in this region.

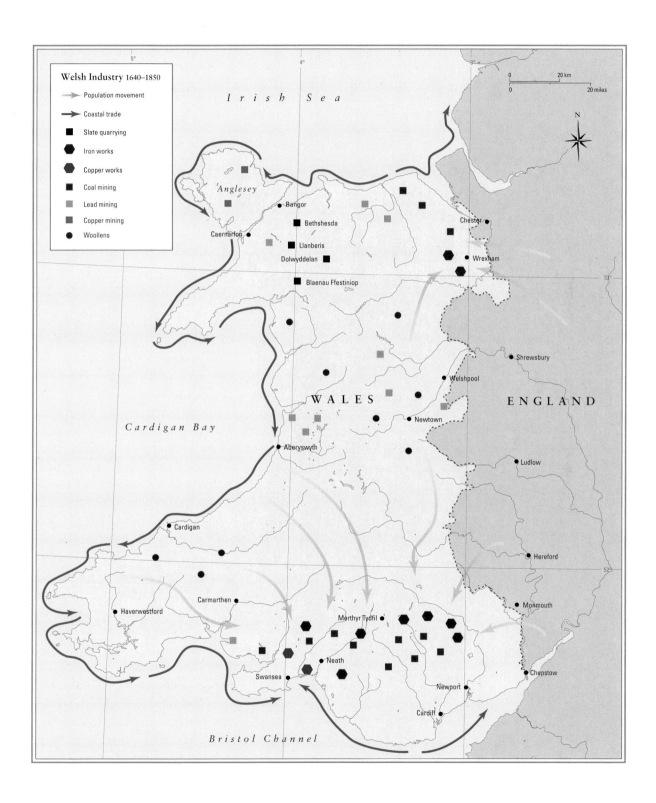

Welsh Industry 1640–1850

→ Population movement
→ Coastal trade
■ Slate quarrying
⬢ Iron works
⬢ Copper works
■ Coal mining
■ Lead mining
■ Copper mining
● Woollens

Irish Sea

Anglesey

Bangor

Bethshesda

Caernarfon

Llanberis

Dolwyddelan

Blaenau Ffestiniop

Chester

Wrexham

WALES

Cardigan Bay

Shrewsbury

Welshpool

Newtown

ENGLAND

Aberyswyth

Cardigan

Ludlow

Carmarthen

Hereford

Haverwestford

Monmouth

Merthyr Tydfil

Neath

Swansea

Chepstow

Newport

Cardiff

Bristol Channel

0   20 km
0   20 miles

N

FRANCE: BRETONS

SOME BRITONS, PURSUED BY THE ROMANS, FLED BRITAIN AND
SETTLED IN NORTHWEST FRANCE, HENCE THE GIVEN NAME FOR
THIS REGION, BRITTANY. THE BRITONS WHO SETTLED IN BRITTANY
EVENTUALLY BECAME KNOWN AS BRETONS. IRON AGE BRITTANY
WAS DIVIDED INTO FIVE TRIBAL CHIEFDOMS.

In classical times, Brittany (*Breizh*), known as Armorica, was rich in pre-historical artifacts and megalithic monuments, the most famous being at Carnac. Gold items have been found, and polished stone axes were exported along a number of river valleys: the Loire, Seine, and Rhône. The Bronze Age witnessed Brittany importing gold from Ireland, silver from Spain and tin from Britain, while the region exported bronze tools, swords, and artifacts as far as Germany and the Low Countries. Brittany was eclipsed technologically by the Greeks, Etruscans, and the Halstatt Celtic cultures. However, Brittany adapted, developing its own iron industry and acquiring cultural influences similar to those defined as Celtic from central Europe. Grave finds, especially skeletal material, demonstrate that Brittany did not experience mass emigrations into the region but became Celtic by evolving its own variant of Celticity from external cultural developments.

By the late fifth century BC, Armorica was divided into five Gallic tribal chiefdoms or kingships. History constantly remembers the Veneti, who inhabited the Morbihan area and are famed for their seamanship and trading systems. This tribe minted its own coins, basing them on Greek examples but with Celtic modifications and additions. Another tribe engaged in trade were the Coriosolitae, whose coins have been found extensively in Britain. This tribe dwelt between the central forests and the north coast. Their pottery has been found in England and the Channel Islands. The Osismii also lived along Brittany's northern coast. The Namnetes controlled the area around the mouth of the River Loire with a capital at Nantes. The Redones resided in the smallest territory, with a tribal capital at modern Rennes.

The Breton region became a target for Roman aggression as Julius Caesar swept through Gaul in his lengthy campaigns. His major obstacle in Armorica was the Veneti fleet but this was defeated. Much archeological evidence suggests that Caesar's reports of having wiped out Brittany's tribes are incorrect and that he was writing for political effect in Rome. The five Gallic tribal chiefdoms were divided into the normal Roman *civitates,* with their capitals transformed into Roman provincial towns: Darioritum (Vannes) for the Veneti; Condate (Rennes) for the Redones; Namnetes (Nantes) for the Namnetes, who lost their lands south of the Loire; Fanum Martis (Corseulles) for the Curiosolitae; and Vorigum (Carhaix) for the Osismii. These centers developed street grid-systems, public baths, administrative buildings, and theaters, together with *basilicae,* temples, and shops; Rennes is a perfect example of this phenomena.

The Romans developed the Breton salt-pan industry and trade generally but when the Romans left Britain, the Angles and Saxons pressured the Britons, many of whom streamed into Brittany, hence the name. Two centuries saw a large migrant population clearing forests and merging with the indigenous Celtic peoples. Three kingdoms were established: Dumnonia in the north; Cornouaille in the south; and Br Erech, the old Veneti area, which became a border conflict area with the Franks.

The history of the British settlement is told in the lives of the early Breton saints, most of whom were born in Cornwall and Wales. These men established monasteries along the Armorican north coast, such as that on Île Modez, named for St. Mawes. Place names provide further evidence to establish areas of British settlement. These are in the north and west, with names commencing with *plou-,* similar to the Welsh *plwyf,* both meaning "people." Other British loans are *lan,* the Welsh *Llan* for "church," *coët,* the Welsh *coed* for "wood" and *ker,* Welsh *caer* for "hamlet." The southeast region of Brittany sees names with the suffixes *–ac, -é* and *–y* from the Roman *–acum,* "place.' Celtic church customs from Briton seriously disrupted religious practices from Rome and gave the province of Brittany even more of a generic identity from the French.

Celtic tribes such as the Osismii dwelled along the dramatic northern coastline of Brittany.

BRITTANY IN THE MIDDLE AGES

THE MEDIEVAL PERIOD IN BRITTANY SAW ECCLESIASTICAL REFORM, MONASTIC ENDEAVOR, AND MASS CHRISTIANIZATION AS MAINSTREAM ROMAN CATHOLICISM ABSORBED AND DESTROYED VESTIGES OF OLD CELTIC PRACTICES.

It is known that the Franks established a border zone in Breton by 778 which was used as a military base to conquer Brittany. These attempts failed and this Breton march remained until the Franks found another way to control the Bretons. Louis the Pious (814-40) gave Vannes to the Breton nobleman Nominoé (831), who rapidly became the most powerful Breton leader. He rebelled against Charles the Bald (823–827) of Francia, defeating him in battle in 845. Nominoé replaced Frankish bishops with Bretons and expanded his territories. His son, Érispoé, defeated Charles again, and was recognized as a vassal King within the Frankish state.

Salomon (857-4) murdered his cousin, Érispoé, so becoming even more powerful than his predecessor. He allied with the Vikings and forced Charles to hand over Jersey and Guernsey. Vikings raided and ruled the land from a capital at Nantes, with other bases scattered through the kingdom (921). Alan's grandson, Alan II, aided by his godfather, King Athelstan of England, raised an army, invaded Brittany and defeated the Vikings (936-7). Alan II ruled as Duke of Brittany, having to compete with increasingly powerful Breton nobles. Thus elements of Frankish feudalism crept into Brittany and Breton feudal society became totally decentralized with ducal power waning for 200 years. However, the monks who had fled from Viking attacks were encouraged to return and establish monasteries. Brittany suffered from having two powerful neighbors: the Vikings and William the Conqueror. William swept through the duchy but was unable to consolidate his gains, as he had more pressing matters to handle in England. The Norman Conquest provided military opportunities for Breton knights because after 1066 some 20 per cent of the land in England was held by Bretons in William's service. The Hundred Years' War between England and France incorporated a Breton war of succession, which broke out in 1341. France supported

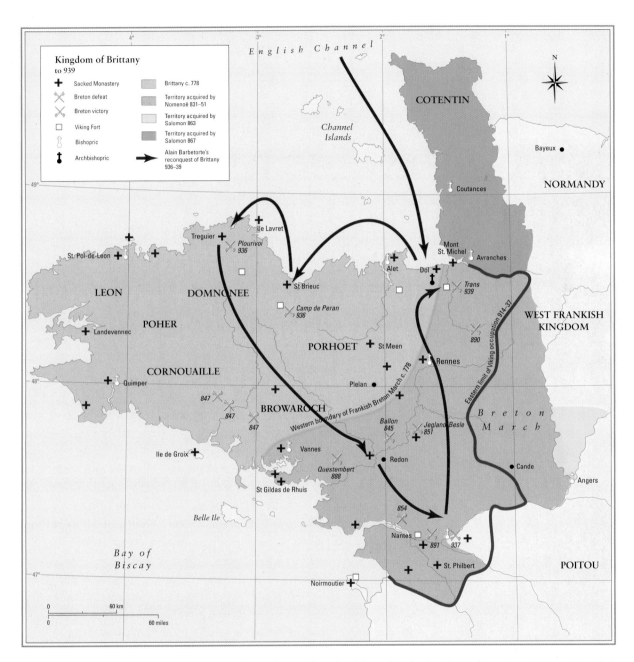

Kingdom of Brittany
to 939

✝ Sacked Monastery
⚔ Breton defeat
⚔ Breton victory
▢ Viking Fort
⚲ Bishopric
⚲ Archbishopric

Brittany c. 778
Territory acquired by Nomenoë 831–51
Territory acquired by Salomon 863
Territory acquired by Salomon 867
➤ Alain Barbetorte's reconquest of Brittany 936–39

English Channel

COTENTIN

Channel Islands

Bayeux

NORMANDY

Coutances

Treguier
Ile Lavret
Plourivoi 936
Mont St. Michel
Avranches

St. Pol-de-Leon
Alet
Dol
Trans 939

LEON
DOMNONEE
St Brieuc
Camp de Peran 936

890

POHER
Landevennec

CORNOUAILLE
Quimper

PORHOET
St Meen
Rennes

Eastern limit of Viking occupation 914-37

WEST FRANKISH KINGDOM

Plelan

Breton March

847
847
847

BROWAROCH

Western boundary of Frankish Breton March c. 778

Ballon 845

Jegland Besle 851

Ile de Groix
Vannes
Redon

Questembert 888

Cande

Angers

St Gildas de Rhuis

Belle Ile

854

Bay of Biscay

Nantes
891
937

St. Philbert

POITOU

Noirmoutier

0   60 km
0   60 miles

Charles of Blois as duke while England supported Jean de Montfort. The defeat of England at the Battle of Formigny (1450) and Castallon (1453) saw the end of English rule in Normandy and Aquitaine. The French then turned on Brittany and annihilated a Breton army at St. Aubin-du-Cormier (1487). French control followed, with the Breton heiress, Anne, being coerced into marriage with King Charles VIII in 1491. The eventual heir to Brittany was also heir to France, and 1532 saw a formal Act of Union.

Brittany (in Roman times called Armorica) suffered population decline toward the end of the Roman rule. At this time a new people appeared, archaeological evidence suggests they were Britons.

BRITTANY AND THE REVOLUTION, 1789

THE FRENCH REVOLUTION GENERATED INCREASING GOVERNMENTAL CENTRALIZATION. BRITTANY WAS DIVIDED INTO FIVE DEPARTMENTS WHICH IGNORED GEOGRAPHICAL, RELIGIOUS, AND LINGUISTIC BORDERS. BRETON AND CELTIC GALLO WERE REGARDED AS INFERIOR LANGUAGES.

In 1789, a Breton leader, Le Chapelier, announced the abolition of all feudal rights, which incited many peasants to attack their former lords. Simultaneously the deputies voted away the special rights that Brittany had enjoyed since the union with France. The revolutionary activity involved dividing France into *departments,* which broke Brittany down into five parts. This division represented the business and commercial interests of the Breton middle class despite the divisions in geography, religious, and linguistic splits between Breton and Gallo speakers.

The peasants' condition was not much changed by the Revolution, with state taxes replacing feudal dues and high rents charged. What pushed many peasants into outright opposition to the new politics were assaults on the Church and monastic property, leading to nationalization. Urban life grew difficult too: bread riots followed the closure of the tobacco factory at Morlaix and large-scale violence occurred in 1793, when 300,000 men were to be conscripted into the army. The threat of federalism was real and the Jacobins commenced employing the guillotine to eradicate actual and potential threats. Hundreds of people were killed in Brittany but thousands in Nantes, with Commissioner Jean-Baptiste Carrier being so extreme that Roberspierre recalled him to Paris. Peasants engaged in guerrilla warfare, which grew stronger as religious persecution increased, became more aggressive.

In 1799, Napoleon Bonaparte seized power in a coup d'état, becoming First Consul. He stabilized Brittany with military force and in 1802 signed the Concordat with the Pope. The years between 1789 and 1815 saw Brittany severely damaged in economic and social terms, with its people divided.

Opposite: The Breton parliament survived until the revolution. Its powers had already been undermined by the centralization policy of the monarchy and the insistance of using French in all legal and government documents.

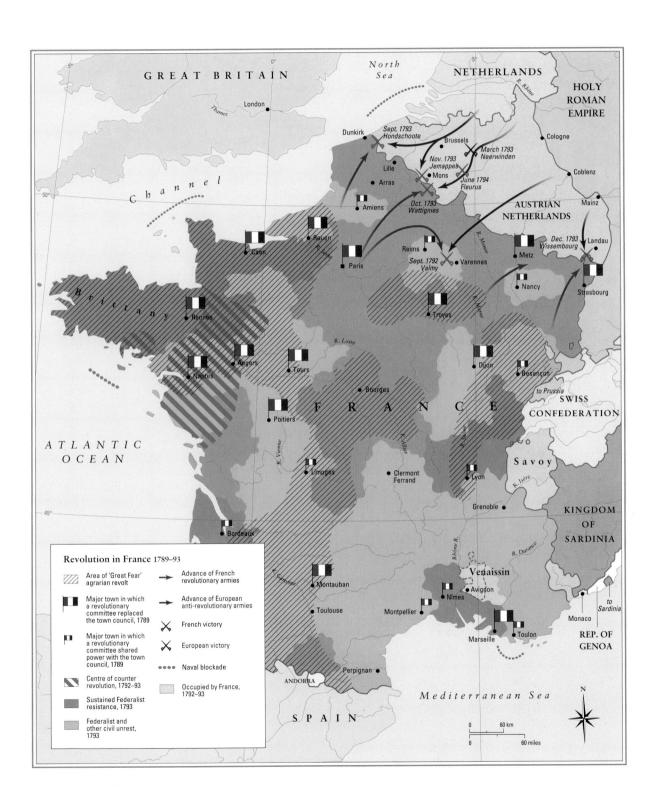

GREAT BRITAIN

North Sea

NETHERLANDS

HOLY ROMAN EMPIRE

London

Thames

C h a n n e l

Dunkirk

Sept. 1793
Hondschoote

Brussels

March 1793
Neerwinden

Cologne

Lille

Nov. 1793
Jemappes

Mons

June 1794
Fleurus

Arras

Amiens

Oct. 1793
Wattignies

AUSTRIAN
NETHERLANDS

Mainz

Coblenz

R. Rhine

Rouen

Caen

R. Seine

Reims

Dec. 1793
Wissembourg

Landau

Metz

Sept. 1792
Valmy

Varennes

Paris

B r i t t a n y

Rennes

R. Meuse

Nancy

Strasbourg

Troyes

R. Marne

ATLANTIC
OCEAN

Angers

Nantes

Tours

R. Loire

F R A N C E

Dijon

Besançon

Bourges

to Prussia

SWISS
CONFEDERATION

Poitiers

R. Vienne

R. Allier

R. Saône

Limoges

Clermont
Ferrand

Lyon

Savoy

R. Isère

Grenoble

KINGDOM
OF
SARDINIA

R. Dordogne

Bordeaux

Rhône R.

R. Durance

Venaissin

Montauban

Avignon

Nîmes

to
Sardinia

Toulouse

Montpellier

Monaco

R. Garonne

Marseille

Toulon

REP. OF
GENOA

Perpignan

ANDORRA

S P A I N

Mediterranean Sea

N

Revolution in France 1789–93

	Area of 'Great Fear' agrarian revolt
	Major town in which a revolutionary committee replaced the town council, 1789
	Major town in which a revolutionary committee shared power with the town council, 1789
	Centre of counter revolution, 1792–93
	Sustained Federalist resistance, 1793
	Federalist and other civil unrest, 1793

→ Advance of French revolutionary armies

→ Advance of European anti-revolutionary armies

✕ French victory

✕ European victory

•••• Naval blockade

Occupied by France, 1792–93

0   60 km

0   60 miles

BRETON TRADE

BRETON TRADE HAS DEVELOPED SINCE THE SECOND WORLD
WAR WITH THE GROWTH OF MIXED FARMS, OYSTER AND MUSSEL
COMMERCIAL FARMING, AND THE HIGHLY SUCCESSFUL BRITTANY
FERRIES CARRYING AGRICULTURAL PRODUCE TO BRITAIN AND
RETURNING WITH TOURISTS.

The Bretons have traded throughout history, generally using the sea and rivers for transportation, with routes linking Brittany to the north and the Newfoundland cod fisheries. Periods of lengthy slump have existed but now Brittany has a thriving, diversified agricultural economy and the farmers own two-thirds of a major shipping line: Brittany Ferries.

The Neolithic period saw gold imported from Ireland, silver from Spain, and tin from Britain while polished stone axes were exported as far as the Low Countries and southern Britain. Many other products were imported and exported, such as wine, pottery, and salt. The Romans improved the transport system and expanded trade routes by using existing Breton roads and built a route to the key Roman center of Lyons in Gaul. The fall of the Roman Empire, barbarian raids, and medieval warfare disrupted economic development but the growth of castles, cathedrals, and stately mansions indicates some prosperity. However, the end of the Hundred Years' War meant the duchy could no longer play off one side against the other and now faced competition. Nevertheless, salt was still exported, as was wine from the Nantes region and cereals. Linen and canvas was exported, as was very fine linen for lace-making.

After annexation by France, Breton wealth accumulated through sea trade and the cloth industry. Trade was conducted with the West Indies and became a veritable gold mine. Breton trade suffered during the American War of Independence, the French Revolution, and the Napoleonic Wars but the sailors of Saint-Malo became renowned as privateers. Since the Second World War, Breton agriculture has progressed, making the region a leading food producer. Better product distribution was pioneered by Alexis Gourvennec, who had the port of Roscoff built and then founded Brittany Ferries, which ships food, heavy goods, and tourists to and from Britain.

Opposite: The Breton peninsula sits astride the main coastal Atlantic seaways. Its safe ports and harbors make an ideal location for north—south trade.

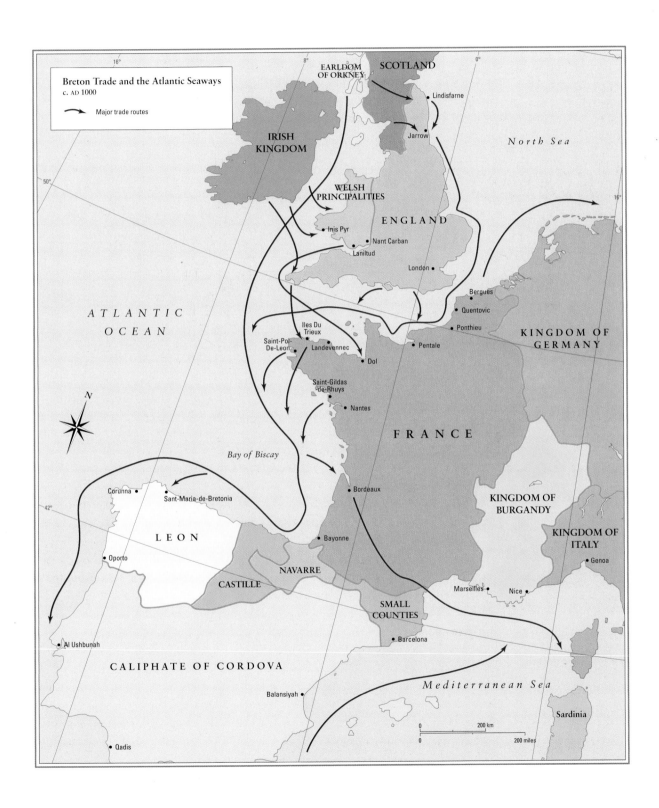

Breton Trade and the Atlantic Seaways
c. AD 1000

→ Major trade routes

EARLDOM
OF ORKNEY

SCOTLAND

• Lindisfarne

• Jarrow

North Sea

IRISH
KINGDOM

WELSH
PRINCIPALITIES

ENGLAND

• Inis Pyr

• Nant Carban

• Laniltud

London •

ATLANTIC
OCEAN

Bergues •

• Quentovic

• Ponthieu

KINGDOM OF
GERMANY

Iles Du
Trieux

Saint-Pol-
De-Leon

• Landevennec

• Pentale

• Dol

Saint-Gildas
-de-Rhuys

• Nantes

FRANCE

Bay of Biscay

Corunna •

• Sant-Maria-de-Bretonia

LEON

• Oporto

• Bordeaux

• Bayonne

NAVARRE

CASTILLE

KINGDOM OF
BURGANDY

KINGDOM OF
ITALY

• Genoa

Marseilles •   • Nice

SMALL
COUNTIES

• Al Ushbunah

• Barcelona

CALIPHATE OF CORDOVA

Mediterranean Sea

Balansiyah •

Sardinia

• Qadis

200 km

200 miles

CELTS AT WAR

THE CELTS HAVE ALWAYS HAD A REPUTATION FOR GREAT BRAVERY
IN BATTLE. IRISH UNITS HAD A PARTICULARLY IMPORTANT ROLE IN
THE AMERICAN CIVIL WAR, AND WERE ALSO ACTIVE IN FIGHTING
THE BRITISH IN CANADA. THE SCOTS SETTLERS IN NORTH AMERICA
WERE INSTRUMENTAL IN THE INDIAN WARS.

The Celts have been renowned for their bravery in battle and their tenacity in military adversity. Their ill-disciplined charges at Telamon or the Highland charge at Culloden are legendary. Throughout time, the Celts have fought invaders of their lands and defended their sovereignty until beaten. Even then, their martial qualities have been utilized by Britain in the French-Indian Wars in America, the Peninsular Wars under the command of Wellington, or in recent times in fighting during the first and second world wars. Their military records are second to none, and the first shot fired by the British army in 1914 was fired by Corporal E. Thomas of the 4th Royal Irish Dragoon Guards just north of Mons on 22 August. Next day, Lientenant Dease, serving with the Royal Fusiliers, died fighting with his machine-gun while attempting to stop a German advance; he was awarded the first posthumous Victoria Cross of the war.

However, the Irish and Scots military histories far exceed that normally recorded. After the French defeat at Agincourt (1415), some 15,000 Scots sailed from the Clyde (1419-24) to fight in France. In 1421, at the Battle of Baugé, they defeated the English, killing the Duke of Clarence. Other Scots were with Joan of Arc at the relief of Orléans and others founded the Garde Écossaise in 1418, which served the French sovereign until the abdication of Charles X in 1830.

Scots were involved in the Northern Crusades, fighting alongside the Teutonic Knights and leave German history until 1577, when the City of Danzig hired a Scots regiment of 700 men to help fight the Polish king. However, the Thirty Years' War (1618-48) saw Scots flooding to Europe as mercenaries, many becoming officers fighting for the Swedish King Gustavus Adolphus. Some romantic historians argue that the Scots mercenary felt loyalty in this war to the King of Bohemia because his wife was a daughter of King James VI of Scotland.

The Irish have an equally interesting military history. A remnant of the Wild Geese, the Hibernia Regiment, fought for Spain during the Napoleonic Wars. Another was the Ultonia, which was virtually wiped out as part of the garrison defending Gerona in 1808. The United States' war with Mexico (1846-48) saw many Irish recruited into the U.S. army as migrants fled the potato famine. Several hundred deserted and formed the San Patricio Battalion in the Mexican army, a body comprising many nationalities. They fought the Americans at Buena Vista, losing a third of their number, and at Churabusco. Captured American deserters from the units suffering hanging, flogging, and branding.

Interestingly, several thousand other American deserters in this war did not suffer such a fate.

The Civil War in the United States saw the formation of Irish units fighting for both the Union and the Confederates. The Irish regiments in the Northern Army of the Potomac suffered dreadful casualties in the battles of Antietam and Fredericksburg in 1862. However, conscription hit the poor Irish, who could not buy substitutes, and this led to Irish riots in New York in 1862.

Irish units went into Canada in 1866, fighting the British in the Fenian rebellion. An inconclusive skirmish at Ridgeway saw an end to the incursion. Other Irish forces fought for the Pope in 1860 against the armies of Garibaldi and Victor Emmanuel of Piedmont-Sardinia. They defended the city of Spoleto and only surrendered when out of ammunition. A so-called Irish Legion joined the French Army of Napoleon III during the 1870-71 Franco-Prussian War. Also, other Irish units sided with the Boers against England in South Africa during the Second Boer War of 1899-1902.

A mass grave at the site of Culloden battlefield. The monument's inscription reads "mixed clans." The battle of Culloden took place on April 16, 1746 and was the final clash between the Jacobites (mainly Highland Scots) and the Hanoverian British government in the Jacobite Rising of 1745.

Robert the Bruce's Invasion of Ireland

THE SCOTS INVASION OF IRELAND CAN BE SEEN AS AN ATTEMPT TO UNITE THE CELTIC WORLD AGAINST THE ENGLISH. THE CAMPAIGNS DIVERTED ENGLISH FORCES FROM ATTACKING SCOTLAND AND DISRUPTED SUPPLIES.

The state of the English colony in Ireland at the end of the fourteenth century was lamentable. Absentee landlords drained resources to the mainland, leaving minimal funding for their bailiffs to defend their lands against Irish attacks. Some English were slipping into Irish ways and the English government and the Irish parliament thought the colony would dissolve if separateness between English and Irish was eradicated.

The English hold on Ireland was tested in 1315 when a fleet of Scottish soldiers, trained up in wars against the English, landed in County Antrim under the command of Edward, Robert the Bruce's remaining brother, the English having killed the other three. Although the Scots-English war continued on the mainland, the Bruce poured scarce resources into Ireland in support of his brother, now the heir to Scots throne as well as styling himself "King of Ireland." Edward was supported by the O'Neills of Tyrone and some minor kings and sought to make his kingship a political reality by driving out the English and winning the support of the Irish leaders.

A major historical problem is an analysis of the Scots' motive in invading Ireland. Did Robert the Bruce expect to coerce Edward II of England into recognizing him as King of the Scots or just to establish his brother on the Irish throne? Were there other possible motives? Historians have suggested that Edward Bruce was so unruly that Robert was glad to see his energies directed elsewhere, especially when he might cause the English a mischief in Ireland. Others maintain that Ireland was a large source of supplies used by the English crown in its campaigns against Scotland and the Irish invasion might disrupt this logistical support. Robert remembered that when he fought with the English against William Wallace, the English forces were saved from starvation by supplies from Ireland. The invasion would require that

Opposite: The weakness of the English colonial establishment was highlighted by Edward Bruce's invasion of Ireland. The Scots joined forces with the O'Neills of Ulster in an attempt to drive out English settlers.

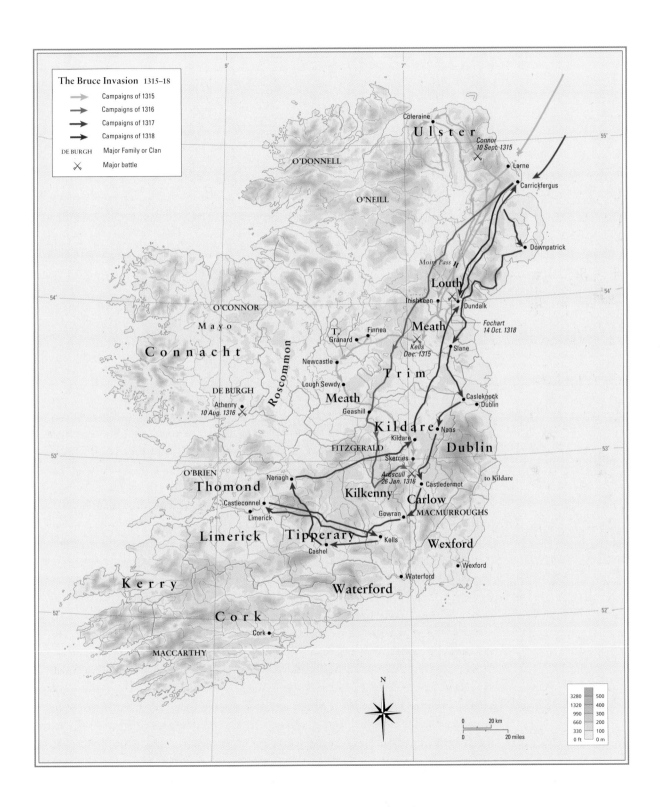

The Bruce Invasion 1315–18

Campaigns of 1315
Campaigns of 1316
Campaigns of 1317
Campaigns of 1318

DE BURGH   Major Family or Clan

✕   Major battle

Coleraine

U l s t e r

Connor
10 Sept. 1315
✕

O'DONNELL   Larne

O'NEILL   Carrickfergus

Downpatrick

Moiry Pass

Louth

Inishkeen   Dundalk

Fochart
14 Oct. 1318

O'CONNOR   Meath

M a y o

C o n n a c h t   T.   Finnea
Granard   Kells
Newcastle   Dec. 1315   Slane

Lough Sewdy   T r i m

DE BURGH   Meath   Casleknock
Athenry   Geashill   Dublin
10 Aug. 1316   K i l d a r e   Naas

                              FITZGERALD
                              Kildare
O'BRIEN   Skerries   D u b l i n
                              Ardscull
Thomond   Nenagh   26 Jan. 1316 ✕ Castledermot   to Kildare
Castleconnel   Kilkenny
Limerick   Carlow
L i m e r i c k   T i p p e r a r y   Gowran MACMURROUGHS
                              Kells
                Cashel   W e x f o r d

K e r r y   Wexford
                        Waterford
C o r k   W a t e r f o r d

Cork
MACCARTHY

N

0   20 km
0   20 miles

3280 500
1320 400
990   300
660   200
330   100
0 ft 0 m

Anglo-Norman forces in Ireland would need to use their entire resource base to counter the invasion rather than raise supplies for England. Again, the very existence of veteran Scots forces in Ireland might split English resources if the English diverted some troops to Ireland.

The Irish in Ireland also had motives for initially welcoming Edward Bruce. Some of the Irish negotiated that they were willing to shift their allegiance to him provided that he drove out the English from Ireland. Hence Edward was granted the high-kingship of Ireland and was crowned near Faughart. Maybe the resurgence of Gaelic Ireland was such that the Irish, seeing that they could not find a native king who would be acceptable to all, found a foreigner from a partly Gaelic country which was itself a child of Dál Riada. Hence the Scots relationship and its new royal family would be an acceptable alternative in raising Irish Gaelic aspirations, the last throw of the dice in re-establishing the high-kingship. Ultimately, the confusion in Ireland is evidenced by the few chieftains who supported Bruce and the large number who remained neutral or who fought against him. Also, Bruce's campaign style was so destructive that many of the Irish turned against him when viewing their ruined economy.

A further interpretation of the Bruce family plans lies in the notion of uniting the Gaelic world against the English. When hiding on Rathlin Island off Antrim in the winter of 130607, Robert the Bruce sent a letter to the Irish explaining that the Scots and Irish came from the same stock with a common Gaelic language and common customs. He thought that this special relationship meant that the Scots and Irish should co-operate in seeking a common liberty from the English; thus, the Scots and Irish were one nation in the same struggle. Robert was also playing upon his half Celtic background from his mother. Later, he used Gaelic gallowglass troops in his 1308 Galloway campaign, and several of these were found when the Isle of Man was re-captured, Bruce having gained the island in 1313. The invasion of Ireland may be seen in this light, and Bruce was also thinking of exploiting these Gaelic links in another theater, Wales. Welsh rebellions had been endemic at the end of the thirteenth century and Bruce thought he might rekindle this spark of resentment. In the end, he attacked Anglesey to no great purpose. Possibly, the leaked diplomacy of a grand Celtic alliance was a threat in itself to the English.

The invasion failed, with the campaign bogged down in bad weather and hunger. Armed uprisings broke out over Ireland but Irish support for Bruce was inadequate. Despite several victories in Edward's annual campaigns, there was never sufficient force to break English rule. Irish support was basically limited to those owing loyalty to the northern O'Neill while the Irishman's enemies were Edward's enemies. Most Anglo-Irish colonists kept their allegiance to the English crown. Another issue was the intense famine ravening through Europe during the Irish campaigns, which sapped military endeavor. The second Battle of Athenry (1316) saw the O'Connors and O'Kellys, Bruce supporters, defeated, leaving western Ireland in the hands of the Anglo-Irish. In 1318, the Battle of Faughart saw the Anglo-Irish under John de Bermingham, Edmund Butler, and Roland Joyce, Archbishop of Armagh, cutting up the three separate Scots divisions in detail because they were so widely separated, with Edward Bruce being killed in the process. Scots interest in Ireland then withered but the campaign was successful in keeping the English occupied outside Scotland.

Robert the Bruce (1274-1329) was the king of Scotland from 1306 and the hero of the Scottish war of independence. Robert tried to unite the Irish and Scottish to fight for liberty from their common enemy, the English. However, the invasion failed, partly owing to lack of support from the Irish but also because of bad weather and hunger.

THE WORLD OF THE GALLOWGLASS, 1150-1600

THE GAELIC-NORSE INHABITANTS OF THE HEBRIDES SUPPLIED GALLOWGLASS MERCENARIES, WHO BROUGHT TOGETHER WEAPONS TECHNOLOGY FROM BOTH CULTURES.

The gallowglass, foreign warriors, were mercenary warriors from the Gallo-Norse clans which had emerged through intermarriage during and after the Viking incursions. They lived in the Western Isles and the Scotttish highlands and were called *gallóglach*, a shortened version of a term meaning "warrior from Inse Gall," the Hebrides. They were noted for their chain-mail coats, iron helmets, and the huge battle-axes they carried. Their weapons were descendants of a Viking's favored weapon. These *sparth* had handles six feet long with foot-long axe-heads. Another common weapon was the *claidheamh mór*, the claymore, a broadsword frequently used two-handed.

An Irish lord often chose a gallowglass guard because he was less likely to be influenced by local feuds and alliances. The gallowglass were often organized into groups of approximately 100, under a captain who would be contracted for military service. The companies of warriors would generally be granted land and were established in Irish lordships. Supplies would be given by local populations, and this was known as *coign and livery*. Although the gallowglass were mercenaries, they became resident and sometimes bolstered their numbers with native Irish. Attached to each gallowglass would be two *kerne* or light infantry armed with javelin, sword, and bow and servants or horse-boys to look after gear.

The gallowglass were so effective that they slowed down the Anglo-Norman expansion and were crucial to the Irish kings' military retinues. During the Middle Ages, they were recruited by the Irish and Anglo-Irish lords alike. In the early sixteenth century, there were 59 battles of gallowglass in service in Ireland. The sixteenth century saw the New Scots or Redshanks, flow into Ireland during the O'Neill wars beginning in 1561. By 1584, some 4,000 gallowglass were in Ulster. By the beginning of the seventeenth century, the gallowglass were a military anachronism, as shown at the Battle of Kinsale (1601).

Opposite: In the fluctuating world of personal loyalties and allegiances, Irish chiefs enhanced their power by importing mercenaries, the Gallowglass, from the west of Scotland.

Allegances of Irish Chiefdoms
c. 1300

| | Irish chiefdoms
● The King of England
● The Earl of Ulster
● The Lord of Connacht
● The Lord of Trim
● The Lord of Thomond

*The Lordship of Meath was partitioned in
1244 into two estates, one administrated
from Trim, the other from Kells*

Counties and liberties

O'Donnell

Carrickfergus ●

O'Neill

*Lough
Neagh*

MacCartan

Down
1260
● Downpatrick

Maguire

O'Connor
of Sligo

O'Hanlon

O'Rourke
MacMahon

O'Reilly

Louth

O'Connor

Meath

● Kells
● Drogheda

O'Farrell

Connacht

Trim
● Trim

Meath

● Dublin

O'Connor
Faly

Kildare

● Galway
● Athenry

Dublin

to Kildare

O'Brien

Thomond

Kilkenny

MacMurrough

Carlow

● Limerick

Tipperary

Kilkenny ●

Limerick

● Cashel

Kilkenny ●

Wexford

Kerry

● Wexford

Waterford

● Waterford

MacCarthy

Cork

Cork ●

N

0   20 km

0   20 miles

THE WILD GEESE, 1691-1745

SARSFIELD PREFERRED TO LEAVE IRELAND UNDER FRENCH
PROTECTION THAN TO LIVE THERE UNDER ENGLISH PENAL LAWS
THAT PREVENTED CATHOLICS FROM OWNING WEAPONS, LAND,
OR PROPERTY. HE VOWED TO MAKE ANOTHER IRELAND IN THE
ARMIES OF THE GREAT KING OF FRANCE.

The Flight of the Wild Geese from Ireland refers to an Irish Jacobite army leaving Ireland under the command of Patrick Sarsfield in October 1691 after King William had conquered Ireland after the Glorious Revolution. However, there had been earlier flights when Irish soldiers quit Ireland to serve overseas for European rulers. The first example of this phenomenon occurred during the Eighty Years' War, the Dutch revolt against Spain. A second occasion was in 1607, when the Irish rebels were defeated in the Nine Years' War and the Flight of the Earls happened. Irish fled to the Spanish Netherlands, where a new Irish regiment was founded. The early seventeenth century witnessed the closure of military and political offices to the Irish in Ireland, and Catholic English officers drifted into Spanish service. Large numbers of these mercenary Irish returned home to join confederate armies after the 1641 rebellion but left again after the Cromwellian boot was placed on the Irish neck. Some 34,000 men sought a military career in Spain although some moved to France. By the Napoleonic Wars three Irish regiments remained in the Spanish army: *Irlanda* (created 1698); *Hibernia* (1709); and, *Ultonia* (1709). These regiments were eventually diluted, becoming mainly Spanish or recruiting other foreigners. The regiments were disbanded in 1815.

After William's conquest of Ireland, Sarsfield took 20,000 people to France, soldiers and their dependents. These Wild Geese were allotted to the court of the deposed James II of England but they were later merged into the Irish Brigade of the French army. James formed 13 infantry regiments, three independent companies of foot, and two troops of Horse Guards but King Louis XIV of France retained control. However, the majority of the Irish served under James against

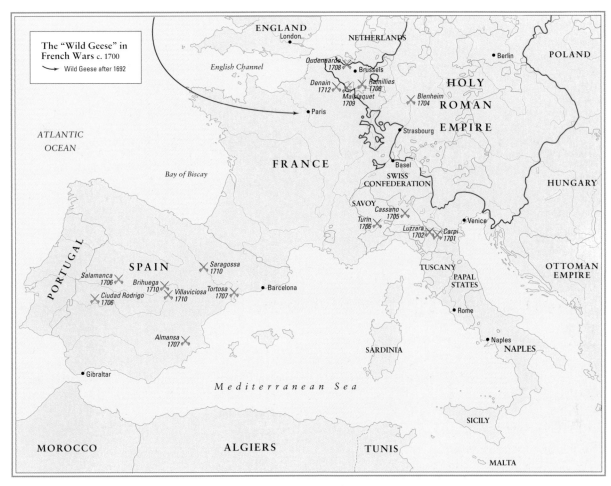

The "Wild Geese" in
French Wars c. 1700

→ Wild Geese after 1692

the Anglo-Dutch forces in Flanders. Sarsfield was made a marshall of France and was killed at the Battle of Neerwinden. The Irish continued their tradition of close-quarter combat, being regarded as ferocious, but their bravery incurred heavy casualties, with one third losses by 1698.

When James II died in 1701, his son asked for the Irish to join the French army. Five infantry regiments and one cavalry regiment were founded and the Irish Brigade was reinforced to full strength. They served in Italy, Flanders, Bavaria, and Spain.

Irish success and valor was demonstrated again in 1704 at the Battle of Bleinheim, where they covered the retreat of that half of the Franco-Bavarian army which escaped Malborough's victory. When the French were defeated at the Battle of Ramillies in 1706, the only flags captured from the Allies were secured by the Irish. By the end of the War of Spanish Succession (1701-14), the Irish had suffered over 35,000 casualties. After the 1745 Jacobite rising, which saw some Irish-French units fighting in Scotland, the British government banned the recruitment for foreign armies in Ireland. From this point, most Irish regiments in France comprised mainly non-Irish soldiers, with officers from Franco-Irish families who had lived in France for several generations.

After the Treaty of Limerick in 1691, many Catholic officers and soldiers decided to leave Ireland, heading southeast to take up service in the armies of France. Many of these men fought in France's wars with Britain, where they occasionally faced their countrymen in British service.

HIGHLANDERS IN THE FRENCH AND INDIAN WARS

THE HIGHLANDERS WERE INSTRUMENTAL IN DEFEATING FRANCE AND ITS ALLIES IN NORTH AMERICA, PART OF THE CAMPAIGN THAT SAW BRITISH VICTORY IN THE WEST INDIES, INDIA, AND EUROPE, TOO.

The French and Indian War erupted in 1755 when British Major General Braddock decided to attack French possessions along the Mississippi. 1756 saw the 42nd Foot (Black Watch) sent to North America with the 77th Foot (Montgomery's Highlanders), and the 78th Foot (Fraser's Highlanders) were despatched next year. The Black Watch was augmented by a second battalion being raised in 1758 while the king awarded the regiment the title of the Royal Highland Regiment. The Royals were employed at the first battle of Ticonderoga (1758), where a much smaller French force drove back the British, with the regiment losing over half its men in the attack. The new battalion sailed to the Caribbean but joined its senior battalion in New York. In 1759, the 1st/42nd Foot joined General Amherst in his capture of Fort Ticonderoga and Crown Point while the 2nd/42nd was sent to Albany to march on Oswego, where the fort had been captured and destroyed by the French in 1756.

Montgomery's Highlanders landed at Charleston, South Carolina (1757) before being ordered to Pennsylvania to join General Forbes's successful campaign against Fort Duquesne (renamed Fort Pitt). The regiment then spent time building roads through the wilderness from Fort Littleton to Pitt. The 77th joined Amherst's expedition against Montréal (1759), being at the capture of Ticonderoga and Crown Point. Fraser's Highlanders sailed to Halifax, Nova Scotia, ending in winter quarters in 1757 in Connecticut. A return to Halifax in 1758 saw the regiment join the campaign against Louisberg, where the 78th landed in the first wave at Kennington Cove before becoming part of the siege force. Fraser's troops, the light company, found an unattended cove as shelter and managed to outflank the French in their trenches and drove them six miles back to Louisberg, being aided by the main body of Highlanders under Fraser. Fraser's Highlanders were next engaged at Montmorency before fighting on the Plains of Abraham in the battle to

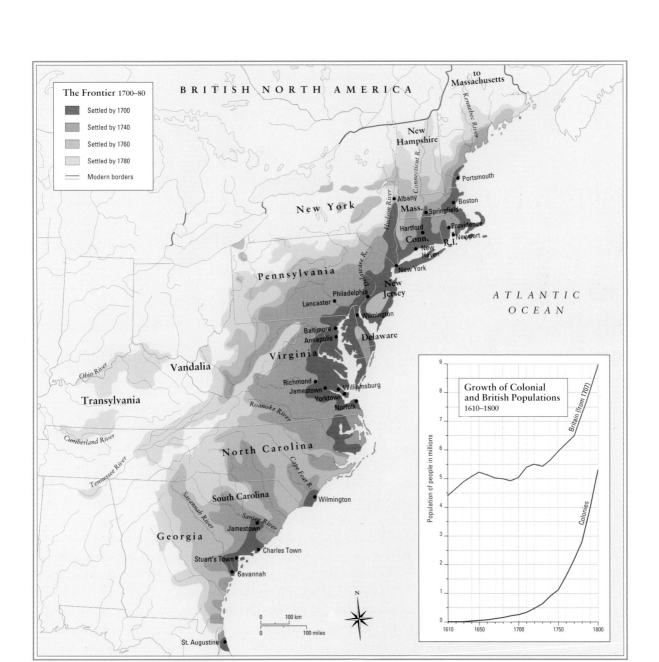

The Frontier 1700–80

- Settled by 1700
- Settled by 1740
- Settled by 1760
- Settled by 1780
- Modern borders

BRITISH NORTH AMERICA

to Massachusetts

New Hampshire

New York

Portsmouth
Albany
Boston
Mass.
Springfield
Hartford
Providence
Conn.
Newport
R.I.
New Haven
New York

Pennsylvania

Philadelphia
Lancaster
New Jersey
Wilmington
Baltimore
Annapolis
Delaware

ATLANTIC OCEAN

Vandalia

Transylvania

Virginia

Richmond
Jamestown
Williamsburg
Yorktown
Norfolk

Ohio River

Cumberland River

Tennessee River

Roanoke River

North Carolina

Cape Fear R.

South Carolina

Savannah River

Santee River
Jamestown

Georgia

Stuart's Town
Charles Town
Savannah

St. Augustine

0   100 km
0   100 miles

N

Growth of Colonial and British Populations 1610–1800

Britain (from 1707)

Colonies

Population of people in millions

seize Québec. After their loss, the French mounted an expedition from Montréal to re-take Québec. The French commander Lévis force-marched to his target and was met on the Plains of Abraham by Murray and his scurvy-ridden troops, his 3,000 facing the French 9,000. This battle of Ste. Foy or Sillery was a hard-fought, with the French capturing all 22 British guns and causing 1,134 casualties. However, the British were rescued by the arrival of a British fleet. The 78th eventually were involved in the peaceful capture of Montréal and saw the surrender of New France to the British (1760).

Britain's expanding colonies in North America inevitably clashed with native Americans and French colonies to the north. Britain deployed its regular army, which included a number of highland regiments.

HIGLANDERS IN PONTIAC'S REBELLION

ON AUGUST 5, 1793, A BRITISH RELIEF COLUMN INCLUDING THE

42ND AND 77TH HIGHLANDERS WAS AMBUSHED BY A LARGE

FORCE OF NATIVE AMERICANS 25 MILES EAST OF FORT PITT. THE

SITE OF THE BATTLE WAS BUSHY RUN.

British-native American relations waned after 1763 because the British had supplanted French traders and now charged high prices for trade goods and lower prices for furs. Additionally, the Indians observed the increasing number of settlers traveling to Kentucky, western Pennsylvania, and Tennessee. An Ottowa chief, Pontiac, and his men lay siege to Detroit while Indian allies took Forts Sandusky, St. Joseph, Miami, Presque Isle, and Michilimackinac. By June 1763, only Detroit remained uncaptured of all the forts west of Fort Pitt.

Colonel Henry Bouquet at Fort Pitt decided to relieve Detroit, and led some 400 regulars, including the Black Watch and Montgomery's Highlanders. Some of the Highlanders had recently survived a Caribbean campaign and displayed symptoms of malaria. This force was ambushed on August 5, 1763 by an alliance of Delawares, Shawnees, Mingoes, and Wyandots, although their numbers have never been ascertained. The attack was one mile south of Bushey Run, a tributary of Bushey Creek. When ambushed, Bouquet had his soldiers repeatedly charging groups of Indians, but the enemy just drifted away, reformed, and attacked again much faster than the soldiers could follow. At dusk, Bouquet moved his force from its position on a hill west of Edge Hill up to the top of Edge Hill, which was a more secure position. August 6 witnessed the Indians apparently encircling the British position and attacking.

Bouquet decided on a *ruse de guerre*, a feigned retreat, to lure the Indians into a position where the Scots could charge home with the bayonet. The Indians, fled being pursued for two miles by the Scots. These Scots charges had proved so effective that they became standard future procedure. Bouquet's force suffered 50 dead and 60 wounded, and so many packhorses were killed that supplies was left so the remaining horses could carry the wounded. The British losses were heavy but the victory boosted frontier morale.

Opposite: The battle of Bushy Run, 1763. Colonel Bouquet, advancing with a relief expedition to Fort Pitt, was surprised by an Indian ambush. He immediately formed his men into a defensive circle. The following day the Indians attacked. The Highlanders caught them in the flank, driving them off the battlefield with considerable loss.

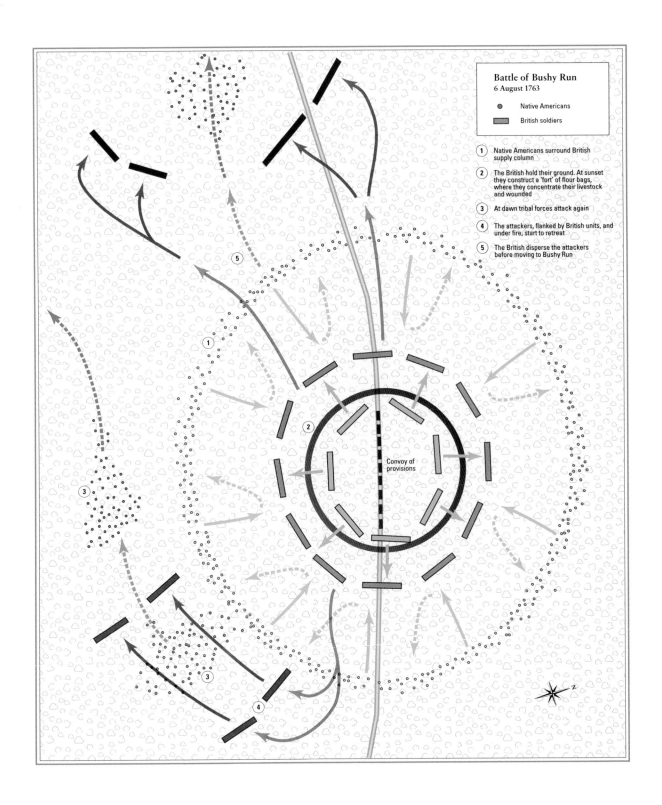

Battle of Bushy Run
6 August 1763

⬤ Native Americans

▬ British soldiers

1. Native Americans surround British supply column

2. The British hold their ground. At sunset they construct a 'fort' of flour bags, where they concentrate their livestock and wounded

3. At dawn tribal forces attack again

4. The attackers, flanked by British units, and under fire, start to retreat

5. The British disperse the attackers before moving to Bushy Run

Convoy of provisions

THE IRISH IN THE AMERICAN CIVIL WAR

THE IRISH-AMERICANS WON ACCLAIM FOR THEIR FIGHTING SPIRIT DURING THE AMERICAN CIVIL WAR. ONE WAR CORRESPONDENT WROTE THAT THE IRISH 69TH REGIMENT FOUGHT LIKE TIGERS IN THE FIRST BATTLE OF BULL RUN.

On the battlefields of the American Civil War, the Irish won acclaim for their fighting spirit and bravery, if not for their discipline, and many Confederate soldiers thought them the best soldiers in the Union army. One of their major achievements was at the Battle of Bull Run. Two Union charges had already been beaten back by a terrible hail of Confederate gunfire when General Tecumsah Sherman called on the Irish to throw themselves into the fight. This regiment became known as "The Fighting 69th." With their green flag flying above them, they were blessed by their priest and then, stripping to their shirtsleeves, barefoot in the July heat, the men charged toward the hill occupied by Confederate artillery, past trees which concealed enemy riflemen. Their battle cry was part-English, part-Gaelic and became as famous as the Rebel yell. They charged and were driven back three times.

At one point in the battle, the colonel ordered the green regimental flag to be lowered, as it had become a target for enemy bullets. The soldier holding it refused, however, and was killed moments later. Another man tried to raise the colors up and he too was shot. John Keefe, a color-bearer, rescued the flag from a group of rebel soldiers and carried it back to the Union line to the sound of cheers from his fellow Irishmen. By facing the Confederate army in battle, and doing their duty bravely, these Irish had also faced down their old enemies, the nativists, and had undoubtedly earned the right to be called Americans. The volunteers of the 69th who survived Bull Run served out their 90 day enlistment period, but many rejoined the regiment when an Irish brigade, made up of the 69th, the 88th, and the 63rd New York volunteers, was formed. The commander, Meagher, declared: "The Irish soldier will henceforth take his stand proudly by the side of the native-born, and will not fear to look him straight and sternly in the face, and tell him that he has been equal to him in his allegiance to the Constitution."

The Irish units were very proud of their unique origins and identity. When Meagher's Irish brigade went to join the Union army in Virginia, they marched under a green banner bearing an Irish harp, sunburst, and wreath of shamrocks as well as their motto in Gaelic: "They shall never retreat from the charge of lances." "Clear the Road" was the Gaelic slogan of the Massachusetts 28th, placed on their flag with an Irish harp.

The most famous Irish corps was the Irish brigade. Their greatest achievement was at the battle of Antietam. Union forces managed to halt the Confederate invasion of Maryland and Pennsylvania, but the fierce fighting left 23,000 dead or wounded on both sides. The Irish were almost swallowed up in the action as they drove the rebels back beyond a sunken road that was strewn with dead bodies from an earlier exchange of artillery fire. Once they had seized it, the the brigade used the depression as a defense, and held it to the end, but one regiment lost nearly 5o percent of its men and another lost more than 30 percent. Indeed the rebels seemed to view the green flag with particular malice, and shot down five of the brigade's color-bearers. Meagher, who had now been promoted to general, led the brigade up a hill into enemy fire. They met first one line of rebel rifles and then a second, and despite a heavy rain of bullets, they carried out Meagher's orders to tear down a rail fence that had been sheltering enemy riflemen and then engaged a force of infantry. The general's horse was shot out from under him and a bullet tore a hole in his uniform; the flag was shot down 16 times, and each time a man rushed in to save it. The battle raged for over four hours, but in the end the Confederate troops were beaten back. The brigade's 69th Regiment had lost 169 of 317 men in the front lines. At Friedericksburg, after signing up new recruits, the brigade was ordered to attack an impregnable Confederate position on Marye's Heights. Meagher urged them on and told them to fasten a sprig of evergreen in their caps to replace their green flags, sadly ravaged by enemy volleys. As they charged again and again, savage rifle fire reduced one regiment of 700 men to 150; of their five regiments, only 200 men remained. The "Fighting 69th" lost 128 out of a corps of 238. The brigade were finally forced to retreat. Their bravery was celebrated in the newspapers of the day, one reporter writing: "After witnessing the gallantry and devotion exhibited by Meagher's troops, the spectator can remember nothing but their desperate courage." After the battle of Chancellorville, only 520 men remained, and heavy losses were also sustained at Gettysburg. Irish-Americans fought well on the side of the Confederacy also: up to 40,000 of its troops were Irish-born,and perhaps an equal number were of Irish descent. Alabama had its Emerald Guards, South Carolina had its Emerald Light Infantry, and Virginia its Emmet Guards.

Irish-Americans contributed to the war effort in other ways, too. Priests said mass on the battlefields before every engagement and nuns nursed the wounded. A Dublin-born musician wrote the lyrics to the famous war song "When Johnny Comes Marching Home" and photographer Matthew Brady created a lasting legacy as he recorded the lives and deaths of valiant Civil War soldiers.

However, tensions broke out when the Union declared its intentions to abolish slavery. The American Irish, still oppressed and fighting for their own status, worried about competing for jobs with African-Americans. They were less willing to volunteer, and following the draft law passed on March 3, 1863, four days of rioting broke out. The famous Irish ferocity in battle had broken out on the streets of New York. Yet once the war was over, the nation was caught up in an euphoria that shaped a new industrial landscape and sent thousands, Irish Americans among them, to make their fortunes in the West.

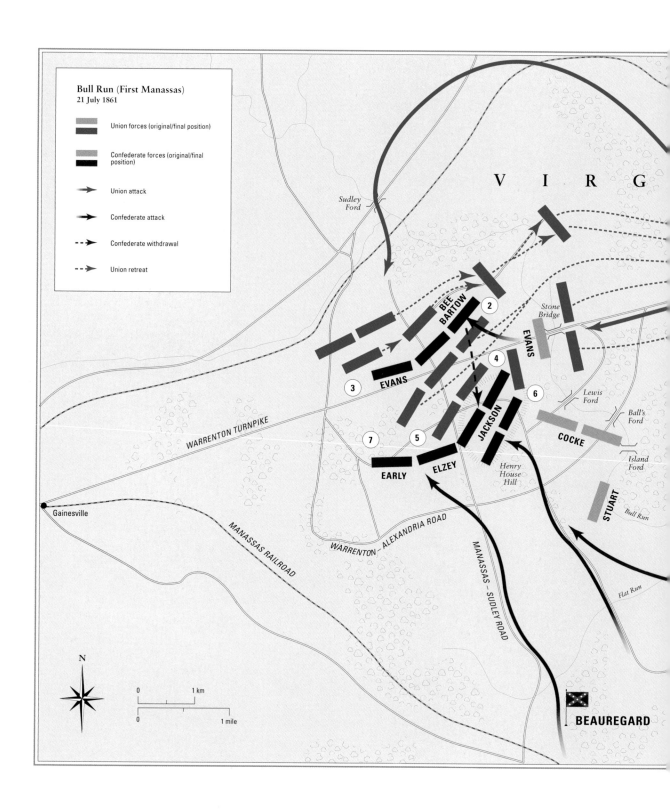

Bull Run (First Manassas)
21 July 1861

Union forces (original/final position)

Confederate forces (original/final position)

Union attack

Confederate attack

Confederate withdrawal

Union retreat

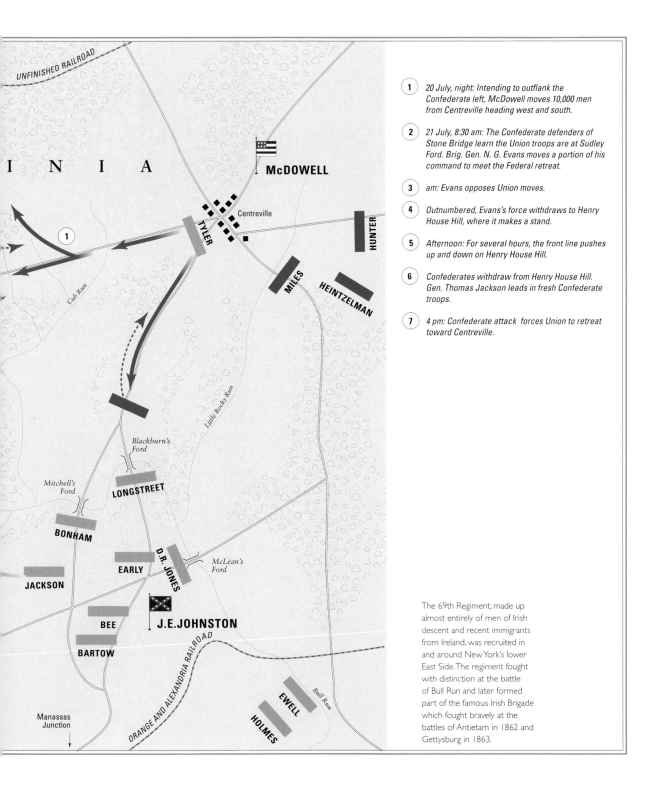

1. 20 July, night: Intending to outflank the Confederate left, McDowell moves 10,000 men from Centreville heading west and south.

2. 21 July, 8:30 am: The Confederate defenders of Stone Bridge learn the Union troops are at Sudley Ford. Brig. Gen. N. G. Evans moves a portion of his command to meet the Federal retreat.

3. am: Evans opposes Union moves.

4. Outnumbered, Evans's force withdraws to Henry House Hill, where it makes a stand.

5. Afternoon: For several hours, the front line pushes up and down on Henry House Hill.

6. Confederates withdraw from Henry House Hill. Gen. Thomas Jackson leads in fresh Confederate troops.

7. 4 pm: Confederate attack forces Union to retreat toward Centreville.

The 69th Regiment, made up almost entirely of men of Irish descent and recent immigrants from Ireland, was recruited in and around New York's lower East Side. The regiment fought with distinction at the battle of Bull Run and later formed part of the famous Irish Brigade which fought bravely at the battles of Antietam in 1862 and Gettysburg in 1863.

Irish Regiments in World War One

World War I saw the Irish Guards in constant action from 1914. They were awarded 30 battle honors, four Victoria Crosses, 67 Military Crosses, 77 Distinguished Conduct Medals, and 244 Military Medals.

Great Britain declared war on August 4, 1914 against the Kaiser's Germany and the Austro-Hungarian Empire. Secretary-of-War Lord Kitchener considered that the war would be long and that the army of 247,000 men would need to be increased by one million soldiers organized into thirty new divisions in the so-called New Armies. The British Army was originally seen as an area of potential employment for working class Irishmen. Joining the army was a chance to increase the status of young men from the working class poor. The pay was very good compared to what was available otherwise and allowances were also paid to the wives while the soldiers were away on duty. Most of the southern Irish Catholics served in Irish regiments, but many Irishmen also served in British regiments, including the Tyneside, Liverpool, and London Irish battalions.

The war occurred just after the Irish Home Rule Bill was given Royal Assent on September 18, 1914 but was adjourned for the war's duration. John Redmond of the Nationalist Party, the putative first prime minister, asked the Irish Volunteers to enlist, knowing that Irish soldiers in the British army had already seen action in Flanders. Some 12,000 of the 180,000 Volunteers kept the Irish Volunteers style, with the rest supporting Redmond. About 80,000 enlisted in Ireland, half from Ulster. The First New Army of 100,000 men was formed in late August 1914 containing the 10th (Irish) Division with its three brigades. The 16th (Irish) Division formed part of the Second New Army being founded in August 1914, followed by the 36th (Ulster) Division in October 1914. Irishmen also joined Irish regiments such as the Irish Guards, the London Irish, the Tyneside battalions of the Northumberland Fusiliers, and the 1st/8th (Irish) King's Liverpool Regiment. Others joined English, Scots, and Welsh regiments, the artillery, the medical corps, the Royal Flying Corps, and the Royal Navy. Women served as nurses and Irish emigrants enlisted in the

An Irish war memorial that was erected in Comber Town Square, Northern Ireland, following World War One.

regiments of Australia, New Zealand, Canada, South Africa, and the United States.

The British Expeditionary Force sent to France in August 1914 contained 14 Irish regiments:

1st Irish Guards,

2nd Royal Dublin Fusiliers,

2nd Royal Munster Fusiliers,

2nd Royal Irish Rifles,

2nd Royal Inniskilling Fusiliers,

1st Royal Irish Fusiliers,

2nd Connaught Rangers,

2nd Royal Irish Regiment,

2nd Leinster Regiment,

4th Royal Irish Dragoon Guards,

South Irish Horse,

8th King's Royal Irish Hussars,

5th Royal Irish Lancers

North Irish Horse.

In 1915, during the Gallipoli campaign, the 1st battalions of the Royal Dublin, Munster, and Inniskilling Fusiliers landed at Cape Helles, with the first two battalions sustaining terrible casualties: the Munsters suffered 637 casualties out of 1,012 men in 36 hours. The 10th Irish Division were landed at Suvla Bay in total chaos and losses were severe. At one stage, the soldiers ran out of ammunition and threw stones at the Turks. The same year witnessed the second Battle of Ypres, with the 2nd Royal Dublin Fusiliers in combat again but near St. Julien in Flanders. May 24 saw a German poison gas attack against the battalion of 666 men. Within seven hours the force was reduced to one officer and 20 other ranks. September observed the 10th Irish Division sailing from Gallipoli for Salonika to fight on the Bulgarian front. In October, the Dublins and Munsters were ordered to capture the village of Jenikoj in modern Macedonia; 385 men were killed, wounded, or missing. A granite Celtic cross now honors the 10th Irish Division at Robrovno, matching those at Wijschate in Flanders and Guillemont in France.

December 1915 had the 16th Irish Division arriving in France, then being assigned to the Loos sector. Later, in April 1916, the division suffered a gas attack, causing 1,980 casualties with 570 deaths and many wounded dying later from respiratory diseases. By August, the division had sustained 6,000 casualties with 1,496 dead. During the Dublin Easter Rising in April 1916, the 4th and 5th regiments and the 10th Royal Dublin Fusiliers fought the Irish Volunteers, as did many soldiers home on leave.

The period between July and November 1916 is known as the Battle of the Somme. After a huge bombardment of the German lines, the British army advanced, with the 36th Ulster Division being given the target of the Schwaben Redoubt. The division gained its objectives but could not hold on because other British attacks failed. Losses reached 5,500, with four Victoria Crosses being awarded. Other Irish battalions joined the July 1 assault, with two Dublin battalions being engaged, the second battalion in the second wave receiving 325 casualties out of a starting force of 503. The 1st Royal Irish Rifles, the 1st Royal Irish Fusiliers, 1st and 2nd Royal Inniskilling Fusiliers, 2nd Royal Irish Regiment, and the 1st, 2nd, 3rd, and 4th Tyneside battalions of the Northumberland Fusiliers were also engaged

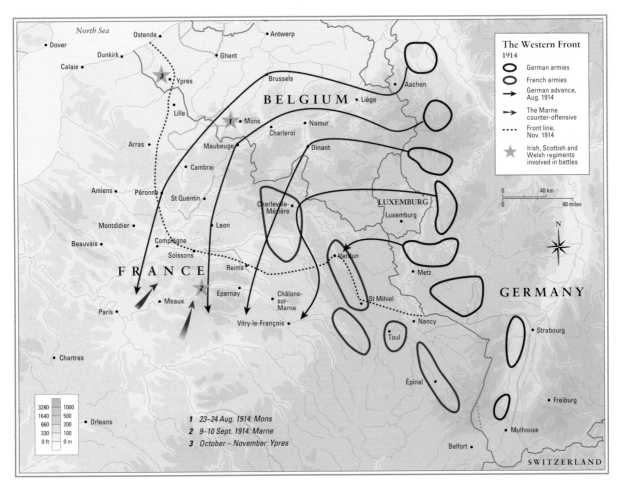

The Western Front
1914

⬭ German armies

⬭ French armies

→ German advance, Aug. 1914

⇒ The Marne counter-offensive

···· Front line, Nov. 1914

★ Irish, Scottish and Welsh regiments involved in battles

1   23–24 Aug. 1914: Mons
2   9–10 Sept. 1914: Marne
3   October – November: Ypres

on that day. The 16th Irish Division took Guillemont in the summer and Ginchy in September, the division receiving 4,314 losses. In November, the 10th Royal Dublin Fusiliers were in an attack capturing Beaumont Hamel.

The 16th Irish and 36th Ulster Divisions were in the June 1917 strike on Messines Ridge, and these two divisions were transferred to the 5th Army in July 1917. Passchendaele in the Third Battle of Ypres saw them engaged again, with the 16th moving against Arras later. Heavy losses were experienced. In September, the 10th Division sailed for Egypt. The Somme in 1918 saw a German assault which wiped out one-third of the 10th and 16th Irish Divisions. Irish battalions took part in the British advances, with the 2nd Dubliners in action at Le Cateau, where they lost 44 percent within two days. The war ended shortly after.ward At least 35,000 Irish died in the war but the figure on the Irish National War Memorial states 49,400.

After the Easter Rising of 1916, many Irish changed their minds about Britain, and this inevitably affected recruitment into the armed forces. Many Irish also disliked the impending prospect of conscription as the war grew worse.

In August 1914, Britain's small professional army marched off to France forming the British Expeditionary Force. This was formed around regiments drawn from countries across Britain such as the Connaught Rangers, the Gordon Highlanders, and the Royal Welsh Fusiliers.

Scottish Divisions in World War One

THE 52ND LOWLAND DIVISION GAINED MANY HONORS, THE MOST IMPORTANT ONE BEING AWARDED BY THE GERMANS. THE GERMANS DREW UP A LIST OF THE DIVISIONS THEIR TROOPS DREADED TO FIGHT. AT THE HEAD WAS THE 51ST HIGHLAND DIVISION, AND THE 52ND LOWLAND DIVISION WAS FOURTH.

At the outbreak of World War One, Kitchener, Secretary of State for War, realized that the conflict would last several years and that the army required considerable expansion. His New Armies were built around raising new battalions for existing regiments in Scottish formations. A 1st Highland Territorial Division was raised before being re-designated the 51st Highland Division; this was followed by the 64th (2nd Highland) Division. The 51st Highland Division first fought at the second battle of Ypres, being at Festubert in May 1915 and Givenchy in June 1915. While between Neuville St. Vaast and Roclincourt, tunneling under trenches, mine explosions, and infantry assaults caused such severe casualties among the 1/6th Argylls that the unit was removed from the division.

From July 1916, the division became involved in the Battle of the Somme. Various battalions of the division engaged in combat at High Wood, Ancre, and Beaumont Hamel. The latter witnessed Gordons, Black Watch, Seaforths, and Argylls grinding their way through German trenches, taking some 7,000 prisoners. The 51st was removed from the Somme, having suffered 8,000 casualties in the 1916 battles, and introduced into the May 1917 Battle of Arras. Together with the 9th and 15th Scottish Divisions and the Canadian Corps, the 51st attacked Vimy Ridge in April. May observed the division engaged in Third Ypres (Passchendaele) while September saw the division moving forward in the battle for the Menin Road Ridge. In November 1917, the division joined the Battle of Cambrai. When the German offensive of March 21, 1918 began, the 51st defended their positions before conducting a fighting retreat, sustaining 5,000 casualties, but it helped fragment the German attacks. Later, in Flanders, the reinforced division

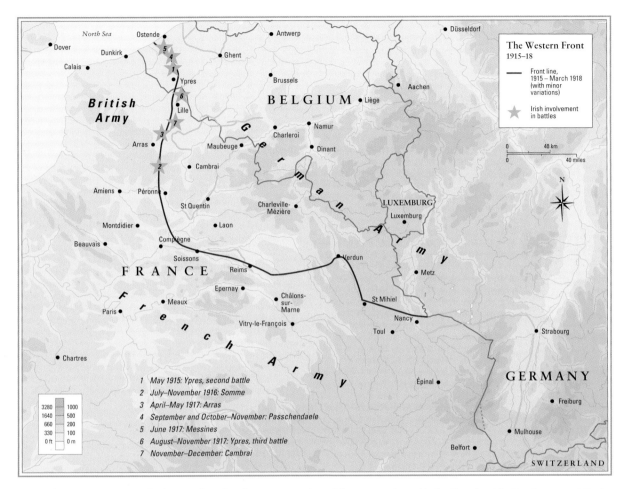

The Western Front
1915–18

— Front line,
1915 – March 1918
(with minor
variations)

★ Irish involvement
in battles

1 May 1915: Ypres, second battle
2 July–November 1916: Somme
3 April–May 1917: Arras
4 September and October–November: Passchendaele
5 June 1917: Messines
6 August–November 1917: Ypres, third battle
7 November–December: Cambrai

fought at Aubers Ridge, then further south in the Champagne region while co-operating with the French. The division's services were required in August at Greenland Hill, and in October an attack thrust back the Germans ten miles. In total, this fighting force sustained over 27,000 casualties in the First World War.

The 52nd Lowland Division fought at the Dardanelles, in Palestine, and the Western Front. Being engaged from June 1915, the division sustained 4,800 dead, wounded, and missing out of 10,900 by July. The entire campaign caused the division 70 per cent of its officers and 50 per cent of its men, excluding those admitted to hospital for sickness. The division next moved to Egypt to fight the Turks again: at Dueidar and at the Battle of Romani. Early 1917 saw the formation engaged at the second Battle of Gaza and later in the town's capture. By April 1918, the division was in France, and helped break the Siegfried Line at Hénin Hill before becoming part of the British advance ending up at Mons.

The 9th Scottish Division was dispatched to France in May 1915 to St. Omer. After spells in the trenches, the division was engaged at Loos, with its 28th Infantry Brigade losing two-thirds of its number. This battle cost the division over 6,000 casualties and a period of re-supply, repair, and reinforcement was sustained at Ypres. In May 1916, the 9th fought at the Somme and were seriously engaged at the Battle of Bazentin Ridge.

The 'Front' became established from September 1914 and existed in much the same place until the major battles of the summer and autumn 1918. The British army's deployment grew from 250,000 to several million, drawing men from all three "Celtic" nations.

The Battle of the Somme, planned as the great breakthrough, in fact turned into the bloodiest day in the history of the British army, with 60,000 casualties and 420,000 dead before the Battle ended.

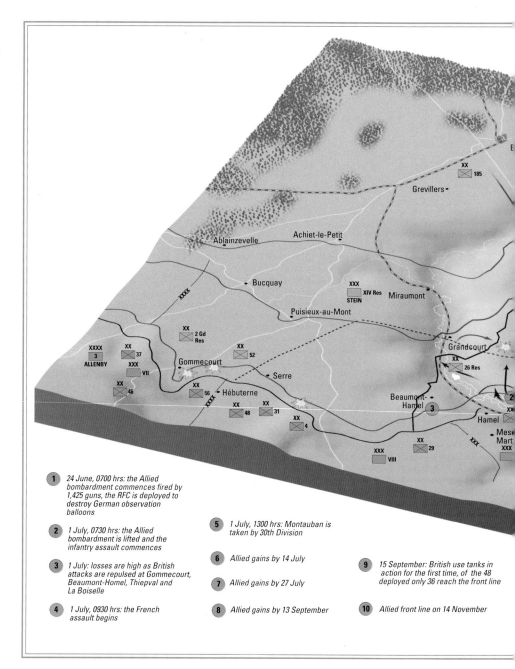

1 24 June, 0700 hrs: the Allied bombardment commences fired by 1,425 guns, the RFC is deployed to destroy German observation balloons

2 1 July, 0730 hrs: the Allied bombardment is lifted and the infantry assault commences

3 1 July: losses are high as British attacks are repulsed at Gommecourt, Beaumont-Homel, Thiepval and La Boiselle

4 1 July, 0930 hrs: the French assault begins

5 1 July, 1300 hrs: Montauban is taken by 30th Division

6 Allied gains by 14 July

7 Allied gains by 27 July

8 Allied gains by 13 September

9 15 September: British use tanks in action for the first time, of the 48 deployed only 36 reach the front line

10 Allied front line on 14 November

Combat between July 1 and July 19 saw the division suffer some 7,600 losses. Action followed at the Battle of Transloy Ridge after which the division left the Somme, moving into a sector at Arras. A successful assault at Arras was followed by engagements around Roeux and Greenland Hill. The division faced the German March 1918 offensive at Gouzeaucourt when it conducted a fighting retreat slowing down the Germans until the attack

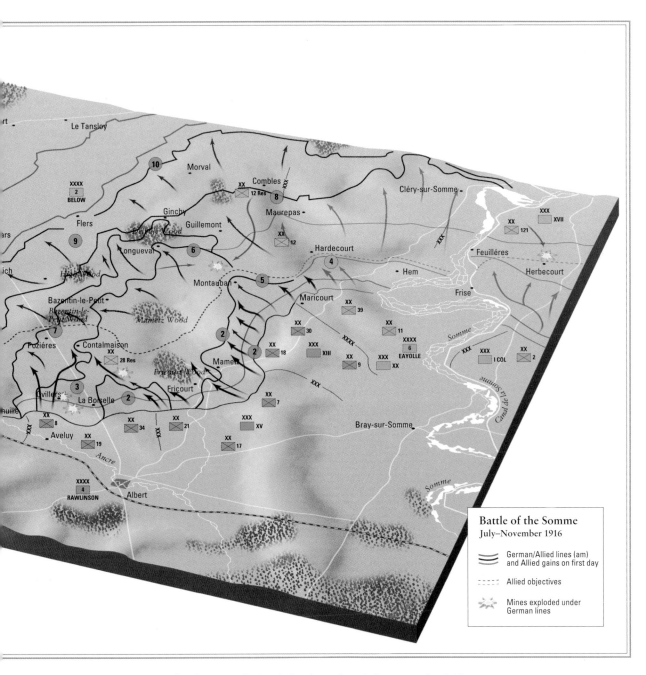

Le Tansloy

10 Morval

XXXX
2
BELOW

Flers   Ginchy
                                    Guillemont
9

Longueval   6

                    Montauban

Bazentin-le-Petit
Bazentin-le-
Petit Wood   Mametz Wood

7
Poziéres   Contalmaison   Mameu
                    XX
                    28 Res
                                Fricourt Wood
3
villers   La Boiselle   Fricourt
                                2
XX
8
XXX   XX   XXX
                34   XXX   21
Aveluy   XX
                19

XXXX
4
RAWLINSON   Albert

Combles
XX   XXX
12 Res   8

Maurepas
XX
12

Hardecourt

5   4

Maricourt
            XX
            39
XX
30   XX
            11
XX   XXX   XXXX
18   XIII   6
        XXX   EAYOLLE
XXX   XX
XV   9   XX

XX
7

XXX

XXX
17

Bray-sur-Somme

Cléry-sur-Somme

XX   XXX
121   XVII

Feuilléres

Hem   Herbecourt

Frise

XXX   XXX   XX
        I COL   2

Somme

Canal de la Somme

Somme

Battle of the Somme
July–November 1916

═══ German/Allied lines (am)
      and Allied gains on first day

- - - - Allied objectives

✳ Mines exploded under
    German lines

was stopped. The division was reduced to 1,340 effectives in five days. After reinforcements, the division went
south of Ypres to help stop another German offensive at Wytschaete and Kemmel. The 9th next joined the
advance to victory, and in December 1918 was part of the division that went to occupy the Rhineland. The 9th
lost 52,055 men, killed, wounded, or missing during the war.

IRISH REGIMENTS IN WORLD WAR TWO

LIEUTENANT-COLONEL BREDIN, DSO, MC OF THE 38TH IRISH BRIGADE, SERVED AS 2I/C OF THE 1ST ROYAL IRISH FUSILIERS. BREDIN ALSO HELD SENIOR COMMAND IN ALL THREE OF THE BRIGADE'S BATTALIONS.

After the foundation of the Irish Free State in 1922, those regiments which traditionally recruited in southern Ireland were disbanded: the Royal Irish Regiment; Connaught Rangers; Prince of Wales's Leinster Regiment; Royal Munster Fusiliers; Royal Dublin Fusiliers, and the South Irish Horse. The remaining Irish regiments went through many amalgamations. The surviving regiments with an Irish identity were the Irish Guards; 5th Royal Inniskilling Dragoon Guards; 8th King's Royal Irish Hussars; Royal Inniskilling Fusiliers; Royal Ulster Rifles; and the Royal Irish Fusiliers. The regimental battalions would often serve in different theaters of war after 1939 and did not comprise an Irish division as occurred in the First World War. They also went through much transformation during the war in terms of becoming armored or mechanized infantry.

The Irish Guards witnessed two of its battalions serving in the Guards Armored Division in 1944. The Irish Guards' 1st Battalion had been involved in the 1940 Norwegian campaign, where it suffered heavy losses like all units involved there. After time spent in London and Scotland, the battalion was sent to North Africa in 1943, arriving in Algiers and eventually fighting in the Tunisian campaign. In 1944, the battalion sailed for Italy and landed at Anzio; severe casualties, despite replacement, led to the unit returning to England for the rest of the war and serving as a training battalion.

The 2nd Guards Battalion joined Harpoon Force to rescue the Dutch Royal family and sustained 63 dead and wounded. The next stop was France, to aid the retreating British Expeditionary Force (BEF) before being evacuated from Dunkirk. In 1941, the 2nd Battalion joined the 5th Guards Armored Brigade with Covenanter tanks while the 3rd Battalion became mechanized infantry. They saw combat in Normandy, being part of Operation Goodwood near Caen, then Operation Bluecoat

Opposite: The British and Allied armies fought their way back into the European mainland in southern Italy in 1943. With them went several Irish units, including the Irish Guards.

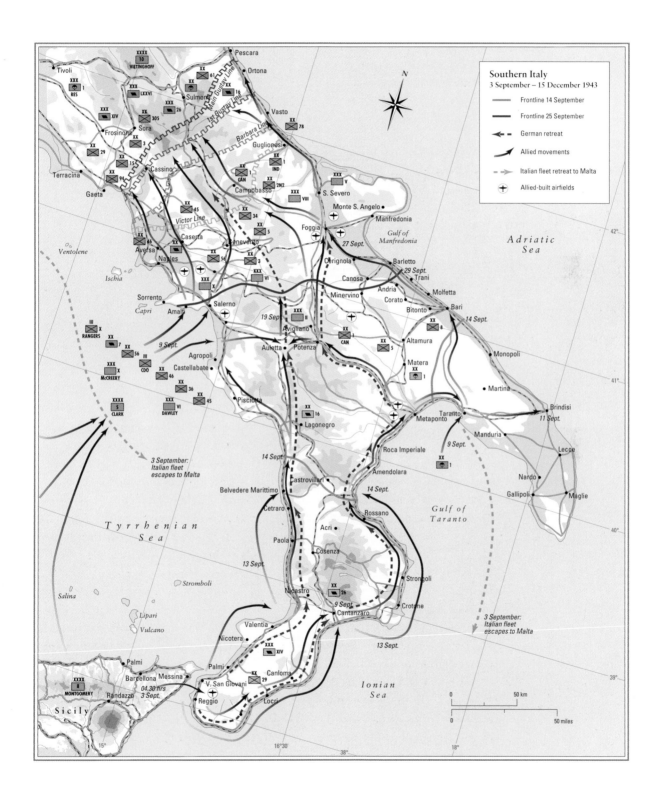

Southern Italy
3 September – 15 December 1943

Frontline 14 September
Frontline 25 September
German retreat
Allied movements
Italian fleet retreat to Malta
Allied-built airfields

in the bocage. The two units saw operations in Normandy and Belgium, being joined together as the Irish Guards Battle Group, which captured a bridge over the Meuse-Escaut Canal. This unit was involved in Operation Market Garden but the advance stalled at Einhoven and, despite a bridge taken by US troops at Nijmegen, was unable to relieve the 1st Airborne Division at Arnhem. Next, these Irish battalions ground their way across the Rhine into Germany. After the war, the 2nd and 3rd Battalions were disbanded. The Irish Guards sustained 845 dead and nearly 1,600 wounded during the war.

The Royal Inniskilling Fusiliers fielded two regular and four wartime battalions. The 1st Battalion saw service in the Far East between 1941 and 1943 in campaigns in Burma but was decimated twice while serving in the 47th Indian Infantry Brigade. The 2nd Battalion went to France with the BEF in the 5th Division. After evacuation, the division sailed to the Middle East and served in Madagascar, India, Syria, and Egypt before joining the invasion of Sicily, the Anzio landing, and the fight up the Italian peninsula. The service battalions played their part, adding in excess of 30 battle honours to the Inniskilling colors.

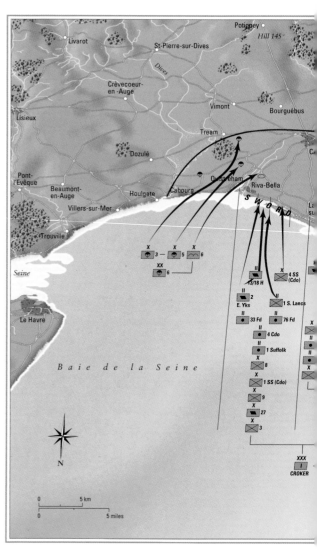

The Royal Ulster Rifles' two Regular battalions fought in northwest Europe while its three reserve battalions provided home defense, with war-time raised battalions becoming training units. The 1st Battalion, serving in India in 1939, was returned to England and was allotted to the air-landing brigade of the 6th Airborne Division, being glidered in on D-Day. The unit saw fierce fighting in France and landed again in the 1945 Operation Varsity and captured an important bridge. As part of the 6th Airborne, the battalion stormed though Germany and met the Russians on the Elbe. The 2nd Battalion saw 1939 in Palestine but was withdrawn to England to serve in the BEF where it sustained light casualties before being evacuated. After extensive training, the battalion landed at Sword Beach on D-Day, followed by gruelling combat in the Normandy bocage. As part of the 3rd Division, the battalion campaigned across France, through the Low Countries, and into Germany, ending the war at Delmenhorst near Bremen.

The Royal Irish Fusiliers 1st Battalion was evacuated from Dunkirk and sent to North Africa. It joined the 38th (Irish) Brigade in 1942 with the 6th Battalion, Royal Inniskilling Fusiliers, and the 2nd Battalion, London Irish Rifles. The Liverpool Irish, the London Irish Rifles, and the North Irish Horse fought in Europe, North Africa, and Italy. Irish Colonial units from Canada and South Africa served with the South African Irish Regiment in Africa, suffering badly at Sidi Rezegh in 1941. More than 43,000 men and women from Eire served in the British forces and 38,000 Irish from the north. Some 4,500 Irish soldiers died divided half and half between north and south of the border.

Operation Overlord, D-Day was the largest seaborne invasion ever undertaken. Among the units landing was Lord Lovat's special service brigade led by their piper, Bill Millan, playing Hielan Laddie.

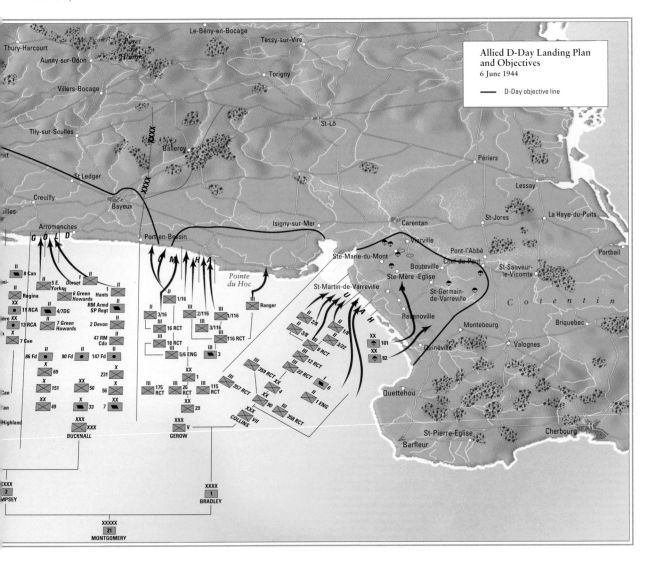

Allied D-Day Landing Plan and Objectives
6 June 1944

—— D-Day objective line

SCOTTISH DIVISIONS IN WORLD WAR TWO

THE 51ST HIGHLAND DIVISION FOUGHT FROM EL ALAMEIN TO THE RHINE CROSSING TO BREMEN. THEY SUSTAINED 15,000 CASUALTIES IN THE BATTLES EN ROUTE AND WON MANY HONORS. THE DIVISION REMAINED IN GERMANY AS PART OF THE OCCUPATION FORCE, RETURNING TO SCOTLAND IN LATE 1946.

The Scottish divisions of the Second World War were the 51st Highland Infantry Division, the 52nd Lowland Infantry Division, the 9th Highland Infantry Division, and the 15th Scottish Infantry Division. The 51st sailed to France in January 1940 and was given a variety of attached units, including an armored car regiment and six artillery regiments. Known as the Saar Force, this amalgamation was sent to the Metz region to defend a section of the Maginot Line. The German army commenced its blitzkrieg attack, to end the Phoney War in May 1940. Pouring through the Netherlands and Belgium, it outflanked the Maginot Line, and the 51st began a withdrawal to the Abbeville area. A fighting retreat saw the division reach the port of St. Valéry-en-Caux, near Dieppe. The army hoped to evacuate the 51st from Le Havre, and its 154th Infantry Brigade with other attached troops went there to safeguard the port. The remainder of the division and its attachments were surrounded at St. Valéry, so the 154th embarked at Cherbourg and reached England. Eventually, the 51st, having used up its artillery shells and surrounded by German armor, surrendered to Major General Irwin Rommel (June 12, 1940).

In Scotland, the 9th Highland Infantry Division was re-designated as the 51st and its brigades as the 152nd, 153rd, and 154th. The captured units were killed and a harsh revenge was to be delivered to the Germans over time. Training was completed when the division was sent to Aldershot in April 1942. Commanded by Major General Wimberley, the division reached North Africa in June 1942 and saw its first combat during the Battle of El Alamein (October–November 1942). Victory over Rommel was sweet, as the 51st helped destroy German armor and take 30,000 prisoners. The formation campaigned across

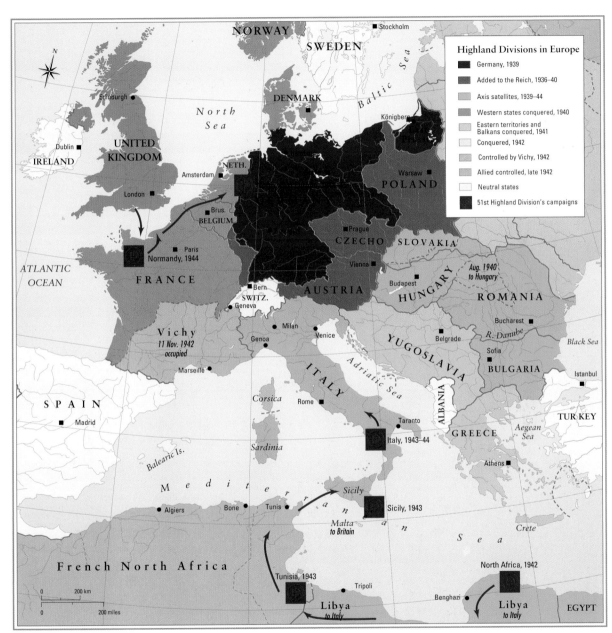

North Africa and fought in battles at Medinine, Mareth, Akarit, Enfidaville, and Tunis.

July 1942 witnessed the 51st landing in Sicily. After the island was captured, the division returned to England to prepare for D-Day. In June 1944, the division fought around Caen before engaging in the breakout from the beachhead which led to so many enemy becoming trapped in the Falaise Pocket. In September, the division was concentrated at St. Valéry-en-Caux before taking on the German garrison at Le Havre. Next, action was taken against similar garrisons at Calais and Dieppe. The 51st was assigned

The 51st Highland Division was deployed from the deserts of North Africa to the crossing the Rhine into northern Germany.

to reach Antwerp but was suddenly sent south to slow the enemy advance in the Battle of the Bulge. That task completed, the division, as part of the 1st Canadian Army, spearheaded an assault on the Reichswald. Afterward, the division was withdrawn to cross the Rhine at Rees. The division then campaigned through Holland, advancing into north Germany and reaching the area of Bremen when war ended.

The 52nd Lowland Infantry Division comprised part of the second British Expeditionary Force in France, moving to Evreux. When the French sought an armistice, a second British evacuation took place, at Cherbourg. The division then became a bastion against possible invasion before being trained as a mountain division, then in combined operations. Next, training followed for air operations to join in Market Garden. The 52nd was withdrawn and entered France as a standard infantry division, being concentrated near Ghent. The division became part of the force with the 1st Canadian Army and was engaged in clearing a route to Antwerp by clearing the south bank of the River Scheldt and then Breskens, South Beveland, and Walcheren ssland. This campaign was a grind, taking several days to clear South Beveland. The assault on Walcheren, included several failed assaults, and reached the island by storming a causeway. Eventually, the Glasgow Highlanders established a bridgehead and the 6th Cameronians crossed to the island elsewhere. The Germans were defeated in a campaign that successfully deployed air power, ship gunnery, and infantry assaults.

The 52nd resisted German attacks during the Battle of the Bulge before destroying the Roer salient knifing into Allied occupied ground where the U.S. and British armies met. Fortified villages were reduced, which opened up a way to attack the Reichwald and reach the River Rhine. A fight to eradicate the Wesel pocket saw the division reaching the Rhine, which it crossed while in support of the 15th Scottish Division and the 6th Airborne. The division finished the war by taking villages and towns, ending up with the battle for Bremen when the cease fire happened. The 15th Scottish Division became a reservoir to provide training and men for other units and was not placed on the register for combat until 1943. The division became part of the follow-up corps after D-Day and eventually reached its objectives in Operation Epsom fighting its way to the Odon bridge at Tourmaville. Having established a Scots controlled corridor, the division faced counter-attacks by Panzer units, finally being relieved by the 53rd Welsh Division. The division had fought various SS Panzer divisions, resisting all counter-attacks in the unit's first battle while sustaining 2,720 casualties.

Moving from the Scottish corridor, the division fought several fierce engagements as the Allies moved forward. The 15th chased the Germans through Belgium, reaching the Albert Canal during Market Garden. The division broke through the Siegfried Line north of the Reichwald and took Cleves. The Rhine was crossed and Germany deeply penetrated, with the division reaching the Baltic after crossing the River Elbe. Here the war ended. The 1,300 men receiving honors and awards must be set side by side with the 11,772 casualties sustained.

The 15th Infantry division formation was as follows:

44th Infantry Brigade: 8th Royal Scots, 6th Royal Scots Fusiliers, and 6th King's Own Scottish Borderers, 46th Infantry Brigade: 9th Cameronians (Scottish Rifles), 2nd Glasgow Highlanders, and 7th Seaforth Highlanders; and 227th Infantry Brigade: 10th Highland Light Infantry, 2nd Gordon Highlanders, 2nd Argyll and Sutherland Highlanders.

The British 2nd Army fought as part of the Allied armies deployed in northwestern Europe. This included many units drawn from Scotland, Ireland, and Wales.

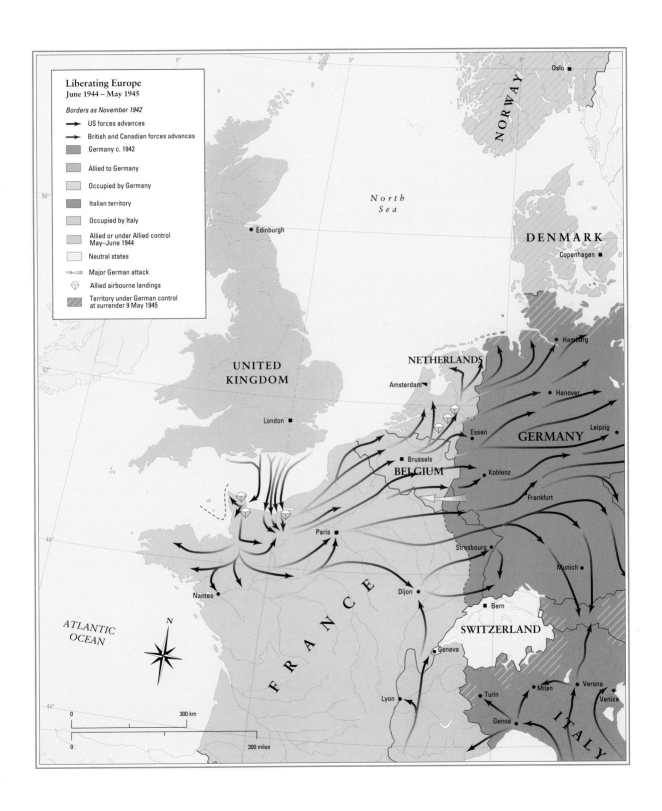

Liberating Europe
June 1944 – May 1945

Borders as November 1942

➤ US forces advances

➤ British and Canadian forces advances

Germany c. 1942

Allied to Germany

Occupied by Germany

Italian territory

Occupied by Italy

Allied or under Allied control
May–June 1944

Neutral states

Major German attack

Allied airbourne landings

Territory under German control
at surrender 9 May 1945

Celtic Diaspora

THE CELTIC COUNTRIES HAVE PROVIDED MILLIONS OF MIGRANTS TO THE UNITED STATES AND OTHER COUNTRIES FROM THE LATE EIGHTEENTH TO THE MID-TWENTIETH CENTURIES. WHETHER AS SOLDIERS, MISSIONARIES, MINERS, OR SETTLERS, THE CELTS HAVE HELPED DEVELOP MANY PLACES WHILE SPREADING THEIR CUSTOMS AND CULTURE. INDEED, CELTIC IDENTITY HAS HELPED TO SHAPE MODERN AMERICA.

Since the seventeenth century, the Celtic peoples have migrated from their homelands in their millions to populate the world, develop new countries, and build two British empires. Wherever the Celts have gone, they have taken their language and culture with them, but they have generally lost their Gaelic in the process although there are probably some 2,000 Gaelic-speakers in the Scots-settled areas in Cape Breton.

Celtic festivals and celebrations have been kept alive and St. Patrick's Day is commemorated globally. A sense of a Celtic identity is alive and well, with Celtic customs and traditions being adopted by other peoples among whom the Scots, Irish, Welsh, Breton, Cornish, and Manx live.

Destination countries have not always kept accurate records of the number of migrants entering them. The Cornish have always been classified as English because Cornwall is an English county and not a country, although it is constitutionally a duchy. The most popular destination by far has been the United States in whatever political guise, but huge numbers have left for England, Canada, Australia, South Africa, New Zealand, Mexico, Argentina, and Puerto Rico. The imagination is normally colored by the millions leaving Ireland during the Great Famine, with the resultant image of migrants fleeing from poverty, hunger, and death. This view is erroneous since many migrants made a positive choice to leave home, with most paying for their own passage on ships. Thus to improve living standards and seize better opportunities with the hopes of higher paid jobs or land were the major reasons for migration.

Ireland sent the most people abroad, with waves of exiles reaching Europe to serve in the armies of Spain and France. Later, approximately eight million left between 1800 and 1922. Additionally, large numbers of Ulster Scots left for America to become the Scotch-Irish, who peopled the mountain chains in the backcountry of the Thirteen Colonies to give Appalachia a marked and distinctive identity. The Great Famine expelled vast numbers, and the Irish faced discrimination in England and in the United States, being resented by the Protestant Scotch-Irish. Ironically, the Irish became the major ethnic group, populating the New York Police Department and police agencies in other major cities.

Many commentators in modern America argue that owing to the large number of Scots and Irish emigrants to North America, Celtic identity has, in some part, shaped the United States. Many modern Americans feel a connection to Celtic identity through their Scottish or Irish ancestry.

Canada became home for Gaelic-speaking Scots highlanders, who were soldiers disbanded in the Americas after 1763 or came as a result of the Highland Clearances. Scots lowlanders, unlike the highlanders settling in Nova Scotia, moved west to create communities in Alberta. The Bretons had been instrumental in building New France and continued to leave France for Québec and Montréal after Britain seized Canada in war. As for the Welsh, Manx, and Cornish, many were miners who left to find mining work abroad and would travel anywhere to find it.

The Welsh settlement in the Chubut Valley in Argentine Patagonia is a superb example of a Welsh-speaking community abroad, although its inhabitants now speak mainly Spanish. A more obscure Welsh community was the town of Hughesovka in imperial Russia. John Hughes, a Merthyr Tydfil engineer, established an ironworks at what is now Donetsk in the southern Ukraine. Taking up a concession from the industrializing imperial government, he created the New Russia Company Limited to raise capital, and in 1870 reached Russia with his equipment and about 100 ironworkers and miners from south Wales. They built a self-sufficient industrial complex with blast furnaces, mines, collieries, and brickworks which grew and prospered. However, the Hughes family and their workers left Russia after the Bolshevik Revolution.

In Australia, some 30 percent of the population claim to have some Irish blood. The years between 1791 and 1867 witnessed some 40,000 Irish convicts transported to Australia, many for political activities. Once there, the Irish tended to become urban workers, leading a far better life than would have occurred in Ireland or England. Whether Catholic or Protestant, they acquired wealth and standing, rising into key positions in the law and politics. Melbourne and Sydney have Irish political associations and 80 percent of the police of the state of Victoria are of Irish origin. The Irish convict, settler, and colonist became important to the survival of Australia, building part of the British Empire when Ireland had become an oppressed part of an earlier British empire.

The Scots attempted an early colony at Darien (1690s) on the Panamanian isthmus, hoping that this settlement would become a focal point for trade. Much Scots capital was sunk into the scheme, but the malarial swamp conditions and the environment meant that the isthmus was difficult to cross and trade was lacking while disease killed many. The Spanish let the colony wither on the vine until it surrendered after ten years of abject failure. In India, Scots after the 1707 Act of Union with England were embraced commercially as well as politically, happily seeking posts in the East India Company, where they eventually controlled half the positions. For example, in 1782, 56 out of 116 officer candidates for the

Company's Bengal army were Scots. Without these men and the Irish in the army, regular or Company, British India would not have survived and expanded.

In the United Arab Emirates, the Dubai Manx Society is run by Gil Salway-Costain. Her Manx name is familiar in Dubai where Manx Sir Richard Costain built a tower in 1969 surrounded by desert. He then

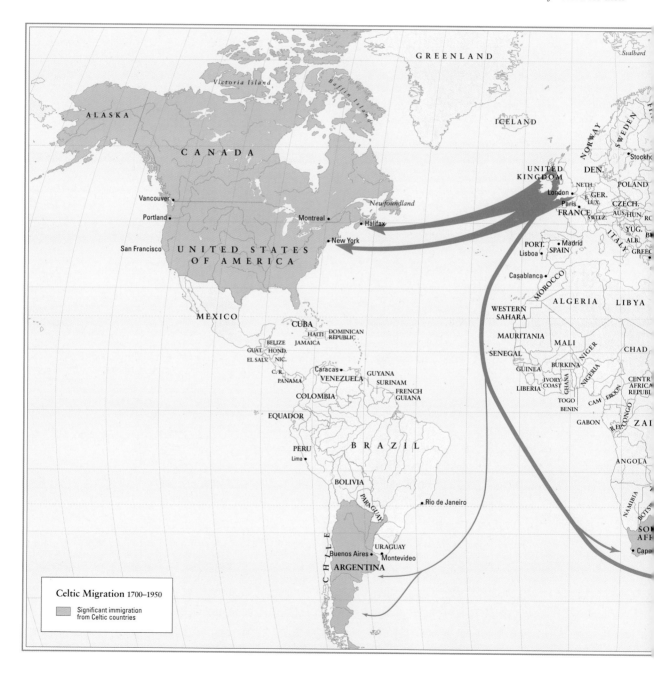

Celtic Migration 1700–1950

Significant immigration from Celtic countries

commenced building the modern infrastructure for the city. The society is not merely a social club; it helps integrate new Manx workers into the culturally different Arab country. Additionally, it acts as an informal agency of the Manx government working to introduce Manx business delegations to the Dubai government. In sum, the society fulfills the same function as early colonists have always done.

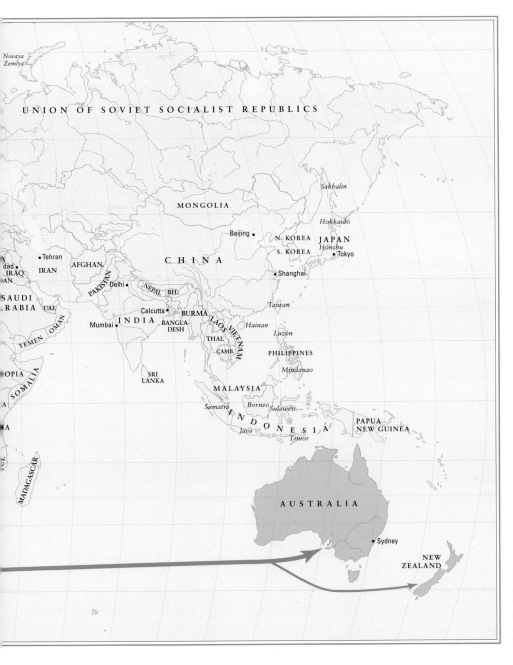

The major direction of Celtic emigration worldwide was westward to North America. Large numbers also went to Australia, New Zealand, and South Africa.

MAKING OF THE BRITISH EMPIRE

BY THE TIME OF THE INDIAN MUTINY, HALF OF THE EAST INDIA COMPANY'S 14,000 SOLDIERS, AND POSSIBLY 40 PERCENT OF THE 26,000 REGULAR BRITISH TROOPS IN INDIA, WERE IRISH. MOSTLY CATHOLICS WITH LOW INCOMES, THEY ENLISTED FOR REASONS OF ECONOMIC NECESSITY RATHER THAN IMPERIAL PATRIOTISM.

The first acquisitions of the British, or originally Stewart, Empire took place with the foundation of tobacco plantations in Virginia. 1624 witnessed the occupying of St. Kitts in the Caribbean, which used indentured labor to produce tobacco. For many years, the Caribbean was seen to be more important than colonies in North America because the importance of the islands for growing tobacco and then sugar. On the Atlantic seaboard of the Americas, the Pilgrim Fathers landed in Massachusetts Bay to establish a Puritan settlement while other foundations were created for other religions or toleration. The colonies were given colonial governors tasked with founding assemblies acting as legislative bodies in this attempt at making what was to be classic English colonial government.

After the English Civil War, Cromwell's English Commonwealth fought Spain and captured Jamaica (1655), which turned into a sugar-growing island rich with plantations staffed by African slaves. Britain had also acquired Barbados, Montserrat, Nevis, and Antigua, gaining an important commercial empire. They remained highly independent in spirit, having to defend themselves in wars against France, Spain, and the Netherlands, which ended in 1670 with the Treaty of Madrid allowing Britain to keep its possessions. One problem emanating from this peace was that the privateers engaged in a quasi-legal role during war now turned to piracy for the next few decades.

After the accession of King William and Queen Mary in England with the ousting of the Stewart monarchy, Britain waged a series of wars with France which sheltered the Jacobite Pretender. In the far north of America, the Hudson's Bay Company was spreading its reach and its intensive trading

Opposite: After the French surrender of Canada and until the America Declaration of Independence in 1776, the British controlled gigantic areas of the North American continent.

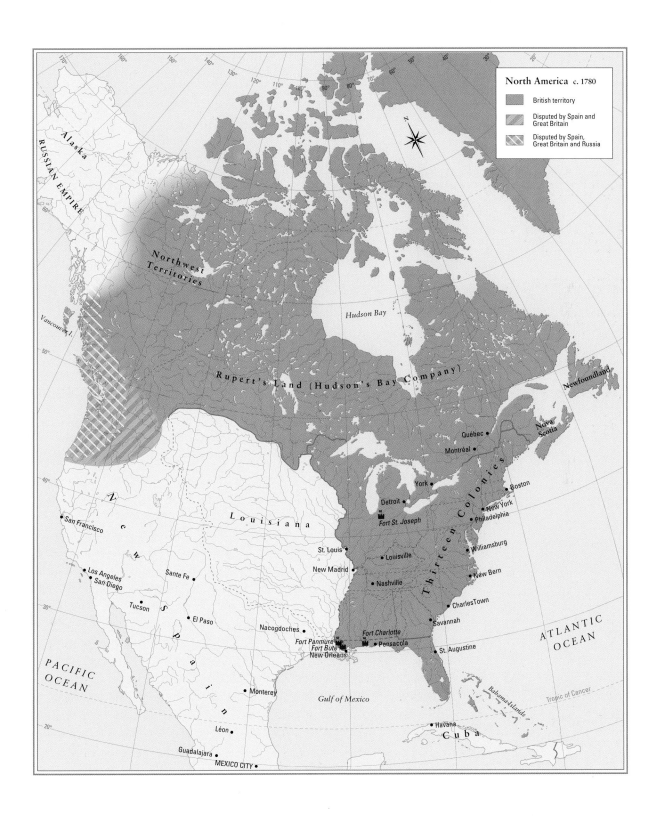

North America c. 1780

British territory

Disputed by Spain and
Great Britain

Disputed by Spain,
Great Britain and Russia

Alaska

RUSSIAN EMPIRE

Northwest
Territories

Vancouver I.

Hudson Bay

Rupert's Land (Hudson's Bay Company)

Newfoundland

Québec

Montréal

Nova
Scotia

York

Detroit

Boston

New York

Fort St. Joseph

Philadelphia

San Francisco

Louisiana

Williamsburg

St. Louis

Louisville

New Madrid

New Bern

Los Angeles
San Diego

Sante Fe

Nashville

Thirteen Colonies

Tucson

CharlesTown

El Paso

Savannah

Nacogdoches

Fort Charlotte

Fort Panmure
Fort Bute
New Orleans

Pensacola

St. Augustine

ATLANTIC
OCEAN

N
e
w

S
p
a
i
n

PACIFIC
OCEAN

Monterey

Gulf of Mexico

Bahama Islands

Tropic of Cancer

Léon

Havana

Cuba

Guadalajara

MEXICO CITY

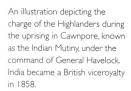

An illustration depicting the charge of the Highlanders during the uprising in Cawnpore, known as the Indian Mutiny, under the command of General Havelock. India became a British viceroyalty in 1858.

caused tension with New France, based upon Montréal and Québec. King William's War (1689-97), part of the Nine Years' War against France became a prelude to Queen Anne's War (1702-13), itself part of the War of Spanish Succession. Britain seized Gibraltar (1704) and Minorca (1708), giving it bases in the Mediterranean for the first time. King George's War (1743-48), a constituent of the War of Austrian Succession and the following French and Indian War (1755-63), the New World component of the Seven Years' War, witnessed a power shift in the world that gave Britain dominance and upset any balance of power. The first conflict saw Louisbourg captured and returned with a peace treaty, but the second struggle gave Britain Canada and also Spanish territories east of the Mississippi, making Britain the hegemonic power in North America.

The aftermath of the birth of the first British Empire witnessed the problem of imperial security, with the British government wanting American resources to pay for defense. A series of poorly thought out acts were passed, upsetting the colonists. The 1754 Sugar and Currency Acts, the 1765 Stamp Act, the 1767 Townshend Acts, and the 1774 Québec Act attacked American constitutional rights and interests, which led to the "shot heard around the world", the Continental Congress, and the American War of Independence, which Britain lost but retained Canada.

Elsewhere, a Second British Empire was being constructed, turning Britain away from its former American- and Atlantic-centered empire into a worldwide global power. By 1696, the British East India Company possessed three fortified trading posts: Calcutta in Bengal, Madras on the Carnatic coast, and Bombay on the west coast. France also began to trade in India, and the War of Austrian Succession and the Seven Years' War spread into an imperial contest in India. The East India Company wanted no further territorial conquests, considering Bengal enough of a bastion to protect its trade. During the French Revolution and Napoleonic Wars, the imperialist policies of Governor-General Lord Wellesley (1798-1805) were introduced, reducing the Nizam of Hyderabad's domains to the status of a virtual protectorate; Mysore became a vassal; Oudh was cut in half; the Carnatic was annexed; and Ceylon was seized from the Dutch. British policy was a mixture of force, extortion, bribery, and manipulation, which was aimed at a subcontinent rife with political and religious disunity. Britain's superior weapons technology, added to a disciplined force of British regulars and Company sepoys, placed Indian resistance at a disadvantage. Further wars followed against the Gurkhas (1814-16) in the Himalayas, after which Nepal was reduced in size and became a protectorate supplying Britain with some of its fiercest troops. Central India's state of disorder and lawlessness led to campaigns subjugating the Maratha and Rajput states. The first Burmese War (1824-26) won Assam and Tennasserim in the Arakan for Britain. Lower Burma was conquered in a second Burmese war (1852), and a third war resulted in the incorporation (1891) of Burma into British India.

In 1854, Britain faced extremely powerful resistance when the Sikhs of the Punjab attacked British possessions. This Sikh military theocracy was defeated in 1846 but fought again in 1848, causing extensive British casualties at the battle of Chilianwala. However, defeat in 1849 led to British annexation of the Punjab. Other territories were acquired on the death of native rulers (the doctrine of lapse) such as Muslim Oudh and Hindu Jaipur, Sambalpur, and the Maratha states of Jhansi, Nagpur, and Satara. Despite the uprising known as the Indian Mutiny (1857-58), where Indian troops rallied to the flag of the last Moghul, Bahadur Shah II, as emperor of India, the British retained control. In 1858, India became

After 1750, British interests in India grew dramatically. Britain also extended its empire in southeast Asia and along the coast of China. The Indian Ocean almost became a British ocean where the Royal Navy protected British interests and trade.

British Possessions in South and Southeast Asia 1800–1900

■ British

▨ Allied to British administration

Sphere of influence c. 1907

▨ British

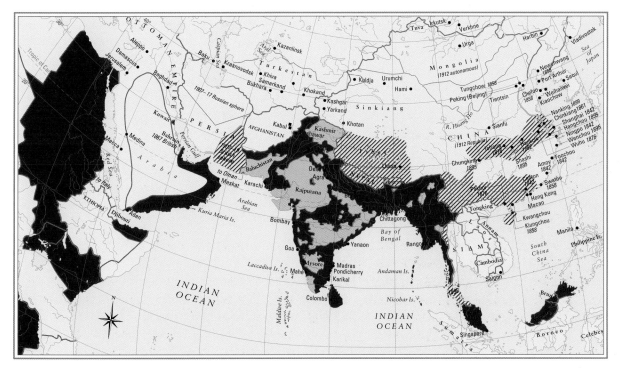

a British viceroyalty, and in 1876 Prime Minister Benjamin Disraeli made Queen Victoria Empress of India.

Britain projected her power through exploration, and Captain Cook's travels in the Pacific led to the First Fleet being sent to Botany Bay in Australia in 1788, leading to a settlement which is now the city of Sydney. Britain used this colony as a penal settlement but those criminals who served their ticket were allowed to make their own way in life, and some felons in England wanted to be transported in order to win a future improvement in their standard of living. New Zealand and the dispossessing of the indigenous Maoris followed. British imperial policy was fueled by the desire for new markets where goods produced by the Industrial Revolution could find purchasers. Consequently, commerce sought not just to retain its trade with the Americas but to move to the Orient too. Part of this policy was realized when Sir Stamford Raffles founded an English colony at Singapore in 1819. This island became a springboard to make a series of treaties with separate Malay states, eventually leading to the Federated Malay States of Perak, Selangor, Negri Sembilan, and Pahang (1896). The power behind the thrones was British, as it was in Kedah, Perlis, Kelantan, and Trengganu, acquired from Siam and Johore. By 1914, British Malaya comprised the Crown Colony of the Straits Settlements of Penang, Singapore, and Malacca and nine states as protectorates. Britain had a secure route to China, and the Opium Wars allowed it to acquire Hong Kong in 1842 and Kowloon and Stonecutters Island in 1860. The New Territories were obtained in 1898 on a 99-year lease.

The other areas associated with the British Empire are Arabia and Africa. Aden was seized in 1839 as a staging post to India and was administered from India while the pirates of the north Arabian coast were crushed by British naval forces. In 1853, a Treaty of Maritime Peace in Perpetuity was signed and after 1873 these Trucial States were administered from India, with Britain controlling their foreign policy. A protectorate was established over Kuwait in 1899 despite it being part of the Ottoman Empire.

Britain acquired Cape Colony from the Dutch during the Napoleonic Wars and gradually Boer settlers moved north in their great treks to establish the Transvaal and Orange Free State, with war eventually following. These states were defeated in the Second Boer War (1899-1902). A British interest lay in the Suez Canal, opened in 1869. Britain occupied Egypt in 1882 to keep and control the Canal. Elsewhere, on the African continent a scramble occurred wherein the major imperial powers attempted to make good their claims to chunks of Africa. British was contained on the west coast by France, but Cecil Rhodes in South Africa acquired Bechuanaland in 1888. Wars with the Zulu and Matabele acquired more land, the second conflict leading to the establishment of Rhodesa in 1894. Other territories grabbed were what became Nyasaland and Uganda (1894) while a colony was established in Kenya. The same period saw a protectorate occurring over Zanzibar in 1890, to ensure the suppression of its slave market.

The British Empire became a reservoir of manpower, which was desperately needed in the First World War. The British dominions supplied troops, with Canadians fighting in France and the Anzacs, Australians and New Zealanders, campaigning in Gallipoli and Palestine. Indian troops were used in France, East Africa, and the Near East. Success in this war led to a further expansion of the empire, with the acquisition of most of the German empire and control over much of the oil-bearing region of the former Ottoman empire. Pressures for decolonization arose and British weakness after the exhaustion of the Second World War saw the empire slip away.

Opposite: Britain had long-established links with Africa. These expanded after the seizure of South Africa from the Dutch. By 1882, large areas of the African continent were part of the British Empire.

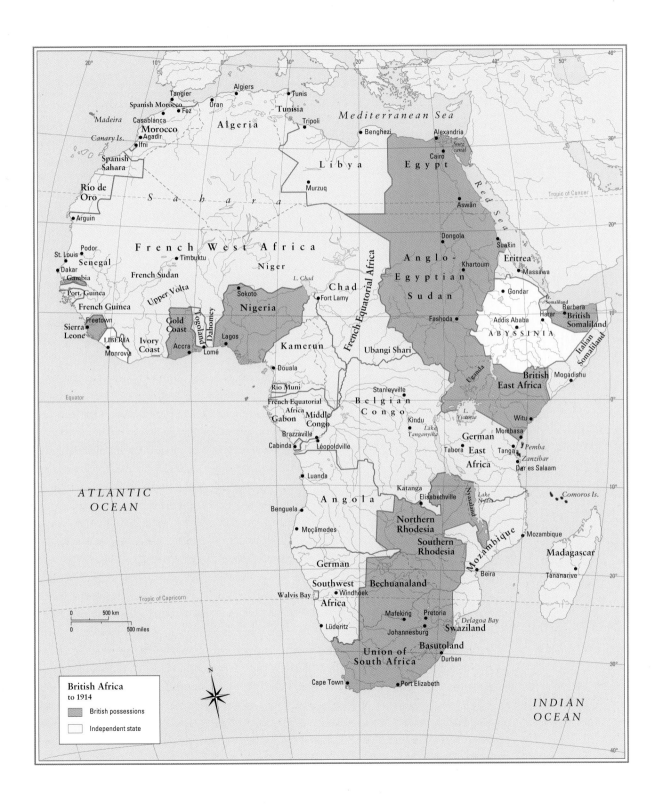

Map labels:

20° · 10° · 0° · 10° · 20° · 30° · 40° · 50°

Tangier
Algiers · Tunis
Spanish Morocco · Fez · Oran
Madeira · Casablanca
Morocco · Tripoli
Canary Is. · Agadir
Ifni
Spanish Sahara
Rio de Oro
Arguin

Mediterranean Sea
Benghazi · Alexandria
Algeria · *Tunisia*
L i b y a · Suez canal · Cairo
E g y p t
Murzuq · Aswân
Tropic of Cancer

S   a   h   a   r   a

F r e n c h   W e s t   A f r i c a
Dongola
Suakin
Eritrea
Podor · Timbuktu · *N i g e r* · Massawa
St. Louis · *Senegal* · Khartoum
Dakar · French Sudan · *L. Chad* · *Chad* · *A n g l o -* · Gondar
Gambia · Upper Volta · Fort Lamy · *E g y p t i a n* · *Somaliland* · Berbera
Port. Guinea · Sokoto · *S u d a n* · Harar · **British**
French Guinea · **Nigeria** · Fashoda · Addis Ababa · **Somaliland**
Sierra · Freetown · *Gold* · *A B Y S S I N I A* · *Italian Somaliland*
Leone · *Coast* · Lagos · *Kamerun* · *Uganda* · Mogadishu
LIBERIA · *Ivory* · Accra · Lomé · Ubangi Shari · **British**
Monrovia · *Coast* · Douala · *East Africa*
Togoland · Dahomey

Equator · Rio Muni · Stanleyville · *L.* · Witu
French Equatorial · *B e l g i a n* · *Victoria*
Africa · *C o n g o* · Kindu · Mombasa
Gabon · *Middle* · *Lake* · **German** · Pemba
Congo · *Tanganyika* · Tabora · *East* · Tanga
Brazzaville · Léopoldville · *Africa* · Zanzibar
Cabinda · Dar es Salaam

Luanda · Katanga · *Lake* · *Comoros Is.*
Elisabethville · *Nyasa*

ATLANTIC OCEAN
A n g o l a
Benguela
Moçâmedes
Northern Rhodesia · Mozambique
Southern Rhodesia · *Mozambique*
German · *Madagascar*
Southwest · **Bechuanaland** · Beira
Walvis Bay · Windhoek
Africa · Tananarive
Tropic of Capricorn
Mafeking · Pretoria · *Delagoa Bay*
Lüderitz · Johannesburg · **Swaziland**
Basutoland
Union of South Africa · Durban
Cape Town · Port Elizabeth

INDIAN OCEAN

Scale:
0 — 500 km
0 — 500 miles

N

British Africa
to 1914
▓ British possessions
□ Independent state

WALES IN PATAGONIA

IN WALES, THE WELSH WERE NOT USED TO HUNTING, BUT
GOOD RELATIONS WITH THE NATIVE TEHEULCHE PEOPLE SAW
THE INDIANS TEACH THEM HOW TO CATCH THE LIVESTOCK
AVAILABLE ON THE PRAIRIE. SOME TEHEULCHE LEARNED WELSH
AND CELEBRATED THE ANNUAL EISTEDDFOD AT TRELEW.

A Welsh non-conformist minister and nationalist, Michael D. Jones, was sad to see Welsh migrants reaching North America, learning English, and losing their Welsh identity. He decided that the only way the Welsh could keep their identity abroad was to built a unified Welsh colony where language and culture could be preserved. His activities resulted in some 150 people from Wales sailing from Liverpool to Patagonia in Argentina in the tea-clipper Mimosa in 1865. These migrants were encouraged by the Argentine government, which wanted Europeans to settle and develop the country outside the area of Buenos Aires.

The Welsh migrants comprised a range of married couples, single or widowed men, and 52 children. Having reached Patagonia, they made their way to the Chubut Valley, where the Argentine government had offered them, or so they thought, a hundred square miles of land. The land was poor and semi-arid, with little water. Nevertheless, a settlement was established on a site which eventually became the town of Rawson, the future capital of Chubut province. Despite flash floods, crop failure, and lack of rainfall, the community survived, being helped by the indigenous Tehuelche, who alleviated food shortages.

More Welsh people arrived between 1865 and 1875. By 1876, there were 690 Welsh in the Chubut Valley. An irrigation system was built which irrigated a band some three to four miles each side of the River Chubut for some 50 miles of its length. The region produced much grain, becoming one of the most fertile agricultural regions of Argentina. Title to the land was given by the Argentine government and the Welsh community became self-governing, with both men and women over 18 having the right to vote. A railway, financed by British funds, was constructed between the Chabut Valley and the coast,

Opposite: In Patagonia, adventurous Welsh colonists saw an opportunity to create new communities based on farming in the vast and almost empty land.

work commencing in 1886 and helped by the arrival of another 465 Welsh migrants. A town named Trelew developed at the railhead which became a commercial center. Further Welsh settlements were founded at Cwm Hyfryd, Esquel, and Trevelin.

Overall, the population grew before the First World War, despite some settlers leaving for Canada. By then, some 4,000 people of Welsh descent inhabited the Chubut Valley. After the war, more settlers were attracted to the region but these came mainly from Italy and other southern European countries, making the Welsh a minority in the valley. However, Welsh identity was preserved by a strong chapel culture and a tight-knit community which looked after itself in times of need. A co-operative society traded on the migrants behalf but it was wiped out in the Great Depression of the 1930s. A major improvement to life was the construction of a dam on the Chubut River in 1963, which removed the danger of flooding which had occasionally devastated the lower Chubut Valley.

The Welsh-Argentine community numbers some 20,000 people, although Welsh speakers number only 1,500. The major communities are at Puerto Madryn, Trevelin, Rawson, Trelew, Dolovon, and Gaiman. Now a co-ordinated attempt has been made by the Argentine government and the National Assembly of Wales to stimulate and maintain the Welsh heritage and identity in Patagonia. The centenary of the colony's birth in 1965 saw many visitors from Wales, and teachers have been sent to keep the language in being. Welsh cultural activities continue, traditionally based around chapel and Welsh tea-rooms, one of which was shown on BBC2 when the *Hairy Bikers* traveled there and cooked Welsh lamb. The Welsh national rugby team played at Puerto Madryn, the settlers' original landfall, with Argentina winning the match. The Welsh colony, *Y Wladfa*, has been portrayed in the works of Eluned Morgan, daughter of the founder of Trelew, who wrote many journal articles and four books.

Wales in Patagonia

Area of Welsh settlement

Welsh Emigration to the United States and Canada

WELSH MIGRANTS MINED THE SLATE QUARRIES AND COAL MINES OF PENNSYLVANIA AND LEAD MINED IN WISCONSIN. SOME JOINED IN THE CALIFORNIA GOLD RUSH. MANY MORE MIGRATED TO SOUTH AMERICA.

T he Welsh have migrated for hundreds of years, especially into the industrial cities and mines of England and Scotland during the Industrial Revolution, which started in the eighteenth century. In fact, there has been an exchange of populations, as many English moved into south Wales in the same period. The Welsh have moved further afield into the coal mining areas of the Pas-se-Calais in France, into Patagonia in the search for religious freedom, and into Canadian Newfoundland. The United States has received many Welsh, with some 1.75 million claiming Welsh ancestry; and 467,000 did the same in the Canadian census in 2006. The Welsh have also found their way south to Australia and New Zealand.

The large Welsh admixture in the U.S.A. has produced eight presidents, with Thomas Jefferson and Abraham Lincoln having Welsh ancestry, and the Confederate president Jefferson Davis also had Welsh genes. A tale about America claims the very name comes from Richard Ameryk, a Welshman and Bristol merchant who was the main investor in John Cabot's second crossing of the Atlantic in 1497. The late seventeenth century witnessed a large influx of Welsh Quakers into Pennsylvania, and one-third of the colony's 20,000 European inhabitants in 1700 are thought to have been Welsh. Pennsylvania was an attractive destination owing to its founder Quaker William Penn, who proclaimed religious freedom in the commonwealth.

Welsh Emigration 170

Significant numbers of emigrants from Wales

The nineteenth century saw a surge of Welsh into Ohio and Utah while Idaho built a Welsh Mormon community in Malad City, Idaho. The Welsh settlers in Columbus, Ohio founded Welsh Congregational, Methodist, and Presbyterian congregations. Likewise, Radnor in Delaware County, Ohio has preserved its Welsh Congregational and Baptist churches. Other noteworthy Welsh-built communities are in Jackson and Gallia Counties, Ohio, known as Little Cardiganshire. The Welsh Mormon community originated from Mormon missionary success in Wales in the 1830s and 1840s. They established a Welsh choir, which eventually renamed itself The Mormon Tabernacle Choir. Tennessee received over a hundred Welsh families from Pennsylvania after the American Civil War. They moved to Mechanicsville and Knoxville, working in heavy industry. A small Welsh coal-mining community from Shawnee, Ohio moved to the gold mines west of Colorado Springs in the late nineteenth century. Culturally, the Madog Center for Welsh Studies at the University of Rio Grande, Ohio, is important, and the National Welsh Gymanfa Ganu Association holds the National Festival of Wales around the country.

Canada has been home to a Welsh community since 1812 although other Welsh had lived there since the end of the American Revolution. A large settlement was founded at Southwald, now London, Ontario and many Welsh coal miners joined in the Cariboo Gold Rush in British Columbia and settled there. Some Patagonian Welsh built a new community at Bangor, Saskatchewan and at Wood River by Ponoka, Alberta. This city has several Welsh societies and Canada enjoys eisteddfodau and Gymanfa Ganu.

The Australian census of 2006 recorded over 25,000 Australians as born in Wales while some 113,242 claimed Welsh ancestry.

Welsh emigration followed the same route as most other European emigration, with the majority heading for North America while significant numbers headed for New Zealand and Australia. Some also settled in Argentina.

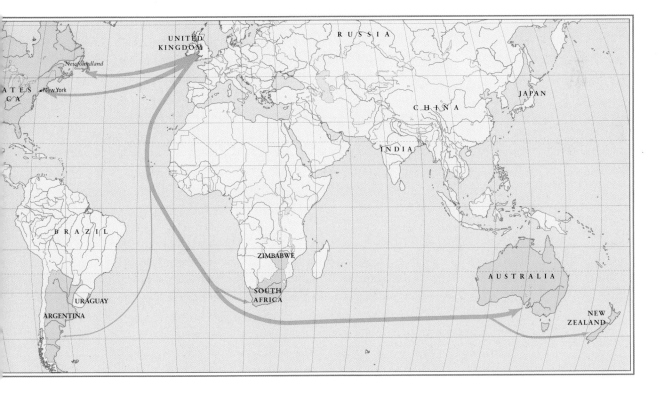

THE MANX IN AMERICA

THERE ARE OVER ONE MILLION PEOPLE WITH MANX ANCESTRY IN THE WORLD, AND THEY CAN BE FOUND PRIMARILY IN THE UNITED STATES. THEY ARE HELD TOGETHER BY THE WORLD MANX ASSOCIATION. THEY ARE INORDINATELY PROUD OF THE ISLAND EVEN IF SOME WILL NEVER SEE IT.

In 2007, John Quirk, a Manxman, published *The Manx Connection*, a book detailing the Manx overseas observed in his research and travel around the world. He found evidence of Manx settlement in Western Australian, Queensland, New South Wales, and Tasmania in Australia and in Christchurch and Auckland in New Zealand. The book demonstrates the strong historical bonds with South Africa where many miners went in the 1870s. There is even a Manx Society in Dubai in the United Arab Emirates, founded in 2000. However, the biggest impact the Manx have made abroad is in the United States.

An early connection with North America was in Myles Standish, who sailed to New England in the *Mayflower* in 1620. His wives were native Manx. A branch of the Christian family from Maughold settled in Virginia in 1655, and one their descendants became a colonel in the American army during the Revolution and was a personal friend of George Washington. However, the majority of Manx settlers were the less wealthy or the poor, and their descendants founded the North American Manx Association in Cleveland Ohio in 1928. The largest concentration of Manx descendants is in Cleveland, Ohio although there are others in northeast Ohio. The next state with a largish Manx group is Illinois, followed by California, New York State, and Michigan. Other states with Manx populations are Florida and Wisconsin, followed by the mining states of Montana, Wyoming, and Arizona. Other states with Manx are Minnesota, Iowa and Nebraska, followed by Massachusetts, New Jersey, Connecticut, Washington DC, and Utah.

Manx migration to Ohio seems to have commenced in 1821-22 when the Corkhill family of Ramsey sailed from Liverpool to Baltimore and went by wagon to Ohio. Poor economic and social conditions, impairing agriculture and fishing in the parishes of Jurby, Andreas, Bride, Kirk Michael, and the area

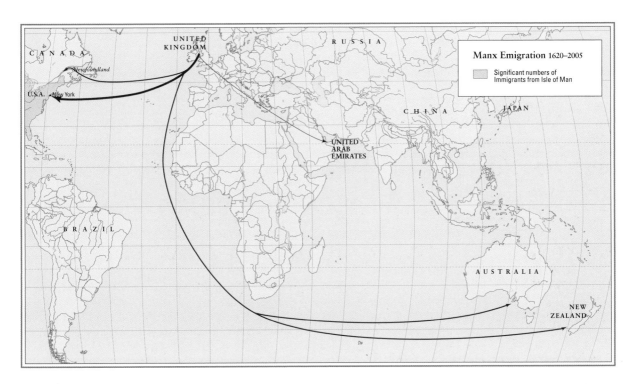

around Peel, created Manx migrants, who found Ohio easy to access by boat after the Erie Canal was cut. 1826 and 1827 saw a virtual exodus to Ohio when people settled near the lake shore in the small mill towns of Madison, moving west to places like Hambden to Elyria. The Manx were initially regarded as rather clannish because they spoke Manx Gaelic and inter-married for generations.

Cleveland saw several types of Manx activity. Five men with Manx names founded the Mona's Relief Society in 1851 in order to aid poor Manx migrants or those in ill health. The migrants were also interested in education and created the Manx Street School. The Manx provided ministers, a medical skin specialist, and a noted lawyer. The Gill family, arriving in the city in 1854, founded a house-building business which provided employment for Manx tradesmen. Illinois was reached via New Orleans and then the Mississippi before railways traveled east to west. Again, migrants came from the poor north of Mann, from Bride and Andreas and from further south (Onchan, Crosby and Peel), taking with them some typical Manx names, such as Crellin, Gelling, Mylchreest, Killip, and Clucas. Wisconsin witnessed an influx of Manx miners from the mines of Laxey and Foxdale, especially when they ceased to flourish. They bought land to build a Methodist church, known as Laxey Church, which later fell into disrepair when the Manx moved on to other mines, at Cripple Creek in Colorado or to Bisbee in Arizona and eventually to the iron mines of northern Michigan. Chicago offered a big opportunity to Manx carpenters, who helped rebuild the city after the 1871 great fire. California has also attracted a large number of Manx, but these tended to reach Los Angeles and San Francisco after having lived elsewhere in the United States In sum, the Manx have been pioneers in the U.S.A. and other parts of the world, and their affection for their home island is shown by the many Manx societies scattered around the world.

Most people leaving the Isle of Man for a new life outside Europe went to the United States. In the modern period, Manxmen, closely associated with the financial industry, have settled in the new financial centers in the Arab Gulf such as Dubai.

Cornish Emigration to Canada, Mexico, and Around the World

Cornish hard-rock miners searched for work all around the world. In Canada they applied their skills to canal-building and to masonry when building fortifications at Halifax, St John's, and Kingston.

Cornwall and its mines have been famous since the Phoenicians traded for tin. The pride and skill of Cornish miners meant that in times of economic distress the miners would search for work in mines around the world. As the tin and copper industries declined, the Duchy exported vast numbers of young people. Between 1861 and 1901, around 20 per cent of the Cornish male population migrated abroad, some quarter of a million people. Although miners were the majority, there were farmers, traders, and skilled craftsmen, too. This mass of people joined their kinsfolk already in the Americas and the Caribbean. The Cornish migrants took their culture with them and their Methodist religion as they worked in gold, silver ,and copper mines overseas. With them went their traditional pasties, their own brand of wrestling, and rugby. Their food has been adopted by the receiving countries, as have their festivals. Those Cornish who remained in England often received remittance money from kin abroad, and by the end of the nineteenth century one million pounds sterling was sent back annually from South Africa. The strength of the Cornish community can be seen in the Cornish Association of Witwatersrand. In addition, Cornish migrants went to the United States, Canada, Mexico, Australia, and New Zealand. They developed tight-knit communities which kept in touch with each other. However, an assimilation process has taken place which has weakened trans-national communications. However, the six million people in the world who claim Cornish ancestors have virtually reinvented their culture with a whole series of Cornish societies worldwide. The South Australian copper triangle, holding the Lowender Kernewek, Cornish Festival attracts some eighty thousand visitors a year.

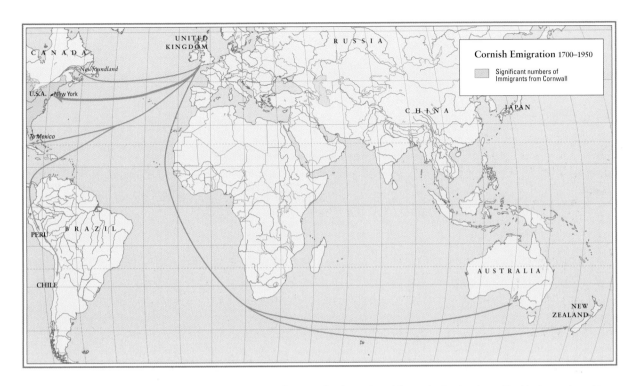

Cornish Emigration 1700–1950

Significant numbers of Immigrants from Cornwall

In South Australia, the towns of Moonta, Kadina, and Wallaroo make the region of the Yorke Peninsula into Little Cornwall, with Cornish vernacular architecture and the mine engine houses. In neighboring New Zealand, its government deliberately encouraged immigrants, and an immigration scheme running between 1871 and 1888 allowed any New Zealand resident to choose a named migrant, who could travel for free if they reached certain criteria. These stated that a migrant should be young, fit, and trained in laboring, farming, or domestic work. Recruiters sent to Britain were instructed to search Cornwall and Scotland for candidates, as these possessed a strong work ethic while the Cornish had a strong chapel culture. As Cornish industry collapsed under declining world prices, particularly the 1866 copper price crash, its miners went to New Zealand to Auckland, Wellington, Lyttleton-Christchurch, and Dunedin.

Latin America has witnessed the arrival of Cornish migrants. The Cornish led the world in mining technology and technological innovation and exported machinery. Richard Trevithick took high-pressure steam engines to the silver mines of Peru in 1816, followed by skilled men to operate them. Mexico possesses its Cornish community, founded in the state of Hidalgo. Miners were contracted to work in the silver mining towns of Mineral del Monte and Pachuca. Most of these miners originated from Cambourne and Redruth and, as elsewhere, Cornish cottage architecture went with the people. Money sent back to Cornwall helped finance the construction of Redruth's Wesleyan Chapel. The two silver-mining communities of Pachuca and Real del Monte are being billed as Mexico's "Little Cornwall" by the Mexican embassy in London. Another Cornish diaspora went to Grass Valley, California to help dig gold mines, and many towns have monuments to their achievements. These miners also established themselves in the copper region of northern Michigan and in the iron-bearing region of that state and Minnesota.

Cornish miners emigrated to wherever their skills were useful, from California to Mexico. Many others went to the goldfields of Australia.

IRISH EMIGRATION TO THE UNITED STATES

THE IRISH WERE AMONG THE VERY FIRST SETTLERS AND
EXPLORERS TO THE UNITED STATES. WORKING ON THE LAND
AND LATER ON THE CONSTRUCTION SITES OF THE RAPIDLY
GROWING CITIES, THE IRISH PLAYED A HUGE PART IN THE
BUILDING OF AMERICA.

Opposite: Between 1820 and
1860, Europe annually sent more
than 120,000 emigrants to the
United States. By 1860, one in
eight of America's 32,000,000
people had been born in Europe.
Of this multitude, 2,000,000
came from Ireland, the bulk of
these people originating in the
least fertile regions of the west.
Irish immigration peaked in the
years following the Great Famine
of 1845, when hundreds of
thousands fled their impoverished
small-holdings.

Two types of Irish came to America, Irish Catholics and Scotch-Irish Presbyterians, and each group thoroughly detested the other. The Irish Catholics were the natives of Ireland; the Scotch-Irish were newcomers from Scotland who, beginning in the early 1600s had crossed the Irish Sea and settled in Ulster, in northern Ireland, on land that had been confiscated from Irish Catholic rebels. The English king, James I, had encouraged the Scots to move to Ireland to counter-balance the influence of Irish Catholics in the north. Between 1606 and 1640, 100,000 Scots Presbyterians had settled in Ulster. By the early 18th century, the Scotch-Irish, chafing under high rents and low wages in Ulster, began emigrating to England's American colonies. By 1775, more than 200,000 Scotch-Irish were in America. While they could be found throughout the thirteen colonies, the majority moved west, into the backwoods of Pennsylvania, Virginia, and the Carolinas and eventually into virgin territory in Kentucky and Tennessee. They carved farms and settlements out of the wilderness and acted as a buffer between the Indians and the more established settlements back east. For the next century the Scotch-Irish were always the advance guard of the pioneers, heading father and farther west. The frontiersman Davy Crocket and presidents Andrew Jackson and Andrew Johnson were Scotch-Irish who began their lives in the backwoods.

The Scotch-Irish had a strong independent streak, and in the years leading up to the American Revolution they were among the most outspoken advocates of severing America's ties to Great Britain. At least five Scotch-Irishmen signed the Declaration of Independence: Thomas McKean, Edward Rutledge, James Smith, George Taylor, Matthew Thornton, and Philip Livingstone.

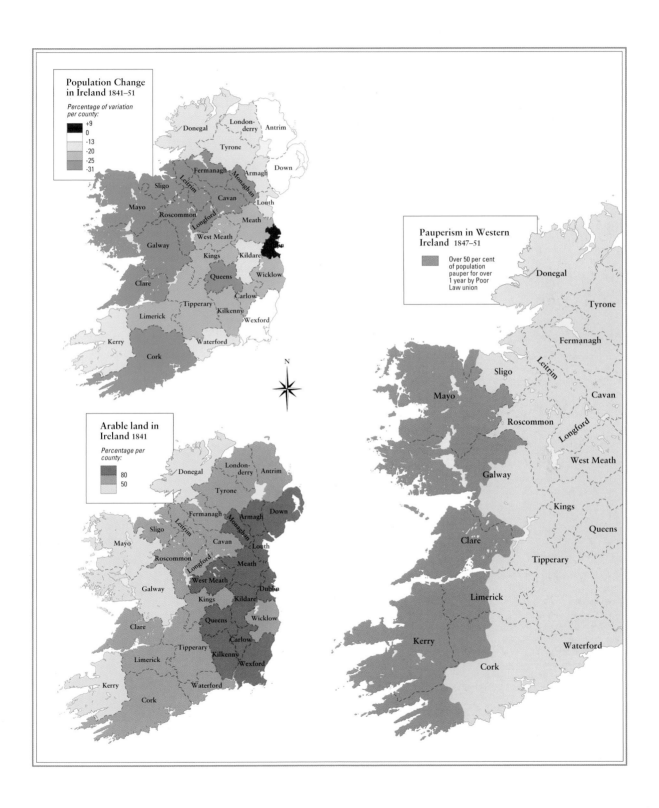

Population Change in Ireland 1841–51

Percentage of variation per county:

+9
0
-13
-20
-25
-31

Pauperism in Western Ireland 1847–51

Over 50 per cent of population pauper for over 1 year by Poor Law union

Arable land in Ireland 1841

Percentage per county:

80
50

In the 19th century the Scotch-Irish were eclipsed by Irish Catholics, who began to come to America to escape poverty and oppression in their homeland. Between 1815 and 1845, 1.3 million Irish, almost all of them Catholic, emigrated to the United States. The potato famine brought another 2.1 million Irish between the years 1846 and 1855. Although most of the immigrants had been farmers in Ireland, in America most of them settled in the cities, where they expected to find more opportunities for work. By 1860, 28 percent of the population of New York, 26 percent of the population of Boston, and 16 percent of the population of Philadelphia had been born in Ireland.

The Irish Catholics transformed the character of America. Catholicism had always been a minority religion in the United States, and often barely tolerated. Now new Catholic churches, schools, convents, hospitals, orphanages, and other charitable institutions were springing up across the country. In the 1840s and 1850s, American Protestants—many of them of Scotch-Irish descent—responded by forming secret associations known as "the True Americans," or "the Native Americans," better known as the Know Nothings because when asked about these secret societies, they replied, "I know nothing." The Know Nothings became a powerful force whose candidates were elected mayors of Boston, Philadelphia, New York, Baltimore, Chicago, New Orleans, and Washington, D.C. They dominated state politics in all the New England states, as well as in Pennsylvania, Indiana, and California. But they did not limit their activities to politics. In cities and towns from Bath, Maine to Galveston, Texas, nativist mobs destroyed Catholic churches and convents and burned the homes of American Catholics; during riots in Philadelphia, dozens of Irish Catholics were murdered by Know Nothings.

The overwhelming majority of Irish immigrants were unskilled labor, and so they took the hardest, dirtiest jobs. Irishmen dug the Erie Canal, laid the railroad tracks that linked the east and west coasts, and labored in the coal mines of Pennsylvania. Irishwomen found work as domestic servants or in mills and factories. By the 1870s Irishmen with some level of education could find more respectable positions as police officers or firefighters. But while many Irish immigrants were striving to get out of the slums into the American middle class, there was also a large semi-permanent Irish criminal underclass. Virtually every city had its Irish crime boss, but even more common were crooked Irish-run political machines. In the 1870s the Irish editor of the Catholic newspaper in Chicago lamented, "The Irish would have occupied a far higher position in America than they do today if, instead of manifesting an extraordinary genius for manipulating primaries and running ward politics, they had devoted their remarkable brightness of mind and cleverness to the task of earning an honest living, outside of politics."

Vast numbers of the migrant Irish flocked to big cities such as Pittsburgh, Detroit, Chicago, St. Louis, Missouri, and San Francisco. Once Irish communities were established, they acted as reception centers for future migrants and staging posts to move migrants westward to other regions. By 1860, the Irish had a large presence in the northeast, and comprised over half the immigrants to the U.S. during the famine years. During the American Civil War, some 150,000 Irishmen joined the Union army, the Irish Brigade being one famous unit, which lost 4,000 officers and men during the conflict. The 69th Infantry Regiment, the Fighting 69th, was known for its ferocity and valor.

Thousands of Irish-Americans joined America's first great push westward. It was Irish-American John O'Sullivan, the founding editor of the *Democratic Review* and later Minister to Portugal, who declared it

Opposite: There was a steady flow of emigrants from Ireland to the British North American colonies. These Irish settled along the western frontier zone forming distinctive communities that have survived into the modern period. From 1845, famine in Ireland touched off a mass migration, with millions of dispossessed peasants arriving in east coast ports, particularly Boston and New York. Many others arrived in Baltimore and as far south as New Orleans. Between 1820 and 1880, almost 3,500,000 Irish people entered the United States.

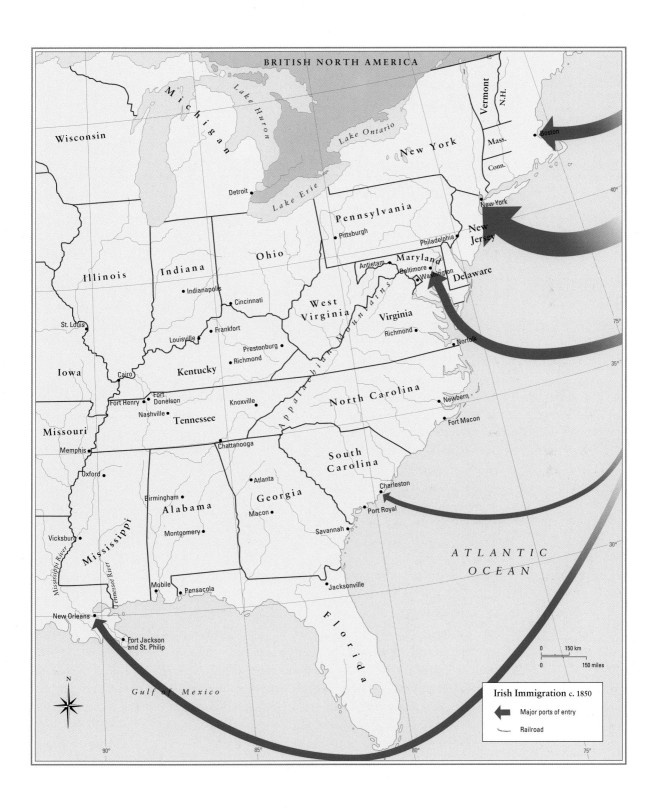

BRITISH NORTH AMERICA

Wisconsin

Michigan

Lake Huron

Lake Ontario

New York

Vermont

N.H.

Mass.

Conn.

• Boston

Detroit •

Lake Erie

Pennsylvania

New York

• Pittsburgh

Philadelphia

New Jersey

Illinois

Indiana

Ohio

Maryland

Antietam •

Baltimore •

Washington

Delaware

• Indianapolis

West
Virginia

• Cincinnati

Virginia

St. Louis •

Louisville •

• Frankfort

Richmond •

Iowa

Cairo

Kentucky

• Richmond

Prestonburg •

• Norfolk

Fort Henry

Fort
Donelson •

Knoxville •

North Carolina

Missouri

Nashville •

Tennessee

• Newbern

Memphis •

Chattanooga •

• Fort Macon

• Oxford

South
Carolina

Appalachian Mountains

Atlanta •

Birmingham •

Georgia

Charleston •

Vicksburg •

Mississippi River

Mississippi

Alabama

Macon •

Port Royal •

Tennessee River

Montgomery •

Savannah •

ATLANTIC
OCEAN

Mobile •

• Pensacola

Jacksonville •

New Orleans •

• Fort Jackson
and St. Philip

Florida

N

Gulf of Mexico

0   150 km

0   150 miles

Irish Immigration c. 1850

◀ Major ports of entry

⌐ Railroad

America's "manifest destiny" to extend her boundaries across the continent, and it was Irish-Americans who built the roads, canals, and railroads that opened her vast heartland to farmers and other settlers. It was Irish laborers who built the Baltimore and Ohio, the Erie, the Illinois Central, the Western and Atlantic, the Wabash and the Chicago and Northwestern. By far their greatest achievement was the transcontinental railroad.

Catholic schools and Democratic politics were the paths the Irish followed to success. Irish priests and nuns in America opened Catholic grammar schools, high schools, and colleges that gave the children and grandchildren of immigrants an education that enabled them to move into the professions. As for Irish would-be politicians, they found that their parish and their neighborhood were natural launching pads for a career in city or state government. By 1924 Irish Catholic politicians were ready for the national stage, or so they believed. The Democrats nominated Al Smith as their candidate for president, an Irish Catholic from a working class neighborhood in New York. Smith was defeated by an anti-Catholic backlash led in many places by the Ku Klux Klan, many of whose members regrettably were Scotch-Irish.

Even so, Irish Catholics continued to permeate every facet of American society: sport, film, music, literature, labor unions, and business. Their crowning moment came in 1960 when John F. Kennedy was elected president of the United States. The election of JFK symbolized the full assimilation of Irish Catholics into the American mainstream. Today over 5.3 million Americans, 2 percent of the population, identify themselves as Scotch-Irish; 36.4 million, more than 12 percent of the population, identify themselves as Irish, and most of these also identify themselves as Catholic. The Irish have been heavily involved in public affairs, especially politics. In association with the Catholic Church, they have been engaged in constructing colleges, orphanages, and hospitals. Irish leadership has been prevalent in labor unions, in the Catholic Church, in educational institutions, and in the Democratic Party in the cities they inhabit. The apex of Irish Catholic political success was the presidency of John F. Kennedy (1961-63). The Irish Catholic community continues its association with the Democratic Party, with one Kennedy brother still a senator and presidents Reagan, Clinton, and Bush all claiming some Irish ancestry. In fact, 23 presidents could make that assertion. An article in the *Washington Post* in May 2007 reported that Barack Obama's great-great-great-grandfather was Fulmuth Kearney from Moneygall, County Offaly, who migrated to the U.S.A. in 1850 aged 19 years. Irish politicians have been elected at every level, and a large number of important cities have elected Irish Catholic mayors, among them Boston, Cincinnati, Houston, Newark, New York City, Pittsburgh, Saint Louis, Saint Paul, Chicago, Boston, and Baltimore.

A well-known Chicago mayor was Richard Joseph Daley, whose tenure lasted from 1955 to 1976. Mayor Daley came to international prominence when he supported a hard-line police reaction to rioting after Martin Luther King's assassination. In 1968, the Democratic National Convention was held in Chicago during a time of national division over the Vietnam war. Anti-war protesters flooded into the city to stop the convention with violent confrontations with the police. The media had a field-day, criticizing the Democratic Irish party machine. However, Daley was re-elected mayor with a slimmed down majority. He ultimately died in office. Daley's son, Richard Daley, was elected mayor in 1989, which office he still holds. Irish contributions to American mass culture are legendary, with the annual St. Patrick's Day celebration held in New York.

From 1870, Irish communities established in the northeast of the United States joined with the rest of American society in looking for land and opportunity westward across the Mississippi River.

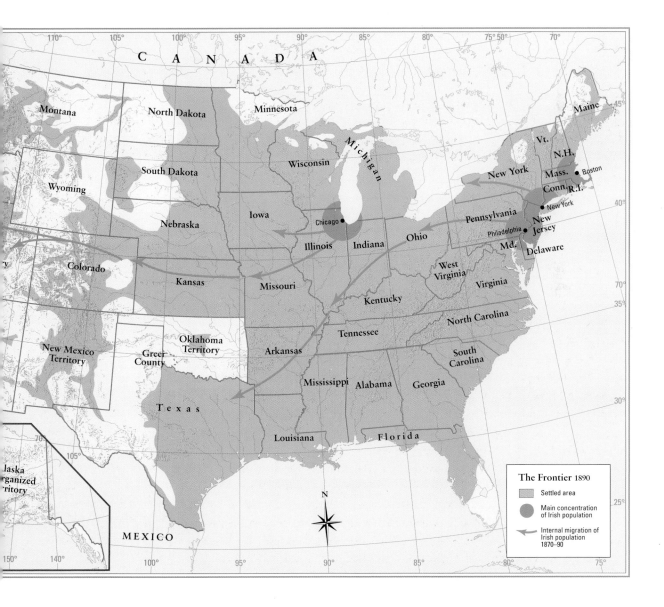

The Frontier 1890

- Settled area
- Main concentration of Irish population
- Internal migration of Irish population 1870–90

THE IRISH IN CANADA

THE GREAT WAVE OF IRISH IMMIGRATION TO CANADA TOOK PLACE IN THE 19TH CENTURY, WHEN IRELAND WAS DEVASTATED BY THE POTATO FAMINE.

The first Irish to settle in Canada came by way of France. In the late 17th century, as the English consolidated their hold over Ireland, those who had the means escaped to the Continent. Some Irish who had taken refuge in France moved on to Canada, where they could practice their Catholic faith, purchase good land at a cheap price, and perhaps have a little adventure. Rough estimates suggest that perhaps as much as five percent of the population of New France was Irish. In fact, surnames that today are considered French Canadian are actually corruptions of Irish names: Riel was originally Reilly and Caissie was originally Casey. Early in the 18th century, Irish seamen and fishermen, most of them from the town of Waterford and the surrounding area, began settling in Newfoundland. Over the next century and a half, Irish immigrants from the Waterford area settled in Newfoundland, establishing a thriving Irish community and the only Irish enclave in Canada where Irish Gaelic was the primary language. In the 18th century, during the wars between France and England, both countries had Irish regiments. Once the wars were over, many Irish soldiers chose to remain in Canada rather than return home where poverty and the penal laws reduced Irish Catholics to second-class citizens in their own homeland. In addition, Scotch-Irish Presbyterians from Ulster in northern Ireland began arriving in Canada shortly after Britain's victory in the French and Indian War. They were joined in the 1770s by Scotch-Irish who originally had settled in the American colonies but during the American Revolution had remained loyal to the British Crown.

The immigrants of the 17th and 18th centuries were only a precursor to the great wave of Irish immigration to Canada during the first half of the 19th century, particularly in the 1840s when rural Ireland was devastated by the potato famine. By 1850 more than 500,000 Irish had arrived in Canada, but most of them moved on to the United States. Their primary reason for choosing Canada as the first stop of their exodus was economic—the fare from Ireland to Canada was cheaper than the direct route to any

U.S. port. Tragically, thousands of Irish immigrants never had an opportunity to reach America. Many of the Irish arrived in Canada malnourished, suffering from typhoid, cholera, or other highly contagious diseases. Those Irish who did stay were concentrated in the Maritime Provinces. Canada was so vast and the newcomers' resources so scant that they could rarely afford passage farther inland.

By and large the Irish remained in the cities and towns where the men could find work on construction and excavation crews and the women as domestic servants or factory workers. By 1871 the Irish were the largest ethnic group in nearly every large city in Canada. It was the presence of so many willing laborers that fueled Canada's expansion in the 1850s and 1860s. The Irish worked as loggers, they built the railroads, and during the building boom of the mid-19th century they found construction jobs in the cities and towns of Ontario. In Canada, just as they had in Ireland, the Scotch-Irish Presbyterians and the Irish Catholics kept apart, nurturing the animosities they had brought with them from the old country. The Irish Catholics prided themselves on their ancient civilization and their fidelity, in spite of persecution, to the Catholic Church. The Scotch-Irish prided themselves on their loyalty to Great Britain, their ancestors' break from "popery," and their ongoing contributions to science, technology, education, and finance in the British Empire. Not surprisingly, there were flare-ups between the two groups; it was not unusual for St. Patrick's Day (March 17) to be observed with brawls and riots. The 20th century saw the Irish assimilate fully into Canadian society, culminating with the election of Brian Mulroney as prime minister. Today more then 4.3 million Canadians, 14 percent of the population, identify themselves as being of Irish descent.

At first the Irish immigrants were concentrated in the coastal provinces; however, they soon began to spread to wherever they could find work.

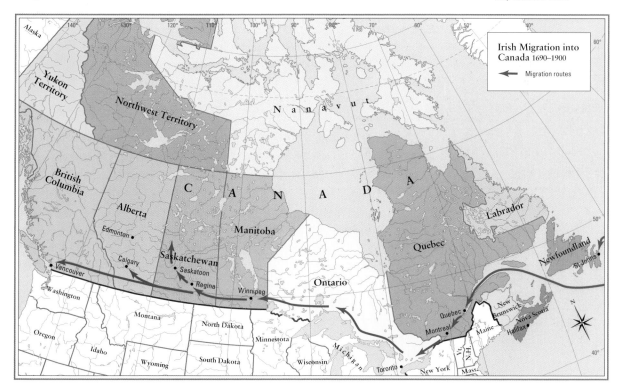

THE IRISH IN LATIN AMERICA

THE TEXAS REVOLUTION OF 1835-36 SAW SOME IRISH COLONISTS BEING LOYAL TO THE MEXICAN GOVERNMENT, TO WHICH THEY OWED ALLEGIANCE AND WHICH HAD GRANTED THEM LAND. THESE IRISH SETTLED ALONGSIDE MEXICAN NEIGHBORS FROM WHOM THEY ACQUIRED THE SKILLS NECESSARY FOR RANCHING.

The Irish diaspora in Latin America has evolved over a long time, with the Irish sometimes serving in Spanish regiments or seeking release from constant British oppression or difficult economic conditions. The major Irish community in Latin America is in Argentina which is home to the fifth-largest Irish community in the world. These came to Argentina, in the hundred years following 1830, with the majority arriving between 1850 and 1870. Traders and mercenaries helping Argentina in its struggle for independence and an Argentine-Brazil war came earlier but they were few. The treatment of the Irish by Britain led many Irish to Argentina, where they could work as laborers on sheep farms, eventually working up to renting and buying their own land. The price of land was cheap, and that was a magnate to landless Irish. Once they were established, word of mouth encouraged further migrants to travel and take advantage of a new life.

Argentine records of immigrants have huge gaps in them, and many Irish told the authorities they were English because Ireland was part of the United Kingdom for so long. Ship lists of passengers and census returns have led researchers to believe that the nineteenth century witnessed the arrival of 10,500 to 11,500 Irish migrants. A complication is that many Irish returned home and sailed back again. More recent estimates have put the nineteenth century Irish influx as high as 45-50,000. Contemporary statistics assert that there are 500,000 Argentines of Irish ancestry. Economically, the Irish were engaged in a range of activities, with some succeeding in the sheep industry or laborers, cattle dealers, and shepherds. Urban settlers became traders and teachers or joined the professional classes. One success story was Eduardo Casey, who recruited, hired, and invited the Irish and other migrants to help open up barren areas to modern agriculture in the provinces of Buenos Aires, Curumalán, Santa Fe, and Venado

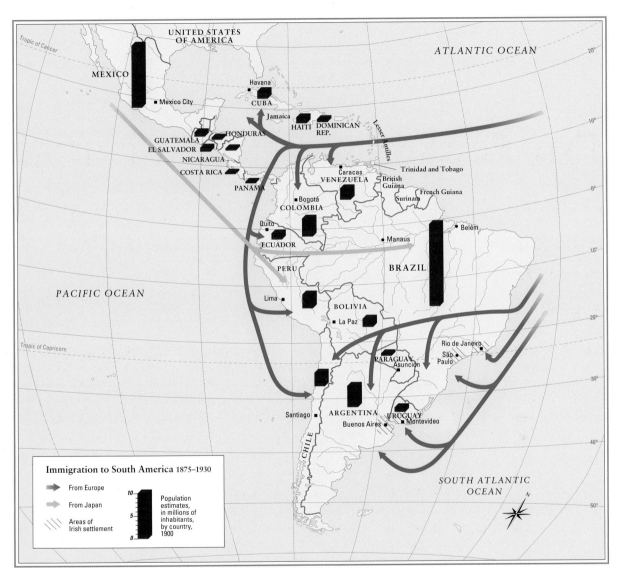

Immigration to South America 1875–1930

→ From Europe

→ From Japan

/// Areas of Irish settlement

Population estimates, in millions of inhabitants, by country, 1900

Tuerto. Although the Argentine Irish retained parts of their identity, when the Falklands/Malvinas War (1982) began, Irish soldiers in the British army were fighting Irish-Argentines.

Two other interesting destinations of the Irish were Puerto Rico and Mexico. After Spain lost its South American empire, its government was determined to keep its Caribbean possessions. The previous Royal Decree of Graces (1815) was renewed which offered free land to non-Hispanic Europeans. The quid pro quo was an oath of loyalty to the Spanish monarchy and Roman Catholicism. After five years, a migrant could become a Spanish subject. After the potato famine in the 1840s, the Irish joined Italians, Corsicans, French, and Germans in settling the island. The Irish rapidly adopted Spanish and married Puerto Ricans; they were very important in the island's sugar industry.

Irish soldiers and adventurers fought in South America's wars of liberation against Spanish colonial rule. From the mid-1800s, Irish communities grew up in and around Rio de Janeiro and Buenos Aires.

THE SCOTS IN CANADA

SCOTS MIGRANTS READILY SETTLED IN CANADA. MANY STARTED BY WORKING FOR THE HUDSON BAY COMPANY WHILE SOME REMAINED IN THE COUNTRY AFTER THEIR REGIMENTS WERE DISBANDED. OTHERS CAME FROM THE UNITED STATES SEEKING REFUGE AS EMPIRE LOYALISTS.

A Scottish courtier of King James VI of Scotland, Sir William Alexander, was granted in 1621 a charter for lands between the St. Croix River and the Gulf of St. Lawrence, the area to be known as Nova Scotia. The late 1620s saw small settlements established on Cape Breton and on the Bay of Fundy, but King Charles I of England surrendered these claims to Nova Scotia in 1632 and the area came into British possession again by the Treaty of Utrecht in 1713. Other early Scots, Jacobite exiles, were those fighting for France in North America. However, the first really solid Scots presence was commenced by the Hudson Bay Company, recruiting many of its employees from the Orkney Islands. By 1800, seventy Orcadians were recruited annually. Some were sojourners but others stayed, particularly if they had relationships with native American women.

Many highlanders came to Canada during the Seven Years' War as British soldiers; and when their regiments disbanded, many took up the offer of grants of land after 1763. During the first years of British rule over the conquered New France, many highland and lowland Scots went to Canada as merchants and government officials. The Scots dominated and consolidated the fur trade and much of the transatlantic trade between Britain and Canada. The year 1770 witnessed the beginning of a large migration from Scotland to North America. Some 25,000 highlanders and lowlanders reached North America but the Canadian region only received about 1,000, to Prince Edward Island, while Highlands on the *Hector* landed at Pictou, Nova Scotia in 1773. In 1774, a party of lowlanders reached St. John's Island. Although some passages were assisted, the bulk of the migrants paid their own way and bought their own land.

New settlers wrote letters home, and such advertisements encouraged other Scots to cross

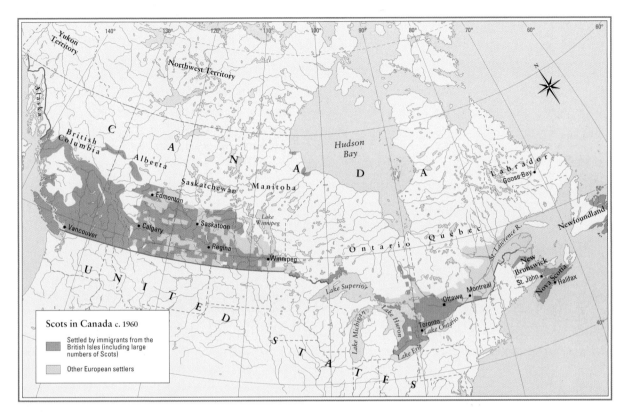

Scots in Canada c. 1960

▨ Settled by immigrants from the British Isles (including large numbers of Scots)

▨ Other European settlers

the Atlantic and settle in regions already Scottish such as Pictou and St. John's Island. During the American Revolution, more highlanders were recruited into the British army, and survivors of the war often stayed and settled. Scots already arrived in the Thirteen Colonies often became Loyalists and moved to Canada for safety. A good number served in American Loyalist regiments or provincial regiments. The 84th Regiment of Foot (Royal Highland Emigrants) joined the regular establishment, and some 25 percent of its soldiers were Scots. One battalion defended Québec while the other campaigned in the Lake Champlain region and in raids into the Mohawk Valley. After the war most of the regiment's soldiers settled in Nova Scotia or Ontario, which became home to many resettled Loyalists, whether Scots or colonists. Prior to the war many Roman Catholic MacDonalds and Macdonnells of Clan Glengarry had settled the Mohawk Valley under the auspices of William Johnson, the Superintendent of Indian Affairs and husband to Molly Brandt, the sister of the Mohawk nation's war chief. These Scots fought the Americans with the utmost ferocity. They were led north by the former Jacobite, Captain John Macdonell.

The Scots enclaves in Canada were peopled by certain distinct areas of Scotland. Hebridean folk settled on St. John's Island; Lochabar and Glengarry people went to Glangarry; and Pictou and Cape Breton Island were supplied with migrants from Skye, Sutherland, and Ross. Highlanders supplied the Montréal-based North West Company with recruits. Run by Simon McTavish, the company eventually merged with the Hudson Bay Company in 1821, which Scots also dominated.

The Highland clearances had established Scots-Gaelic-speaking communities in Nova Scotia from the mid-1700s. Later, from the early 1800s, Canada became a destination of choice, with many Scots contributing to the pattern of settlement that reached from Toronto across the prairies and the Rocky Mountains to Vancouver.

Prince Edward Island, Canada. During the Highland clearances, 800 colonists were shipped here in 1801 by Lord Selkirk.

A wave of Scots left the western highlands and islands in 1791, with a second wave in 1801. Whole families tended to move together, and they generally left from small ports near their homes. In 1803, Lord Selkirk felt so strongly about the fate of crofters dispossessed by landlords intent on improving their lands that he shipped 800 colonists to Prince Edward Island. The highland and lowland clearances also fueled immigration while the 1846 potato blight with its famine caused other Scots to leave. Continued crop failures throughout the 1850s, together with famine relief programs, saw thousands of Scots shipped to both Canada and Australia.

From the mid-nineteenth century to 1914, more and more lowlanders left for Canada, the Highlands having already given up its surplus population. Displaced by agricultural transformations in Scotland, the lowland farmer and laborer went to Ontario and increasingly the Canadian west. Various emigration societies encouraged women to migrate. and the Aberdeen Ladies' Union sent several hundred Scottish women to Canada. Evidently, hard-working, God-fearing women were at a premium as domestic servants. Orphaned children were another element of the population which was shipped to Canada. The Quarrier's Orphan Homes at Bridge of Weir sent 7,000 children to Canada between 1878 and 1933.

Toward the end of the nineteenth century, a steady influx of Scots went into the west, and 1904 saw 12,627 Scots leaving Glasgow for Canada. One group headed for Manitoba and another to Alberta and Saskatchewan. After the Second World War, 260,000 Scots left for Canada between 1945 and 1993, with many of these having high levels of education and professional skills. Rather than having traditional Scots areas as their destination, they have relocated to urban centers in Ontario, Alberta, and British Columbia. A higher standard of living compared to that on offer in Scotland occasioned this wave. Canada has benefited from a Scots work ethic which has imbued many successful business ventures. In 2001, the Canadian census claimed that 4,157,210 Canadian citizens recorded full or partial Scottish ancestry, but this is considered to be a low figure.

Below: Vintage map showing parts of Canada that received an influx of Scottish immigrants. Nova Scotia is Latin for "New Scotland".

SCOTS EMIGRATION WORLDWIDE

SCOTS HAVE BEEN WELCOMED EVERYWHERE AS INDUSTRIOUS, GOD-FEARING PEOPLE. THEY HAVE BECOME PROMINENT CITIZENS WHEREVER THEY HAVE SETTLED.

There are two types of United States citizen with origins in Scotland: the Scots-Irish coming via Ulster, numbering about 5.4 million, and the 25 million Scottish-Americans sailing direct from Scotland. The Scottish-Americans moved down the eastern seaboard from Canada, arriving after the First World War, or those descended from nineteenth-century incomers have tended to move west. The states now with large Scottish-American descendants are California, Florida, Texas, Michigan, and New York, with pockets in Maine, Vermont, Utah, Oregon, Wyoming, and Idaho. Elements of Scottish culture remain as in the haggis-fed Burns Supper, pipe-bands in full Highland dress with tartan sometimes being worn. Highland Games with tossing the caber and throwing the hammer are held throughout the United States, with the games held at Pleasanton, California, being the largest.

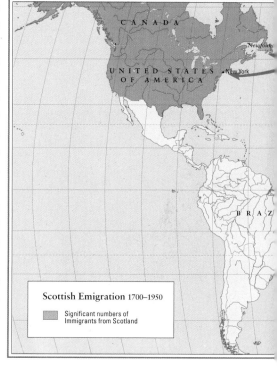

Scottish Emigration 1700–1950

Significant numbers of
Immigrants from Scotland

Large numbers of Scots have emigrated to the southern hemisphere to Australia and New Zealand. Quite a number of Scots landing were felons with seven years' labor to serve. Census 2006 stated that some 1.5 million Australians claimed Scottish ancestry. The fifth governor, from 1809 to 1821, was Lachlan Macquarie. An enlightened despot, he transformed New South Wales from a prison camp into a reformatory, allowing convicts to become citizens in a land of opportunity. Macquarie built Sydney, creating a colonial city. John McDouall Stuart led six major expeditions from South Australia, reaching the center of Australia and making a crossing of the entire continent. Like Scots in America, the Australian Scots have their pipe-bands, celebrate Scots festivals, and have Highland Games.

In New Zealand, many people enjoy Scots ancestry, as evidenced by the large number of Scottish place names, particular areas of Scots settlement being Southland and Otago. The port of Invercargill became one of the world's southernmost cities, but Dunedin, the Scots name for Edinburgh, is a major city in Otago, with a university founded by Scots in 1869.

The period between 1853 and 1870 saw 30 per-cent of the population of New Zealand as Scottish. Many came having heard of the discovery of gold. Highlanders came to be shepherds while the settlement of Waipu encouraged others. Migration slowed down after the Second World War, especially when assisted passages ended in 1975. Although Otago and Scotland retain many aspects of Scots culture, Scots descendants are now spread evenly across New Zealand, with one-third engaged in professional or business occupations, one-third in white collar jobs, and the rest in working class jobs. The sheep and wool industry has always absorbed many Scots.

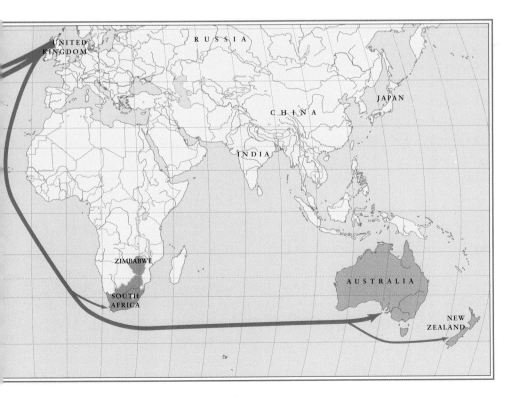

The Scottish worldwide diaspora is concentrated in Canada and the United States. Many more settled in South Africa, Australia and New Zealand.

Scots in the Deep South and Appalachia

The Scotch-Irish established a culture which was independent, kin-based, and hostile to British rule. They supplied many soldiers for the American armies during the American Revolution.

The Scotch-Irish sent the best part of 400,000 Irish Protestants to America in the eighteenth century. They were the descendants of mainly Scottish families who had been settled on the Irish plantations of Ulster in the 1600s. These Scotch-Irish were Presbyterian dissenters from the Anglican Church, and they supplied large numbers of troops for General George Washington during the American Revolution. Owing to their dissenting faith, the Presbyterians suffered penal laws which gave full rights of land ownership to members of the established church. Religious disharmony, poor weather, low crop yields, and rising rents from English or Anglo-Irish absentee landlords were motives sending the Scotch-Irish across the Atlantic.

The Scotch-Irish entered America via Philadelphia, Pennsylvania and New Castle in the state of Delaware. The best agricultural land had been taken by earlier settlers, so these later arrivals were forced to the borders of the colonies where land was cheaper or they could squat. The Scotch-Irish moved away from the coastal lowlands and moved inland; they became the major ethnic group in parts of Pennsylvania. They formed the major culture in the Appalachian Mountain chain.

Although life on the frontier was hard, the Ulster migrants thrived. Coming from a land where they had been a minority and endangered, the fears of native American raids were readily faced. North Carolina observed the arrival of most of its Scotch-Irish settlers during the years 1735 to 1775. Often being second- or even third-generation settlers, they moved south to find affordable land. After building farm houses and barns, they founded churches, schools, sawmills, and tanneries. So many Ulster settlers entered North Carolina that the state legislature created five new counties for them: Johnston and Granville (1746), Anson (1750), Orange (1752), and Rowan (1753). On its creation, Rowan was inhabited

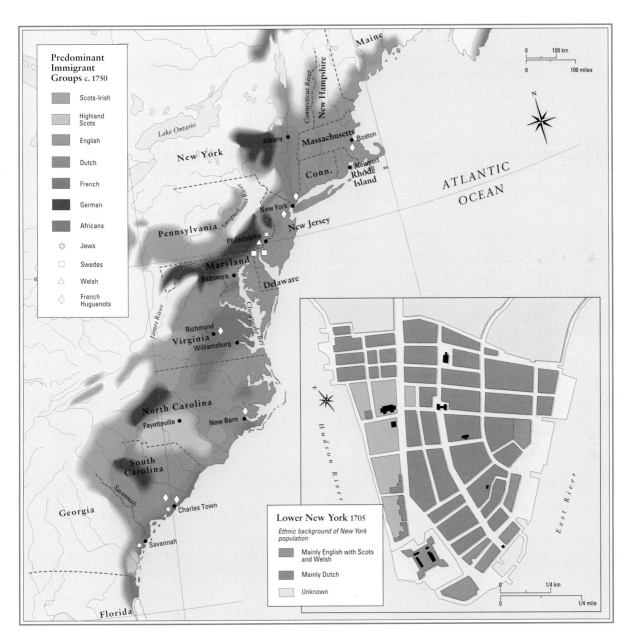

Predominant Immigrant Groups c. 1750

- Scots-Irish
- Highland Scots
- English
- Dutch
- French
- German
- Africans
- ✡ Jews
- ☐ Swedes
- △ Welsh
- ◇ French Huguenots

Lower New York 1705

Ethnic background of New York population

- Mainly English with Scots and Welsh
- Mainly Dutch
- Unknown

by at least 3,000 people. In 1754, Mecklenburg County was created.

That the Scotch-Irish were related to or of the same stock as others inhabiting Appalachia meant that they provided a type of cement uniting so many colonies, maybe in the belief that independence from Britain was essential. Over the years, the Scotch-Irish have moved from Presbyterianism to become Baptists and Methodists. The community has spread far and wide and supplied many presidents, and it has been suggested that the traditional Scotch-Irish "Celtic" music is the source of bluegrass and gospel.

The Scotch-Irish became a major element in the peopling of the frontier in the southern part of the United States. Their music contributed to the emerging culture of the Appalachian Mountain region.

Bretons in Montréal and Québec

Jacques Cartier explored Newfoundland, establishing a settlement at today's Québec. By 1754, there were 85,000 colonists and a thriving fur trade with the help of the Native American Huron and Ottowa.

From early times, Bretons were using the coasts of North America in their fishing expeditions, establishing permanent settlements at Plaisance in Newfoundland, which encouraged King Louis XIV of France to appoint a governor in 1655. The settlement was taken by Britain in 1713 in the Treaty of Utrecht, leaving the entire colony to move to Île Royale (Cape Breton) . This Louisbourg became a key trading partner with the port of Saint-Malo in Brittany, so much so that the Gulf of St. Lawrence was a Breton seaway. Between 1713 and 1792, Saint-Malo despatched 4,654 fishing vessels and more than 106,967 people to North America, along the coasts of Newfoundland, Labrador, the Gaspé, and Île Royale, with Bretons forming the largest contingents of settlers in the colony of New France, as it was called.

A French colony in the St. Lawrence Valley was originally proposed by the explorer Jacques Cartier. Located at Cap Rouge in 1541, it ended with the settlers being massacred by native Americans. From then on, colonization was left to individuals, and some 1,040 Bretons settled in Canada. Poor economic conditions and political disturbances do not seem to have motivated Bretons to emigrate, but government policies did have an impact. By 1663, New France had only 3,000 inhabitants when Intendant Jean Talon commenced a recruitment campaign. For defense, the colony hosted the Carignan-Salières Regiment, and any officer who stayed in the colony after his discharge was offered a seigneury, and enlisted men free land. Of the soldiers who took up the offer, 19 came from Brittany. Similarly, 262 Breton soldiers from marine detachments settled, as did 40 Bretons who served under General Montcalm. Talon also persuaded those tradesmen and women who were contracted to work in Canada for three years to remain, and more than ten Bretons settled. Talon also began a recruitment campaign in Brittany aimed at young women, *les filles du roi*, and 15 traveled to the St. Lawrence Valley. More and more weddings

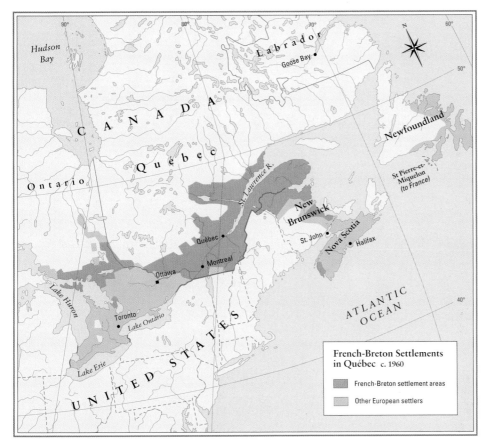

French-Breton Settlements
in Québec c. 1960

☐ French-Breton settlement areas
☐ Other European settlers

Breton fishermen had long been taking advantage of the fishing grounds off the coast of Newfoundland, where they founded a number of small colonies. When New France was established along the banks of the St Lawrence River, further Bretons settled in Canada as part of general French migration.

were celebrated and the population began to increase naturally.

The 1730s witnessed the largest number of Bretons reaching Canada in the eighteenth century. Even after the British conquest, soldiers still came into the country, and Breton men were marrying Canadian women. After 1875, the Roman Catholic Church sent missionaries to Brittany to acquire recruits to settle the Canadian West. Additionally, colonization societies stimulated Breton emigration to Canada. The *Société d'Immigration Française* and the *Société Foncière du Canada* were responsible for several hundred Bretons migrating to Canada before 1929.

The two world wars diminished Breton migration but the 1950s saw it increase again. The Association of Relatives of Emigrants to North America (*Amicale des Parents d'Émigrés d'Amérique du Nord*), with its headquarters in Courin in Brittany, has estimated that 45,000 Bretons emigrated to Canada between 1870 and 1900, and 8,000 Bretons now dwell or work in the Montréal area. Since the Second World War, Breton migrants have left rural France and moved to the eastern Canadian cities, particularly the Montréal region. The migrants have not just been rural workers; they have such diverse vocations as managers and civil servants, butchers, pastry chefs, and restaurant owners. However, young farmers were being attracted in the early 1990s, as the Québec Department of Agriculture wanted to revitalize the region's agriculture, especially in the St. Lawrence Valley.

THE IRISH IN AUSTRALIA

MOST OF THE IRISH IMMIGRANTS TO AUSTRALIA CAME
THROUGH TRANSPORTATION FOR PETTY CRIMES AT HOME.
DESPITE A DIFFICULT START, THE IRISH SOON TOOK ADVANTAGE
OF THE MANY OPPORTUNITIES THE COUNTRY HAD TO OFFER.

Between 1791 and 1867, approximately 50,000 Irish convicts, men and women, were transported from the British Isles to Australia. It is traditional in Ireland to regard all of them as martyrs to the cause of Irish freedom, yet historians have found that only about twenty percent were convicted of political crimes. The bulk of Irish convicts were found guilty of offenses that ranged from petty theft to posting threatening notices against landlords or government officials to assault and murder. In the first years of the 19th century, a large group of Irish convicts broke out from the Castle Hill government prison farm and began raiding settlements in the area. In 1804, the escaped convicts planned major attacks on Sydney, Hawkesbury, and Parramatta. Major George Johnston, an officer of the colony's military administration, led a small detachment of 26 men against the escapees and found himself facing more than 250 well-armed convicts. He called on the convicts' leaders to join him in a parley, and when these men presented themselves, he had them arrested, then sent in his troops to cut down the leaderless rank and file. Subsequently, nine of the chief Irish rebels were tried and hanged. One of the most famous of the transported Irish was William Smith O'Brien, for twenty years a member of the House of Commons. In 1848 he led a botched insurrection in County Tipperary, was found guilty of high treason, and sentenced to life in Tasmania. After serving six years he was granted a conditional discharge and permitted to return to Ireland.

The Irish convicts have passed into the folklore of Australia and Ireland. Escapees such as Bold Jack Donahoe had a successful career as a highwayman until he was tracked down and shot by police officers. He is said to have been only 23 at the time, and his life became the inspiration for the Irish ballad The Wild Colonial Boy. Even more famous is Ned Kelly, son of an Irish convict, who led an outlaw gang before he was caught and hanged for the murder of three policemen. Ironically, for all their associations with criminality, by the 1880s many Irish Australians were drawn to careers in the police force.

Between 1840 and 1914, approximately 300,000 Irish emigrated to Australia, a piddling number compared to the millions who poured into the United States, Canada, and Britain. But Australia was so far away, the passage so expensive, the land so unfamiliar and even frightening that for most Irish it was the destination of last resort. Those who did settle in Australia followed a pattern that was being repeated in other parts of the English-speaking world: founding parishes, mutual benefit societies, and political organizations. As in America and Canada, the Irishmen in Australia were unskilled and took any heavy labor jobs they could find. They followed the same settlement pattern as the English, Scots, and Welsh in Australia, tending to concentrate in New South Wales, Victoria, and Queensland, where the Irish found so many opportunities for work that they began writing bragging letters home. Two sisters in Geelong assured their family in Ireland, "[In this] Colony… you would think no more of five pounds than you would of one penny at home."

The Irish saw themselves as nation-builders, but many of their neighbors regarded them as a drain on Australian society. There were a disproportionate number of Irish in jails, in insane asylums, and on poor relief. But the upwardly mobile Irish kept at it: by the end of the 19th century, there were Irish businessmen's associations, athletic leagues, cultural organizations, as well as societies that raised funds for the Home Rule movement back in the old country. Irish immigration to Australia dropped off sharply in the 20th century after Ireland gained its independence from Britain. Yet it was an Irish-Australian, Prime Minister John Curtin, who saw the country through the dangerous years of World War II. Today about one-third of Australians are of Irish descent, among them Sir Gerald Brennon, former Chief Justice of Australia, Sir William Deane, former Governor General of Australia, author Thomas Keneally, and the actors Mel Gibson and Nicole Kidman.

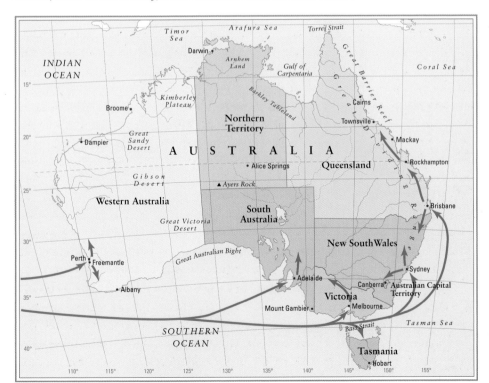

Most of the immigrants from Ireland to Australia came into ports scattered along the southern coast.

Irish Migration into Australia 1791–1950

➤ Migration routes

Celtic Legacy – Celtic Future

The Celtic past survives in archeological evidence but also in a Celtic revival. School children are being taught their ancestral language, and music, literature, and poetry are being kept in publication.

Evidence of the Celtic past dots Europe in terms of archeological sites, Greek and Roman writing, *keeils*, Celtic crosses, design, and living languages, albeit spoken by few. The term "Celt" is riddled with difficulty in the modern world, with some groups claiming a Celtic past but with no living language. Europeans as a whole have Celtic blood and genes coursing through their bodies in diverse quantities. Even the names of Belgium and Aquitaine, home of troubadours and the *langue d'oc*, have their origins in *Gallia Belgica* and the Celtic tribe, the Aquitani. The Helvetii, turned back by Julius Caesar, are commemorated in the Latin *Helvetica*, a term found on Swiss stamps.

Modern times have seen the term "Celt" being adopted as a means of identification by minority groups in struggles with centralized governments in Britain and France. Fashion can dictate the use of the term: an Irish passport is sometimes thought to be a protection against terrorism and a Manx passport has the distinction of making its carrier a citizen of the oldest parliament in the world, the Tynwald, based on a form of Norse democracy. At times, the Manx have been designated as Norse or Viking, and even the museum complex at Peel tends to play down the dominance of Manx in personal names and place names. Another connotation of "Celt" is nationalism, which has received a bad press, with associations of Irish Republican Army terror tactics, the Breton *Bezen Perrot* collaborating with the Nazis and fighting the *Maquis*. On the other hand, some Manx even believe that money carrying images of Queen Elizabeth II's head is occupation currency.

The six Celtic nations have found togetherness in their position of European periphery, making the seaways again the traditional means of communicating between them as they did before the Romans and in the Hiberno-Norse world of the Viking period and the domain of the Lord of the Isles. Pride in their past and roots manifests itself in sport in the Highland Games in Scotland and in Scots communities around the world while hurling, Gaelic football and shinty are celebrated as "Celtic." Cultural festivals are held in Celtic communities everywhere and Celtic music is played with the Welsh bagpipe, the Breton *biniou*, the Irish *uillean* pipes, and the Highland bagpipe, and also the Irish *bodhran*. Festivals such as the Breton *fest noz*, the Scottish *mod*, the Irish *fleadh*, the Manx *Yn Chruinnacht*, and the Welsh *eisteddfod* are increasingly well developed and supported. Europe received an injection of Celt culture with Michael Flatley and Jean Butler's *Riverdance,* performed in the interval in the 1994 Eurovision Song Contest. Accompanied by the Celtic choral group *Anùna*, the dancers received a standing ovation. The performance was turned into a full show and has toured the world ever since in both large and small venues. The group *Clannad* and the singer *Enya* are other Irish exports with haunting layers of sound.

In more political terms, devolution has occurred to a considerable extent with the creation of the Welsh Assembly and Scottish Parliament. Eire is totally independent, the Manx have Tynwald, Ulster has the Good Friday Agreement, the Bretons now have a Regional Council but the Cornish remain an English county and demand constitutional revision. In an internationally organized sense, the Celtic League has sought to promote the interests of the six nations. Membership is only open to those communities which retain a Celtic language, which leaves out Galicia and the Asturias. Founded in 1961 and originating in older Pan-Celtic organizations, the League aims to help members of the six nations in their various struggles to achieve degrees of political, cultural, social, and economic freedom. Major tasks include fostering co-operation among themselves, developing solidarity, publicizing the various national struggles, creating a formal association when more Celtic nations achieve full self-government, and striving to ensure that resources deriving from each nation are used for the benefit of that nation.

The Celtic League publishes news concerning its political struggles in the quarterly magazine, *Carn,* and an American branch publishes its own quarterly newsletter, *Six Nations, One Soul.* Major political campaigns are waged by the League: the reunification of Ireland, the return of the Loire-Atlantique department to Brittany, and support for keeping Celtic languages alive. Another bone of contention is the British Museum's holding of the *Chronicles of Mann,* compiled by monks at the Cistercian Rushen Abbey in Mann. This is a record of Manx history from 1016 to 1316. A key success was the island known as the Calf of Man, separated from Mann's southern tip by Calf Sound, being transferred from the English National Trust to the Manx National Trust.

Wales Millennium Center is a performing arts center in Cardiff. The strikingly original architecture was designed by the Percy Thomas Partnership. The inscription contains the English words "In these stones horizons sing" alongside the Welsh words "Creu Gwir Fel Gwydr O Ffwrnais Awen" (Creating truth like glass from the furnace of inspiration). The building is a symbol of modern Welsh identity.

KEILLS AND CROSSES

"THE SHAPE IS RECTANGULAR WITH NO DIVISION BETWEEN NAVE
AND CHANCEL. THE DOOR, WHICH IS NARROW AND TAPERING
TOWARD THE TOP, IS USUALLY SITUATED IN THE WESTERN GABLE.
THE WINDOW – AS THE RULE ONLY ONE – IS BUILT AT A HEIGHT
OF 2-3 FEET ABOVE THE FLOOR. THE ALTAR IS INVARIABLY AGAINST
THE EASTERN WALL, ATTAINING A HEIGHT OF ABOUT 2 FEET."
(MARSTRANDER, A NORWEGIAN ARCHEOLOGIST)

A *keeill* is a small, very simple chapel situated on the Isle of Man, where the remains of some two hundred exist. The chapels were about 15 feet long and ten feet wide. Next to the *keeill* would be a small cell or oratory where the reclusive missionary would live while serving his small flock. Some historians believe that these spiritual leaders came from the monastic order the Culdee (*Céli Dé*, the vassals or servants of God). Ancient Irish manuscripts combined with island evidence suggest that the Manx Celtic Church had bishops, of which four are named: Germanus, Conindrus, Romulus, and Maughold. Some *keeill* sites have been lost, especially when a later church was built on top of the old construction. Also, Victorian and Edwardian antiquarians destroyed sites in their search for buried treasure and they failed to keep site plans and records.

The Celtic cross is a design combining a cross with a ring circling the intersection. The design can be seen in monumental free-standing crosses or incised into cross-slabs. They can be found all over the Celtic fringe-land but reached Brittany much later than the British islands. Free-standing upright crosses were erected by Irish monks as an expression of faith or to mark the limit of monastic lands. Their erection commenced in the seventh century, and some Manx Celtic crosses carry inscriptions in Norse runes. The symbolism of the cross can be compared with the sun cross found in Bronze Age Europe, when the cross was entirely encircled by the ring. This design is sometimes called a sun-disc.

Opposite: Keills are simple, small chapels and are unique to the Isle of Man. Around 200 are known to exist; the main ones are shown on the map.

Manx Surnames

PATRONYMIC MANX SURNAMES HAVE SEEN NAMES CONTRACTED
WHEN THE ORIGINAL MAQ WAS LOST, TO CONSTRUCT PECULIARLY
MADE NAMES WHICH ARE READILY RECOGNIZABLE. MACISAAC
HAS BECOME KISSACK, MACGILLCHRIST IS NOW MYLECHREEST,
MACHENRY IS KINRY, AND MAC GIOLLA HAS SHORTENED TO MYLEY.

Manx surnames are difficult to identify unless certain facts and rules are taken into consideration. The Manx language was accepted from Ireland and is thus Q-Celtic Goedelic. During the period of Christianization, Irish missionaries gave their names to the old Manx *keeils* or churches, and this influenced the formation of many Manx surnames. The Viking period saw the introduction of Norse as the elite language of rule and governance, but Manx Gaelic swallowed it up although some place names have Scandinavian origins. The Norse language arrived with the Viking invaders and became the elite language but Gaelic was used by women and in child-rearing. Eventually, Norse died away, especially after the break up of the kingdom. Then Scots Gaelic influenced the Manx variety, pulling it partially away from its kindred Irish Gaelic. The island became entirely Gaelic again but retained its mixed genetic heritage and many Norse place-names. Many farms end in the suffix *by,* meaning farm, as opposed to the Manx prefix *balla.* The tallest Manx mountain is Snaefell, which is Norse for snow-mountain. Records of genealogy in the Isle of Man are few before the sixteenth century, but it is likely that surnames were in use by 1300, as they were in Ireland.

Manx surnames are patronymics because the Celts linked their name with their father, as exemplified by the Irish *O'* and *Mc,* the Scottish *Mac,* and the Welsh *Map,* which has diminished to the initial letter *P* (*Map Howell* is now *Powell*). The Manx for this custom is *Maq,* later *Mac,* but this will not be found in any Manx names now, as erosion has left just the last hard sound expressed as *C, K* or *Q.* Two expert philologists who have written books about Manx surnames are Moore and Kneen. Moore makes the case that of the 170 surnames used at the beginning of the nineteenth century, about 100 were Celtic and 30 Norse-Celtic, but he has a name list totaling 212 names, with 166 arguably Manx and 44 off-island. Of the rest he is uncertain. If one looks at the initial letter of Moore's names, the largest number begin with *C* (75), followed by *K* (34), *M* (16), and *Q* (16). Other letters found are *S* (13) and *G* (11). An examination of names with other initial letters shows names English, Irish, or Scottish in origin, and probably they derive from those serving in the island's garrison or as administrators by the Church or Lords of Man. Many came from Lancashire, where the Earls of Derby, Lords of Man, had their estates, but some families might have anglicized their names to promote their own standing.

Moore lists few Manx names with an initial having less than a 5 percent impact and represented in some form on the island before 1515, and these are: Allen, Brew, Bridson, Duggan, Duke, Far(a) gher, Farrant, Fayle, Gale, Garrett, Gawne, Gell, Gelling, Gick, Gill, Gorree (Gorry), Halsall, Harrison, Hudgeon, Joughin,, Lace, Leece, Lewin, Looney, Lowey, Lucas, Nelson, Norris, Radcliffe, Taggart, Teare, Thompson, Vondy, Waterson, Wattleworth, and Wood(s). A similar list for the letters *M* and *S* is brief: Maddrell, Martin, Moore, Morrison, Moughtin, Mylxh(a)raine, Mylchreest, Mylrea, Mylroi, Mylvoirrey, Sansbury, Sayle, Scarff, Shimmin, Skelly, Skillicorn, Skinner, Stephen, Stephenson, and Stowell. The great mass of Manx names commence with the sound "*k*." *Qu* is only used when the following vowel is "*a*" or "*i*." *K* can be followed by *a, e, i,* or *n.* There are three names beginning with *Ch*: Chrystal, Christory, and Christian, the last name being notorious, as found in the mutineer on HMS *Bounty.* The following list shows the Manx names normally found, which help genealogists as they trace families in the Manx diaspora.

Cain(e)	Connelly,	Creer,	Kaighan,	Kinvig,	Quaggin,
Calcot(t),	Cooil,	Creetch,	Kaighin,	Kissack,	Qualtrough,
Caley,	Coole,	Cregeen,	Kaneen,	Kneal(e),	Quane,
Callin,	Corjeag,	Crellin,	Karran,	Kneen,	Quark,
Callister,	Corkhill,	Crennell,	Kay,	Knickell.	Quarry,
Callow,	Corkish,	Cretney,	Kee,		Quay,
Cammaish,	Corlett,	Criggal,	Kegeen,		Quayle,
Cannan,	Cormode,	Cringle,	Kegg,		Quiggin,
Cannel,	Corooin,	Croghan,	Keig,		Quill,
Cannon,	Corran,	Crow(e),	Keigeen,		Quillrash,
Carine,	Corrin,	Crye,	Kelly,		Qwilliam,
Carran,	Corris,	Crystal,	Kannaugh,		Quillin,
Casemenr,	Corteen,	Cubbon,	Kennish,		Quine,
Cashen,	Cosnahan,	Curghey,	Kermeen,		Quinney,
Cashin,	Costain,	Curphey.	Kerruish,		Quirk.
Castell,	Costean,		Kew,		
Caveen,	Cotteen,		Kewin,		
Clague,	Cotter,		Kewish,		
Calrk(e),	Cottier,		Kewley,		
Cleator,	Cowell,		Key,		
Cleg(g),	Cowen,		Kie,		
Clerk,	Cowin,		Killey,		
Clucas,	Cowle,		Killip,		
Cogeen,	Cowley,		Kinley,		
Collister,	Craig,		Kinnish,		
Colvin,	Crain)e),		Kinred,		
Comish,	Crebbin,		Kinry,		

CELTIC DESIGN – KNOTS AND SPIRALS

THE INTERLACED KNOT WORK PATTERNS WITH THEIR
UNBROKEN LINES SYMBOLIZE THE PROCESS OF MAN'S ETERNAL
SPIRITUAL GROWTH. WHEN THE CORD IS UNRAVELED, IT LEADS
ONE ON – AN AID TO CONCENTRATION OCCUPYING THE
CONSCIOUS MIND WITH A DEMANDING REPETITIVE TASK AS YOU
MIGHT USE A ROSARY OR MANTRA.

Celtic knots are an endless interlace patterning used for decoration on metalwork, Christian stone crosses, and illuminated manuscripts like the *Book of Kells* and the *Lindisfarne Gospels*. Prior to any Christian influence, the Celts used spirals, step patterns, and key patterns; in fact, they drew influences from wherever they found them, including designs from the Near East as they worked their way north and west in trade goods. It is difficult to date when a particular influence reached the Celtic world. Suffice it to say that plaits and knot work can be found in Roman mosaics in early Roman Britain and were later used in Celtic Christianity. As well as knots and interwoven lines, there were depictions of animals, plants, human beings, and mythical beasts such as dragons, all becoming part of the interlaced work.

Early plaits predate knot design and can be found in different parts of the world. However, the broken and reconnected knotwork began in northern Italy and southern Gaul and then spread northward until it reached Ireland by Christian times. Once developed in religious terms, it was spread to Europe by Irish monks and their heirs the Northumbrian monks. Many have philosophized about the meaning of the different designs but no evidence exists to support these conjectures. Any spiritual meaning must lie with the designer of any specific piece of artwork.

A basic Celtic design is the key pattern, which is really spirals in straight lines. They appear to

Opposite: Note the distinctive Celtic design on these crosses in a cemetery on Aran island, Ireland. This fairly simple design is based upon the Celtic knot, consisting of unbroken lines to symbolize the eternal spiritual growth of man.

Opposite: A Celtic manuscript detailing St. John the Evangelist. Zoomorphic and anthropomorphic design are used frequently in Celtic art; in this image note the eagle in the background, standing over St. John. Animals were sacred to the Celts, and medieval designs depict the four evangelists, using animal symbols. The eagle is John's particular symbol.

be a virtual processional path through a complicated maze or labyrinth leading to a center point. In Christian practice, walking a sacred labyrinth was akin to a pilgrimage in terms of mental and spiritual concentration until the center was reached. At the center truth or faith was revealed, or the navel of the world was met as if it were Jerusalem itself.

The Celtic spiral has been found marking the entrance to the Newgrange megalithic tomb in County Meath, Ireland. The spiral is an organic form found in nature in the way many plants grow. Some say the spiral is symbolic of eternal life. It can also be seen in the whirlpools and eddies of a stream or river. The Christian monks in Ireland used the spirals and whorls to represent the continuous creation and disintegration of the world, a virtual circle or cycle of life itself. The whorls suck you into a more contemplative state as you reflect upon the center of a design. In this sense, the spiral is akin to the Buddhist mandala, which is a microcosm of the universe for the beholder in their search for the source of life.

Zoomorphic and anthropomorphic designs are common in Celtic art, as animals and birds were sacred to the Celts. Many of their gods and creatures of the spirit world are depicted with animal or bird parts. Shape-shifting was said to be a druidic power and pertained to their gods, so their mythical beings were said to adopt an animal form. The patterns with plants turning into tails which are interlaced with animals developing hands and feet appeared in the Bronze Age art of Britain and Ireland. The *Book of Kells* continues this tradition in which the four evangelists are shown symbolically: the man for Matthew; the lion for Mark; the calf for Luke; and the eagle for John.

As Irish missionary activity spread under Saint Columba through western Scotland and the land of the Picts, the highly decorated Celtic crosses appeared in monumental form, and small stone churches were built as the north was Christianized, carrying with the faith the new developments in art forms. Water motifs appear in Celtic art, and here one should remember the ancient Celtic custom of throwing weapons and jewellery into lakes and wells, and the custom of throwing coins into wells and fountains persists even today. The springs which had life-giving properties to cure sickness and aid fertility were taken over during missionary times and given saints' names as the old and new faiths blended together.

The Celtic cross, the iconic Celtic design object, especially in jewelry today, is not just the symbol of Christianity, the symbolism being much older. The oldest examples are those incised or painted on flat pebbles, dating from about 10,000 BC, found in a cave in the French Pyrénées. These ancestor stones were believed to contain the spirits of the dead. The cross symbolizes four routes; it is derived from quartering the circle through the navel, or *omphalos*, at the center. The cross in the wheel has been used as a sun symbol and for Christ's rule over everything, including length, breadth, height, and depth.

When Christianity reached Britain and Ireland from the fifth century AD onward, the old druidic faith or religion was not necessarily abandoned. Christianity was regarded as the fulfillment of Druidism, and Saint Columba called Jesus the Archdruid. By the sixth century, Pope Gregory allowed a fusion of Christian and Celtic beliefs without destroying the old, as seen in the wells, springs, groves, clearings, and standing stones, which became the bones of the Celtic Church. With the spread of Christianity, the Gospels needed to be duplicated, and the missionaries asked the same artisans who worked for pagan gods and chiefs to decorate the Gospels. Highly skilled artists executed the Irish alphabet and illuminated the texts with supreme artwork using old Celtic designs.

CELTIC MUSIC

"I STARTED WITH ROCK 'N' ROLL ... THEN YOU START TO TAKE IT APART LIKE A CHILD WITH A TOY AND YOU SEE THAT THERE'S BLUES AND THERE'S COUNTRY ... THEN YOU GO BACK FROM COUNTRY INTO AMERICAN MUSIC, AND YOU GO BACK FROM AMERICAN FOLK MUSIC AND YOU END UP IN SCOTLAND OR IRELAND EVENTUALLY." (ELVIS COSTELLO)

Celtic music might be considered to be the totality of music in all its styles emanating from all Celtic regions and countries and parts of the world to which Celts have migrated. This means that Celtic music also incorporates English roots as in Scots and Irish music, certainly through the Scots lowland language. The music of the Celtic peoples is kept alive through national and international festivals, especially Brittany, where there are festivals throughout the year and an annual Celtic festival in Lorient. The Welsh have their traditional *eisteddfodau*, the Manx the *Yn Chruinnaght*, the Cornish their *troyls*, the Bretons the *fest noz*, and so on.

In Cornwall, minstrelsy was common in the medieval period, with the production of miracle plays By the nineteenth century, religious dissenters and temperance movements frowned upon dance and music but choral and brass bands flourished, with traditional tunes being used for carols and hymns. Cornish *ceilidhs*, called *troyls*, were common. Community music and dance are still alive in Padstow and Helston, with the Furry or Flora Dance on 8 May. Cornish music is similar to Breton music, which fits with a common history and people. The instruments can be the traditional fiddle, *bombarde*, *bodhrán*, bagpipes, harp, and accordion. One popular band is *Hevva*, and contemporary music is put to Cornish with *Skwardya* and *Krena*. Top of the Hill Recordings promotes traditional and modern Cornish music, and it can be heard on *Radyo an Gernewegva*.

Manx music covers all genres, not just folk. The earliest-known forms of music were fiddle music and folk dances, with ballads, jigs, and reels. Church music has been a major influence from the nineteenth

The fiddle, one of the most important instruments used in traditional Irish music, is played differently, depending on the style of a particular region.

century but modern versions of rock, blues, jazz, and pop exist. Manx music is promoted by the Manx Heritage Foundation (*Undinys Eiraght Vannin*) and takes a major place in *Yn Chruinnagt*. Exponents of Manx music are many, and well known are the *King Chiaullee* band and *Mactulladh Vannin*.

Welsh traditional music is linked in most people's minds with male voice choirs and brass bands in the colliery areas. More recently a fifty-strong mixed gender choir of school pupils from Bangor, Ysgol Glanaethwy, reached the final in a TV program, *Last Choir Standing*, and its members' first language was Welsh. Traditional Welsh music is played on the triple harp, the stringed *crwth*, Welsh bagpipes and *pibgorn*, a reed pipe, and the fiddle. Music and singing competitions take place at *eisteddfodau* while pop music is represented by such singers as Shirley Bassey, Tom Jones, Catatonia's Cerys Matthews and, more recently, Duffy, among many others. There has also been a folk revival with performers such as *Moniars*, *Carreg Lafar*, and *Bob Delyn A'r Ebyllion*.

Scots music is often associated with massed military pipe bands. One must never forget that bagpipes are common throughout Europe, North Africa, the Arab Gulf, and the Caucasus, but the great highland bagpipes developed exclusively in Scotland. Scotland has a large repertoire of Gaelic songs, with music being part of dances. This music is played at *ceilidhs*, balls, and weddings. The instruments used are the pipes, accordion, fiddle, and tin whistle, often with cello and keyboards. A traditional Scottish instrument is the *clàrsach*, the harp, which was the national musical instrument until displaced by the pipes in the fifteenth century. The harp might have originated with the Picts, and a harper is incised into the Monifeith Pictish stone, dating from somewhere between AD 700 and 900. Folk music has seen a revival since the 1960s and Scotland's performers are legion. Pop singers are numerous, with names such as *Eurythmics*' Annie Lennox, Franz Ferdinand, and the Glasgow band, *Texas*, with their lead singer, Sharleen Spiteri.

Ireland has enjoyed the good fortune, in one sense, of remaining an agricultural community with a strong oral tradition, which helped in the survival of native music. But folk music did not gain widespread favor commercially until the 1970s. Irish music has developed, incorporating other styles to produce the sounds of singers like *Thin Lizzy*, the *Corrs*, *Clannad*, and Enya. Music comes in many forms such as *ar sean nós* a capella singing while dance music is more widely experienced, with reels and jigs being common. Irish musical instruments are numerous; there are the fiddle, flute, tin whistle, *Uilleann* pipes, harp, accordion, concertina, banjo, guitar, *bodhrán,* and, more recently, the *bouzouki*. Irish folk music has blended with other genres, exponents being Van Morrison, Enya, Sinéad O'Connor, and the *Pogues*.

Breton music is rich in its variety of vocal and instrumental styles. A call and response (*Kan ha diskan*) style of singing is very old but has survived. Hymns comprise an expected form of music in what was a traditionally Catholic area. These *kantikoù* are accompanied by harp, pipes, and organ. Ballads, laments, and sea shanties comprise other forms of song. Instrumental music is provided by the harp, a leading player being Alan Stivell, the violin, clarinet, guitar, flutes, whistles, accordion, and two types of bagpipe. These are the *biniwhere kozh*, a small bagpipe played with the *bombarde*, and the *biniou braz*, a highland bagpipe imported in the late nineteenth century. The *veuze*, a diatonic accordion, is also played. The most important musicians are Alan Stivell, who has blended Breton folk with Celtic harp and rock and inspired other musicians to innovation. A well-known name is the Nantes group *Tri Yann*, whose lyrics have demanded that Nantes be returned to Brittany. *Tri Yann* also perform some Gallo songs.

Although the bagpipes are most frequently associated with the Scots, it must not be forgotten that bagpipes have been used throughout Europe, northern Africa, the Arab Gulf and the Caucasus. The great highland bagpipe is probably the most well-known type of bagpipe and is found in Scotland. The less familiar uilleann pipes are Irish.

BEZEN PERROT

SOME BRETON NATIONALISTS SAW THE NAZI OCCUPATION OF
FRANCE AS AN OPPORTUNITY TO BUILD A BRETON STATE AND
SHED FRENCH JACOBIN RULE. OTHERS, LIKE *BEZEN PERROT*,
NAMED AFTER A PRIEST MURDERED BY THE *RÉSISTANCE*, FOUGHT
ALONGSIDE GERMAN POLICE IN BATTLES AGAINST THE *MAQUIS*.

The Second World War witnessed the development of a Breton collaborationist force, the *Bezen Perrot*, the Perrot Unit. Led by the nationalist leader Célestin Lainé, aka Neven Henaff, these Breton militants saw themselves as a national force continuing Breton military resistance against France, and thus they refused to identify themselves with French collaborationist organizations. Those forces were considered to be "Jacobin" and enemies of Brittany.

The Breton nationalist imagination found inspiration in tales of Irish rebellion, especially MacBride's Brigade, which fought for the Boers in South Africa, and one nationalist, Louis Le Roux, saw the Irish Easter uprising as a sign of resurrection in which its martyrs died for Celtic Bretons, too. Lainé and his fellow militants fought with opponents of Paris, in this case Nazi Germany, and served in the ranks of France's enemies. Initially, Lainé and his friends created *Gwenn-ha-Du* (white and black after the colors in the Breton flag), which made a spectacular political debut when it destroyed a monument in August 1932 at Rennes. In November the group cut a railroad line at Ingrandes, which delayed Prime Minister Herriot's train on its way to Nantes. *Gwenn-ha-Du*'s militancy inspired young Breton nationalists who were exasperated with the constitutionalist *Parti national Breton* (PNB). The growth of fascism in Italy also aroused the admiration of the younger generation. In May 1933, a secret *Kuzul Meur* (Grand Council) of Breton nationalism met, and the PNB hoped to control the militants through it. Lainé and his friends chose to found a new underground force which would train Bretons to create a nucleus of a future Breton army. This *Kadervenn* then created yet one more organization, the *Service Spécial*, which made links

Opposite: Many Bretons saw the period of German occupation as an opportunity to throw off the shackles of French rule. Brittany was home to an extremely large German garrison, which reached its peak in May–June 1944.

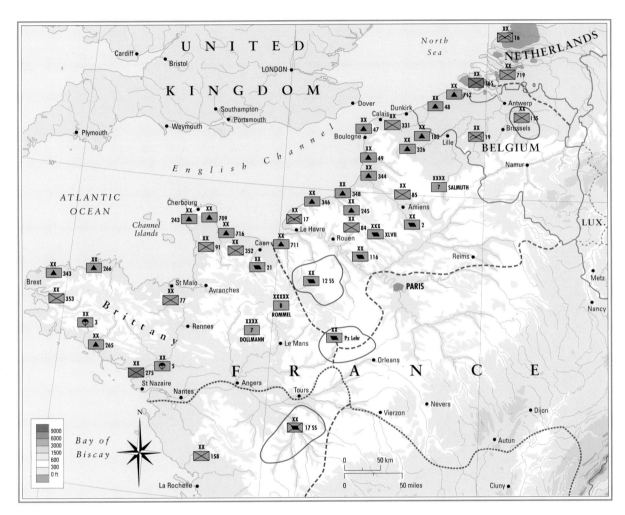

Festung Europa, German Defences in France
June 1944

with German intelligence, seeing it as a better supporter of the Bretons than relations with the IRA. Weapons were imported into Brittany by sea, sent from Hamburg by the Abwehr. During the German occupation of France, Lainé's band offered their services to the *Sicherheitsdienst der SS* and undertook campaigns against members of the French resistance.

This virtual civil war in Brittany pushed Lainé's group into a strong anti-communist, anti-Semitic stance with a belief in an ultimate German victory after which Brittany would become a separate state. Accused of massacring captured *maquis* members, the force earned a reputation for brutal anti-Resistance operations and the hostility of most Bretons. After D-Day, *Bezen Perrot* fled to Germany, and many members ended up in the French zone of occupation. Some members were executed or given long prison sentences, but the original members of *Gwenn-ha-Du* escaped to enjoy Irish asylum or fled abroad. The wartime activities of *Bezen Perrot* condemned militant Breton nationalism for many years after the war.

CELTIC FLAGS AND SYMBOLS

NATIONAL EMBLEMS AND FLAGS SYMBOLICALLY REPRESENT A NATION. THE IMAGES GENERALLY COME FROM THE NATURAL WORLD, USUALLY PLANTS, TREES, AND ANIMALS, LIKE THE GOLDEN EAGLE FOR SCOTLAND. PATRIOTIC SYMBOLS COMPRISE THE IRISH HARP, THE BRETON ERMINE, THE MANX TRISKELION, THE IRISH SHAMROCK, AND SAINTS SUCH AS PIRAN, PATRICK, DAVID, AND ANDREW.

Brittany (*Breizh*)

The flag of Brittany was designed in 1923 by Morvan Marchal, who was a founding member of a nationalist movement called *Breizh Ato* (Brittany Forever). The flag is called the *Gwen-ha-Du* or Black and White, which colors are almost a thousand years old, as is the heraldic ermine. The flag was first flown publicly in 1925 and was affirmed by the Bretagne Regional Council in 1997 as the regional flag, although the Council's logo is different. The black and white colors were used by Breton warriors in the ninth century, and the Breton Crusaders used the *Kroaz Du*, a flag of white carrying a black cross; this design is the exact mirror opposite of St. Piran's flag in Cornwall. Heraldically, the flag is described as sable, four bars argent; the canton ermine. Traditionally, the flag is carried at arm's length over the head. Marchal claimed that his design was inspired by the flags of the United States and Greece.

The ermine motif dates from 1213, when French King Philippe-Auguste gave Brittany to Pierre de Dreux Mauclerc as a duchy. Mauclerc's personal coat of armor depicted the ermine motif, *Irs Herminois Plain*, which became the provincial banner between 1532 and 1789. Most *Gwen ha Du* feature eleven ermine spots, which could represent the number of letters in *Breizh Dieuh* (Free Brittany). The nine stripes represent the nine Breton counties and the four white stripes symbolize the four Breton counties of Leon, Trégor, Kernov, and Vannetais (Genev) while the five black stripes depict the Gallo areas of

Rennes, Nantes, Dol, Saint-Malo, and Penthièvre.

Another Breton symbol is heather, and the anthem *Bro Gozh ma Zadoù* (Old Land of My Fathers) and is sung to the tune of the Welsh national anthem, *Hen Wlad Fy Nhadau* (Land of My Fathers). The Cornish use the same tune for their anthem, *Bro Goth Agan Tasow* (Dear Land of Our Fathers). In religious terms, the Bretons uniquely have a *Pardon,* which is a procession through a parish in honor of its saint, followed by a Catholic mass. An older pilgrimage is the *Tro Breizh* (The Breton Tour), where the pilgrims walk to all the graves of Brittany's founder saints.

Cornwall (*Kernow*)

Cornwall is represented by the white cross of Saint Piran (Petroc). He was an Irish missionary who is supposed to have brought Christianity to Cornwall in the fifth century. Saint Piran was also a tinsmith, appropriate in a tin-mining county/duchy. Legend suggests that while he was smelting in his kiln, a white fluid seeped out in the shape of a cross on black ashes. Reputedly, Cornish soldiers carried a flag of that design into battle at Agincourt in 1415. The flag is similar to the Breton flag and that of St. David. Certain French families had coats of arms which have similarities to St. Piran's flag: Geoffrey le Borgne; the Arnèke family; and Rouvroy de Saint-Simon. Another flag associated with Cornwall is the flag of the Duke of Cornwall with its black ground charged with an inverted pyramid of 15 golden bezants, which represent the ransom paid for a Cornish Duke captured by the Saracens during the Crusades. The chough, a species of crow, is another Cornish emblem; it is supposed to incorporate the spirit of King Arthur. Its red beak and feet are said to represent the blood shed in Arthur's battles.

Isle of Man (*Ellan Vannin*)

The Isle of Man incorporates the triskelli into its flag, like Sicily. When Sir William le Scrope was Lord of Man, he changed the triskelli into the three conjoined armored and spurred legs. The triskelli's origin can be Celtic or Norse, since both cultures used it. Possibly the symbol represents the Celtic sea god Mannanan MacLir, who lives on the island shrouding it mist to hide it from dangerous enemies. Another coat of arms bearing a triskelli belonged to Sir Thomas Randolph, Earl of Moray, who was allegedly related to the early Manx kings. He was Lord of Mann when Robert the Bruce gained control of the island. Moray's triskelli had mailed not armored legs.

The Manx flag became fashionable after 1929 when it was flown at Peel Castle, Tynwald Hill, and Castle Rushen. The current design was fixed in 1966, and its associated motto is *Quocunque jeceris stabit* (Whichever way you throw it, it still stands). A red ensign with the triskelli in the fly is used as a civil ensign. The coat of arms of the Isle of Man were granted by Queen Elizabeth II in 1996 and sees the triskelli augmented by additions, chiefly in the supporters of a peregrine falcon and a raven. The first bird refers to 1405, when King Henry IV gave the Isle of Man with all its rights to Sir John Stanley provided he paid homage and gave two falcons to him and to every future king of England on his coronation. The presentation of the two falcons continued until the coronation of King George IV in 1822. The raven is the bird which accompanied the god Odin. The bird was also present in the modern Viking long-ship, Odin's *Raven*, which sailed to Norway and is now preserved on the island. The other Manx emblem is the Sword of State, which is carried before the Lieutenant Governor at each meeting of Tynwald Day at St. John's.

The Isle of Man also has a parliamentary flag depicting a Viking warship on a blue background.

The triskelli's legs depict the waves of the sea, the breath of the wind, and the flame of fire, with earth at the join. Other Celtic meanings see the circle of life with birth, death, and rebirth. Another Manx emblem is the national flower, the yellow, daisy-like *Cushag,* and there is the national anthem, *Arrane Ashoonagh dy Vannin* (Land of Our Birth).

Ireland (*Eire*)

The Irish tricolor dates from 1848, with the three stripes symbolizing freedom, brotherhood, and equality, like the French Revolutionary flag. The flag's designer, Thomas Francis Meagher, a leader of Young Ireland, created the pattern, which represented the Protestants in the orange stripe and the Catholics in the green one. The green also stands for Ireland itself. The white stripe represents a truce between the two faith communities, with the stripe uniting the communities as one nation. The orange also was the dynastic color of King William of the House of Nassau, whose forces were victorious at the 1689 battle of the Boyne, which helped consolidate English rule in Ireland. The tricolor became the national flag of Ireland in 1919, and this was confirmed in 1937 by the Dail Erinn and is known as *An Bhratach Náisiúnta.* The Easter uprising of 1916 saw the tricolor raised over the General Post Office in Dublin, which gained it much respect.

Two other flags feature in Irish history. The first is a green flag charged with a gold harp; it dates back to Confederate Ireland and the activities of Own Roe O'Neill from 1642. It was later adopted by the Irish Volunteers and the United Irishmen. The second flag is Saint Patrick's, which features a white ground blazoned with a red saltire cross. Some say the flag is relatively recent, dating from the foundation of the Order of Saint Patrick in 1783. Another view exists, pointing to the red saltire appearing on the seal of Trinity College Dublin from 1612, as well as being in the arms of the cities of Enniskillen and Cork. The saltire is also present in the arms of the Geraldine Dukes of Leinster. Other emblems of Ireland include the Irish wolfhound and setter, the harp, Sessile Oak, and shamrock.

Wales (*Cymru*)

Apart from flags, Wales has a series of national symbols. St. David's Day on March 1 sees a leek worn. Legend states that St. David ordered Welsh soldiers to identify themselves by attaching a leek to their helmets before battling Saxons. The national flower of Wales is the daffodil, which is also worn on St. David's Day and is known as Peter's leek, *Cenhinen Bedr.* The Welsh Oak (Sessile Oak) is the national tree while the red kite is the national symbol of wildlife. As well as the national anthem, other songs and hymns represent Wales: *Men of Harlech, Cwm Rhondda, Calon Lan,* and *Sosban Fach.* A more formal Welsh symbol is the heraldic badge of the Three Feathers, once worn by King John of Bohemia but taken by Edward, the Black Prince and first Prince of Wales. The King of Bohemia, although blind, fought with the French against the English at the Battle of Crécy (1346), where he was killed in a brave but futile charge. The Prince of Wales's badge is used by the Welsh Rugby Union, the game being considered the national sport, as in Cornwall too.

The red dragon or *Y Ddraig Goch* is an ancient Welsh symbol, with Nennius stating that the Britons used it as a standard when fighting the Saxons. The term *ddraig* means warrior; and with the prefix

The national flag of Ireland is a tricolor of green, orange, and white and dates from 1848. The green stands for a Gaelic tradition, the orange represents supporters of William of Orange, and the white in the middle symbolizes peace, that is the truce between the orange side and the green.

The Scottish flag is a white saltire against a blue background. The white cross represents Saint Andrew, the patron saint of Scotland.

pen-, the word *pendragon* or *warlord* is attained. In the Arthurian legends associated with Wales, Uther Pendragon was Arthur's father. The flag of Wales uses the red dragon of Prince Cadwalader together with the Tudor colors of green and white, carried by Henry VII Tudor at the Battle of Bosworth in 1485, after which he became King of England. Welsh archers at the Battle of Crécy wore a green and white livery.

Other flags used in Wales now are the royal standard, which is used in England, Wales, and Northern Ireland, and St. David's Flag, which is a black field charged with a gold cross. Historic Welsh flags include the standard of the Prince of Wales, which is the banner of the princely House of Aberffraw and the Kingdom of Gwynedd and was used by Llywelyn among others. The Prince of Wales uses this emblazoned with a crown on a green shield. The flag of Owain Glyndwr was similar to Gwynedd's, sporting four lions rampant gold (2) and red (2) in four quarters with the colors counter-charged. The lion turns up red on a gold field as the banner of the princely house of Mathrafal. It is used by the rulers of Powys and as a gold lion on a red field and for the princely house of Dinefwr and the Kingdom of Deheubarth. The thirteenth-century personal banner of Llywelyn ap Gruffudd saw three red lions passant on a silver field while Madog ap Gruffud Maelor had a silver field with a black lion rampant. A final interesting banner is the *Y Groes Nawdd* (The Cross of Neith), used as a battle flag by Llywelyn the Last with a gold Celtic Cross on a purple ground.

Scotland (*Alba*)

Apart from flags, the Scots possess many national symbols in the tartan, Scots pine, thistle, lion, unicorn, the golden eagle, red deer mand maybe the Loch Ness monster. The national anthem is Flower of Scotland (*Flùr na h-Alba*), but *Scotland the Brave* is also popular. The first lines of Flower of Scotland are:

O Flower of Scotland
When will we see your like again
That fought and died for
Your wee bit of hill and glen.

The national saint, Andrew, is represented by the saltire cross on which he was martyred: a white cross on a blue ground. Legend claims that King Angus led the Picts and Scots against the Anglo-Saxons under Athelstan in 832. The Scots became surrounded and the cross appeared to both sides, presumably in the form of a cloud against the sky. The Scots were uplifted and defeated their enemy and took the saltire design for the Scottish flag ever since. Records show that the cross was used in 1165, and by 1180 it appeared on the seal of St. Andrews. The year 1385 witnessed the Scots parliament decreeing that Scottish soldiers should wear the saltire.

The saltire appears in the provincial flag of Nova Scotia, where there is a blue saltire on a white field which is emblazoned with the shield from the Royal Arms of the Kingdom of Scotland. The Scottish saltire is a component of the Union Flag, which had different designs in Scotland and England after the crowns were unified in the person of King James I and VI. After the 1707 Act of Union, the English version was adopted and the current 1801 Union flag unites the English Cross of St. George, the Scots Saint Andrew, and Saint Patrick of Ireland, which is the adopted flag of the United kingdom of Great

Britain and Ireland. The flag was not modified to take account of the 1921 partition of Ireland nor the creation of the Irish Free State. The royal standard of the King of Scots is the lion rampant. It shows a red lion with blue tongue and claws on a yellow field surrounded by a double border. In heraldry, the description is: *Or, a lion rampany Gules armed and langued Azure within a double tressure flory counter-flory of the second*. The flag was incorporated in the royal standard of the United Kingdom and is used officially at the royal houses of Holyrood Palace and Balmoral Castle when the Queen is not in residence.

Celtic Traditional Dress

NATIONAL DRESS COMMUNICATES AN IDENTITY THROUGH FOLK DRESS OR REGIONAL COSTUME AND RELATES TO A CELTIC AREA DURING A PERIOD OF TIME, GENERALLY THE NINETEENTH CENTURY. THE CLOTHING CAN DEMONSTRATE SOCIAL AND MARITAL STATUS, AND THE COSTUMES CAN COME IN THE FORM OF EVERYDAY CLOTHING OR FOR FESTIVALS, LIKE BRETON PARDONS, AND FORMAL WEAR.

Traditional dress comprises a glimpse of the past, of the customs and lifestyle of older generations; when looking at Welsh dress, a snapshot is obtained of the nineteenth century. Most traditional dress is worn by women rather than men, especially in tourist resorts, fairs, markets, and religious festivals. In Brittany, the men tend to wear black trousers and a jacket with a black hat. The women wear dresses with tiered skirts, elaborate bodices, and a whole variety of aprons, normally made of satin or velvet and brocaded, embroidered, or edged with lace. Women of Quimper wear no bib with the apron while at Pont-Aven they have a small one, and at Lorient the bib reaches to the shoulders. The most striking component of Breton costume is the headdress or *coiffe*, made from intricate lace patterns. The Pont-Aven headdress looks like a waitress's hat with two ribbons hanging down the back, accompanied by a large, starched collar covering the shoulders but with the edges flared up. The *coiffe* at Bigouden in the Pont-l'Abbé area is exceedingly tall but at Quimper a small *coiffe* is worn on the crown of the head; in Plougastel the headdress has long ribbons at the side. Douarnenez headdress is small and wrapped around a bun, and the one from Huelgoat is like a hairnet.

In the Isle of Man, traditional dress can be seen in the National Museum and is actually worn at the working Folk Museum at Cregneash. The men wore coats, the *Perree bane*, of white flannel and woolen

The traditional Scottish kilt originated in the Scottish highlands in about the 16th century. Kilts are found in Scottish traditions but are popular in many other Celtic nations, such as Wales, the Isle of Man, and Cornwall. Wearing the kilt enables the wearer to feel a strong sense of Celtic identity.

keear lheeah knee breeches, and rawhide brogues and felt hats. The women wore petticoats of linen and wool mixed together and a short jacket called a beggon, with a chequered apron. Some wore black silk bonnets as big as an inverted coal scuttle. Another form of dress was a laced shawl, with married women wearing a white muslin mob cap.

Cornwall witnessed a variety of clothing styles, and the styles worn in Victoria's reign continued into the twentieth century in west Cornwall. Women's blouses were buttoned at the front with no cuff on the sleeves, which were worn generally rolled up. Pastel colors with grays and browns seem to be traditional hues. Skirts were made from serge, flannel, or heavy cotton drill with a gored front and the fullness at the back. These would be accompanied by petticoats and an apron that would reach around the entire front and would often be made from boiled flour sacks to cover cotton aprons when dirty work was being done. Shawls were generally checked and pinned under the chin while the hats could be any style, although straw hats were favored. Men's shirts were very basic and drab in color. Serge trousers would be accompanied, for fishermen, by a smock made from sailcloth or a woolen Guernsey. Agricultural workers would wear vests made from wool, leather, or suede and these would be dark in color. A variety of hats were worn, from a sou'wester or a tam-o'-shanter to a deep derby hat or cap.

The standard vision of Welsh national dress is a woman dressed in a red cloak and a tall black hat, an image created during a deliberate revival of Welsh culture when it was seen to be under threat. The nineteenth century costume for Welsh countrywomen included a striped flannel petticoat, worn beneath a flannel open-fronted bed-gown or beggon, with an apron, shawl, and kerchief or cap. The bed-gown could be a loose coat-style gown, a gown with a fitted bodice and long skirts, or short, like a riding habit. The wearing of such attire was encouraged by Lady Llanover, the wife of a Gwent ironmaster, who maintained that it should be worn at eisteddfodau. The shawls worn by Welsh women varied in quality, from silk Paisley to machined lace to woolen shawls with check patterns. A tradition which still exists in some parts is to carry babies in a shawl.

In Ireland, images of clothing can be found in the *Book of Kells,* and there are carvings in churches. Additionally, the Ilbreachta sumptuary law stated how many colors people of different states could wear: a slave one, a bard five. The types of clothing worn were a range of belted plaids, types of tunics or saffron shirts, trews, cloaks, and mantles. The richer men wore a shin length tunic, which might be pleated below the belt, and a sleeveless cloak. Those who did physical work wore trews and a jacket with full legs or with them stopping just above or below the knee. Women wore ankle-length dresses with a large cloak or mantle. By Elizabethan times the long tunic had shortened, not reaching beyond the thigh and was accompanied by a bright cloak with a fringe with a contrasting collar. Tudor rule meant the proscription of Irish garb, which became purely historical. Now traditional Irish costume is associated with the bright, elaborate, and flamboyant dresses worn by traditional Irish dancers.

Scotland sports traditional highland dress, with the kilt developing from the belted plaid and being kept alive by the highland regiments. The Dress Act was repealed and Scots dress became a fashion experiment among the elite of English society. Traditional dress then became the kilt of tartan with shirt, waistcoat, tweed jacket, and stockings/hose with a garter, brogue shoes, and a sporran. A bonnet was often sported displaying the clan crest. Women wore dresses or pleated skirts of tartan with a plaid or shawl of tartan material.

The distinctive traditional costume of Bretons can still be seen at festivals and special occasions. The men generally wear black with embroidered waistcoats and broad-brimmed hats, and the women wear dresses and very elaborately decorated aprons, as seen in this photograph. This particular image was taken at the "festival interceltique" in Lorient, France.

Tartans and Clans

TARTAN CONTINUES TO BE AN APPROPRIATE STYLE OF CONTEMPORARY DRESS AND IS VIRTUALLY SACRED WHEN COMBINED WITH A CLAN LINEAGE. THE SETTS HAVE SURVIVED AND RETAIN A HEROIC QUALITY, BEING ASSOCIATED WITH GROUP IDENTITY AND SCOTTISH MILITARY ÉLAN.

The history of Scottish tartans is fraught with dispute and subject to commercial interests, with people expecting individual clans to have an identifiable tartan. The growth in genealogy has fueled the debate over the origin or etiquette of wearing tartan, so researchers can find what is "theirs." Some historians suggest that tartans are a recent innovation, an invention of the Victorians in the nineteenth century when Queen Victoria and the Prince Consort visited Scotland and commenced the highland fever, a passion for all things Scottish.

The first reference to highland clothing comes in the 1093 *Saga of Magnus Barefoot,* when the king adopted the dress of the western lands visited and afterward went barelegged "having a short tunic and also upper garments." The tartan is a pattern created by criss-crossed horizontal and vertical bands in several different colors. Originally, natural plant dyes would have been used, meaning that different localities had access to different dyes, leading to different colors being used. The earliest documented tartan dates from the third century AD; it is known as the Falkirk tartan, found stuffed into the mouth of an earthenware pot containing some 2,000 Roman coins. This Falkirk tartan comprised two different colors of wool, pale cream and dark brown. An early eighteenth-century description of dress in the Western Islands remarked that that setts and tartans varied from island to island, and the author did not mention that any one pattern was attributed to a family or clan. It seems likely that the most numerous family in an area would adopt a pattern and call it their own as part of an identity, so the tartan would originally come from a district not from a family. As industry produced more and more tartans, no one can be sure if they were based upon original patterns. The notion of a clan tartan could possibly originate in the use of specific tartans for highland regiments.

Opposite: Scottish clans were closely associated with where they lived. Tartans woven in those areas began to have associations with particular clan names.

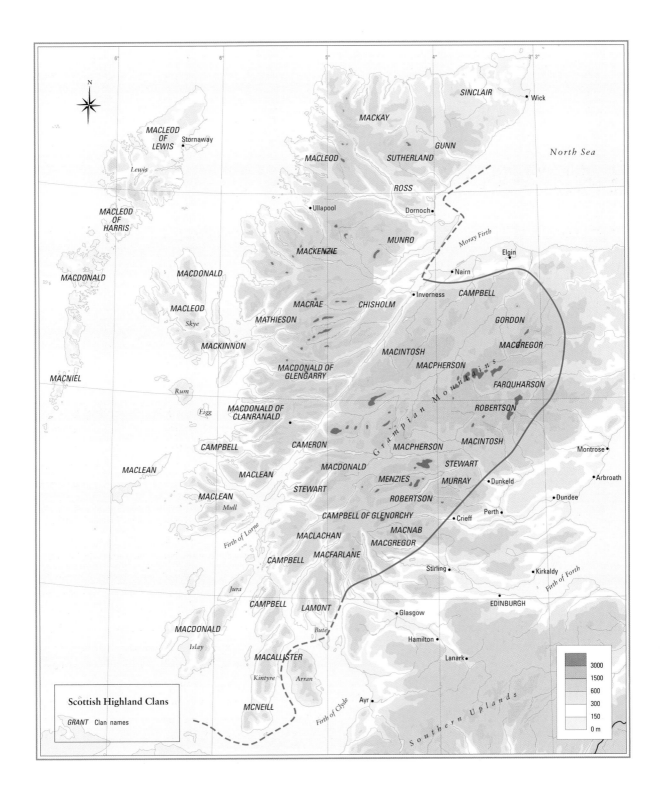

N

MACLEOD
OF
LEWIS • Stornaway
Lewis

MACLEOD
OF
HARRIS

MACDONALD

MACDONALD

MACLEOD
Skye

MACKINNON

MACNIEL

CAMPBELL

MACLEAN

MACLEAN
Mull

MACLEAN

MACDONALD
Islay

MACALLISTER
Kintyre   Arran

MCNEILL

SINCLAIR
• Wick

MACKAY

GUNN

MACLEOD   SUTHERLAND

ROSS
• Ullapool   Dornoch

MUNRO

MACKENZIE

North Sea

Moray Firth

Elgin
• Nairn
• Inverness   CAMPBELL

MACRAE   CHISHOLM

MATHIESON   GORDON

MACINTOSH   MACGREGOR
MACPHERSON

MACDONALD OF   FARQUHARSON
GLENGARRY

Rum   ROBERTSON

Eigg   MACDONALD OF
CLANRANALD

MACINTOSH

CAMPBELL   CAMERON   MACPHERSON   Montrose •

MACDONALD   STEWART

MACLEAN   MENZIES   MURRAY   Dunkeld •   Arbroath •

STEWART   ROBERTSON   Perth •   Dundee •

Firth of Lorne   CAMPBELL OF GLENORCHY   Crieff •

MACLACHLAN   MACNAB
MACGREGOR

CAMPBELL   MACFARLANE   Stirling •   Kirkaldy •
Firth of Forth

Jura   CAMPBELL   LAMONT   EDINBURGH
Bute   • Glasgow

MACDONALD   Hamilton •
Islay

Lanark •

Firth of Clyde   Ayr •   Southern Uplands

Grampian Mountains

	3000
	1500
	600
	300
	150
	0 m

Scottish Highland Clans

GRANT Clan names

CELTIC TRADITIONS IN THE UNITED STATES AND CANADA

AS THE IRISH, SCOTS, WELSH, BRETONS, AND CORNISH EMIGRATED TO THE UNITED STATES AND CANADA, THEY TOOK THEIR UNIQUE CUSTOMS WITH THEM. MANY OF THESE TRADITIONS ARE OBSERVED IN THOSE COUNTRIES TODAY.

Perhaps the most significant import to the United States and Canada of Celtic origin is the music. The Appalachian mountains received a huge influx of Scots-Irish settlers, and this Celtic presence is felt in the music of the region. The fiddle does play a prominent role both historically and currently, as well as the lilting Appalachian style that has its foundation in Irish and Scottish reels. Many American musicians are of Irish descent, and there are a large number of folklore bands that play traditional Celtic music, using fiddles, harps, and even bagpipes. Music festivals proliferate throughout the United States. Wisconsin holds the Milwaukee Irish fest, and there is the Cincinnatti Irish fest in Ohio. The Celtic Colors festival takes place annually in Cape Breton, Nova Scotia. Celtic folk music has also influenced other genres of American music. Bands such as Seven Nations and Needfire do American adaptations in the form of Celtic rock. Mil a h-Uile Rud are a Scottish Gaelic punk band from Seattle, and they recorded in Gaelic in 2004.

There are also many hundreds of St Andrew's and Caledonian Societies, independent organizations that have sprung up across the United States. A consistent thread running through their objectives is their encouragement of the study of Scottish culture and their acting as organizing bodies for sporting events and social gatherings. Many of the North American organizations have a long and illustrious history. The Illinois St Andrew Society is a good example: "Organized in 1854 to sustain the Scottish heritage in music, literature, history, cultural exchanges, and dance and to assist fellow Scottish immigrants in adjusting to the rugged pioneer mid-west. Offers a wide variety of programs, groups, and committees for Scottish genealogy, history, and business, as well as the Scottish Home for elderly Scots."

New Yorkers have their own unique way of celebrating Saint Patrick's Day, the Irish national day, called "the Wearing of the Green." Green clothes, green flowers, and green hats are standard, but you will also find unique green beers, green bagels, green water fountains, and even a green Empire State Building. Traditionally, Saint Patrick's Day is celebrated as a religious holiday in Ireland and other areas. Ironically, scores of Irish citizens make the trip across the pond to experience the more festive American flavor of Green Day, akin to the pilgrimage to New Orleans for Mardi Gras. Whether you go to church, the parade or a pub, this is one of the city's most exuberant annual celebrations. The parade marches up 5th Avenue, clan by clan, from 44th to 86th streets starting at noon on March 17th. The first official parade in the city was held in 1766 by Irishmen in a military unit recruited to serve in the American colonies. For the first few years of its existence, the parade was organized by military units until after the war of 1812. At that time, Irish fraternal and beneficial societies took over the duties of hosting and sponsoring the event. Originally, Irish societies joined together at their respective meeting places and moved in a procession toward St. Patrick's Old Cathedral, St. James Church, or one of the many other Roman Catholic churches in the city. However, as the years passed, the size of the parade increased, and around the year 1851, as individual societies merged under a single grand marshal, the size of the parade grew sharply. Each year a unit of soldiers marches at the head of the parade; the Irish 165th Infantry (originally the 69th Regiment of the 1850s) has become the parade's primary escort, and they are followed by the various Irish societies of the city. Some of the other major sponsors and participants in the parade are the Ancient Order of Hibernians, the thirty Irish county societies, and various Emerald, Irish-language, and Irish nationalist societies. Currently floats, automobiles, and exhibits, the usual elements that most people associate with parades, are not permitted in the parade, yet more than 150,000 marchers participate in the parade each year.

The tartan, which originated in Scotland, has also found its way into the culture of the United States and Canada. Every province of Canada, with its Scottish heritage, has a registered tartan, and some U.S. states have tartans, not surprising with the number of Scot migrants, especially the Scotch-Irish of Appalachia. There is even an American national tartan, taking its inspiration from the American flag.

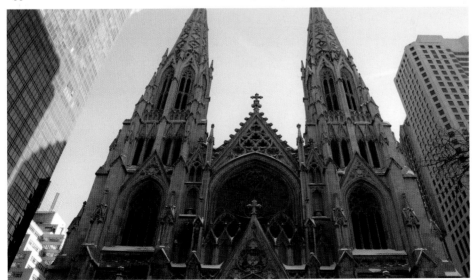

St Patrick's Cathedral, New York City. Traditionally, Irish societies moved in procession toward the cathedral during the annual St Patrick's Day parade.

HIGHLAND GAMES IN AMERICA AND CANADA

THE HIGHLAND GAMES BEGAN IN THE ELEVENTH CENTURY
IN SCOTLAND. NOWADAYS, THE CUSTOM HAS SPREAD FAR AND
WIDE. HIGHLAND GAMES TAKE PLACE IN ALMOST EVERY STATE OF
NORTH AMERICA AND THROUGHOUT CANADA.

Games and cultural festivals are important to the Celtic nations, and the events foster solidarity and communal spirit. The most awe-inspiring occasion is the Highland Games, which celebrate heritage and culture and show the military training incorporated in the games, with iconic events such as tossing the caber, stone-putting, massed pipe bands, dancing, and singing contests. The games are essentially Victorian-inspired events held annually in Scotland at Dunoon with some 3,500 competitors and audiences of between 15,000 and 20,000 people. This event is modest compared withthe 50,000 attending the games at Grandfather Mountain in North Carolina and the even bigger gathering hosted by the New Caledonian Club in San Francisco.

The heavy events are joined by the Scottish hammer throw, the weight throw, weight over the bar, and the sheaf toss. These events attract both men and women, and top athletes join to extend their careers after international and national athletic retirement. Pipe band and drumming competitions make for much noise, but quieter music can be found with fiddling and harping. Highland dancing with its balletic movements, especially the sword dance, are governed by the Scottish Official Board of Highland Dancing. Arts and crafts are normally present together with the traditional *ceilidh* and highland animals.

Other forms of games and festival are celebrated in Wales and Ireland. The most well-known cultural events are the Welsh *eisteddfodau* festival of literature, music, and performance. The national Eisteddfod of Wales attracts some 150,000 visitors, with thousands competing. The 2009 event takes place at Bala, with 2010 at Blaenau Gwent. Poetry, harping, singing, orchestras are all in competitions, and *eisteddfodau* keep alive an interest in Welsh music and poetry. An international Eisteddfod is held at Llangollen annually, and *eisteddfodau* can be found in Australia and in Argentine Patagonia with the Chubut Eisteddfod at

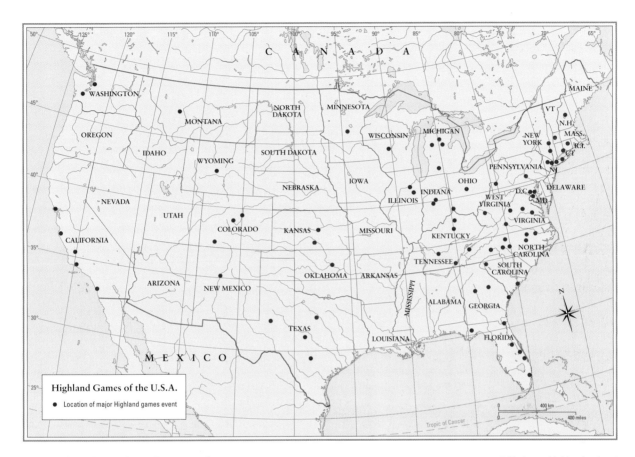

Highland Games of the U.S.A.
● Location of major Highland games event

Trelew and another in the Andes in Trevelín.

Ireland hosts the Pan Celtic Festival, the *Féile Pan Cheilteach*. Performers from each Celtic nation compete in singing and choral competitions, with others playing pipes, fiddling, or dancing. The event is similar to the mod, Lowender Peran, the Breton *Kan ar Bobal,* and the Manx *Yn Chruinnaght*. The Manx *Yn Chruinnaght* is an inter-Celtic festival, with contributions from all six nations.

Nowadays, with an estimated Scottish diaspora of some 60 million, the appetite for games and Celtic festivals continues unabated. In the United States, 44 out 50 states have their own events — an amazing 257 stretching the length and breadth of the country. From the Athena Caledonian Games in Oregon, 2,400 miles south east to the Peace River Celtic Festival in Florida and from the San Diego Highland Games in California, 2,700 miles north-ast to the Maine Highland Games.

Canada has over 70 such events. They reach from the Victoria Highland Games in British Columbia, 2,800 miles east to the Gathering of the Clans in Pugwash, Nova Scotia. A quick detour of 5,300 miles would take you to Waikiki, Hawaii and the Hawaiian Scottish Festival. Australia, Barbados, Czechoslovakia, England, France, Japan, Portugal, the Netherlands, New Zealand, Spain, and of course the "old country" itself, Scotland. In total, there are almost 480 Scottish events, inspired by the "almost lost" culture of a tiny Celtic nation in the North Sea.

With the worldwide migration of Scottish people went the Highland Games, a celebration of traditional highland sports.

SEPARATISTS

NATIONAL SELF-DETERMINATION REQUIRES THAT A NATION CAN PURSUE ITS OWN FUTURE WITHIN A FREE AND INDEPENDENT STATE. THE CORNISH AND THE BRETONS HAVE NOT ACHIEVED THIS WHILE NATIONALISTS IN EIRE WAIT FOR THE DAY WHEN THE REPUBLIC ABSORBS ULSTER, AS IT MUST DEMOGRAPHICALLY.

After the First World War, the Wilsonian principle of self-determination became a major political slogan in redrawing the map of Europe after the collapse of Austria-Hungary, Tsarist Russia, and imperial Germany. The post-1945 process of decolonization reinforced this principle when many mini- and micro-states were created. Within the demand for autonomy at any level is a sentiment of nationalism, which seeks a route to freedom via federalism, regionalism, or separatism. The Celtic nations of Europe have been largely ignored for much of recent history, but some of them have achieved degrees of self-rule. Nevertheless, some Cornish, Manx, and Breton nationalists are still not satisfied with their political conditions.

The position of the Bretons and their language has been difficult. During the French Revolution, the Jacobins sought to reduce Breton to the status of an inferior, uncivilized tongue during a process of excessive centralization. One official notice said: "It's forbidden to spit or speak Breton." Expressions of Breton identity have been few and far between since 1789. There is a flag and some car stickers with the letters BZH (*Breizh*), but political activities have been nowhere as strong as in Scotland. In the past, the Bretons failed to win self-determination at Versailles in 1919, but in 1965 some young left-wing militant nationalists formed the clandestine Breton Liberation Front (*Front de Libération de Bretagne*), which damaged a television mast at Roc-Tredulon in 1974 and blew up the Hall of Mirrors in Versailles in 1978. They kept attacking property until 1981. A comparable organization was the ARM (*Armée Révolutionnaire de Bretagne*). The year 2000 saw Breton nationalists being accused of bombing a McDonald's restaurant near Dinan, with one fatality resulting. Such violence has proved unappealing to most Bretons, although the legal persecution of the perpetrators has won some sympathy among various nationalist groups.

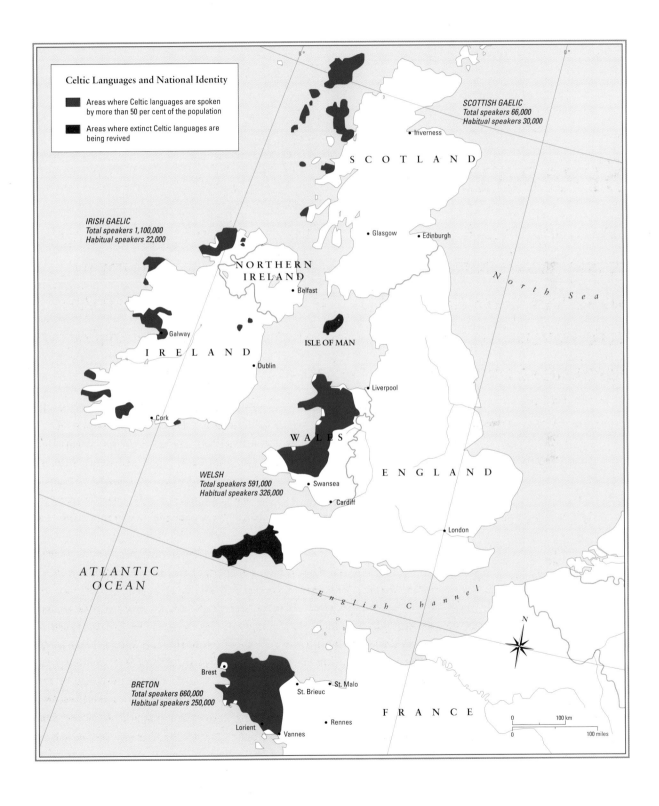

Celtic Languages and National Identity

■ Areas where Celtic languages are spoken by more than 50 per cent of the population

▨ Areas where extinct Celtic languages are being revived

SCOTTISH GAELIC
Total speakers 66,000
Habitual speakers 30,000

• Inverness

S C O T L A N D

• Glasgow   • Edinburgh

IRISH GAELIC
Total speakers 1,100,000
Habitual speakers 22,000

NORTHERN
IRELAND

• Belfast

N o r t h   S e a

I R E L A N D

• Galway

ISLE OF MAN

• Dublin

• Liverpool

W A L E S

• Cork

WELSH
Total speakers 591,000
Habitual speakers 326,000

• Swansea

• Cardiff

E N G L A N D

• London

ATLANTIC
OCEAN

E n g l i s h   C h a n n e l

N

Brest ○

BRETON
Total speakers 660,000
Habitual speakers 250,000

St. Brieuc •   • St. Malo

F R A N C E

Lorient •

Vannes •

• Rennes

0   100 km

0   100 miles

However, the legacy of some Breton nationalists collaborating with the Germans during the Second World War has been fairly damning.

More orthodox expressions of Breton political feeling have been the socialist-green Breton Democratic Union (*Union Démocratique Bretonne*), which was founded in 1964, and the conservative SAV (*Strollad ar Vro*), which emerged in 1973. Their electoral success has been minimal. Emgann, founded in 1983, desires complete Breton independence and the *Parti Breton*, established in 2001, looks to Plaid Cymru in Wales and the Scottish Nationalist Party for political inspiration. Other examples of Breton expression can be found in Breton being taught in an increasing number of schools. Breton medium schools are run by Diwan, which opened its first school in 1977, and bilingual streams commenced in state schools in 1984 (*Div-yezh*) and in Catholic schools (*Dihun*) in 1990. By 2005, some 9,700 school children were receiving some or all of their education in Breton in five departments.

In the Isle of Man, 1962 observed the formation of *Mec Vannin*, Sons of Man, which is a political party seeking the revocation of the Manx status as a British crown dependency in an attempt to create a totally sovereign state. That the Isle of Mann is a tax haven has stimulated a range of anti-immigration policies in the party program. The fast growth of the finance sector, especially in the capital, Douglas, Mec Vannin states, has placed an intolerable burden on the island's infrastructure and environment while damaging community life too. The party wishes to establish a separate Manx nationality and strengthen environmentalist policies in the areas of silviculture, fishing, farming, and tourism. A Manx university is desired despite the island's small population being unable to sustain one. Political decentralization, with more power being given to local councils, is desired. However, the party has lacked political success. In 1976, ten candidates were put up for the House of Keys but only Peter Craine was successful. He eventually quit the party and joined the very short-lived Manx National Party (1977-81). Mec Vannin publishes a newsletter (*Yn Pabyr Seyr*) twice a year and can be accessed via its website, www.mecvannin.im.

In Cornwall, Mebyon Kernow (MK), Sons of Cornwall, was founded in 1951. It claims to campaign for all residents of Cornwall while seeking greater autonomy through a legislative assembly following the Welsh or Scottish models. The party virtually fails to use Cornwall's unique constitutional status or Celticity. Nevertheless the MK has adopted a variety of postures over culture: fostering the Cornish language and literature; pushing the idea of the Celtic character of Cornwall as one of the six Celtic nations; fostering Celtic concerts and entertainment; and preserving the true nature of the Duchy.

The party has contested local elections and won seats, but originally it acted more like a pressure group than a regular political party. The 1970s saw the party fighting national elections, and 2005 witnessed an electoral pact with the Greens: the MK did not contest St. Ives while the Greens reciprocated in the remaining four Cornish constituencies. In May 2007, the party put forward 24 candidates in Cornwall's district, town, and parish councils, winning seven district council seats. MK is a member of the European Free Alliance and enjoys close relations with Plaid Cymru.

MK has issued a declaration for a Cornish Assembly and has collected signatures in support from about ten percent of the Cornish electorate. Supporters claim that the South West Regional Assembly and South West Regional Development Agency are unelected quangos and thus undemocratic and unaccountable.

The Saint Piran's flag, which is the flag of Cornwall. Historically the flag has had strong links with the Cornish separatist party Mebyon Kernow, but today the flag is considered more a symbol of Cornish pride. The design of the flag is similar to the old Breton flag and the flag of Saint David, a further example of the strong cultural ties between these Celtic communities.

Mebyon Kernow also wishes to contest Westminster excluding Cornwall from the Framework Convention for the Protection of National Minorities. One day, this issue may be taken to the European Court of Human Rights after all UK legal avenues have been explored.

THE SCOTTISH PARLIAMENT AND DEVOLUTION

DEVOLUTION HAS MEANT THE TRANSFER OF SOME POWER TO SCOTLAND FROM THE CENTRAL GOVERNMENT AT WESTMINSTER, BUT THE LATTER RETAINS SOVEREIGNTY.

Despite the union of the crowns of Scotland and England in 1603 and the full union of the two states and parliaments in 1707, Scotland kept its distinctive national character, reflected in a separate legal system, education system, and church. Scottish nationalism was expressed weakly until after the Second World War, when the decline of the British Empire and the cost of financing the war caused industrial decline. The 1979 referendum to establish a devolved Scottish Assembly required support from 40 percent of the electorate. The vote saw 32.5 percent in favor, and failure to reach the threshold killed the proposal. After the Labour Party won the May 1997 general election, Scots voted for a Scottish Parliament with tax-varying powers, with the seat of government in Edinburgh. Power was transferred from Westminster on May 6, 1999.

The electoral system uses proportional representation, with 73 Members of the Scottish Parliament (MSP) representing individual geographical constituencies and another 56 MSPs returned from eight additional regions. The Scottish Parliament has devolved powers in areas such as education, agriculture, health, and the legal system. Areas reserved to Westminster include: all forms of energy; defense and the military; employment; foreign policy; transport safety; social security, and the monetary system. Some critics of devolution feel full independence might be achieved incrementally, which would leave just the crowns unified. The damage done to the Bank of Scotland and the Royal Bank of Scotland in the 2008 credit crunch suggests independence would be unsustainable economically. Another problem is the "West Lothian Question". Scottish MPs sitting in the House of Commons can vote on domestic legislation applying to England, Wales, and Northern Ireland while English, Scottish, Welsh, and Northern Ireland MPs cannot vote on domestic legislation in the Scottish Parliament.

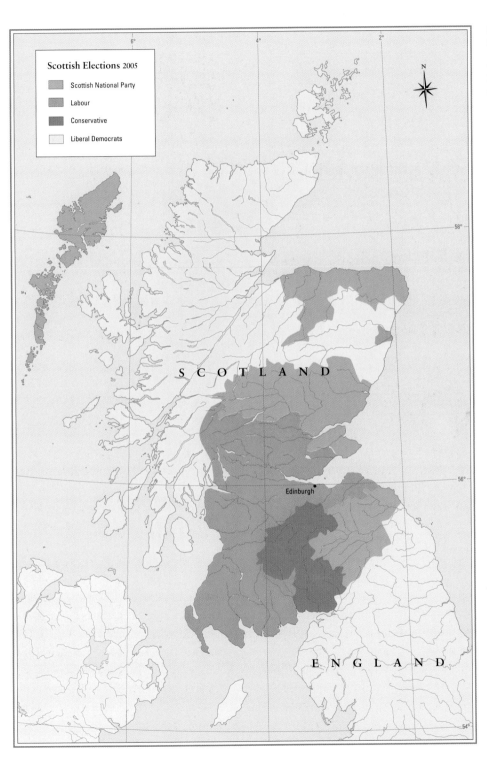

Scottish Elections 2005

- Scottish National Party
- Labour
- Conservative
- Liberal Democrats

N

S C O T L A N D

Edinburgh

E N G L A N D

Scotland did not have a parliament between 1707 and 1999. It was not until 2007 that the Scottish National Party became, only just, the largest party in the Scottish Parliament.

THE WELSH ASSEMBLY

"OWEN GLYNDYR ... ENVISAGED A WELSH FUTURE IN A EUROPEAN CONTEXT ... SIX CENTURIES LATER WE ARE STARTING TO THINK IN THOSE TERMS AGAIN." (RHODRI MORGAN, LABOUR LEADER, WELSH ASSEMBLY, APRIL 17, 2000).

Original support for modern Welsh nationalism was more concerned with protecting and preserving Welsh culture and language than with Welsh self-government. Support for Plaid Cymru, the Welsh nationalist party, was meager until the 1960s, when it developed a following mainly in the Welsh-speaking areas. In 1964, the Welsh Office was created, providing an unelected agency for Welsh affairs but not necessarily staffed by Welsh. However, it did establish a basis for the territorial stewardship.

The 1969 Royal Commission on the Constitution, the Kilbrandon Committee, recommended devolution for Wales, but a proposed assembly was rejected by the Welsh electorate in 1979. After the 1997 general election, Tony Blair was determined to enact laws that would democratize politics by giving devolution to Wales, Scotland, and Northern Ireland. A second referendum was held on September 18, 1997 in which the electorate just approved the foundation of a national assembly for Wales. The executive powers of the Welsh Office were transferred to the assembly. The Government of Wales Act 2006 altered the electoral system. The first-past-the-post electoral system was changed to a version of proportional representation, the additional member (AM) system: 40 assembly members elected from single-member constituencies on a plurality voting system, with constituencies the same as those used for the House of Commons at Westminster and 20 AMs elected from regional closed lists. The Welsh Assembly has been criticized by Plaid Cymru for not having full powers, and opinion polls suggest that most Welsh people desire full legislative powers while the AMs would be happy to obtain further powers from Westminster. In the meantime, Wales might demand powers similar to the Scottish Parliament, with both countries moving incrementally to gaining more power in different areas with a dream of full autonomy.

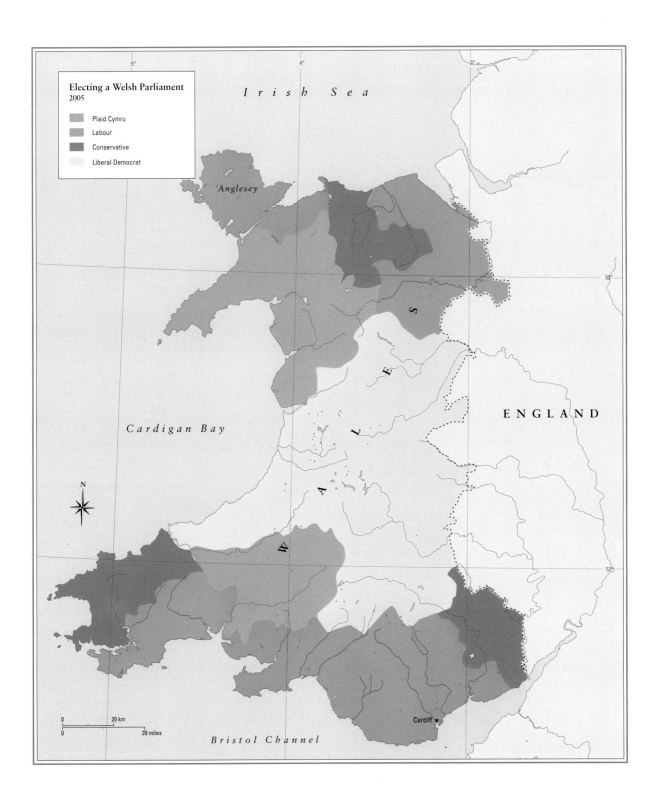

Electing a Welsh Parliament
2005

Plaid Cymru
Labour
Conservative
Liberal Democrat

Irish Sea

Anglesey

ENGLAND

Cardigan Bay

W A L E S

N

Cardiff •

Bristol Channel

0   20 km
0   20 miles

Cornish Stanneries: The Past and the Dream

"A good sword and a trusty hand! A faithful heart and true! King James's men shall understand what Cornish lads can do!" (Trelawny, a Cornish anthem, by Hawker)

A form of Cornish self-government existed in the Stannary Parliaments and Courts, which had legislative and legal functions in the county. They oversaw the area's tin miners and tin mining interests and were the courts of record for towns dependent upon tin mining. Executive authority was held by the Lord Warden of the Stannaries. These institutions demonstrate the importance of tin to the economy during the Middle Ages. In 1201, King John gave the tin miners of Cornwall and Devon, who had similar institutions, a charter authenticating their just and ancient customs and liberties. The tin miners of both counties would congregate at Hingston Down to create a parliament. King Edward I (1239-1307) separated the counties, providing them with identical sets of institutions. The jurisdiction of the Cornish Stannary institutions covered the whole county. King Edward III (1312–77) re-affirmed the privileges of the Stannaries when he created the Duchy of Cornwall in 1337. Tin miners were exempt from all civil-state jurisdiction except in cases affecting land, life, or limb. Cornwall rebelled, with the Stannaries suspended in 1497. Cornwall did not wish its taxes to finance a war against Scotland. The institutions were restored upon payment of a fine by King Henry VII (1457-1509). Henry's Charter of Pardon (1508) stated no new laws affecting miners could be made without the approval of the 24 Stannators. The last Stannary Parliament sat at Truro in 1752; but since English law does not recognize that laws lapse through lack of use, the Stannary Parliament still exists. The 1508 Charter of Parliament remains on the statute books, and the Attorney General for England and Wales stated that a stannator's right to veto the Westminster Parliament has never formally ceased (1977).

Cornish nationalists have attempted to revive the Stannary Parliament, claiming its renewed existence since 1974. The Stannary Parliament is interested in greater local autonomy and the diminution of

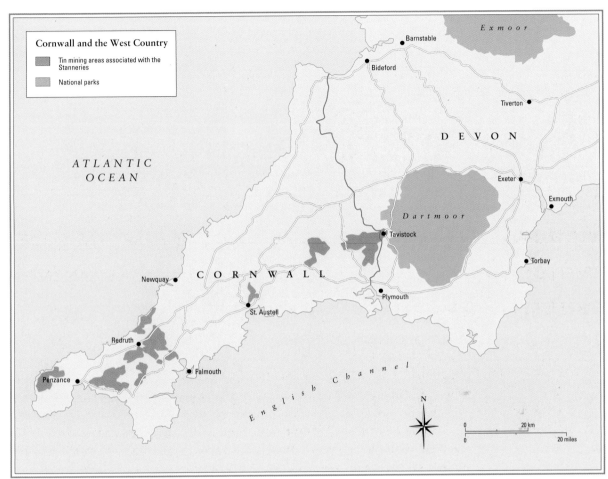

Cornwall and the West Country

Tin mining areas associated with the Stanneries

National parks

The Cornish Stanneries were a series of local parliaments and courts which passed laws and oversaw legal functions across the county. Among other things, they oversaw Cornwall's tin mining interests.

centralized government. It wants to change the constitutional status of Cornwall in line with other regions in Great Britain and Europe, such as Wales and Scotland. The revived institution has argued that the Court of Chivalry sat in 1952 for the first time in 200 years, and thus the Stannary Parliament has the right to exercise its legal authority.

The revivalist members want all taxes raised in the Duchy to be spent in Cornwall. They also seek the rights over all mineral wealth, including oil and natural gas, and want St. Piran's flag (a black ground with a vertical white cross) to be the standard of the Cornish nation. When taken to court, one defendant stated that he had staked out moor land acres as a potential tin mining area and was outside English law. The magistrates agreed they had no jurisdiction, but the English High Court had the decision rescinded. Other campaigns have asked why the Duchy of Cornwall has transferred property to English Heritage, to protect the interests of the Queen's heir. Other cases have been taken to the European Court of Human Rights and the European Court of Justice. Here, the feudal position of the Duke of Cornwall, it is argued, brings Prince Charles privileges and exemptions from the law in Cornwall which indirectly and directly discriminate against the indigenous Cornish.

Manx Tynwald

THE ISLE OF MAN POSSESSES ITS OWN FORM OF HOME GOVERNMENT, AND ITS TYNWALD IS A SCANDINAVIAN FORM OF LEGISLATURE WHICH HAS BEEN ESTABLISHED SINCE THE NINTH CENTURY. IT IS THE OLDEST DEMOCRACY IN THE WORLD. THE LORD OF MANN IS QUEEN ELIZABETH II OF ENGLAND.

Tynwald, the Manx parliament, sits in session throughout the year, but each July 5 it meets outdoors on Tynwald Hill at St. John's, when the year's enacted laws are read out. This political institution and its convocation extend back over 1,000 years to the Viking ancestors who arrived around AD 800, making the Isle of Man the oldest recorded democracy in the world. It is not part of the United Kingdom but a crown dependency, with Queen Elizabeth II acknowledged as the Lord of Mann. The Norse settlers in Mann inter-married with the Celtic inhabitants, and Celto-Norse dynasties ruled the island for four and a half centuries, until the island was gained by the king of Scotland in 1266. This lengthy period allowed an administrative structure to develop. Today's Tynwald possesses a number of branches, the Legislative Council, and the House of Keys.

The Queen is represented by the Lieutenant Governor, who grants Royal Assent. The Legislative Council elects its President, responsible for order and business in the Council. The Legislative Council is the Upper Branch of Tynwald, comprising the President, the two ex-officio members of the Queen's Attorney General, and the Lord Bishop of Sodor and Man, plus eight members elected by the House of Keys. The House of Keys comprises 24 members elected from single-member and multi-member constituencies. Other important officers are the Clerk of Tywald, who is Secretary of the House of Keys and Counsel to the Speaker. There is a *Yn Lhaider*, the Reader, who promulgates the acts in Manx. Finally, the Chief Judge of the Island's High Court of Justice is First Deemster and acts as Deputy Governor in the absence of the Governor. The Parliament has a flag depicting a Viking warship on a blue ground, which harks back to the origins of Tynwald when the ancient arms showed a ship with sails furled; the current flag represents the ship under full sail.

Opposite: The Manx Tynwald, the parliament of the Isle of Man, is located in Douglas, its capital. It has been functioning for over 1,000 years, making it the oldest democracy in the world.

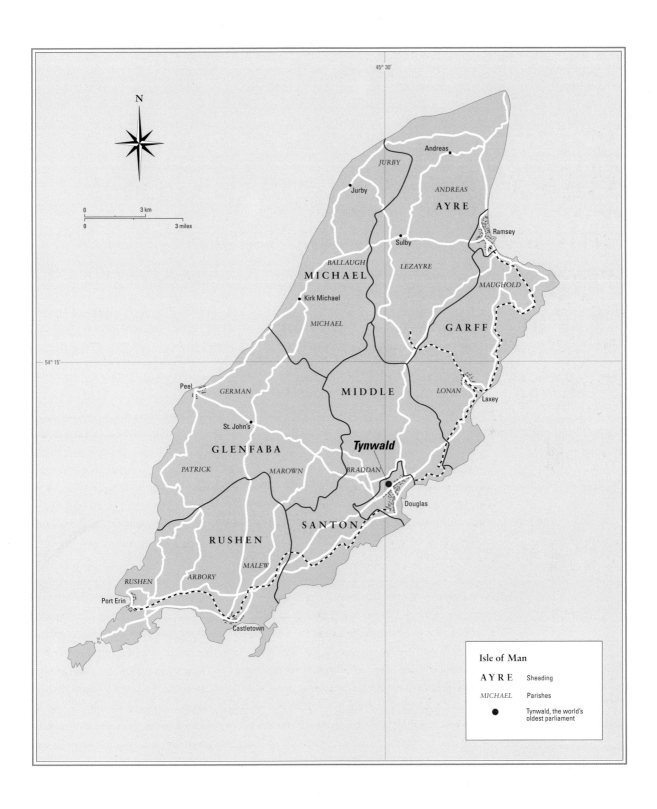

N

0   3 km
0   3 miles

45° 30'

JURBY

Andreas

Jurby

ANDREAS

AYRE

Sulby

Ramsey

BALLAUGH

MICHAEL

LEZAYRE

MAUGHOLD

Kirk Michael

MICHAEL

GARFF

54° 15'

Peel

GERMAN

MIDDLE

LONAN

Laxey

St. John's

Tynwald

GLENFABA

PATRICK

MAROWN

BRADDAN

Douglas

SANTON

RUSHEN

MALEW

RUSHEN

ARBORY

Port Erin

Castletown

Isle of Man

AYRE   Sheading

MICHAEL   Parishes

●   Tynwald, the world's oldest parliament

STORMONT AND THE GOOD FRIDAY AGREEMENT

THE MAJOR POLITICAL DIVISION IN ULSTER IS BETWEEN THE UNIONISTS, WHO DESIRE TO SEE THE PROVINCE REMAIN PART OF THE UNITED KINGDOM, AND NATIONALISTS/REPUBLICANS, WHO WISH TO SEE NORTHERN IRELAND JOIN EIRE.

The origins of the Irish troubles lie in the past, and the partition of Ireland in 1922 failed to solve the problem. Then a sizeable Catholic, basically republican minority still lived in the north and felt threatened by the Protestant majority. Simultaneously, these Protestants saw themselves as a minority in Ireland as a whole. The intransigence of each side has been characterized by competing flags, ceremonies, ritual marches, and hostility. The Catholics in Ulster were discriminated against in terms of employment, welfare, and housing while political rights were infringed by gerrymandering.

The 1960s saw the Unionist leader and prime minister, Terence O'Neill, pursuing moderate unionism, which was detested by militant Ulster loyalists. Rioting resulted in British troops being sent to keep the peace, but they outstayed their welcome and lost Catholic support, becoming perceived as ultimately the defense force of a Protestant state. Increasing violence caused many Catholics to look to the IRA as their defense force. The policy of internment and imprisoning suspected terrorists without trial won the IRA further support. That the 1st Battalion of the Parachute Regiment opened fire on a peaceful civil rights march in Derry on January 30, 1972, Bloody Sunday and killed 13, including seven teenagers, merely served to exacerbate political tension, leading the British Prime Minister Edward Heath to suspend Northern Ireland's parliament at Stormont.

Northern Ireland dissolved into aggression, with the Provisional IRA attacking British soldiers and the Royal Ulster Constabulary. Social segregation along religious lines and inter-faith murder increased, and parts of Belfast and Derry became no-go territory, with paramilitaries on both sides policing their areas with corporal punishment, including knee-capping by gun shot. During these troubles, Ian Paisley founded the Democratic Unionist Party in 1971 while Catholics supported the constitutional nationalism

Opposite: The balance between Catholic and Protestant populations in Northern Ireland inevitably affected voting sentiments from the 1920s onward. Population change continues to influence the political reality of daily life up to the present day.

Religious Denomination per County 1926 and 1971

■ Roman Catholic, 1926/1971   ■ Church of Ireland, 1926/1971   ▨ Presbyterian, 1926/1971   ▨ Others, 1926/1971

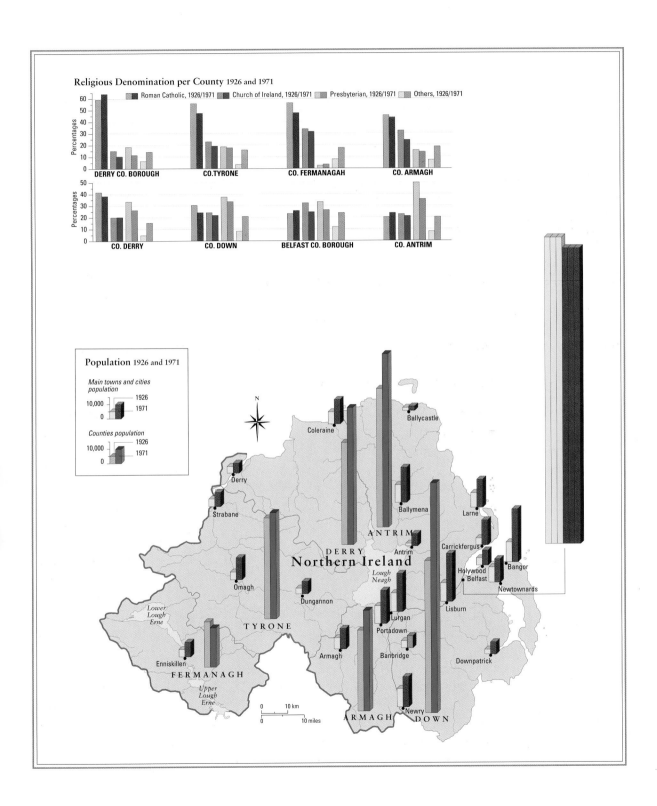

DERRY CO. BOROUGH   CO.TYRONE   CO. FERMANAGAH   CO. ARMAGH

CO. DERRY   CO. DOWN   BELFAST CO. BOROUGH   CO. ANTRIM

Population 1926 and 1971

Main towns and cities population

10,000 — 1926
0 — 1971

Counties population

10,000 — 1926
0 — 1971

N

Ballycastle

Coleraine

Derry

Strabane

Ballymena

Larne

ANTRIM

Antrim

Carrickfergus

DERRY

Northern Ireland

Lough Neagh

Holywood
Belfast
Bangor

Newtownards

Omagh

Dungannon

Lower Lough Erne

TYRONE

Lurgan

Portadown

Lisburn

Enniskillen

Armagh

Banbridge

Downpatrick

FERMANAGH

Upper Lough Erne

ARMAGH   DOWN

Newry

0   10 km
0   10 miles

of the Social Democratic Labour Party (SDLP) or of Sinn Féin (SF), which is republican and was linked to the IRA.

The 1970s and 1980s witnessed a search for peace, but it was not until the Labour general election victory in 1997 that a process commenced, leading to the 1998 Good Friday Agreement, or Belfast Agreement. Crucial elements included a devolved assembly for Northern Ireland elected by the single transferable vote system of proportional representation and with legislative and executive powers; an executive comprising ten ministers, to be allocated according to the d'Hondt process to ensure proportionate power sharing; and parallel referendums in both parts of Ireland to ratify the agreement. The electorates endorsed this political program but Ian Paisley's hostility and the issue of decommissioning IRA weaponry remained on the agenda.

Since the Northern Ireland Assembly has been created, it has been suspended on four occasions: February 11-May 30, 2000; August 10, 2001 for 24 hours; September 22, 2001 for 24 hours; and October 14, 2002-May 7, 2007. Unionists refused to participate in the institution until the IRA decommissioned its arms, ended its activities, and disbanded. On July 28, 2005, the IRA stated that it had ordered an end to the armed campaign and had instructed its volunteers to assist the development of purely political and democratic programs through exclusively peaceful means. Three elections have been held, in 1998, 2003, and 2007. The last election saw Ian Paisley's DUP and Sinn Féin agreeing to enter a power-sharing government, with Paisley as First Minister and Martin McGuinness (SF) as Deputy First Minister.

The assembly has several means of ensuring power-sharing. The d'Hondt system apportions ministers between the various parties, and certain resolutions must have cross-community support, with a certain percentage of MLAs from both the Catholic and Protestant communities. Money bills all go through this process. The assembly can legislate in any area not reserved to Westminster, these issues being either "excepted matters" or "reserved matters," the latter possibly being transferred to the assembly in the future. Unlike Westminster, Northern Ireland law is subject to judicial review. Laws can be axed if they exceed the powers of the assembly, break European Union law, violate the European Convention on Human Rights, or discriminate against a person on the grounds of their political opinion or religious belief.

Transferred matters are covered by the ten ministerial portfolios of education; health; agriculture; enterprise, trade and investment; environment; regional development; employment; finance; social development; and culture, arts, and leisure. Reserved matters comprise criminal law; police; navigation and civil aviation; international trade and financial markets; telecommunications and postage; the foreshore and seabed; disqualification from assembly membership; consumer safety; and intellectual property. Excepted matters are the royal succession; international relations; defense and armed forces; nationality, immigration and asylum; taxes levied across the United Kingdom; appointment of senior judges; all elections held in Northern Ireland; currency; and the conferring of honors.

The future of Northern Ireland is uncertain. Demographic trends suggest that a nationalist Roman Catholic majority will emerge, and Irish unification might be demanded although this dream has been deleted from Eire's constitution. Currently, Eire seems less threatening to unionists owing to its development. The Catholic Church has lost much of its clout, and Eire has prospered as the Celtic tiger and through European Union membership.

The south is no longer anyone's poor relation, although pockets of poverty do still exist. The two Irelands might eventually blend together since it is unlikely that the north will remain as part of the United Kingdom. Future joint-sovereignty might aid a transition and Anglo-Eire co-operation as enshrined in the Belfast Agreement's inter-governmental British-Irish Council could continue in areas where there is mutual interest.

Stormont; the parliament buildings of Northern Ireland are located in the Stormont area of Belfast. This building now houses the Northern Ireland Assembly and the Executive Committee.

THE BRETON REGIONAL COUNCIL

REGIONAL COUNCILS ARE BECOMING HIGH STATUS INSTITUTIONS, WITH POLITICIANS SEEKING POSTS IN THEM. RECENTLY, SEVEN NATIONAL ASSEMBLY DEPUTIES HELD REGIONAL PRESIDENCIES WHILE NINE SENATORS HELD PRESIDENCIES.

France suffers from a Jacobin tendency that fears central government taking control of its geographical periphery lest local autonomy might undermine the integrity or the political stability of the national territory. A second element of this national view is that local autonomy is an anti-national concept that could weaken Jacobin centralization, which developed during the French Revolution. However, these notions are weakening since President Pompidou, in 1972, enacted a reform creating unelected regional councils. Further reforms in 1982 envisaged direct elections to regional councils, with the transfer of several important policy-making powers devolved to regional level.

The initial form of proportional representation led to fragmented party politics with an inbuilt impossibility of coalition building. The system was reformed in 1999, with a set of regional elections in 2004, and the elections take place every six years. If a party wins more than 50 percent of the votes cast at the first ballot, that list will win 25 percent of the total number of council seats, with the rest distributed proportionally among all parties that win more than 3 percent of the votes cast, including the winning list. If no party wins more than 50 percent, there is a second ballot in which the seats are distributed in a similar fashion, even if the winning list wins less then 50 percent of the votes cast. At the second ballot, only lists that won more than 5 percent at the first ballot can re-stand. The powers of the Brittany Regional Council are the same as for other regions. The council is responsible for the upkeep and maintenance of secondary schools and main oversight over regional economic development. Additionally, the council has responsibility for professional training and apprenticeships, employment, research and innovation, transport, tourism, the environment, culture, and sport. The Brittany Council has incorporated certain basic values in its operations such as solidarity, sustainable development, openness to Europe and the

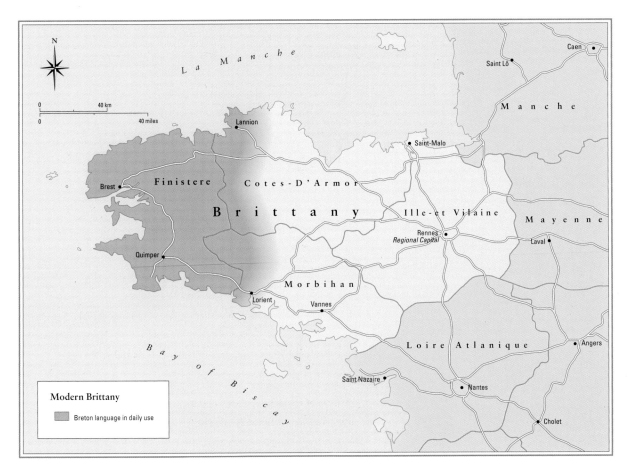

world, gender equality, and better access for people to information technology. Thus although the Breton Regional Council does not possess the taxation powers of the Welsh Assembly, Scottish Parliament, and Manx Tynwald, it still owns a variety of important competencies and can apply for European regional funding. One issue facing those Breton nationalists who want more devolved powers is to redress the manner in which regions were constructed. The government seemed to deliberately break up historic regions in order to ensure that they could not re-establish a competing identity with France. Brittany incorporates four departments: Côtes-d'Armor, Ille-et-Vilaine, Morbihan, and Finistère, with the capital at Rennes. A fifth department of Brittany, the department of Loire-Atlantique, has been placed in the Pays-de-la-Loire region, with the old Breton city of Nantes as its capital. A re-incorporation would add rivalry between Rennes and Nantes but could improve the business of the region. A problem would be to face the difficulty of a rump Pays-de-la-Loire, which would, however, retain a coastline in the Vendée.

The Breton Regional Council has other interesting qualities; the region voted "yes' to the European constitution in the 2005 Referendum and is very pro-European and outward looking, as it used to be historically. Furthermore, an agreement with Wales since 2004 involves town-twinning, culture and language exchanges, European projects, and links between Welsh and Breton schools.

Modern Brittany consists of four "departments" of the French Republic. The region has its parliament in Renne and is involved in promoting the Breton language and cultural identity.

CELTIC TIGER

THE ECONOMY OF THE REPUBLIC OF IRELAND IS TRADE-
DEPENDENT, AND MOST OF ITS CITIZENS' WEALTH IS IN
PROPERTY. THE RECESSION OF 2008 IS LIKELY TO SEE THE BUBBLE
OF SPECULATION BURST AS THE CREDIT CRUNCH DEEPENS.

The term "Celtic Tiger" has been applied to two periods of economic boom in Ireland: the 1990s to 2001 and 2003 to 2007, turning Eire from one of the poorest European countries into one of the richest. A prime reason was Eire's support for the European Union and the single European market, which won it funding to invest in education and an infrastructure of roads and to develop conditions attractive to foreign investors. Eire created a well-educated population that spoke English. It also projected an aura of stability. The social partnership created a virtual corporate state where economic interests co-operated in negotiating pay rises, welfare reform, and industrial peace. That different governments came and went did not matter; no party rocked this political and economic boat because all sought to retain conditions favorable to foreign investment. Eire benefited from investment in telecommunications in the 1980s, changing from older industries to those based upon information technology. Taxes, especially corporate tax, are low, which favors the investor. The creation of the International Financial Services Center turned the capital into a focal point of European banking and investment. Dublin has become a modern, cultured city, European in its opportunities and its multi-cultural population, a trend that has affected Cork, Limerick, and Galway too. Migrants poured into the country, especially from Poland and the Baltic states. However, the "tiger" has a downside. As unemployment fell and wages grew, Eire's prices were pushed higher, to match northern Europe, which may eventually diminish returns. The gross domestic product has soared, but foreign-owned companies are responsible for 93 percent of Eire's exports, making the country dependent on trade. Links with the U.S. economy have strengthened, maybe at the expense of ties with Europe. A U.S. downturn in economic activity and the collapse of the sub-prime market has yet to show its knock-on effects.

Opposite: Ireland's economic boom of recent decades has been promoted largely by full membership of the EU. Ireland enjoyed development grants and access to a market which now reaches eastern Europe.

Ireland in the European Union

Development of the European Community

- Signature of the Treaty of Rome, 1957
- EC member added 1973
- EC member added 1986
- Became part of the EC after unification of Germany, 1990
- EC member added 1995
- EC membership added May 2004
- EC membership approved January 2009
- ■ Membership pending

200 km
200 miles

N

Arctic Circle

Norwegian Sea

FINLAND

Oslo
Helsinki
St. Petersburg
Stockholm
Tallinn
ESTONIA
RUSSIAN FEDERATION

LATVIA
Riga

Baltic Sea

LITHUANIA
Vilnius

Kaliningrad
RUSSIA
BYELORUSSIA

Gdánsk
Warsaw

North Sea

Scotland
Glasgow
Edinburgh

DENMARK
Copenhagen
Hamburg

POLAND

UKRAINE

UNITED KINGDOM

Dublin
IRELAND

Liverpool
Birmingham
Wales
Bristol
London
Amsterdam
The Hague
NETHERLANDS
GERMANY
(GERMAN FEDERAL REPUBLIC)
Berlin
(GERMAN DEMOCRATIC REPUBLIC)

Cracow
Lvov

Prague
CZECH REP.
SLOVAKIA
Bratislava

Calais
Brussels
BELGIUM
L.
Frankfurt

Paris

ATLANTIC OCEAN

Brittany
FRANCE

Bern
SWITZERLAND

Vienna
AUSTRIA
HUNGARY
Budapest
ROMANIA

Bucharest

Lyon
Bordeaux

Milan
Genoa
Venice
Trieste
SLOVENIA
Ljubljana
Zagreb
CROATIA
BOSNIA HERZEG.
Sarajevo
SERBIA
Belgrade

Black Sea

BULGARIA
Sofia

Marseille
Monaco
ITALY
Adriatic Sea

ANDORRA

MONTE NEGRO
ALBANIA
Tiranë
Skopje
Istanbul

Barcelona

Corsica

Rome
Naples

TURKEY

PORTUGAL
Lisbon
SPAIN
Madrid

Sardinia

Aegean Sea
GREECE
Izmir
Athens

Alicante

Balearic Is.

Sicily

Cádiz
Almeria
Gibraltar
to United Kingdom
Tangier

Mediterranean

Crete

Sea

MALTA
Joined 1990

MOROCCO
ALGERIA
TUNISIA
LIBYA

CYPRUS

New Findings

NEW FINDINGS IN ARCHEOLOGY CONTINUE TO ADD TO THE STORE OF KNOWLEDGE ABOUT THE ANCIENT CELTIC WORLD. NEW THINKING ABOUT FINDS CONSTANTLY CHANGES VIEWS ABOUT THAT SOPHISTICATED AND ARTISTIC CIVILIZATION.

Ancient artifacts are often found by accident, leading to an archeological investigation. On August 5, 2005, Island Trust 2000, on the Isle of Wight, started to create a pond for water voles and dragon flies at Alverstone. Excavations revealed an ancient, possibly Roman, cobbled road. Some 1,887 square meters of marshland were dug four meters down, with the removal of 7,500 metric tons of mud. Underneath was found a network of fashioned, carved, jointed, and drilled wooden causeways pinned down by long oak dowels that are thought to range from the Iron Age (700 BC) to Saxon (1066). 1,840 pieces of wood have been recovered, components from different ages and alignments.

The site has been investigated using metal detectors, which does tend to skew findings, but hundreds of finds have been made, including buckles, bracelets, flint cobbles, nails, spear heads, crossbow bolts, a coin dated to AD 383, one of Magnus Maximus, the Roman emperor who withdrew Roman forces from Britain, and a rivet from Roman armor plus much organic matter. The site has also produced a chert hand axe and a bronze ax head, found on the sand bar of the site. The structures at Alverstone come from seven different phases of construction, with four Iron Age causeways and a probable fish trap. The site is considered to be of national importance, and the analysis of the finds will take years, but eventually a picture of the flora and climate of this part of the Isle of Wight will be pieced together.

Provisional interpretations of the Alverstone site suggest the site is Briton Iron Age and Roman from 700 BC to AD 400. The large number of structures point to a trading center of the Celtic period, and comparisons with post alignments, causeways, and fish traps in inter-tidal mud found over recent years indicate a possible maritime center despite Alverstone being five kilometers from a river mouth.

Historical evidence shows that the island had a more extensive shoreline, which has shrunk over time.

Rising sea levels some 12,000 years ago during the last Ice Age flooded not just the Solent Valley but the river valleys flowing into the Solent such as the Itchen-Test network, now Southampton Water, and the estuaries of the lower Medina, Wootton, and West Wight. Geological evidence shows the historic silting up and layers of alluvium found. Scientific evidence shows a much larger former Isle of Wight and a narrower Solent, with much of the interior of the island being flooded twice a day by high tides. Thus old maps show an island of Bembridge with another at Freshwater. This Isle of Wight of 1,000-3,000 years ago puts Alverstone at the lowest point on the Eastern Yar River, where the river could be crossed by road and where small sea vessels could reach on a high tide before resting on the mud at low tide for unloading. An important trading center needs protection and record keeping. Thus the site provides weapons and styli, the latter in large numbers, showing a degree of literacy of the island.

The site seems to be a communication hub because the alignment of the cobbled section points to Wroxall in the south and Nunwell in the north, This road crosses the east-west alignment of the downs. Here Roman villas are found such as the huge site at Brading and the partially excavated site on Mersley Down at the renowned Garlic Farm, where several different ages have been unearthed.

The Alverstone site is difficult to work, with a high water table flooding the dig, and more funds are required in order to initiate a full geophysical survey to detect any other underground structures.

Elsewhere, a remarkable find was made at an Iron Age grave near Colchester in Essex, England. The find was made in 1996 but has been kept under wraps for twelve years to allow a full and thorough investigation of the archeological site. Experts think that the man interred was a druid. If so, this is the only druid burial ever found. Little is known about druids since the Roman emperor Claudius ordered the druids to be exterminated after Boudicca's uprising in AD 61. Excavators found a board game with glass counters laid out, and no others have ever been found in Roman-era sites in Great Britain. Included in the grave were a series of surgical instruments: scalpel, surgical saw, hooks, and forceps. A jet bead is thought to have magical connotations. There was a set of metal rods positioned in a particular order, and these might have been used for divining. A tea strainer there contained Artemisia pollen, which is associated with herbal remedies. So this man was a doctor, surgeon, and probable shaman, a druid. Thus new digs keep adding to information about the old Celtic world.

One of the most significant sites of the last century is the Hayling Island site in Hampshire. Owing to drought crops being stunted, the outlines of buried walls were revealed when seen from above. Aerial photographs of Hayling Island in 1976 revealed a rectangular walled enclosure of some 40 square meters (48 square yards) surrounding a circular structure. The material evidence suggests that this enclosure was not a "roundhouse" as first thought but a Celtic temple, typically oriented toward the rising sun and in use during Roman times. It may have been used for storaging booty from the battlefield, which explains the discovery of spearheads at the site. Contemporary sources explain how the Celtic Gauls used to bring such things to their sacred places, where they would dedicate them to a war god and accompany the ritual with animal sacrifice (explaining also the animal bones found). The spearheads were intentionally bent, to signify the defeated enemy. The Temple of Vesunna in France is a rare surviving example of a Celtic-Roman temple, giving an idea of the appearance of the Hayling Island temple.

There is a general lack of archeological evidence concerning the Celts, and there are no direct literary sources. The ancient Celts are a people that continue to be shrouded in mystery.

BIBLIOGRAPHY

The author readily acknowledges the work of the many scholars and published works which have been consulted in preparation of this atlas. Among this selected bibliography are books recommended for further reading and study of the Celts and their history and culture from ancient times to the present.

Allen, Stephen, *Lords of Battle: The World of the Celtic Warrior*, Oxford: Osprey Publishing, 2007

Arnold, Bettina (ed), *Celtic Chiefdom, Celtic State*, Cambridge: Cambridge University Press, 1998

Aughey, Arthur, *The Politics of Northern Ireland*, London: Routledge, 2005

Barry, Terry (ed), *A History of Settlement in Ireland*, London: Routledge, 1999

Bennett, Martyn, *Oliver Cromwell*, London: Routledge, 2006

Bersu, Gerhard, *Three Iron Age Round Houses in the Isle of Man. Excavation Report*, Douglas: The Manx Museum and National Trust, 1977

Bain, Ian, *Celtic Knotwork*, London: Constable, 1986

Bradley, Ian, *Celtic Christianity. Making Myths and Chasing Dreams*, Edinburgh: Edinburgh University Press, 1999

Brooke, Christopher, *The Saxon and Norman Kings*, Oxford: Blackwell Publishing, 2001

Bryce, Derek, *Symbolism of the Celtic Cross*, Lampeter, Cribyn: Llanerch Press, 2006

Caesar, Julius, *The Conquest of Gaul*, Penguin, 1982

Campbell, James (ed), *The Anglo-Saxons*, London: Penguin, 1991

Campey, Lucille H., *After the Hector. The Scottish Pioneers of Nova Scotia and Cape Breton, 1773–1852*, Toronto: Natural Heritage Books, 2004

Campey, Lucille H., *The Scottish Pioneers of Upper Canada, 1784–1855*, Toronto: Natural Heritage Books, 2005

Cassius Dio, *History of Rome*, London: Loeb Classical Library, 1989

Castleden, Rodney, *King Arthur*, London: Routledge, 2003

Chadwick, Nora, *The Celts*, London: The Folio Society, 2002

Chandler, David & Beckett, Ian (eds), *The Oxford History of the British Army*, Oxford: Oxford Paperbacks, 2003

Christiansen, Eric, *The Norsemen in the Viking Age*, Oxford: Blackwell Publishing, 2001

Clanchy, M. T., *England and its Rulers, 1066–1307*, Oxford: Blackwell Publishing, 2006

Collingridge, Vanessa, *Boudicca*, London: Ebury Press, 2006

Crowley, Tony, *The Politics of Language in Ireland, 1366–1922*, London: Routledge, 1999

Cunliffe, Barry, *The Ancient Celts*, London: Penguin, 1999

Cunliffe, Barry, *The Oxford Illustrated History of Prehistoric Europe*, Oxford: Oxford University Press, 1994

Davies, John, *A History of Wales*, London: Penguin, 2007

Davis, Courtney, *The Celtic Art Source Book*, London: Blandford Press, 1988

Delaney, Frank, *The Celts*, London: Grafton Books, 1986

Diodorus Siculus, *World History*, London: Loeb Classical Library, 1989

Duffy, Seán, *Robert the Bruce's Irish Wars: The Invasions of Ireland 1306–1329*, Gloucestershire, Stroud: Tempus Publishing Ltd., 2002

Duffy, Seán, *The Concise History of Ireland*, Dublin: Gill & Macmillan, 2000

Duffy, Seán (ed), *The World of the Galloglass. Kings, Warlords and Warriors in Ireland and Scotland*, Dublin:Four Courts Press, 2007

Dyer, James, *Hillforts of England and Wales*, Buckinghamshire, Princes Risborough: Shire Publications Ltd., 1992

Edwards, Ruth Dudley & Hourican, Bridget, *An Atlas of Irish History*, London: Routledge, 2005

Elgie, Robert, *Political Institutions in Contemporary France*, Oxford: Oxford University Press, 2003

Favereau, Francis, *Bretagne contemporaine. Langue, culture, identité*, Morlaix: Skol Vreizh, 1993

Ferguson, Niall, *Empire. How Britain Made the Modern World*, London: Penguin, 2004

Glassie, Henry (ed), *The Penguin Book of Irish Folktales*, London: Penguin, 1985

Green, Miranda, *Exploring the World of the Druids*, London: Thames and Hudson, 2005

Green, Miranda (ed), *The Celtic World*, London: Routledge, 1996

Griffin, P. D., *Encyclopaedia of Modern British Army Regiments*, Gloucestershire, Stroud: Sutton Publishing Ltd., 2006

Haywood, John, *The Historical Atlas of the Celtic World*, London: Thames & Hudson, 2001

Herodotus, *The Histories*, London: Penguin, 1954

Hirschman, Elizabeth, *Two Continents, One Culture: The Scotch-Irish in Southern Appalachia*, Tennessee, Johnson City: Overmountain Press, 2007

James, Simon, *Exploring the World of the Celts*, London: Thames & Hudson, 2005

James, Simon, *The Atlantic Celts: Ancient People or Modern Invention?* London: British Museum Press, 1999

Keneally, Thomas, *The Commonwealth of Thieves: The Story of the Founding of Australia*, New York: Vintage, 2007

Kenny, Kevin (ed), *Ireland and the British Empire*, Oxford: Oxford University Press, 2004

Kinvig, R. H., *The Isle of Man. A Social, Cultural and Political History*, Liverpool: Liverpool University Press, 1975

Kneen, J. J., *The Personal Names of the Isle of Man*, Oxford: Oxford University Press, 1937

Konstam, Angus, *British Forts in the Age of Arthur*, Oxford: Osprey Publishing, 2008

Konstam, Angus, *The Historical Atlas of the Celtic World*, London: Mercury Books, 2003

Kramer, Jürgen, *Britain and Ireland. A Concise History*, London: Routledge, 2006

Kruta, Venceslas, *Celt: History and Civilization*, London: Hachette Illustrated, 2005

Laing, Lloyd, *The Archaeology of Celtic Britain and Ireland, c. AD 400–1200*, Cambridge: Cambridge University Press, 2006

Laing, Lloyd & Jenny, *The Picts and the Scots*, Gloucestershire, Stroud: Alan Sutton Publishing Ltd., 1994

Le Glay, Marcel et al., *A History of Rome*, Oxford: Blackwell Publishers, 1996

Lehmberg, Standford, *A History of the Peoples of the British Isles: From Prehistoric Times to 1688*, (3 vols) London: Routledge, 2002

Leyburn, James Graham, *The Scotch-Irish: A Social History*, North Carolina, Chapel Hill: University of North Carolina Press, 2004

Livy, *History of Rome*, London: Penguin, 1969

McGrail, Seán, *Ancient Boats and Ships*, Buckinghamshire, Princes Risborough: Shire Publications Ltd., 2006

McWhiney, Grady, *Cracker Culture: Celtic Ways in the Old South*, Tuscaloosa; University of Alabama Press, 1988

MacAulay, Donald (ed), *The Celtic Languages*, Cambridge: Cambridge University Press, 2008

Mackenzie, Alexander, *Stories of the Highland Clearances. Bloodshed and Betrayal in the Glens*, Glasgow: Lang Syne Publishing, 2005

Mackey, James P., *An Introduction to Celtic Christianity*, Edinburgh: T & T Clark, 1995

MacIntyre, *A Concise History of Australia*, Cambridge: Cambridge University Press, 2004

Macraild, Donald & Delaney, Enda (eds), *Irish Migration Networks and Ethnic Identities since 1750*, London: Routledge, 2007

Markale, Jean, *Women of the Celts*, Vermont, Rochester: Inner Traditions Bear & Co., 1987

Marren, Peter, *Battles of the Dark Ages. British Battlefields, AD 410 to 1065*, Barnsley: Pen & Sword, 2006

Mathieson, Kenny, *Celtic Music*, San Francisco: Back Beat Books, 2001

Maund, Kari (ed), *The Welsh Kings: Warriors, Warlords and Princes*, Gloucestershire, Stroud: Tempus Publishing Ltd., 2006

Megaw, Ruth, *Celtic Art: From its Beginning to the Book of Kells*, London: Thames & Hudson, 2001

Mitchison, Rosalind, *A History of Scotland*, London: Routledge, 2002 (3rd ed.)

Moscati, Sabatino et al. (eds), *The Celts*, Milan: Bompini, 1991

Moscati, Sabatino (ed), *The Phoenicians*, London: I. B. Tauris, 2001

Negra, Diane (ed), *The Irish in the US*, Durham, NC: Duke University Press, 2006

NicDhàna, Kathryn Price et al., *The CR FAQ-An Introduction to Celtic Reconstructionist Paganism*, River House Publishing, 2007

Ó Cróin'n, Dáibh', *A New History of Ireland. I. Prehistoric and Early Ireland*, Oxford: Oxford University Press, 2005

Pausanias, *Description of Greece*, London: Loeb Classical Library, 1989

Payton, Philip, *A History of Cornwall*, Cornwall, Fowey: Cornish Editions Ltd., 2004

Payton, Philip, *The Cornish Overseas*, Cornwall, Fowey: Cornwall Editions Ltd., 2005

Piette, Gwenno, *Brittany. A Concise History*, Cardiff: University of Wales Press, 2008

Polybius, *The Histories*, London: Loeb Classical Library, 1989

Power, Daniel, *The Norman Frontier in the Twelfth and Early Thirteenth Centuries*, Cambridge: Cambridge University Press, 2004

Pryor, Francis, *Britain BC: Life in Britain and Ireland before the Romans*, London: Harper Perennial, 2004

Quilliam, Leslie, *Surnames of the Manx*, Isle of Man, Peel: Cashtal Books, 1989

Quirk, John, *The Manx Connection*, Onchan, Isle of Man: The Manx Experience, 2007

Ralston, Ian, *Celtic Fortifications*, Gloucestershire, Stroud: Tempus Publishing Ltd., 2006

Richards, Eric, *The Highland Clearances*, Edinburgh: Birlinn Ltd., 2007

Ross, Robert, *A Concise History of South Africa*, Cambridge: Cambridge University Press, 1999

Sadler, John, *Culloden: The Last Charge of the Highland Clans 1746*, Gloucestershire, Stroud: The History Press, 2008

Sawyers, June Skinner, *Celtic Music. A Complete Guide*, New York: Da Capo Press, 2001

Seaborne, Malcolm, *Celtic Crosses of Britain and Ireland*, Buckinghamshire, Princes Risborough: Shire Publications Ltd., 1994

Shotter, David, *Roman Britain*, London: Routledge, 2004

Smith, Philippa Mein, *A Concise History of New Zealand*, Cambridge: Cambridge University Press, 2005

Strabo, *Geography*, London: Loeb Classical Library, 1999

Tacitus, *Agricola, Germania, Dialogus*, London: William Heinemann Ltd., 1970

Tacitus, *The Annals*, Indiana, Indianapolis: Hacket Publishing Co., Inc., 2004

Toulso, Shirley, *The Celtic Alternative*, London: Century Hutchinson, 1987

Vitali, Daniele, *The Celts. History and Treasures of an Ancient Civilization*, Italy, Verceli:White Star, 2007

Webb, James H., *Born Fighting: How the Scots-Irish Shaped America*, New York: Broadway Books, 2005

INDEX

ACKNOWLEDGMENTS

For Cartographica Press
Maps: Jeanne Radford, Alexander Swanston, Malcolm Swanston, and Jonathan Young

The publishers would like to thank the following picture libraries for their kind permission to use their pictures and illustrations:

Corbis 11, 25, 47, 49, 77, 119, 135.

Istock 19, 71, 102, 123, 127, 141, 149, 153, 168, 173, 185, 199, 205, 233, 257, 265, 269, 306, 339, 344, 350, 351, 359, 362, 363, 383.

Photos.com 193, 203, 236, 346, 358.

Every effort had been made to contact the copyright holders for images reproduced in this book.
The publishers would welcome any errors or omissions being brought to their attention.